Tradition Kept

Priest Abisha ben Phinahas holding a Torah scroll case in front of his wooden shelter on Mount Gerizim at the 1934 Samaritan Passover. Standing next to Abisha is his daughter, Azziah. Abisha became High Priest of the Samaritans in 1943 until his death in January 1961. Used by permission of Eduard Fischer.

ROBERT T. ANDERSON
and TERRY GILES

Tradition Kept

*The Literature of
the Samaritans*

HENDRICKSON
PUBLISHERS

© 2005 by Hendrickson Publishers, Inc.
P. O. Box 3473
Peabody, Massachusetts 01961-3473

1-56563-747-X

Printed in the United States of America

First Printing — March 2005

Cover Art: The cover photograph depicts the waving of the Torah scrolls at the Samaritan celebration of Pentecost on Mt. Gerizim, ca. 1980–1997. © Hanan Isachar/Corbis. Used with permission.

English translations of the Hebrew Bible are the authors' except where otherwise noted. Scripture quotations marked NRSV are from the New Revised Standard Version of the Bible, copyright © 1989 by the Division of Christian Education of the National Council of the Churches of Christ in the United States of America, and are used by permission. Scripture quotations marked RSV are taken from the Revised Standard Version of the Bible, copyright 1952 (2d ed., 1971) by the Division of Christian Education of the National Council of the Churches of Christ in the United States of America. Used by permission. All rights reserved.

Library of Congress Cataloging-in-Publication Data

Anderson, Robert T., 1928–
    Tradition kept : the literature of the Samaritans / Robert T. Anderson, Terry Giles.
        p. cm.
    Contains commentaries on various Samaritan works and selections from them in English.
    Includes bibliographical references and indexes.
    ISBN 1-56563-747-X (alk. paper)
    1. Samaritan literature—History and criticism. 2. Samaritan literature—Translations into English. 3. Samaritans—History. 4. Samaritans. I. Giles, Terry. II. Title.
BM935.A53 2005
296.8'17—dc22
                                                                2004028784

Table of Contents

111983

Part Two: Samaritan Theology and Worship

List of Abbreviations

GENERAL

A.H.	*anno hegirae,* in the year of the Hegira (622 C.E.)
ca.	circa
ch(s).	chapter(s)
diss.	dissertation
DSS	Dead Sea Scrolls
ed(s).	editor(s), edited by
e.g.	*exempli gratia,* for example
esp.	especially
et al.	*et alii,* and others
etc.	*et cetera,* and the rest
frg(s).	fragment(s)
i.e.	*id est,* that is
ibid.	*ibidem,* in the same place
LXX	Septuagint (the Greek Old Testament)
MS(S)	manuscript(s)
MT	Masoretic Text (of the Old Testament)
n(n).	note(s)
n.p.	no place; no publisher; no page
no(s).	number(s)
NRSV	New Revised Standard Version
NS	new series
OG	Old Greek
p(p).	page(s)
repr.	reprinted
rev.	revised
RSV	Revised Standard Version
SJ	Samaritan Joshua *(Chronicon samaritanum)*
SP	Samaritan Pentateuch
trans.	translator, translated by; transitive
vol(s).	volume(s)

PRIMARY SOURCES

Talmudic Tractates and Targumic Texts

b.	Babylonan Talmud
Sanh.	*Sanhedrin*
Sotah	*Sotah*
Tg. Ps.-J.	*Targum Pseudo-Jonathan*

Josephus

Ant.	*Jewish Antiquities*

Biblical Books

Gen	Genesis
Exod	Exodus
Lev	Leviticus
Num	Numbers
Deut	Deuteronomy
Josh	Joshua
Judg	Judges
2 Chr	2 Chronicles
Isa	Isaiah
Matt	Matthew
1 Cor	1 Corinthians
Col	Colossians
2 Pet	2 Peter
Rev	Revelation

SECONDARY SOURCES

ABD	*Anchor Bible Dictionary.* Edited by D. N. Freedman. 6 vols. New York, 1992
AbrN	*Abr-Nahrain*
BJRL	*Bulletin of the John Rylands University Library of Manchester*
BO	*Bibliotheca orientalis*
BZAW	Beihefte zur Zeitschrift für die alttestamentliche Wissenschaft

CW	Chamberlain-Warren collection at Michigan State University
ER	*The Encyclopedia of Religion*. Edited by M. Eliade. 16 vols. New York, 1987
HTR	*Harvard Theological Review*
JA	*Journal asiatique*
JAOS	*Journal of the American Oriental Society*
JBL	*Journal of Biblical Literature*
JQR	*Jewish Quarterly Review*
JSOT	*Journal for the Study of the Old Testament*
JSOTSup	Journal for the Study of the Old Testament: Supplement Series
MW	*Muslim World*
NedTT	*Nederlands theologisch tijdschrift*
NovT	*Novum Testamentum*
NTS	*New Testament Studies*
OTP	*Old Testament Pseudipigrapha*. Edited by James H. Charlesworth. 2 vols. New York, 1983
RB	*Revue biblique*
REJ	*Revue des études juives*
TSK	*Theologische Studien und Kritiken*
TZ	*Theologische Zeitschrift*
ZAW	*Zeitschrift für die alttestamentliche Wissenschaft*

Preface

Samaritan history is a rather slender cultural thread wandering through Middle Eastern history, but its trail is better marked than was once believed. Occasionally the archaeologist unearths a building at Delos or Gerizim, a cave at Wadi Daliyeh reveals its grim evidence, or an inscription is found at Emmaus or Delos. Early literary evidence appears, often in the same archaeological finds—a bit of information on the refugees in the cave or an inscription once part of a building. Among the texts at Qumran are recensions of the Pentateuch with a distinctive Samaritan flavor. Bursts of literary activity appeared in the third and fourth centuries and again in the thirteenth century, when theological questions become more urgent to the struggling community.

This study describes and illustrates a wide variety of Samaritan literature, including the various versions of the Pentateuch, biblical commentaries, liturgical texts, theological works, and chronicles. Various methods of literary and historical criticism have greatly enhanced our knowledge of the Bible, and the same approaches can illuminate the context and significance of Samaritan writings. In turn, these texts inform our understanding of Middle Eastern culture. Parallel Islamic, Jewish, and Christian traditions are noted. For example, some say that the first part of the Muslim short creed comes from the Samaritans or that many ideas in the *Memar Marqah* are taken from Christianity. Often the extensive biographical information that is available about authors and transmitters of the text reveals familial networks across a large geographical area.

We discover that the Samaritans were not an incidental part of the Roman world, that their Pentateuch was central to the birth of textual criticism in the West, and that their traditions may offer a corrective on several points of the history of the Middle East. Much of what we know about the Samaritans derives from non-Samaritan sources, particularly Josephus, Roman and Byzantine official documents, and the accounts of travelers through their lands. But their own words can tell a new story that enhances the overall picture.

MANUSCRIPTS

The words of the Samaritans, their literature, are preserved in hundreds of manuscripts copied over the past thousand years and studied by Western scholars since the sixteenth century. The manuscripts have experienced a diaspora much more extensive than that of the community that produced them. There are collections in Australia, Canada, Denmark, England, France, Germany, Israel, Italy, Russia, Sweden, Turkey, and the United States.[1]

LANGUAGE AND PROBLEMS OF TRANSLATION

All the English translations have their problems because the texts themselves are very problematic. They were often carelessly copied and contain many arbitrary spellings, misspellings, and other errors. The shift in languages among Aramaic, Hebrew, and Arabic as well as the changing vocabulary and idioms of the languages themselves over a period of time present continuing difficulties.

DIVISIONS WITHIN SAMARITAN LITERATURE

This book contains two main sections. The first is a presentation of the narrative works that tell the Samaritan story: the Samaritan Pentateuch, the Samaritan Joshua (also called the *Chronicon samaritanum*), and the *Annals* and chronicles. The first of these three works, the Samaritan Pentateuch, is the sacred text of the Samaritans. It is the basic source of Samaritanism. The Samaritan Pentateuch gives the Samaritan community its identity and begins the Samaritan story. The Samaritan Joshua continues this story from the time of Joshua up until the Roman domination of Palestine. It takes the reader from the "period of divine favor" to the "period of divine disfavor" through the retelling of fantastic acts of heroism, deliverance, and disappointment. The *Annals* of Abu'l Fath, the *New Chronicle (Chronicle Adler)*, and *Chronicle II* pick up the story where the Samaritan Joshua left off and continue the Samaritan story right up to modern times. The cumulative

---

[1] See J. G. Fraser, "A Checklist of Samaritan Manuscripts Known to Have Entered Europe before A.D. 1700," *AbrN* 21 (1982/1983): 10–27; Jean-Pierre Rothschild, *Catalogue des manuscrits samaritains* (Paris: Bibliothèque Nationale, Department des Manuscrits, 1985).

effect of placing these three narrative works back-to-back is a window into the Samaritan self-understanding.

The second section of the book deals with religious writings that concern Samaritan ritual and theology. The core texts in this section of the book are the *Tibat Marqe* and the liturgy. *Marqe* presents the theology of the Samaritan community and the liturgy provides examples of how this theology expressed itself in the collective worship of the Samaritans. The final chapter discusses a miscellany of religion-related writings, inscriptions, amulets, and astrological writings.

CHOICE OF SELECTIONS FOR THIS BOOK

An introduction demands decisions about what to include and what to omit. Sometimes these decisions are very difficult (especially when something is omitted), but it is impractical, and in an introduction not very helpful, to include a detailed examination of all Samaritan religious and sacred literature. Consequently, we have had to be selective in the literature presented and in the extent of the introduction for each Samaritan writing. Our choice was guided by three questions:

1. How significant is the particular work of Samaritan literature to the Samaritan community itself?

2. How accessible is that work to the general reading audience?

3. How helpful is that work for the beginning student's understanding of the Samaritans?

The manner in which all three questions came together determined our selection of material for this introduction. For example, the Samaritan Pentateuch is tremendously valuable to the Samaritan community and is absolutely vital for the beginning student's understanding. In its major variations from the MT, however, the Samaritan Pentateuch is readily available to the beginning student. Therefore the whole text of the Samaritan Pentateuch is not reproduced here but only the sections that best illustrate its unique character. Conversely, the Samaritan Joshua, though not as important to the Samaritan community as the Samaritan Pentateuch, is nonetheless very important for the beginning student yet is not as readily available. The text of the Samaritan Joshua thus appears in this introduction much more extensively than does the text of the Samaritan Pentateuch. Samaritan Joshua along with the other chronicles is a rather straightforward narrative and needs little commentary along the way. *Tibat Marqe* is considerably less narrative and more conceptual and benefits from interspersed commentary. The chapters on the liturgy and more particularly the chapter including inscriptions and amulets contain less text to illustrate the accompanying commentary. Excerpts and discussions of some less important works of Samaritan religious literature appear as sidebars scattered throughout the book. They are placed next to or within presentations of Samaritan literature where they have either historical or theological connections.

In the *Tibat Marqe,* the *Asatir,* and liturgical works אלהים is translated as "God," both אדוני and מרי as "LORD," and יהוה as "YHWH." We have used brackets to indicate our editorial additions and the words we have supplied that are not found in the text. Except in quoted translations, an attempt has been made to standardize Samaritan names according to Alan D. Crown's spellings in "Studies in Samaritan Scribal Practices and Manuscript History: IV. An Index of Scribes, Witnesses, Owners, and Others Mentioned in Samaritan Manuscripts, with a Key to Principal Families Therein," *Bulletin of the John Rylands University Library of Manchester,* 68 (1986): 317–72.

List of Illustrations

Part One

The Samaritan Story

Chapter 1

Samaritan Pentateuch

INTRODUCTION

The Samaritan Pentateuch (SP) constitutes the entire canon of sacred text for the Samaritan community. Its prominent role within the Samaritan community is clear. Public reading of the Pentateuch is a central component of communal worship and religious festivals. Inscriptions taken from the Pentateuch decorate public buildings and private homes alike. Devotees memorize portions from the Pentateuch and incorporate these memorized texts into prayer and private piety. The importance of the SP as a living and vibrant part of the Samaritan community cannot be overstated. The symbiotic relationship between the Samaritans and the SP makes it impossible to conceive of the community without the SP or the SP without the Samaritan community.

Despite its close ties to the Samaritans, the SP's influence is not limited to the Samaritan community. Referred to in the writings of the early Christian patristic authors as well as in the Talmud and by early Jewish writers, the SP was a recognized textual tradition known throughout the Levant in the early centuries of the Common Era. Lost to the West for hundreds of years, the SP reemerged in the seventeenth century and found itself immediately embroiled in religious debates between the various branches of Christianity. For the better part of 150 years, this unfortunate controversy among Roman Catholic and Protestant scholars over the preferred reading of the Old Testament text sidetracked investigation away from the SP as a tradition and text valuable in and of itself. Fortunately, this religious polemical veil has been removed, and once again the SP has drawn the attention of scholars, religious and nonreligious, as an important text in its own right and as an important textual witness to the vibrant and tenacious Samaritan community.

Scholarly attention given to the SP grew exponentially during the last two decades of the twentieth century and promises to grow even further in the opening years of the twenty-first century. Literary critics investigating the text transmission of the Hebrew Bible are consulting the SP, as are sociologists and anthropologists interested in the history and cultures of the Hellenistic

Levant. Publications of the DSS have provided tantalizing evidence to suggest that the SP textual tradition was a major participant in the literature of the Hellenistic and post-Hellenistic Levant.

ORIGIN

The text that became the SP is the result of expansions and alterations made to a text type that had a considerable history of use prior to its adoption by the Samaritans as their sacred text.[1] Comparisons with the LXX, the MT, and, more recently, the Qumran materials have demonstrated that the text adopted by the Samaritans was part of a group of texts that existed side by side and, in various ways, related to each other in the centuries before the turn of the eras.

Several attempts have been made to diagram the history of the text prior to its sectarian Samaritan identification.[2] None of the proposed reconstructions have won unanimous support, but a generally accepted outline has emerged within a scholarly consensus.[3] In broad terms, the path that led to the four texts we know today (LXX, MT, SP, and that represented by the appropriate DSS, such as 4QExod) developed as follows. A loose, but common, text tradition circulated that encompassed the Old Greek (OG) text, the MT, the 4QExod, and the SP. From this the OG text split off first, developing its own set of unique expansions and characteristics. For a time, the textual tradition common to the MT, 4QExod, and the SP continued developing until the 4QExod and SP traditions followed a path of their own, marked by a number of expansionist tendencies that distinguish it from the tradition later resulting in the MT. Finally, the traditions behind 4QExod and the SP went their separate ways, with the addition of major expansions in the SP, such as those found in Exod 20, intended to make clear the legitimacy of worship on Gerizim.[4] These "textual trajectories" are, as it were, the footprints of social

---

[1] Judith E. Sanderson, *An Exodus Scroll from Qumran: 4QpaleoExod and the Samaritan Tradition* (Atlanta: Scholars Press, 1986), 308; James Purvis, *The Samaritan Pentateuch and the Origin of the Samaritan Sect* (Cambridge: Harvard University Press, 1968), 69.

[2] See the survey presented by Sanderson, *Exodus Scroll*, 31–34.

[3] The major alternative to the theory presented here is a theory of regional or local texts. See Frank Moore Cross Jr., *The Ancient Library of Qumran and Modern Biblical Studies* (rev. ed.; Garden City, N.Y.: Doubleday, 1961); Purvis, *Samaritan Pentateuch*, 80–81; and Frank Moore Cross Jr. and Shemaryahu Talmon, eds., *Qumran and the History of the Biblical Text* (Cambridge: Harvard University Press, 1975).

[4] Sanderson, *Exodus Scroll*, 311.

groups that developed their own self-identity and used the respective textual traditions as a means of articulating their identity and legitimacy in the face of competing groups and ideologies.

If this reconstruction is correct, it is best to consider the SP as a tree branch coexisting with other branches that developed from a common trunk.[5] Indeed, the text of Qumran and that of the Samaritans are so similar that they may well be considered articulations of one single text type.[6]

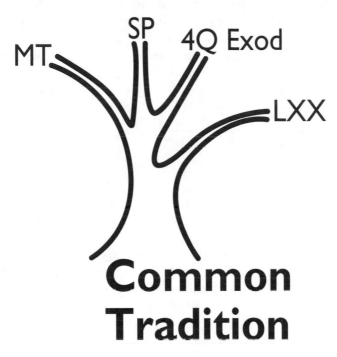

Figure 1. Schematic of the "manuscript tree"

The Samaritans held their Scriptures in common with other groups within Palestine during the last several centuries B.C.E.[7] The expansions contained in the Samaritan and Qumran texts include challenges to the supremacy of Jerusalem as the preferred site of worship and to the cult stationed there. The presence of these challenges within the texts makes it easy to

---

[5] See Frank Moore Cross Jr., "History of the Biblical Text," in *Qumran and the History of the Biblical Text* (ed. Frank Moore Cross Jr. and Shemaryahu Talmon; Cambridge: Harvard University Press, 1975), 181.

[6] Sanderson, *Exodus Scroll*, 314.

[7] Ibid., 317.

imagine that the various text types used by groups in Palestine had become weapons by which the struggle for religious legitimacy was fought.

Comparing the differences between the SP and the 4QExod material may help furnish clues to the historical circumstances surrounding the sectarian recension that finally resulted in a text fit for the Samaritan community.[8] The last major recension, and the one that separates SP from 4QExod, is the expansion, found in Exod 20, that creates a new tenth commandment and elevates Gerizim as the legitimate place of worship. Once the Samaritan community canonized this text recension, it assumed a static quality allowing it to function as an identifying hallmark of the Samaritan faithful. Just when this final recension took place is difficult to say, but at present all signs point to a process that began in the late Hasmonaean period, during the late second or early first century B.C.E., but may not have finally become static or complete until the second century C.E.[9]

HISTORY

The SP is known outside the Samaritan community already in early patristic and Jewish writings.[10] Care, however, must be taken when reviewing these writings, for the term "Samaritan" can be used to refer to inhabitants of the region of Samaria or to the ethnic and religious group. For example, Justin uses the term several times, but only in chapter 53 of the *First Apology* can it be concluded that by the term "Samaritan" he means the religious group. Origen, writing in the third century, seems to have at least a passing acquaintance with the SP. He recognizes that the Samaritans revere the Pentateuch but not the Prophets.

---

[8] Sanderson, ibid., 319, contributes observations in this direction.

[9] See Frank Moore Cross Jr., "The History of the Biblical Text in the Light of the Discoveries in the Judean Desert," *HTR* 52 (1964): 287–92. Ingrid Hjelm has presented very interesting arguments in *The Samaritans and Early Judaism: A Literary Analysis* (JSOTSup 303; Sheffield: Sheffield Academic Press, 2000), 93. See also Purvis, *Samaritan Pentateuch,* 85. Alan D. Crown ("Redating the Schism between the Judaeans and the Samaritans," *JQR* 82 [1991]: 17–50) has argued for a date as late as the third century C.E. for the schism between Judaeans and Samaritans.

[10] As an initiation into the subject of the SP in patristic writings, see Bruce Hall, "The Samaritans in the Writings of Justin Martyr and Tertullian," in *Proceedings of the First International Congress of the Société d'Études Samaritaines* (ed. Abraham Tal and Moshe Florentin; Tel Aviv: Tel Aviv University Press, 1991), 115–22. A survey of rabbinic material can be found in Robert T. Anderson and Terry Giles, *The Keepers: An Introduction to the History and Culture of the Samaritans* (Peabody, Mass.: Hendrickson, 2002), 42–50.

Likewise, in the rabbinical literature, care must be taken to discern when the term "Samaritan" refers to the religious sect and when it does not. Within this literature, the SP is certainly not accepted as an authoritative text. Two of the best known examples will suffice to illustrate.

> Mar Zutra or, as some say, Mar 'Ukba said: "Originally the Torah was given to Israel in Hebrew characters and in the Sacred [Hebrew] language; later, in times of Ezra, the Torah was given in the Assyrian script and the Aramaic language. [Finally], they selected for Israel the Assyrian script and the Hebrew language, leaving the Hebrew characters and the Aramaic language for the *hedyototh*." Who are meant by the hedyototh—R. Hisda answers: "the Cutheans (Samaritans)." *b. Sanh. 21b–22a*[11]

In this passage, it is apparent that the very script used by the Samaritans is clear evidence that the SP text is different and not to be preferred over the MT.

The second example bases the rabbinical rejection of the SP on the content of the Samaritan text.

> R. Eleazar son of R. Jose said: "In this connection I proved the Samaritan Scriptures to be false. I said to them, 'You have falsified your Torah but you gained nothing thereby. You declare that "the terebinths of Moreh" means Shechem. We have learned this by an inference from analogy; but how have you learned it'!" *b. Soṭah 33b*

Deuteronomy 11:30 is the subject of the contention mentioned by R. Eleazar.[12] The MT ends simply with the phrase, "the terebinths of Moreh" whereas the SP adds a clarifying explanation, "over against Shechem" and so locates the exact spot. R. Eleazar's point is that even though the identification specified by the Samaritans is correct, they confirmed that location by adjusting their sacred text, making the SP less than reliable.

For centuries the SP was preserved solely in the Samaritan communities themselves and was unknown to Western scholarship. That all changed, however, in the early part of the seventeenth century. In 1616 the scholar, statesman, and adventurer Pietro della Valle purchased a SP manuscript from a merchant in Damascus. Little did della Valle anticipate the central role it would play in Samaritan studies. The manuscript originated in Damascus and reports to have been completed in 1345/1346. European scholars received it enthusiastically, and seven years after its purchase by della Valle, the manuscript was presented to the Paris Oratory and published in

---

[11] All quotes from the Babylonian Talmud are from Isidore Epstein, ed., *The Babylonian Talmud,* London: Soncino Press, 1936.

[12] A discussion of Deut 11:30 appears later in this chapter.

the *Paris Polyglot,* edited by Morinus. A second polyglot, the *London Poly-glot,* edited by Walton, appeared in 1675. Von Gall used this manuscript as his Codex B, and it served as the basis for his edited version of the SP, published early in the twentieth century.

Both seventeenth-century editions of the SP quickly became embroiled in controversies between Protestants and Roman Catholics, each group seeking to gather evidence supporting its own contentions regarding the content of Sacred Scripture. The dispute raged over the merits of the MT, on one hand, upon which Protestant translations of the Bible were based, and the LXX and Vulgate, on the other, the textual traditions preferred by Catholic scholars. The fact that the SP agrees with the LXX in a limited number of readings led certain scholars, such as Capellus and Morinus, to advocate the value of the text, for it was thought to support their contention of the primacy of the LXX.[13] Protestant scholars, however, such as Hottinger, argued against the reliability of the SP tradition on the basis of these same common readings of the SP and the LXX.[14]

This controversy continued for the better part of two centuries, based on the assumption of SP's similarity to LXX although the SP reads, in fact, closer to the MT than to the LXX. The latter point became lost to those with more sectarian agendas to debate. Thus a mistaken description of the SP was used as fuel to fire controversy between Catholics and Protestants. An important exception to this argumentative trend was the work of Kennicott in the middle of the eighteenth century.[15] He attempted to move the discussion about the SP away from sectarian considerations with a careful consideration of the SP text on its own merits. Despite Kennicott's efforts, however, the SP remained embroiled in these religious disputes.

The delay in textual criticism of the manuscripts came to an end with the groundbreaking work of W. Gesenius in 1815.[16] Gesenius constructed categories by which to examine the variants between the MT and the SP: (1) grammatical emendations made in the SP, (2) glosses added to the SP text, (3) variations added to the SP removing ambiguities in the MT, (4) the elimina-

---

[13] A. L. Cappelus, *Diatriba de veris et antiquis Hebraeorum literis* (Amsterdam, 1645); Joannes Morinus, *Exercitationes ecclesiasticae in utrumque Samaritanorum Pentateuchum* (Paris, 1631).

[14] Johann Heinrich Hottinger, *Exercitationes antimorinianae de Pentateucho samaritano* (Zurich, 1644).

[15] B. Kennicott, *The State of the Printed Hebrew Text of the Old Testament Considered: Dissertation the Second Wherein the Samaritan Copy of the Pentateuch Is Vindicated* (Oxford, 1759).

[16] William Gesenius, *De Pentateuchi samaritani origine, indole, et auctoritate commentatio philologico-critica* (Halle, 1815).

tion of inconsistencies in the MT based upon parallel passages, (5) SP expansions from parallel passages, (6) changes made in chronologies, (7) changes based upon Samaritan grammar and morphology, and (8) variations based upon sectarian Samaritan theology.

These categories are still used in comparative examinations, although the conclusions offered about the variations have changed since Gesenius's time. Gesenius was of the opinion that the SP is a fairly late corruption of a standard Hebrew text and, as such, of very little, if any, value for textual criticism. As in other areas of biblical text criticism, the shadow Gesenius cast influenced the better part of a generation of SP scholarship.

Later in the nineteenth century, Paul de Lagarde made significant strides in establishing the science of the textual criticism of the Old Testament.[17] His work led to a greater appreciation of both the LXX and the SP as early witnesses to the textual tradition that would become stabilized in the MT.

Without doubt, the most important publication for SP studies in the early part of the twentieth century was von Gall's edited version of the SP in 1916–1918.[18] Criticized at times for its unevenness and although significant manuscripts were not available to von Gall (notably the Abisha Scroll), this remains the standard published edition available to Western scholarship.[19] Von Gall's edition appeared at a time when Western scholarship was experiencing an explosion in textual criticism of the Bible, of related texts such as the SP, and of inscriptions recovered by the archaeologist's trowel. P. Kahle argued the case for what he believed to be the antiquity of the SP.[20] He recognized that the SP represented a popular text existing side by side with the tradition that would later become the MT. Kahle concluded that in comparison with the MT, the SP preserved many more than the four original readings allowed by Gesenius. He explained the similarities to the LXX by suggesting that the earliest Greek translations were based on popular versions of the Hebrew text, such as the one represented by the SP. In general, Kahle was followed by the Old Testament exegetes O. Eissfeldt, E. Würthwein,

---

[17] Paul de Lagarde, *Anmerkungen zur griechischen Übersetzung der Proverbien* (Leipzig: A. Brockhaus, 1863).

[18] August von Gall, *Der hebräische Pentateuch der Samaritaner* (5 vols.; Giessen: Töpelmann, 1914–1918; repr., 1 vol., 1966).

[19] As pointed out by Abraham Tal ("Samaritan Literature," in *The Samaritans* [ed. Alan D. Crown; Tübingen: J. C. B. Mohr, 1989], 435), von Gall's predilection for the MT led him to choose readings that were closer to the grammar of the MT, and so he may have unwisely established the MT as the standard by which to measure the SP.

[20] Paul Kahle, "Untersuchungen zur Geschichte des Pentateuch-textes," *TSK* 88 (1915): 399–439.

R. H. Pfeiffer, F. F. Bruce, and M. Greenburg.[21] The recovery of the materials from Qumran, including texts that read very much like the SP, has supported Kahle's reconstruction in at least one respect: even if the hypothesis of a popular and an official text existing side by side can no longer be supported,[22] Kahle was correct in that the SP represents a pre-Masoretic textual tradition that circulated well beyond the Samaritan sect.

The recovery and dissemination of the scrolls from the Dead Sea has provided a new, much more complete, and somewhat surprising context by which to understand better the SP and the textual tradition of which it was a part. In 1955 P. Skehan concluded, on the basis of his work with the scrolls, that 4QExod belonged to the Samaritan recension.[23] J. Sanderson, who made a detailed comparison between the 4QExod material, the LXX, the MT, and the SP, concluded that the shared expansions of the SP and 4QExod link the two texts and that 4QExod represents an earlier stage of development of the same tradition later expressed in the SP.[24] In 1965 B. Waltke made a strong case that the LXX should not be ignored in the reconstruction of the textual context of the SP.[25] Such examples of recent scholarship fostered a renewed interest in, and appreciation for, the common textual tradition out of which emerged the text types that we know and recognize today. This common pool of religious texts speaks of the lively social dynamics characterizing Hasmonean Palestine.

Gall's *Der hebräische Pentateuch der Samaritaner,* remains the most widely known edition of the SP outside the Samaritan community, continuing to provide the best available access to the SP for most.[26] Augmenting von Gall's edition are two more recent scholarly publications of the SP. The first is the edition produced by Abraham and Ratson Tsedaqa in 1962–1965.[27] This in-

---

[21] Otto Eissfeldt, *Einleitung in das Alte Testament* (Tübingen: Mohr, 1934); E. Würthwein, *The Text of the Old Testament: An Introduction to the Biblia hebraica* (trans. E. F. Rhodes; Grand Rapids: Eerdmans, 1979); Robert H. Pfeiffer, *Introduction to the Old Testament* (New York: Harper & Brothers, 1941); F. F. Bruce, *The Books and the Parchments* (Westwood, N.J.: Fleming H. Revell Publishing, 1953); M. Greenburg, "The Stabilization of the Text of the Hebrew Bible in the Light of the Biblical Materials from the Judean Desert," *JAOS* 76 (1956): 157–67.

[22] Purvis, *Samaritan Pentateuch,* 79.

[23] Patrick Skehan, "Exodus in the Samaritan Recension from Qumran," *JBL* 74 (1955): 182–87.

[24] Sanderson, *Exodus Scroll,* 307–311.

[25] Bruce Waltke, "Prolegomena to the Samaritan Pentateuch" (Ph.D. diss., Harvard University, 1965).

[26] Gall, *Der hebräische Pentateuch.*

[27] Abraham and Ratson Tsedaqa, *Samaritan Pentateuch* (Holon, Israel, 1962–1965).

teresting but unfortunately out-of-print edition places the Samaritan text alongside an Old Hebrew and an Arabic translation of the text. The second is that of Abraham Tal in 1994.[28] Tal's publication presents an edited version of MS 6 (C) of the Shechem synagogue. This highly regarded thirteenth-century manuscript is presented with relatively few but carefully chosen editorial notes. Although Tal's work is commendable, he is quick to note that a thoroughly updated critical edition to improve upon that of von Gall's is desirable.[29]

MANUSCRIPTS

The manuscript most venerated by the Samaritans, from which all other copies are reported to originate, is the Abisha Scroll, housed in the synagogue at Nablus. This scroll presents itself as written by Abisha, son of Pinhas,[30] son of Eleazar, son of Aaron, in the thirteenth year after the Israelites entered the land of Canaan. Its reputed antiquity, traced back to the very earliest days of the Israelite experience, gives the scroll a place of honor within the Samaritan community. Unfortunately, modern scholarship has been unable to substantiate this claim of the scroll's ancientness. Although the scroll gives the appearance of "great antiquity"[31] and the scribal notation dates the scroll to 1065 C.E., a significant portion of modern research dates the scroll to no earlier than the middle of the twelfth century C.E.[32] Even if it cannot be attributed to the great-grandson of Aaron, the scroll's great age and its special place within the Samaritan community make the scroll worthy of high regard.

The Abisha Scroll is only one manuscript among many that have become available to the scholarly community, and the last decades of the twentieth century witnessed an increase in scholarly interest directed toward the various Samaritan manuscripts. In collections around the world, there are just under one hundred manuscripts of the SP that date from before the eighteenth century.[33] With few exceptions (notably the Abisha Scroll and

---

[28] Abraham Tal, *The Samaritan Pentateuch, Edited according to MS 6 (C) of the Shekhem Synagogue* (Tel Aviv: Tel Aviv University Press, 1994).

[29] Ibid., vi.

[30] The name Pinhas often appears with alternate spellings; Phineas or Phinehas. For consistency, we will use Pinhas throughout.

[31] R. E. Moody, "Samaritan Material at Boston University: The Boston Collection and the Abisha Scroll," *Boston University Graduate Journal* 10 (1957): 158–60.

[32] F. Pérez Castro, *Séfer Abisha* (Madrid: C.S.I.C., 1959); Alan D. Crown, "The Abisha Scroll of the Samaritans," *BJRL* 58 (1975): 36–55.

[33] Jean-Pierre Rothschild has compiled a very useful guide to Samaritan manuscripts, "Samaritan Manuscripts: A Guide to the Collections and Catalogues," in *The Samaritans* (ed. Alan D. Crown; Tübingen: J. C. B. Mohr, 1989), 771–94.

modern copies sold to tourists), most existing pre-twentieth-century manuscripts are in codex form. The earliest of the manuscripts date from the perhaps the eleventh century C.E. (the Abisha Scroll), and a sizable quantity
come from the fourteenth and fifteenth centuries C.E. Typically, these are
written in the Paleo-Hebrew script with the text appearing in two columns
per page. It is not uncommon for the manuscripts to include Arabic or Aramaic renditions of the text in columns next to the Hebrew text. Sometimes
the text is written in Arabic using Samaritan (Paleo-Hebrew) script. The text
is divided into paragraphs. The end of a paragraph is frequently marked by a
"-:" sign followed by a blank space. Within a paragraph, a ":" sign is used to
separate between sentences. A single "." level with the letters is used to separate words. Scribes were at liberty to create visually interesting patterns
within the text by aligning letters in a column on a page or by decorating
margins in some manner. (See figure 2, p. 13.)

The fact that pre-twentieth-century SP manuscripts are scattered around
the world, substantial collections are in the Samaritan synagogue at Nablus,
the John Rylands Library of the University of Manchester, the British National Library in London, the Bibliothèque Nationale in Paris, the State Public Library in St. Petersburg, and the Michigan State University Library in
East Lansing. The manuscripts in these collections not only contain the text
of the SP; scribes usually included valuable information concerning the production of the scroll or codex. Many of the manuscripts contain scribal colophons, cryptograms, honorific titles given to the buyer or commissioner of
the manuscripts, or bills of sale. These notations are useful in dating the
manuscript and identifying the scribe who prepared it and the manuscript's
place of origin. It turns out that many of the manuscripts existing today were
copied between the twelfth and fifteenth centuries, with production reaching
its peak in the fourteenth and fifteenth centuries.[34] Whether an accident of
history or a result of the tumultuous times, there are no extant manuscripts
produced between 1231 and 1321.

The majority of the pre-twentieth-century manuscripts in these collections come from four centers of manuscript production: Damascus,
Egypt, Shechem (Nablus), and Zarephath.[35] Shechem, as a site for manuscript production, is quite understandable, as it is the Samaritan holy
place, nestled in the valley between Mounts Gerizim and Ebal. Damascus

---

[34] Robert T. Anderson, *Studies in Samaritan Manuscripts and Artifacts: The
Chamberlain-Warren Collection* (Cambridge, Mass.: American Schools of Oriental
Research, 1978), 10.

[35] Robert T. Anderson, "Samaritan Pentateuch: A General Account," in *The
Samaritans* (ed. Alan D. Crown; Tübingen: J. C. B. Mohr, 1989), 395.

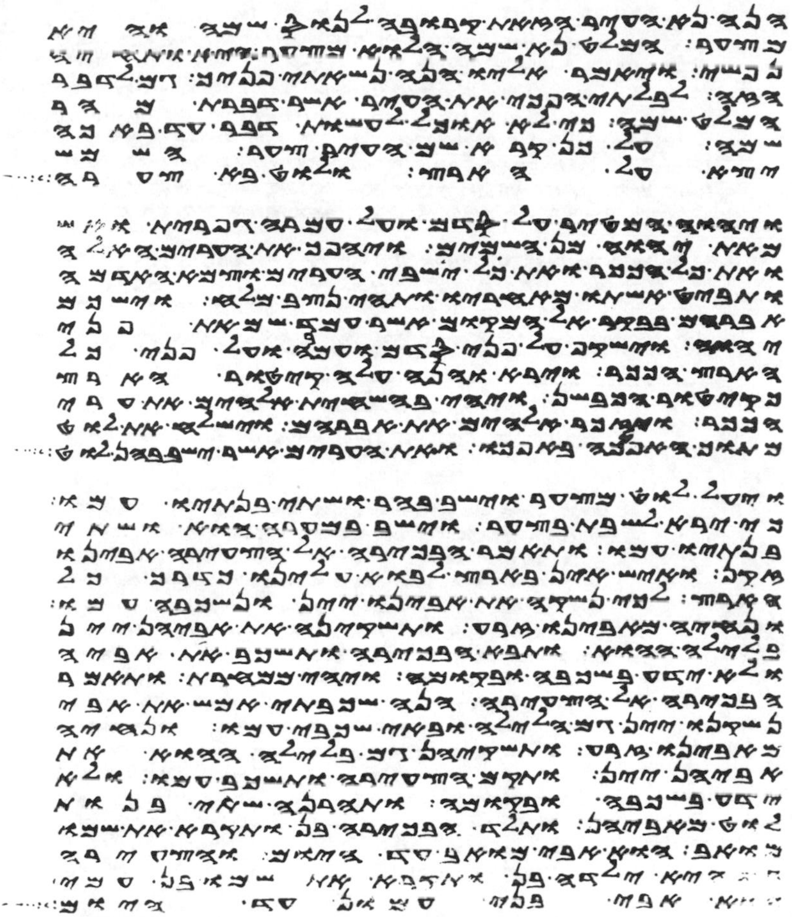

Figure 2. Genesis 19:20–38 in the fifteenth-century manuscript CW 2473 in the Chamberlain-Warren collection at Michigan State University. There are several examples of skipped spacing to align similar letters in a vertical column. Four *alefs* are aligned in the last four lines of the first paragraph along with two *ayins* in the last two lines. Toward the end of the last paragraph, four *vavs* are seen and two *bets* are columned in the last two lines. *Courtesy of Special Collections, Michigan State University Libraries.*

must have been favored as a secure and relatively peaceful location, for about twice as many of the manuscripts come from there as from any other center of production. Those originating from Zarephath all come from a sixty-five-year span and may reflect the vicissitudes of the family of scribes settled there, although its beauty and pleasant coastal location certainly

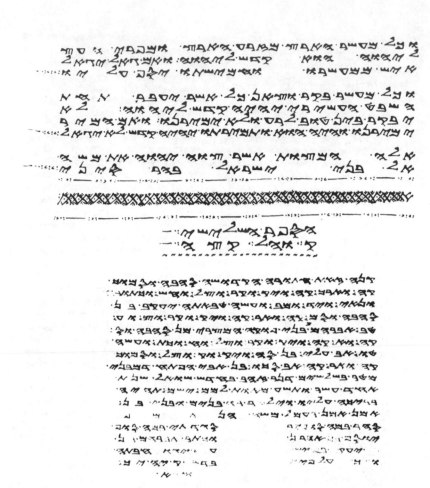

Figure 3. The last page of Leviticus in CW 2473, illustrating Samaritan decorative patterns and a bill of sale. *Courtesy of Special Collections, Michigan State University Libraries.*

make it an attractive spot. The manuscripts coming from Egypt attest to the wide dispersion of the Samaritan community and must have been intended to meet the needs of these Samaritans to the far south. (See figure 4, p. 15.)

Some of the information provided by the scribes is presented in the form of acrostics woven into the text of the scroll or codex. The Abisha Scroll has such an acrostic woven into the text of Deut 6:10:

I am Abisha son of Pinhas son of Eleazar son of Aaron the priest; on them be the favor of the Lord and his glory.

Figure 4. Deuteronomy 8:3–16 in CW 2484, a fifteenth-century manuscript in the Chamberlain-Warren collection at Michigan State University. A central vertical channel has been created into which the scribe has dropped letters from the horizontal biblical text to create a vertical text describing himself. The vertical text on this page identifies the scribe's family (Munes) and the fact that he copied the manuscript in Egypt. *Courtesy of Special Collections, Michigan State University Libraries.*

I wrote this holy book at the door of the tent of meeting on Mount Gerizim in the year thirteen of the reign of the children of Israel in the land of Canaan to all its boundaries round about. I praise the Lord. Amen.[36]

---

[36] Anderson and Giles, *The Keepers,* 111.

Likewise, bills of sale also provide information regarding the circumstances of the manuscript's production. The following is found at the end of the book of Exodus in CW 2478a:

> This Holy Torah was bought by (..) (..) (..)
> (..) Joseph son of (..) (..) (..) (..) (..)
> Obadiah son of Abd Hehob of the family Iqara from (..)
> (..) (..) (..) (..) (..) (..) (..)
> Obadiah son of (..) (..) (..) (..) (..)
> Abd Hehob son of Sedaqa of the family Remach, all of them from among the inhabitants of Egypt, for 24 dinars in the month of Rajab in the year 892 [C.E. 1487].
> May there be a blessing upon it. Amen.
> Abraham son of Ab Uzzi son of Joseph son of Jitrana of Damascus wrote this.[37]

In an effort to group the manuscripts into families related by common place of origination, scribal affiliation, and chronology, scholars have considered information provided by acrostics, bills of sale, and other incidental pieces of information included in the manuscripts, along with stylistic characteristics. Anderson's work in the 1980s, which established early criteria for "clusters," was successful in placing several of the manuscripts used by von Gall into three clusters.[38]

Limited access to the collections of manuscripts afforded to scholars have, however, handicapped Samaritan studies. The geographical distances between the collections and the fragile condition of some of the scrolls and codices have prevented a thorough comparison of manuscripts. There have been notable attempts to overcome this dilemma. A. D. Crown has made extensive use of microfilm to record images of the manuscripts and so retain access to the valuable materials even when thousands of miles removed from the collections themselves. The publication of an updated critical edition and text-critical inquiries that investigate the history and relationships between the various SP manuscripts will be aided by efforts to electronically disseminate photographic images of the scrolls and codices.

---

[37] (..) indicates an honorific title.

[38] Robert T. Anderson, "Clustering Samaritan Hebrew Pentateuchal Manuscripts," in *Études samaritaines: Pentateuque et targum, exégèse et philologie, chroniques* (ed. Jean-Pierre Rothschild and Guy Dominique Sixdenier; Louvain: Peeters, 1988), 57–66.

A new generation of communication technology promises to remove the barrier of limited access altogether. The Rare Collections division of the Michigan State University Library is conducting a pilot project aimed at digitizing images of the fifteenth- and sixteenth-century Chamberlain-Warren scrolls. The plan is to preserve these images on a specially designed Web site hosted by the university and available to any interested scholar. The images are clear and sharp and can be manipulated to reveal even more detail than what is available to the naked eye when examining the manuscripts in person. This project may well be a harbinger of a developing trend.

CHARACTERISTICS

Early in the last century, the influential Samaritan scholar James Montgomery wrote that the SP's "variations will never be of interest to more than the textual scholar."[39] Montgomery here clearly missed the mark, for in recent years scholars have recognized the SP as an important participant in the literary milieu of the Hellenistic Levant. But Montgomery could not have foreseen the recovery of the DSS, nor could he have imagined that those materials would, because of similar readings to the SP, cast new light not only upon the Samaritans and their text but upon text transmission as a whole in the Hellenistic Levant.

The SP is commonly characterized in terms of its variations from other textual traditions, primarily the MT. At times, this tendency to compare the SP with only the MT has obscured the fact that the SP is actually closer to the MT in its readings than it is to the LXX. Further, with the widespread publication of the DSS, it has become obvious that a simple comparison with the MT is inadequate, for the SP shares a considerable part of its textual tradition with the tradition represented by the collection of materials recovered at Qumran. Nevertheless, ever since Gesenius, it has been customary to describe the variations between the MT and the SP in terms of Gesenius's eight groupings.[40]

---

[39] James Montgomery, *The Samaritans, the Earliest Jewish Sect: Their History, Theology, and Literature* (Philadelphia: Winston, 1907; repr., New York: KTAV, 1968), 290.

[40] Gesenius, *De Pentateuchi samaritani origine.* Recent comparisons with the materials from Qumran, especially 4QExod, are refining Gesenius's categories. See Sanderson, *Exodus Scroll,* 17–52.

Scribal Errors

Many of the approximately six thousand variations between the MT and the SP are a confusion of letters that when spoken sound very much the same, for example, between labials, gutturals, dentals, or palatals; such as between ס (s) and שׁ (sh, sometimes s), or between צ (ts) and ז (z), or a confusion between letters that sound different but in writing appear similar such as between ד (d) and ר (r), or between י (y) and ו (w).

Figure 5. Hebrew characters "r," "d," "y," and "w" (reading left to right) with SP equivalents below. A careless or idiosyncratic hand in either script could produce confusion between *resh* and *dalet* or *yod* and *vav*.

Often the confusion results in a nonsensical construction that is easily remedied:

In Gen 10:27 the SP reads א (the glottal stop) in אדורם for the ה (h) in the MT rendition, הדורם.

The SP of Gen 31:40 reads a nonsensical חרף, having placed a פ (p) for the ב (b) in חרב ("harvest") as found in the MT.

A common scribal error is illustrated in Gen 14:2, where a ד (d) has become substituted for ר (r) in the SP reading שמאבד for the MT reading שמאבר.[41]

There are probably several reasons for confusions between letters. At times, the confusion seems to be between letters that sound the same (ס [s] and שׁ [sh, sometimes s]). At other times, the confusion seems to be a result of a mix-up between letters that appear the same (ד [d] and ר [r]). These mixtures

---

[41] See also Gen 47:21 and Num 24:17.

of letters with the same sound and of letters with similar appearance may provide insight into the scribal means for copying manuscripts. On occasion, the scribe may have been copying from an original that was being read to him aloud whereas at other times the original was copied by sight. If the original was being copied as the scribe heard, confusion between letters with the same sound may appear more frequently, but it is likely that errors in grammar would be minimized. The scribe may not remember the correct spelling for a particular word, but the scribe would have understood the sentences that were being read to him, and grammatical forms such as agreement between verbs and subjects and pronouns would more likely be written correctly. If the scribe was copying by sight from an original presented before him, confusion of letters with the same sound would not be expected as frequently as confusion between letters of similar form. Further, that scribe would not need to understand the text that was being copied, but only have a commitment to faithfully transcribe the forms of the letters. In this case, grammatical errors could be expected much more frequently, and there would be little to prevent nonsensical renditions as in Gen 31:40 above.

Grammatical Variations Prescribed by Samaritan Grammar

Attempting to explain the grammatical differences between the SP and the MT, Gesenius was of the opinion that "the Samaritan scribes [acted] according to the norms of an unlearned and inaccurate grammar."[42] This evaluation will no longer do. Instead several theories have been developed that attempt to explain the grammatical differences evident in the MT and the SP. Some scholars have thought that the differences reflected a northern dialect whereas others have considered the differences to be chronological, either preceding or, more recently, following the tradition resident in the MT.[43] Ben-Hayyim, in his most helpful discussion of the grammatical differences between the SP and the MT, concludes that the

> SP, the sole literary source extant among the Samaritans that dates from the First Temple period, is presented to us in a linguistic redaction that

---

[42] Gesenius, *De Pentateuchi samaritani origine,* 26.

[43] For the opinion in favor of a northern dialect, see D. W. Thomas, "The Textual Criticism of the Old Testament," in *The Old Testament and Modern Study* (ed. H. H. Rowley; Oxford: Clarendon, 1951), 238–63. For the opinion that the differences preceded the MT tradition, see Paul Kahle, "Die überlieferte Aussprache des Hebräischen und die Punktation der Masoreten," *ZAW* 39 (1919): 230–39. For the opinion that it followed, see Ze'ev Ben-Hayyim, *A Grammar of Samaritan Hebrew* (rev. ed.; Winona Lake, Ind.: Eisenbrauns, 2000), 3.

reveals, to the extent possible, features particular to the Hebrew of the
Second Temple period, even though its external appearance, the formation
of the letters, and the divisions of words by means of a dot, antedates that
of the Jewish Pentateuch.[44]

Some of the linguistic characteristics that were previously thought to be
peculiar to the SP tradition are, in fact, features of the language from the Second Temple times. The SP reflects a vocalization later than the Tiberian (i.e.,
MT) tradition but nevertheless incorporates elements (particularly in morphology) of an older stage.[45]

Several examples of the types of grammatical difference between the SP
and MT follow:

1. In the SP, all vowels in open syllables are long whereas vowels in
closed syllables are short, except for those closed at a late stage of linguistic development. Final closed syllables, which may contain long
vowels in the MT because of the stress on the final syllable, will be
short in the SP because the stress is there placed on the penultimate,
or next-to-last, syllable.[46] The SP will avoid consonant clusters either
at the beginning or at the end of a word.[47]

2. Morphological differences occur as well. Generally, the MT prefers a
"long" form of 2ms (second person, masculine, singular) and 3fs
(third person, feminine, singular) pronominal suffix endings whereas
the SP shows a preference for the "short" form, that is, a form without a final vowel. In verbal forms, differences occur as well. For
instance, the 2fs (second person, feminine, singular) perfect per-
formative form of the verb as appears in MT is xxxת (t—), whereas
the SP consistently uses xxxתי (yt—).

3. Certain particles, for example, SP כן (kn) for the MT אם ('m), the SP
לא (l') and ל (l) for the MT לא (l') and אל ('l), prepositions, and
nominal forms vary (typically, the vowels of a word tend to remain
constant throughout its declension in SP).[48]

---

[44] Ben-Hayyim, *Grammar*, 4.

[45] Ze'ev Ben-Hayyim, *The Literary and Oral Tradition of Hebrew and Aramaic
amongst the Samaritans* (5 vols. in 6; Jerusalem: Academy of the Hebrew Language,
1957–1962), 3:7; Purvis, *Samaritan Pentateuch*, 71.

[46] Waltke, "Prolegomena," 283.

[47] Ben-Hayyim, *Grammar*, 60–61.

[48] Ibid., 314–22, 239.

4. Sentence syntax in the SP is at times different from that found in the MT. As noted by Ben Hayyim, the differences at times seem to be the result of differences of interpretation, but at other times, the different readings may have given rise to differences in interpretation (Gen 42:22; Deut 24:5).[49]

Modernization of the SP through Updated Philology in Comparison with That Found in the MT

Distinct from the types of variation mentioned above, this group of grammatical variations between the SP and the MT can with certainty be accounted for by recognizing in the SP an "updated" form of the Hebrew linguistic tradition when compared with that of the MT. Ben-Hayyim's observation has ample support: "SP . . . is presented to us in a linguistic redaction that reveals, to the extent possible, features peculiar to the Hebrew of the Second Temple period."[50] The grammar of the SP is closer to the Mishnaic Hebrew than is the Tiberian (i.e., MT) tradition. A great many of the differences between the SP and the MT are a result of this linguistic leveling. One interesting example of the leveling process involves the 3ms (third person, masculine, singular) pronominal suffix (the vowel sound long "o"). In early Hebrew a final ה (h) was used to mark this "o" sound instead of the later and more common use of a final ו (w). There are rare instances where the older form for marking this sound is preserved in the MT (Gen 9:21; 49:11; Exod 22:26). In all of these, the SP replaces the ה with the more typical ו. Other examples of modernization include the following:

1. The SP demonstrates a preference for full spelling rather than the defective or short spelling frequently used in the MT.

2. The SP occasionally replaces a *waw*-consecutive (conversive) with the normal verb tense (Gen 27:22; Exod 8:12, 23).[51]

3. The SP uses the internal *matres lectionis* י (y) and ו (w) more frequently than does the MT and occasionally uses א (glottal stop) as an internal *mater*.[52]

---

[49] Ibid., 328–29.

[50] Ibid., 4.

[51] See ibid., 169–72, for a discussion of differences between Tiberian Hebrew and Samaritan Hebrew tenses and moods.

[52] See, however, M. Cohen, "The Orthography of the Samaritan Pentateuch: Its Place in the History of Orthography and Its Relation with the MT Orthography," *Beth Miqra* 64 (1976): 50–70; 66 (1976): 361–91.

4. SP replaces the infinitive absolute with an imperative or finite verb form (Num 15:35; 25:17; Gen 8:3, 5, 7).

5. The SP uses the long form of the imperfect rather than the MT preference for the short form with *waw*-consecutive (Num 16:10; 31:50).

6. The SP eliminates the rare MT use of the indefinite pronoun with more customary forms (Deut 33:11; Exod 15:16).

7. The SP eliminates the rare form of נחנו (nḥnw = "we") of the MT, found only in Gen 42:11; Exod 16:7, 8; Num 32:32.[53]

8. The SP is inconsistent in its use of the locative (a particle used to show direction) ה (-h) as in Exod 10:19; 33:9; 37:24.[54]

Removal of Grammatical Difficulties Found in the MT

Consistent with the process of "updating" mentioned above, the SP also eliminates some of the grammatical difficulties found in the MT. These variations include a more consistent presentation eliminating the differences between full and defective spelling (i.e., Gen 1:14, 15, 16), correction of a verbal form to agree with noun (Gen 13:6; 49:20; 49:15) and subject (Gen 30:42; Exod 4:29; Num 9:6) and with other syntactically related verbs (Exod 39:3; Lev 14:42; Num 13:2; 21:32). The SP regularly replaces passive verbal constructions with active ones (Exod 27:7; Num 3:16; 28:15, 17; Lev 11:13). The SP also tends to even out various forms of spelling. Where the MT may render the same word with two different spellings, the SP opts for a single rendition (Gen 1:14, 15, 16; 7:2; 8:20).

Removal of Objectionable Passages of Historical Difficulties

The variations resident in this category are interesting, for they seem to be guided by the scribe's sense of propriety. Several examples will suffice.

MT Gen 50:23 [NRSV]: Joseph saw Ephraim's children of the third generation; the children of Machir son of Manasseh were also born on Joseph's *knees.* (על־ברכי יוסף)

---

[53] Bruce Waltke ("Samaritan Pentateuch," *ABD* 5:936) supports Ben-Hayyim's observation with his own conclusion, "The Samaritan text-type is clearly modernized relative to the MT."

[54] Ben-Hayyim, *Grammar,* 326.

SP Gen 50:23: Joseph saw Ephraim's children of the third generation; the children of Machir son of Manasseh were also born in Joseph's *days.* (בימי יוסף)

In MT Gen 50:23 the births of Joseph's grandchildren are described as occurring on *Joseph's knees.* The SP changes "knees" to "days." The reason for the change is unclear. Perhaps, as some have suggested, the verse was considered unseemly for the Patriarch, and so the change was made. Or perhaps the verse refers to an adoption custom that placed the children of Machir in a special position of privilege with the patriarch, and this position of privilege was not wanted by the Samaritan scribe.[55]

> MT Deut 25:11 [NRSV]: If men get into a fight with one another, and the wife of one intervenes to rescue her husband from the grip of his opponent by reaching out and grabbing his *genitals* (במבשיו).
>
> SP Deut 25:11: If men get into a fight with one another, and the wife of one intervenes to rescue her husband from the grip of his opponent by reaching out and grabbing his *flesh* (בשריו).

A sense of propriety must have guided the Samaritan scribe writing Deut 25:11. Considering it improper to describe a brawl in which a woman became involved and grabbed her male opponent's genitals (MT), a simple substitution rendered the verse more appropriate.

> MT Gen 2:2: And God completed on the seventh day the work that he had done, and he rested on the seventh day from all the work which he had done.
>
> SP Gen 2:2: And God completed on the *sixth* day the work that he had done, and he rested on the seventh day from all the work which he had done.

A similar sense of what was right may have guided the Samaritan scribes in Gen 2. Verse 2 of this chapter in the MT is so worded that it may lead to confusion about the divine creative activity. One might get the idea that God concluded his work on the seventh day, finishing up perhaps by midmorning or a little later, and then took the rest of the day off and so finished the seventh day at rest. The SP scribes apparently wanted no such confusion to take place and so made it clear that the divine labor was concluded on the sixth day.

---

[55] A similar episode is recorded in Gen 30:3, where Rachel seeks to establish a special closeness to the anticipated child of Bilhah.

The genealogies of Gen 5 and 11:10–26 are well known for the problems they pose. The systems of reckoning that were used to construct the genealogical tables found in Gen 5 and 11:10–26 as presented in the MT, LXX, and SP are not the same and, at least according to Gesenius, seem to operate according to their own patterns of "physiological and chronological knowledge, which were sometimes similar and sometimes contradictory to each other."[56] Whatever the "patterns of knowledge" were that the editors of the MT, LXX, and SP each tapped into, it is evident that the end result is different for each tradition. The reasons for the differences are yet to be explained.[57]

MT Exod 12:40:

ומושב בני ישראל אשר ישבו במצרים שלשים שנה וארבע מאות שנה

And the time that the people of Israel dwelt in the land of Egypt was 430 years. (RSV)

SP Exod 12:40:

ומושב בני ישראל ואבתם אשר ישבו בארץ כנען ובארץ מצרים שלשים שנה וארבע מאות שנה

The time that the children of Israel and their fathers dwelt in the land of Canaan and the land of Egypt was 430 years.

Another chronological notation that has caused considerable debate is that found in Exod 12:40. The LXX agrees with the SP except that it reverses the order for "the land of Canaan" and "the land of Egypt." Attempts to account for this variation frequently assume that the SP and the LXX represent a gloss that has as its intent the removal of the difficulty in imagining that this 430-year stay in Egypt consumed only four generations (Exod 6:15–19; Num 26:58).[58] The tradition of the 430-year stay in Egypt is present also in Ezek 4:5, but the Apostle Paul appears to favor the chronology of the SP and the LXX (Gal 3:17).

Small Variations Clarifying and Interpreting the SP

This category of variant from the MT seemed to Gesenius straightforward and a result of tendentious Samaritan scribal activity. At times, the variants are quite simple—for example, the insertion of a preposition (Gen 48:5; Exod 12:43), a noun (Exod 15:22; Lev 5:4; Num 23:26), the sign of the direct object (Gen 44:26; Lev 4:17), or one of a variety of particles (Gen 2:12, 19; Exod 29:33) in order to render the sentence clearer.

---

[56] Gesenius, *De Pentateuchi samaritani origine,* 48.

[57] Waltke ("Prolegomena," 314–15) provides helpful charts showing the differences in the three traditions.

[58] Gesenius, *De Pentateuchi samaritani origine,* 49.

On other occasions, the variations result in the harmonization of parallel passages without altering the meaning of each. For example, SP Gen 18:29 reads לא אשחית (I will not destroy) for the MT לא אעשה (I will not do). The SP has imported the reading from verses 28, 31, and 32, thereby harmonizing the entire passage. Similarly the MT reads several names for the father-in-law of Moses whereas the SP consistently refers to him as Jethro (יתרו).

In SP Exod 21:20, 21 a change in the text compared with the MT clarifies an ambiguity. The paragraph in Exodus concerns capital offenses and considers the appropriate punishment due for injury to a pregnant woman. The MT of verse 20 reads נקם ינקם (He shall be punished) and uses the verb יקם (punished) in verse 21 whereas the SP of verse 20 reads מות ימות (He shall be killed) and uses יומת (killed) in verse 21. Although it may be that the SP represents a simple removal of ambiguity, clarifying the intent of the MT, it may also be the case that in removing the ambiguity, the SP goes further than the MT writers intended and began an interpretive trajectory carried further by the LXX.

At other times, the clarifications are even more complex. The Qumran materials have brought a whole new body of literature to bear on the comparison. Sanderson has demonstrated, through her work on 4QExod, that the interplay among the SP, 4QExod, the MT, and the OG predecessor of the LXX is very complex. Her conclusion that 4QExod and the SP coexisted for a time within a common textual tradition after the MT and OG had begun their own trajectories suggests that only some of the clarifying and interpretive variants in the SP are a result of Samaritan sectarian scribal activity.[59]

On several occasions, the insertion of an introductory sentence or phrase renders the clarification. In Exod 24:1 and 24:9, Aaron's sons Eleazar and Ithamar are introduced as accompanying the procession summoned to meet the Lord. The inclusion of these two sons of Aaron is not found in the MT.

> MT Exod 24:1: And he said to Moses, "Come up to the LORD, you and Aaron, Nadab and Abihu, and seventy of the elders of Israel." (NRSV)

> SP Exod 24:1: And he said to Moses, "Come up to the LORD, you and Aaron, Nadab and Abihu, *Eleazar and Ithamar,* and seventy of the elders of Israel."

> MT Exod 24:9: Then Moses and Aaron, Nadab and Abihu, and the seventy elders of Israel went up. (NRSV)

> SP Exod 24:9: Then Moses and Aaron, Nadab and Abihu, *Eleazar and Ithamar,* and the seventy elders of Israel went up.

---

[59] Sanderson, *Exodus Scroll,* 85–88.

It is significant that the SP and 4QExod share both of these variations as opposed to the MT and the LXX, which read the same to the exclusion of Eleazar and Ithamar. This expansion seems intent on making sure that these younger sons of Aaron, who would eventually replace the older sons (Nadab and Abihu) in their religious offices (Lev 10:1–7), were present at the great theophany at Sinai and so were worthy replacements.[60]

A less understood expansion at the end of Exod 27:19 is found in the SP:

ועשית בגדי תכלת וארגמן ותולעת שני לשרת בהם בקדש

And you will make garments blue and purple of fine linen for their holy service.

The reading seems oddly out of place. It follows a lengthy discussion about the tabernacle and its measurements and utensils (27:9–19) and is positioned to introduce a paragraph describing the oil used to keep the lamp in the tabernacle continually burning. It is only in Exodus 28:2 that the paragraph discussing the priestly vestments begins. Consequently, the expansion of 27:19 appears two verses too soon. Although fragmentary in 4QExod, it seems apparent that this scroll from the DSS collection shares the SP expanded reading. This shared reading thus stands in contrast to the reading preserved in the MT and the LXX.[61]

Genesis 22:2 serves as a well-known example of a small variant that results in support of Samaritan beliefs and priorities. The place of Abraham's sacrifice of Issac is rendered in the MT as המריה (Moriah) whereas in the SP the place is המראה (Morah). The effect of this variant is to change the association of the place of sacrifice from the Temple Mount of Jerusalem (Jerusalem is Moriah) by way of 2 Chr 3:1 to the preferred Samaritan site, Shechem (a city often associated with Morah). On the other hand, 4QExod avoids the dilemma by eliminating the mention of Moriah/Morah altogether.[62]

Interpolations from Other Texts

Perhaps the most intriguing and significant variations between the MT and the SP are the occasions where the redactors of the SP interpolate into the text selections culled from other passages of the Pentateuch. When compared

---

[60] Sanderson (ibid., 213) uses these two insertions of Exod 24 to make a convincing argument for the literary affiliation between the SP and the 4QExod text.

[61] Ibid., 209–10.

[62] Michael Wise, Martin Abegg, and Edward Cook, *The Dead Sea Scrolls* (San Francisco: Harper Collins, 1996), 262–63.

with the MT, many of these interpolations have the effect of altering the *structure* of the text but not its *words*. The technique is also evident in some of the DSS and accounts for some of the shared readings between the SP and the DSS.[63] The expansions unique to the SP give the text a distinct theological and literary focus. Presumably for political or sectarian reasons, they were accomplished to set forth more clearly the group's agenda without altering or violating reverence to the sacredness of the words of the received text. One of the key passages to invoke this interpolation technique is the Decalogue of Exod 20.[64] The following is a sampling of some of the other passages where the interpolations are found; interpolations are in italic in this section.

Gen 30:36 Adding Gen 31:11–13

> And he set a distance of three days' journey between himself and Jacob, while Jacob was pasturing the rest of Laben's flock. (NRSV) *And the Angel of God said to Jacob in a dream and he said, "Jacob," and Jacob replied, "Here I am." He said, "Lift up your eyes and look, all the goats that leap on the flock are striped, speckled or spotted for I have seen all that Laben is doing to you. I am the God of Beth-El where you anointed a pillar and made a vow to me. And now rise up and leave this land, return to the land of your father, to the land of your birth."*

Gen 42:16 Adding Gen 44:22

> "Let one of you go and bring your brother, while the rest of you remain in prison, in order that your words may be tested, whether there is truth in you; or else, as Pharaoh lives, surely you are spies." (NRSV) *And they said to him, "The boy cannot leave his father, for if he leaves his father, his father will die."*

In a number of instances, text from Deuteronomy is inserted into Numbers. The insertion has the effect of expanding or amplifying the corresponding story in Numbers. Several examples follow.[65]

Num 10:11 Preceded by Deut 1:6–8

> *And the LORD God spoke to Moses saying, You have stayed long enough at this mountain. Resume your journey, and go into the hill country of the Amorites as*

---

[63] For a summary of the 4QExod scroll, see Sanderson, *Exodus Scroll,* 312.

[64] The Exod 20 passage is dealt with separately because of its importance and relative length.

[65] In addition to the examples cited above, the reader may also consult Num 21:12, followed by Deut 2:17–19; Num 21:20, followed by Deut 2:24–29, 31; Num 27:23, followed by Deut 3:21–22; and Num 20:13, followed by Deut 3:17–18.

> well as into the neighboring regions; the Arabah, the hill country, the Shephelah, the Negeb, and the seacoast—the land of the Canaanites and the Lebanon, as far as the great river, the river Euphrates. See I have set the land before you; go in and take possession of the land that I swore to your fathers, to Abraham, to Isaac, and to Jacob, to give to them and to their children after them. In the second year, in the second month, on the twentieth day of the month, the cloud lifted from over the tabernacle of the covenant. (NRSV)

This example of interpolation also contains several other editorial marks. In both the MT and the SP versions of Deut 1:6, God speaks to the people, not to Moses, and identifies Horeb as the location of the camp. In the interpolated version that finds its way into SP Numbers, God speaks to Moses and there is no mention of Horeb.

Num 13:33 Followed by Deut 1:27–33

> There we saw the Nephilim (the Anakites descend from the Nephilim). And the children of Israel grumbled before God and they said, "It is because the LORD hates us that he brought us from the land of Egypt to give us into the hands of the Amorites to destroy us. And now, where are we going? Our brothers have made our hearts melt by saying, 'The people are greater and more numerous than we are. The cities are greater and fortified up to the heavens. And also, the sons of the Anakim we saw there.'" And Moses said to the sons of Israel, "Do not have dread or be afraid on account of them. The LORD your God who goes before you will fight for you just as he did in Egypt before your eyes and in the wilderness where you saw the LORD your God carried you just as a man carries his son all the way that you traveled until you reached this place. But still you do not trust the LORD your God, who goes before you in the way to seek a place for you to camp in fire by night and in a cloud by day to show you the route to take."

Num 14:41 Preceded by Deut 1:42

> The LORD said to Moses, "Say to them, 'Do not go up and do not fight, for I am not in the midst of you; otherwise you will be defeated by your enemies.'" But Moses said, "Why do you continue to transgress the command of the LORD? That will not succeed." (NRSV)

The interpolation is not always from Deuteronomy to Numbers. Sometimes Deuteronomy seems to borrow from Numbers.

Deut 2:8 Preceded by Material from Num 20:14–18

> And I sent messengers to the king of Edom saying, "Permit us to pass through your land. We will not trample your field or vineyard or drink from your well. We

will go along the King's Highway, not turning aside to the right hand or to the left until we have passed through your borders." And he said, "You may not pass through or we will come against you with the sword." We passed by our relatives, the sons of Esau who live in Seir, leaving the way of the Arabah that comes from Elath and Ezion Geber. And we headed out along the route of the wilderness of Moab.

Deut 10:6–8 Incorporating Material from Num 33:31–38a

The Israelites journeyed from Moserah and came to Bene-Jaakan. From there they journeyed and came to Gudgodah. From there they journeyed to Jotbathah, a land with flowing streams of water. From there they traveled and came to Abronah. From there they traveled and came to Ezion Geber. From there they traveled and came to the wildernesss of Zin, that is, Kadesh. From there they traveled and came to Mount Hor. There Aaron died. There he was buried. And Eleazar was made priest after him.

A large harvest of these additions is found in Exodus, where the redactor has added passages taken from elsewhere in Exodus or from another book in the Pentateuch.[66] The added passages are still found in their original sites. The insertion of passages from one part of the Pentateuch into another effects a change in the emphasis of the modified text.

Exod 6:9 Adding Exod 14:12

Moses told this to the sons of Israel, but they would not listen to Moses because of their broken spirit and their cruel slavery. And they said to Moses, "Let us alone and let us serve the Egyptians. It would have been better for us to serve the Egyptians than to die in the wilderness."

There are several instances where the text of SP Exodus includes passages found in both the SP and MT versions of Deuteronomy. Two examples will illustrate this practice.[67]

Exod 18:25 Incorporating Deut 1:9–18

Appropriate changes in verbal forms and other small variations are made, allowing a smooth narrative.

Moses said to the people, "I am unable by myself to bear you. The LORD has multiplied you so that today you are as numerous as the stars of the heavens. May

---

[66] Gesenius, *De Pentateuchi samaritani origine*, 45.

[67] Perhaps the best-known example of this interpolation appears in the Exod 20 rendition of the Decalogue. The Exod 20 text will be dealt with separately.

the LORD *God of your fathers increase you a thousand times more and bless you as he has said. How can I by myself bear the burden of your disputes? Choose for each of your tribes men who are wise, discerning, and knowledgeable to be your leaders." They replied and said, "What you have said is good."* He took the leaders of the tribes, men who were wise and knowledgeable, and gave them as leaders over them, officers of thousands, officers of hundreds, officers of fifties, officers of tens, and officers throughout the tribes. *He made them judges and said to them, "Listen fairly between your brothers and judge righteously between a man and his brother and between the citizen and the sojourner. Do not be partial in judgment between the small and the great. Do not fear any man because judgment is God's. If a matter is too great for you, bring it to me and I will hear it." He commanded them at that time all that they should do.*

Exod 32:10 Including a Portion from Deut 9:20

"Now therefore let me alone that my anger may burn against them and I will consume them. But of you I will make a great nation." *The* LORD *was very angry against Aaron and was ready to destroy him, but Moses prayed for Aaron.*

As mentioned, many of the alterations, insertions, or expansions noted above may have been made with the goal of enhancing the narrative in some way.[68] Often the purpose of the alteration is to make more explicit some valued idea or belief and so produce text more suitable for sectarian purposes.[69] This is the effect created in Exod 32:10 above. Aaron is cast in a role quite dependent on Moses. By extension, the expected prophet, the Taheb, because of his connection to Moses, is to be preferred over a priesthood that relies upon its Aaronic descent.

One type of interpolation consists of a repeating phrase that does not occur in the corresponding MT text. A fascinating example of such repetition occurs in the plague narratives of Exodus, in 7:18, 29; 8:19; 9:5, 19; and 10:2. Although constructed with variations, all of these repetitions contain a description of Moses and Aaron (although the verbal forms are at times awkward) approaching Pharaoh and pronouncing a message from the Lord, כה אמר יהוה ("Thus says YHWH"). The pronouncement is a repetition of the command

---

[68] Sanderson, *Exodus Scroll,* 313.

[69] Jeffrey H. Tigay ("An Empirical Basis for the Documentary Hypothesis," *JBL* 94 [1975]: 327–42, here 334–35) notes that the interpolation of Deut 1:9–18 into Exod 18:21–27 allows the redactor to "preserve the version of Deuteronomy and drop that of Exodus."

given by God and issued earlier to Moses. The expansion commands the release of the Hebrews, the people of God, so that they may go and serve the Lord (sometimes in the desert and sometimes under threat of retribution from the hand of the Lord). The elements of the repeating insertion seem to be rehearsals of the formula found in Exod 7:16: "The LORD, the God of the Hebrews, sent me to you saying, 'Let my people go that they may serve me in the wilderness: and behold you have not yet obeyed me.'" Sanderson makes the point that the nature of these expansions is to emphasize the conflict between the Lord and Pharaoh.[70]

As in other Exodus readings, the expansion found in the SP shares characteristics with readings preserved in 4QExod. Sanderson argues that this reading shared by SP and 4QExod was made by a single author before the separation of these two text traditions, and she suggests that they may have been intended to assist in a dramatic recitation of the text or its liturgical use.[71]

Changes Advancing the Theology of the Samaritans

Several significant variations in the SP from the MT support the sectarian theology of the Samaritans. Conventional wisdom indicates that the changes were made in order to legitimize the theological distinctiveness of the Samaritans. Examples of the five most widely recognized theologically motivated variations appear here.

Legitimizing Gerizim as the Proper Place of Worship

MT Deut 12:5: But you shall seek the place that the LORD your God *will choose* out of all your tribes as his habitation to put his name there. (NRSV)

SP Deut 12:5: But you shall seek the place that the LORD your God *has chosen* out of all your tribes as his habitation to put his name there.

Perhaps the best-known variant fitting into this category is the group that, like Deut 12:5, renders a past tense of one verb and thereby elevates Gerizim as God's chosen site.[72] The SP affirms God's past choice, Gerizim, as identified in 11:29–30, and so removes the future "will choose," reading instead "has chosen." The implication is that Jerusalem is not a legitimate location for the proper worship of God, as it was not "chosen" before the crossing of the Jordan by the wandering Israelite nation.

---

[70] Sanderson, *Exodus Scroll,* 204.

[71] Ibid., 203–4.

[72] There are twenty-one such instances: Deut 12:5, 11, 14, 18, 21, 26; 14:23, 24, 25; 15:20; 16:2, 6, 7, 11, 15, 16; 17:8, 10; 18:6; 26:2; 31:11.

> MT Exod 20:24: You need make for me only an altar of earth and sacrifice on it your burnt offerings and your fellowship offerings, your sheep and your oxen; in *every place* where I *will cause* my name to be remembered, I will come to you and bless you. (NRSV)

> SP Exod 20:24: You shall make for me an altar of earth and sacrifice on it your burnt offerings and your fellowship offerings, your sheep and your oxen; in *the place* where I *have caused* my name to be remembered, I will come to you and bless you.

Exodus 20:24 presents a variant that has much the same effect as that found in Deut 12:5. The variants are relatively simple—במקום ("in the place") for בכל־המקום ("in every place") and אזכרתי ("I will cause to remember") for אזכיר ("I will remember")—but make quite plain that there is one proper place of worship and it is there that God's blessing can be expected. The act of remembering is not simply bringing to mind but constitutes a dedication or commitment.

> MT Deut 27:4: So when you have crossed over the Jordan, you shall set up these stones, about which I am commanding you today, on Mount *Ebal,* and you shall cover them with plaster. (NRSV)

> SP Deut 27:4: So when you have crossed over the Jordan, you shall set up these stones, about which I am commanding you today, on Mount *Gerizim,* and you shall cover them with plaster.

Deuteronomy 27:4 is a classic example of a variation made for sectarian purposes. The verse reads the same in the SP except for the all-important change from Ebal to Gerizim. If the tradition represented by the MT is the variant, then it was intended to detract from the Gerizim site, but if the SP is the variant tradition, then this change must have been made by Samaritan scribes in order to emphasize the priority of Gerizim against all competing places of worship.

> MT Lev 26:31: I will lay your cities waste, will make your *sanctuaries* desolate, and I will not smell your pleasing odors. (NRSV)

> SP Lev 26:31: I will lay your cities waste, will make your *sanctuary* desolate, and I will not smell your pleasing odors.

Likewise Lev 26:31 seems to point to a variation designed to substantiate a theological bias. Here the point of a single, divinely approved place of worship is made by a simple change of a plural form, "sanctuaries," to the singular form, "sanctuary." Even in the midst of threatened divine punishment, the text asserts only one place of legitimate and actual worship—Gerizim.[73]

> MT Deut 11:30: As you know, they are beyond the Jordan, some distance to the west, in the land of the Canaanites who live in the Arabah, opposite Gilgal, beside the oak of Moriah. (NRSV)

> SP Deut 11:30: As you know, they are beyond the Jordan, some distance to the west, in the land of the Canaanites who live in the Arabah, opposite Gilgal, beside the oak of Moriah *opposite Shechem.*

This one last example illustrates the concern that was expressed about making sure that the right location for worship was preserved. Once again the verse is repeated in the SP except for one important addition. After "Moriah" and to make sure that the location is clear to all is added the phrase "opposite Shechem." The association of Moriah and Jerusalem is not given any opportunity to flourish here.

Avoidance of Plural Predicates to elohim

Occasionally, plural verbal forms are used with the noun *elohim* in the MT. The SP tends to avoid these verbal forms, using singular forms and so asserting the singularity of God. For example, Gen 20:13 reads in the MT התעו (third person, plural), "caused to go." The SP eliminates the plural, using instead the third person, singular התעה. Similar occurrences are found in Gen 20:13, 31:53, and 35:7 and Exod 22:8.

Avoidance of Anthropomorphisms

Anthropomorphic presentations of God are shunned in Samaritan theology, and in a manner consistent with that theological sensibility, anthropomorphic representations of God are avoided in the SP as well. A favorite text with the Samaritans, used in liturgies and appearing on stone inscriptions, Exod 15:3, also serves as an example of anthropomorphic avoidance.

MT Exod 15:3:   יהוה איש מלחמה יהוה שמו

The LORD is a man of war. The LORD is his name. (RSV)

SP Exod 15:3:   יהוה גבור במלחמה יהוה שמו

The LORD is mighty in warfare. The LORD is his name.

---

[73] A similar change occurs in Exod 20:24 for the same reason as in Lev 26.

Other examples of this kind of anthropomorphic avoidance can be found in (1) Exod 4:22, which reads in the SP, "my own people," instead of the MT's "my first born son," (2) Exod 15:8, which reads in the SP, "breath from you," instead of the MT's "breath from your nostrils," (3) Deut 32:8, which reads in the SP, "your creator," instead of the MT's "your father," (4) Deut 32:36, which reads in the SP, "he forgave," instead of the MT's "he repented."

The Agency of the Angel of the Lord Preserving the Transcendence of God
In certain episodes of the SP, the angel or messenger of the Lord appears as the actor where in the MT the Lord acts or speaks directly without the benefit of mediation (Num 22:20; 23:4, 5, 16). This presentation of the transcendent God is in accord with the theology of the Samaritans.

Protecting the Honor of Moses
Samaritan theology holds Moses in the highest regard. The SP, by a subtle change in word order in Deut 34:10, enhances the status of Moses by asserting his lasting uniqueness.

MT **Deut 34:10:**   ולא־קם נביא עוד בישראל כמשה

Never since has there arisen a prophet in Israel like Moses. (NRSV)

SP **Deut 34:10:**   ולא־קם עוד נביא בישראל כמשה

Never again will there arise a prophet in Israel like Moses.

The SP projects the special position of Moses into the future. Not only does this rendition of Deut 34:10 enhance the stature of Moses; it presents a trajectory for the future. The Taheb, the one who will restore divine favor to the Samaritans, will be in the tradition of Moses but not replace Moses. All others, prophets, priests, and kings alike, regardless of their stature and influence, must assume secondary positions in light of the divinely sanctioned role played by these two: Moses and the "one to come."

DECALOGUE

The SP Decalogue of Exod 20 is a composite literary piece, inserting into the Exodus text selections from Deut 5, 11, and 27. The resulting rendition of the Ten Commandments accomplishes three important tasks. First, with clarity and geographical precision, Mount Gerizim is identified as the only legitimate and divinely ordained place of sacrifice. Worship on Gerizim becomes the concern of the tenth and final command in the Samaritan rendition, and in this manner the importance of Gerizim as the distinctive place for Samaritan worship is secured. Second, Moses is elevated to an even higher status than that presented in the MT. Only he can speak with God, and the community grants only to Moses the status of intermediary to the divine. The third accomplishment of this text is to invest the promised prophet to come with all the authority of the ten sacred words. The promise of the prophet in Samaritan theology becomes a significant social construct by which the Samaritans offer critique against the Davidic dynasty and all such social-power structures that detract from the centrality of the one who will restore divine favor, the Taheb. The SP insertions are in italic in this section,

(Exod 20:1) And God spoke all these words saying,

(2) I am the LORD your God, who brought you out of the land of Egypt, out of the house of bondage.

(3) [First command] You shall have no other gods before me.

(4) You shall not make for yourselves a graven image, or any likeness of anything that is in heaven above, or that is in the earth below, or that is under the water under the earth;

(5) you shall not bow down to them or serve them; for I the LORD your God am a jealous God, visiting the iniquity of the fathers upon the children to the third and fourth generation of those who hate me,

(6) but showing steadfast love to thousands of those who love me and keep my commandments.

(7) [Second command] You shall not take the name of the LORD your God in vain; for the LORD will not hold him guiltless who takes his name in vain.

(8) [Third command] Remember the Sabbath day, to keep it holy.

(9) Six days you shall labor and do all your work,

(10) but the seventh day is a Sabbath to the LORD your God; in it you shall not do any work, you, or your son, or your daughter, your manservant, or your maidservant, or your cattle, or the sojourner who is within your gates;

(11) for in six days the LORD made heaven and earth, the sea, and all that is in them, and rested the seventh day; therefore the LORD blessed the Sabbath day and hallowed it.

(12) [Fourth command] Honor your father and your mother, that your days may be long in the land that the LORD your God gives you.

(13) [Fifth command] You shall not kill.

(14) [Sixth command] You shall not commit adultery.

(15) [Seventh command] You shall not steal.

(16) [Eighth command] You shall not bear false witness against your neighbor.

(17) [Ninth command] You shall not covet your neighbor's house; you shall not covet your neighbor's wife, or his manservant, or his maidservant, his ox or his ass, or anything that is your neighbor's. [Tenth command] *[Deut 11:29] And when the* LORD *your God brings you into the land of the Canaanites, which you are entering to take possession of it, [Deut 27:2–7] you shall set up these stones and plaster them with plaster, and you shall write upon them all the words of the law. And when you have passed over the Jordan, you shall set up these stones, concerning which I have commanded you this day on Mount Gerizim. And there you shall build an altar to the* LORD *your God, an altar of stones; you shall lift no iron tool upon them. You shall build an altar to the* LORD *your God of unhewn stones; and you shall offer burnt offerings on it to the* LORD *your God; and you shall sacrifice peace offerings and shall eat there; and you shall rejoice before the* LORD *your God. [Deut 11:30] That mountain is beyond the Jordan, west of the road, toward the going down of the sun, in the land of the Canaanites who live in the Arabah, over against Gilgal, beside the oak of Moreh in front of Shechem.* (Exod 20:1–17 RSV with SP inserted)

(18) Now when all the people heard the thunderings and the sound of the trumpet and saw the lightnings and the mountain smoking, all the people were afraid and trembled; and they stood afar off, and said to Moses, *[Deut 5:24–27] "Behold, the* LORD *our God has shown us his glory and his greatness, and we have heard his voice out of the midst of the fire; we have this day seen God speak with man, and man still live. Now, therefore, why should we die? For this great fire will consume us; if we hear the voice of the* LORD *our God anymore, we shall die. For who is there of all flesh who has heard the voice of the living God speaking out of the midst of the fire, as we have, and has still lived? Go near and hear all that the* LORD *our God will say, and speak to us all that the* LORD *our God will speak to you; and we will hear and do it,*

(19) *but let not God speak to us lest we die."*

(20) And Moses said to the people, "Do not fear; for God has come to prove you, and that the fear of him may be before your eyes, that you may not sin." (RSV)

Figure 6. From Exod 20:7 to the end of the Decalogue, including the unique Samaritan addition, in CW 2484. The commandments are numbered in the right margin. *Courtesy of Special Collections, Michigan State University Libraries.*

(21) And the people stood afar off while Moses drew near to the thick darkness where God was. (RSV)

(22) And the LORD spoke to Moses, saying, [Deut 5:28–29] "I have heard the words of this people, which they have spoken to you; they have rightly said all that they have spoken. O, that they had such a mind as this always, to fear me and to keep my commandments, that it might go well with them and with their children for ever. [Deut 18:18–22] I will raise up for them a prophet like you from among their brethren; and I will put my words in his mouth, and he shall speak to them all that I command him. And whoever will not give heed to his

words while he shall speak in my name, I myself will require it of him. But the prophet who presumes to speak in my name that which I have not commanded him to speak, or who speaks in the name of other gods, that same prophet shall die. And if you say in your heart, 'How may we know the word that the LORD has not spoken?' When a prophet speaks in the name of the LORD, if the word does not come to pass or come true, that is a word that the LORD has not spoken; the prophet has spoken presumptuously, you need not be afraid of him. [Deut 5:30–31] Go and say to them, return to your tents. But you, stand here by me, and I will tell you the commandments, the statutes, and the ordinances that you shall teach them, that they may do them in the land that I give them to possess."

(23) You shall not make gods of silver alongside me, nor gods of gold shall you make for yourselves.

(24) You shall make for me an altar of earth and sacrifice on it your burnt offerings and your fellowship offerings, your sheep and your oxen; in the place where I have caused my name to be remembered, I will come to you and bless you.

(25) If you make an altar of stone for me, do not make it of hewn stone, for if you use a chisel on it, you profane it.

(26) And do not go up on steps to my altar, so that your nakedness is not exposed on it.

Several interesting observations are evident when a comparison is made between the SP's Decalogue in Exod 20 and Deut 5 and that of the MT.

The commands that prohibit other gods, the vain use of God's name, killing, committing adultery, stealing, and bearing false witness are the same in the MT and the SP renditions. Beyond these instances of exact replication, there are occasions where it seems that the SP has chosen a middle road, negotiating between the differences resident in the MT. John Bowman characterizes the Samaritan treatment of the Ten Commandments as "no more than the result of the application of a general principle which . . . affects the whole Pentateuch. . . . That principle is harmonization."[74] Although there is certainly harmonization at work, the exact nature and purpose of the harmonization are not as simple as one might suppose. The harmonization is designed to do more than eliminate differences. Further, the harmonizing principle becomes more complex when the SP Deuteronomy and the SP Exodus versions of the Decalogue

---

[74] John Bowman, *Samaritan Documents Relating to Their History, Religion, and Life* (Pittsburgh: Pickwick, 1977), 16.

are compared. At times, the SP preserves the differences found in the MT versions, and at other times the SP eliminates those differences. Several examples of the various renditions are these: (1) SP Deut 5:8 differs from MT Deuteronomy by inserting ו ("and") before כל ("all") and is in agreement with SP and MT Exod 20:3; (2) SP Deut 5:10 agrees with SP Exodus 20:6 and MT Exodus 20:6 מצותי ("my commands"), not מצותו ("his commands") as found in MT Deut 5:10; (3) SP Deut 5:12 has לקדשהו ("to keep it holy") in agreement with SP Exodus instead of לקדשו ("to keep it holy") as in MT Deut 5:12; (4) SP Deut 5:14 inserts בו ("in it," "during it") in distinction to MT Deuteronomy, MT Exodus, and SP Exodus; (5) SP Deut 5:14 lacks ו ("or") before "servant" and "donkey," like SP Exodus and MT Exodus.

The point of these simple comparisons is to demonstrate that there is no consistent agreement in the readings between the SP and the MT. Some of the differences in reading are due to grammatical characteristics of Samaritan Hebrew, and some appear to be the result of scribal preferences for a variety of reasons. The SP makes much use of MT Deuteronomy, but the preference is not consistent.

A comparison of two of the commandments proves especially interesting. The SP Exodus version uses MT Exodus for the Sabbath commandment, but SP Exodus favors MT Deuteronomy in the prohibition against coveting.

The Sabbath Command

This command offers an interesting example of Samaritan scribal editing. Just as in the MT Deut 5:12 command, SP Deut 5:12 inserts כאשר צוך יהוה אלהיך ("as the LORD your God commanded you"), not found in SP Exod 20:8 or in MT Exod 20:8. In this instance, SP Exodus and MT Exodus agree. Still, within the same verse, SP Exodus is free to prefer MT Deuteronomy over MT Exodus. The SP Exodus version begins with שמור as does SP Deuteronomy and MT Deuteronomy, but MT Exodus begins with זכור. The preference of שמור ("keep") over זכור ("remember") is quite understandable, for שומרים ("Keepers") is the self-designation of the Samaritans. Is the harmonization in this verse (the use of אשמר ["I will keep"]) nothing more than a device to emphasize the legitimacy of the sect known as the שומרים? If so, this rescension must have followed the formation of the Samaritan sect and been designed to legitimize the sect.

The Covet Prohibition

The second command that shows interesting comparisons is the command not to covet. The following comparison indicates that the relationship

between the Deuteronomy and Exodus renditions of the covet commandment is multifaceted.[75]

SP Deut 5:21:   ולא תחמד בית רעך ולא תחמד אשת רעך שדהו עבדו

Do not covet your neighbor's house, do not covet your neighbor's wife, *his
field,* or his servant

SP Exod 20:17:   לא תחמד בית רעך ולא תחמד אשת רעך שדהו עבדו

Do not covet your neighbor's house, do not covet your neighbor's wife, *his
field,* or his servant

MT Exod 20:17:   לא תחמד בית רעך לא תחמד אשת רעך ועבדו

Do not covet your neighbor's house, do not covet your neighbor's wife or
his servant

MT Deut 5:21:   ולא תחמד אשת רעך ולא תתאוה בית רעך שדהו ועבדו

Do not covet your neighbor's wife, do not *desire* your neighbor's house, *his
field,* or his servant

Both SP Exodus and SP Deuteronomy present the same reading. And
both are at variance with MT Deuteronomy (the ordering of "house" and
"wife" and the insertion of תתאוה ["desire"] as the offense against the neighbor's house and property to follow) in the first part of the commandment,
agreeing instead with the MT Exodus reading. The MT Deuteronomy version
itemizes the neighbor's field as one of the things that should not be coveted.
Both Samaritan renditions mention the neighbor's field as well. Apparently,
the Samaritan scribe felt free to follow either MT Deuteronomy or MT Exodus when need demanded. Since the SP reading does not appear in any other
recovered texts, including the DSS, it is quite probable that this recension
is late and took place after the Samaritan sect developed a sense of self-
awareness. The appropriate text from the DSS (4Q158, frgs. 7–8) is reproduced below. The lengthy text is presented here to provide a comparison to
the SP rendition. These texts provide valuable information for the attempt to
understand the development of the SP in its own literary context.

(Honor) your [father] and your mother [so that your days may be long
in the land that the LORD your God is about to give to you. You shall not
murder. You shall not commit adultery. You shall not steal. You shall

---

[75] Bowman (ibid., 19) is aware of the above differences but does not consider
the range of implications that arise from these textual observations.

not bear] false witness [against] your [neighbor]. You shall not covet [your] nei[ghbor's] wife, [male or female slave, ox, donkey, or anything that belongs to your neighbor]. And the LORD said to Moses, "Go say to them, 'Return to [your tents.' But you, stand here by Me, and I will tell you all the commandments, the statures] and the ordinances that you shall teach them, so that they may do them in the land that [I am about to give them as a possession."] . . .

So the people returned to their individual tents, but Moses remained be-fore [the LORD, who said to him, "Thus shall you say to the Israelites,] 'You have seen for yourselves that I spoke with you from heaven. You are not to mak[e gods of silver alongside Me, nor make for yourselves gods of gold. You need make for Me only an altar of earth, and sacrifice] on it your burnt offerings and offerings of well-being, your sheep [and oxen; in every place where I cause My name to be remembered I will come to you and bless you. But if] you make for Me [an altar of stone], do not build it of hewn stones; for by [using] a chisel [upon it you profane it. You are not to go up by steps to My altar lest your nakedness be exposed] on it.'"[76]

As shown in these fragments, 4Q158 does not include "field" in its ren-dition of the Exodus passage but reads much more like the MT rendition.[77] Later in Exod 20, however, 4Q158 does share substantial agreement with the SP. Does the agreement with MT in the covet command mean that, unlike the Samaritan editors, the Qumran editors felt no such threat to their cherished land holdings? Does deliberate inclusion of "field" in SP Exodus indicate that the SP Exodus recension can be dated to a time when the Samaritans were threatened with losing their property to the hands of pious neighbors and that the specification of "field" is in protest to this threatened loss? If so, is this evidence that the recension of the covet prohibition, like that of the Sab-bath command, took place after a sense of self-awareness had developed for the Samaritan sect and not before?[78]

The Tenth Commandment

Following the prohibition on coveting, SP Exodus inserts a lengthy sec-tion (in italic) taken from Deut 11 and 27. The reworked material appears

---

[76] Wise, Abegg, and Cook, *Dead Sea Scrolls,* 202.

[77] Nor, because of the lacuna, does the DSS version appear to mention "neigh-bor's house" but this is not central to the issue.

[78] This argument is provisional, given the partial condition of fragments 7–8.

after verse 17 and forms the tenth commandment in the Samaritan presentation of the Decalogue.

> (17) [Ninth command] You shall not covet your neighbor's house; you shall not covet your neighbor's wife, his field, his manservant or his maidservant, his ox or his ass, or anything that is your neighbor's. [Tenth command] *[Deut 11:29] And when the LORD your God brings you into the land of the Canaanites, which you are entering to take possession of it, [Deut 27:2–7] you shall set up these stones and plaster them with plaster, and you shall write upon them all the words of the law. And when you have passed over the Jordan, you shall set up these stones, concerning which I have commanded you this day on Mount Gerizim. And there you shall build an altar to the LORD your God, an altar of stones; you shall lift no iron tool upon them. You shall build an altar to the LORD your God of unhewn stones; and you shall offer burnt offerings on it to the LORD your God; and you shall sacrifice peace offerings and shall eat there; and you shall rejoice before the LORD your God. [Deut 11:30] That mountain is beyond the Jordan, west of the road, toward the going down of the sun, in the land of the Canaanites who live in the Arabah, over against Gilgal, beside the oak of Moreh in front of Shechem.*

The material inserted from Deuteronomy makes quite clear that Gerizim is the appropriate place for worship. The material identifies the location of Gerizim precisely, thereby eliminating any possibility of rival sites, presumably and particularly Jerusalem. The inclusion of the Deuteronomy material here in the Exodus Decalogue elevates the status of Gerizim by identifying it as the uniquely appropriate place for worship, and it does so with the weight of authority no less than that granted to the ten words spoken directly by God.[79]

It is intriguing to try to reconstruct the origin of the redaction presented in the SP reading of the tenth command. The orthography and script used in the SP point to a production in the late part of the Hasmonean era. It may well be that the SP tradition developed from a Palestinian textual tradition from as far back as perhaps the fifth century but finally underwent a sectarian redaction no earlier than the first century B.C.E.[80] From a comparison with the DSS, it is clear that not all the changes appearing in the SP were made by the Samaritans, for many of the alternate readings are shared by the Qumran material. This tenth commandment may be one of the best examples for the intermingling of the changes that are both shared with other traditions and unique to the SP.

[79] Sanderson, *Exodus Scroll*, 317.
[80] Purvis, *Samaritan Pentateuch*, 85.

THE SAMARITAN PENTATEUCH AND THE
DEAD SEA SCROLLS

Compared with the MT, the SP presents an expanded form that was, before the 1940s, unknown in any other textual tradition. With the recovery and examination of the DSS, however, this all changed. One of the most significant expansions found in the SP is the rendition of the Ten Commandments found in Exod 20. Unexpectedly, the DSS revealed a version of Exod 20 much more like that found in the SP than that found in the MT. The scroll fragment containing Exod 20, 4QExod, with its similarities to the SP, shows that the SP was much more part of the mainstream textual dialogue of the first century than was previously thought. The SP and presumably the Samaritans themselves were part of the cultural conversation within the religious community of Palestine during the two centuries before the turn of the eras. A good illustration of this textual dialogue between the various literary traditions is the tenth commandment, including a description of the prophet to come. The SP version of the relevant portion of Exod 20 is once again reproduced below.[81]

(18) Now when all the people heard the thunderings and the sound of the trumpet and saw the lightnings and the mountain smoking, all the people were afraid and trembled; and they stood afar off, and said to Moses, *"Behold, the LORD our God has shown us his glory and his greatness, and we have heard his voice out of the midst of the fire; we have this day seen God speak with man, and man still live. Now, therefore, why should we die? For this great fire will consume us; if we hear the voice of the LORD our God anymore, we shall die. For who is there of all flesh who has heard the voice of the living God speaking out of the midst of the fire, as we have, and has still lived? Go near and hear all that the LORD our God will say, and speak to us all that the LORD our God will speak to you; and we will hear and do it,*

(19) *but let not God speak to us lest we die."*

(20) And Moses said to the people, "Do not fear; for God has come to prove you, and that the fear of him may be before your eyes, that you may not sin."

(21) And the people stood afar off while Moses drew near to the thick cloud where God was.

---

[81] Bowman, *Samaritan Documents,* 24–25.

(22) *And the* LORD *spoke to Moses, saying, "I have heard the words of this people, which they have spoken to you; they have rightly said all that they have spoken. O, that they had such a mind as this always, to fear me and to keep my commandments, that it might go well with them and with their children for ever. I will raise up for them a prophet like you from among their brethren; and I will put my words in his mouth, and he shall speak to them all that I command him. And whoever will not give heed to his words while he shall speak in my name, I myself will require it of him. But the prophet who presumes to speak in my name that which I have not commanded him to speak, or who speaks in the name of other gods, that same prophet shall die. And if you say in your heart, 'How may we know the word that the* LORD *has not spoken?' When a prophet speaks in the name of the* LORD, *if the word does not come to pass or come true, that is a word that the* LORD *has not spoken; the prophet has spoken presumptuously, you need not be afraid of him.*

This text should now be compared with the DSS text appearing below. Even though extremely fragmentary, with substantial elements missing, fragment 6 of 4Q158 does appear to include the promise of the prophet in a fashion very similar to the SP rendition of Exod 20.

[like us, and live? Approach and hear everything that the LORD our God says. Then you can tell us everything the LORD our God says] [to you, and we will listen and obey. But do n]ot let [God] speak to u[s, or we will die." Moses said to the people, "Do not fear; for God has come only to test you] [and t]o put the fear of [Him upon you so that you do not sin." The people stood at a distance, while Moses drew near to the thick darkness where] God was.

And the LORD [spoke] to Moses, s[aying, "I have heard this people's words, which they have spoke to you; they are right in all they have spoken. If only] they had such a mind as this, to fear [Me and to keep all My commandments always, so that it might go well with them and with their children forever! Now, as you have heard] My words, s[ay to them, 'I will raise up for them a prophet like you from among their own people; I will put my words in the mouth of the prophet, who shall speak to them everything that I command. Anyone] who does not heed the words [that the prophet shall speak in My name, I Myself will hold accountable.

But any prophet who presumes to speak in My name a word that I have not commanded] him [to] speak, or who shall sp[eak in the name of other gods—that prophet shall die. Perhaps you will say to yourself, "How can we recognize a word that the LORD has not spoken?"] If a [prophet]speaks [in the name of the LORD, but the thing does not take place or prove true, it is a (sig.) not a word that the LORD has spoken. The prophet has spoken presumptuously; do not be frightened by it."][82]

As with many of the expansions found in the SP, the expansions found here in 4QExod come mainly from Deuteronomy. The inclusion of the passages from Deuteronomy into the Exod 20 text has the effect of elevating the status of Moses by giving to him greater credibility as a prophet approved by God. Further, the inclusion of the discussion about the prophet gives utmost priority to the expectation of a future prophet following in the footsteps of Moses, while at the same time recognizing that false prophets are a possibility and the community has no obligation to follow their leadership. Preference for one or another of the identified successors to Moses was central to sectarian Jewish groups of Hellenistic and early Roman Judaism, and texts such as this version of Exod 20 helped articulate the perceived differences between the groups.

As pointed out by Sanderson, the 4QExod text of Exod 20 shares all of the major expansions found in the SP, with several minor variants, except that of the peculiarly Samaritan expansion of the tenth commandment, in which the SP adds material gleaned from Deut 11 and 27.[83] In particular, 4QExod lacks the peculiarly Samaritan inclusion of Gerizim.

A detailed comparison of the SP and the appropriate DSS will undoubtedly shed additional light upon the recensions of the major textual traditions of the Hebrew Bible. The similarities between the SP and 4QExod lead to two important conclusions: (1) The fact that the text used by the Samaritans was so similar to other texts of the first century helps us to see the sect within the overall umbrella of the Judaism of the first century.[84] (2) The text that later became identified with the Samaritans has a considerable amount in common with the appropriate DSS material. Still, the instances of unique readings, particularly those that advocate Gerizim and other elements peculiar to Samaritan thought, argue for a community that must have experienced a sense of solidarity and self-awareness before the adoption of the edited text.

Perhaps one of the most revealing conclusions that study of the DSS has produced about the SP and the Samaritan community is the relationship of the Samaritans to other religious groups at the turn of the eras.

In one more way their group [i.e., Samaritans] has been shown to be quite at home in the "rich complex of Judaism." They were not the only

---

[82] Wise, Abegg, and Cook, *Dead Sea Scrolls*, 201–2.
[83] Sanderson, *Exodus Scroll*, 307.
[84] Ibid., 32.

ones to treat their Scriptures as they did. Or, at very least, even if they were the creators of all of the major expansions, a scroll with all but the Gerizim expansion was accepted and used in a different and very isolationist and hostile group. Even the most tendentious aspect of their Scripture followed a pattern also found at Qumran and, we may suppose, elsewhere as well.[85]

These observations about the SP have led to a general consensus about the beginnings of the Samaritan community. The estimated points of origin range from the second to the first century B.C.E.[86]

SIGNIFICANCE

The text adopted by the Samaritans as their holy book has had a long and influential history. It is no exaggeration to say that the Samaritan community owes its continued existence to the unifying function played by the SP.[87] The honor given to the Abisha Scroll, kept safe and revered in the Nablus synagogue by the Samaritan community, illustrates the important role played by the SP textual tradition. Quite literally, the SP is the fountain from which flows the religious identity of the Samaritans.

The influence of the SP is by no means limited to the Samaritan community. As early as Origen and Jerome, the SP has been an important part of Hebrew Bible studies. The SP continues to be an important source for the investigation into formation of the Hebrew Bible. Already the SP has provided significant evidential support to the Documentary Hypothesis for the con-

---

[85] Ibid., 319–20.

[86] James Purvis ("The Samaritan Problem: A Case Study in Jewish Sectarianism in the Roman Era," in *Traditions in Transformation: Turning Points in Biblical Faith* [ed. Baruch Halpren and Jon Levenson; Winona Lake, Ind.: Eisenbrauns, 1981], 333) concludes that the Samaritans must have been "a community whose self-understanding was not clearly defined until around 100 B.C.E." Morton Smith (*Palestinian Parties and Politics That Shaped the Old Testament* [New York: Columbia University Press, 1971], 182–90) traces the origins of the Samaritans to their refusal to engage in the Maccabean revolt. Richard Coggins (*Samaritans and Jews: The Origins of Samaritanism Reconsidered* (Atlanta: John Knox, 1975) finds that the religious context of the Hasmonean period is a reasonable time for the Samaritan origin. Ferdinand Dexinger ("Limits of Tolerance in Judaism: The Samarian Example," in *Aspects of Judaism in the Graeco-Roman Period* [ed. E. P. Sanders, A. I. Baumgarten, and Alan Mendelson; vol. 2 of *Jewish and Christian Self-Definition,* ed. E. P. Sanders; Philadelphia: Fortress, 1981], 108–14) points to the destruction of Shechem under John Hyrcanus as the "breaking point" that resulted in the Samaritan sect.

[87] Reinhard Pummer, *The Samaritans* (Leiden: Brill,1987).

struction of the Pentateuch.[88] The SP has contributed to the investigation of other parts of the Hebrew Bible as well. Comparative studies have shown that the pentateuchal text used by the Chronicler in 1 Chr 1–9 has a greater resemblance to the SP than to the MT.[89]

In the textual criticism of the Hebrew Bible, the SP has played an invaluable role.[90] Although the SP is of disputed worth for establishing original readings,[91] the SP, in conjunction with the other recovered textual traditions, is helping scholars understand the relationship between text types of the Hasmonean period. Recent research into the readings shared by the DSS and the SP have been especially fascinating. Not only shared readings but editorial techniques employed in the formation of the SP are evident in some of the Qumran scrolls. And together the SP and the DSS may help provide a useful trajectory by which to better understand the literary practices that were used in the formation of some of the Christian New Testament literature from the first and second centuries.

The significance of the SP has reached beyond the world of textual studies. Sociologists and anthropologists interested in understanding the dynamics of the Samaritans as a social group must consider the SP as an integral part of the investigation. The SP gives researchers an important tool in understanding the manner in which a group maintains its identity in the midst of the vicissitudes of cultural change.

Those interested in the history of religions also find in the SP a wealth of information that can be used in understanding sectarian movements. The interaction between text and community, each affecting the expression of the other, forms a vital laboratory in which to investigate a tenacious and enduring textual tradition and its religious community.

---

[88] Tigay, "Empirical Basis."

[89] Gillis Gerleman, *Synoptic Studies in the Old Testament* (Lund: C. W. K. Gleerup, 1948), 9–12.

[90] Moshe Goshen-Gottstein, "The Textual Criticism of the Old Testament: Rise, Decline, Rebirth," *JBL* 102 (1983): 372–75.

[91] Sanderson, *Exodus Scroll*, 58.

Chapter 2

Samaritan Joshua

INTRODUCTION

The Samaritan book of Joshua (SJ) is a wonderful, if uneven and eclectic, collection of stories in the form of a chronicle that reaches back to the time of Moses and continues through to the Roman occupation of Palestine and the career of Baba Rabba. Its fifty chapters present the story of the Samaritans, beginning with God's blessing upon the Israelite nation at the time of the conquest of Canaan, continuing through the early kings (biblical judges) and the period of divine favor, moving to the Israelite religious infidelity and the removal of divine favor, and finally concluding with the beginning of divine disfavor under the conquests by Nebuchadnezzar, Alexander, and the Romans. The stories recount episodes of heroism, betrayal, and supernatural and magical wonders and include songs of praise and portrayals of utter despair, all effectively presenting Samaritan values and a sense of Samaritan self identity. It is not an overexaggeration to say that the SJ presents a community memory and, as such, articulates a description of what it means to be Samaritan.

The early chapters of the book read much like targumaic writings, steeped in the pentateuchal texts. Later chapters reflect traditions similar to those found in Josephus's *Antiquities*. And on several occasions at least, the SJ brings to mind apocryphal and New Testament texts both in its content and in its style.

HISTORY

Joseph J. Scaliger first brought the SJ to the attention of the West in 1584. He obtained a manuscript of the work from the Samaritan community in Cairo and brought it to Europe, where the manuscript eventually made its way to the University Library of Leiden. For many years, this manuscript (itself a composite, with part dating from 1362 and part from 1513) was the only copy of the SJ available in Europe.[1] In the middle of the nineteenth century,

---

[1] John Bowman, *Samaritan Documents Relating to Their History, Religion, and Life* (Pittsburgh: Pickwick, 1977), 62.

several other manuscripts were obtained; one became resident in the British National Library, and one in the library of Trinity College in Cambridge.

It was Johann Heinrich Hottinger who, in the mid–seventeenth century, first published the contents of the SJ, albeit in condensed and abbreviated form.[2] For years, Hottinger's publications were the only scholarly treatments of the SJ available.[3] During the nineteenth century, however, the additional copies of the SJ that became available in Europe allowed greater scholarly access to the work. It fell to T. W. J. Juynboll to provide the next major advance in SJ studies. In 1848 Juynboll edited the Arabic text of the Leiden manuscript and published it together with a Latin translation.[4] His masterful edition, in turn, provided the basis for the English translation of the SJ made by Oliver T. Crane in 1890.[5] The English translation found in this chapter is Crane's. The authors have modernized the language, corrected typographical errors, leveled the spelling of names, and provided explanatory footnotes.

DESCRIPTION

The earliest surviving manuscripts of the SJ are written in Arabic. At times, that Arabic is awkward and appears to be a translation from an earlier edition. Indeed, chapter 1 of the SJ acknowledges that at least this first section (chs. 1–8) is a translation from a Hebrew original. Thus Theodore Gaster's uncovering of a Hebrew text of the SJ near the beginning of the twentieth century met with initial excitement. Though itself very valuable, this manuscript proved, upon later examination, to be of no earlier origin than the already available Arabic manuscripts. The whole of the SJ, as it now exists, can be dated to no later than the thirteenth century although undoubtedly parts of the work were composed far back in antiquity. Similarities between portions of the first twenty-five chapters and the LXX version of the biblical book of Joshua suggest that the writer of that part of the SJ was aware

---

[2] Johann Heinrich Hottinger, *Exercitationes antimorinianae de Pentateucho samaritano* (Zurich, 1644); and *Smegma orientale* (Zurich, 1657).

[3] This despite the unfortunate and failed duplicity exhibited by Robert Huntington and Thomas Marshall, each of whom attempted to procure additional Samaritan manuscripts from the Nablus community by presenting themselves as representatives of the "English Samaritan" community. See Robert T. Anderson and Terry Giles, *The Keepers: An Introduction to the History and Culture of the Samaritans* (Peabody, Mass.: Hendickson, 2002), 94–96.

[4] T. W. J. Juynboll, *Chronicon samaritanum* (Leiden: S. & J. Luchtmans, 1848), 72.

[5] Oliver T. Crane, *The Samaritan Chronicle; or, the Book of Joshua the Son of Nun* (New York: John Alden, 1890).

of the LXX version or, more likely, the pre-Masoretic Hebrew version that served as the basis for the LXX.

The book gives evidence of several different authorial hands, each of which may have relied upon other independent sources. The varieties of readings present in available manuscripts make the issue even more complicated. Most agree that chapters 1–8 were added to preface the "Book of Joshua the Son of Nun," which receives an internal title at the beginning of chapter 9. Some are of the opinion that the section beginning with chapter 9 continues to chapter 15 whereas others see it concluding at chapter 25.[6] The remaining chapters (either 16–50 or 26–50) are subdivided at either 46b–50 or 47–50 respectively. The scheme suggested here considers major sections: 1–8; 9–25; 26–46 (with a subsection at 38–46), and 47–50, each seeming to represent distinct periods of creative authorship.[7] These sections are separated from one another by major breaks either in the form of an introduction, as seen, for example, in the introduction to chapter 9 ("The Beginning of the Book of Joshua the Son of Nun"), or in the form of a conclusion or transition, such as those found at the end of chapters 25 and 37. In addition to these major compositional sections, there is evidence of editorial work in a variety of places.[8] At times, the editing is seen in the use of later Arabic titles within sections that seem otherwise to have been written much earlier.[9] In other instances, it is evident in the editorial remarks that often conclude a chapter and offer the editor's assessment of the events just recounted (e.g., at the end of chs. 40 and 44) or a doxology to God for his beneficence on behalf of the Samaritans (e.g., at the end of ch. 32). The uneven style among the chapters of the SJ also suggests various stages in redaction. Some chapters— for instance, chapter 1—certainly appear to be Arabic translations of an earlier work. At places in these early chapters, the style is rough and the grammar awkward. This awkwardness all but disappears later in the book, particularly from chapter 38 to the end.

Chapter 1 of the SJ provides a particularly interesting example of editorial work. The whole chapter functions as an introduction to the work, much

---

[6] For ch. 15, Juynboll, *Chronicon,* 82ff.; for ch. 25, Bowman, *Samaritan Documents,* 63.

[7] These major sections can be subdivided, and recognizable units of material can be observed throughout.

[8] Alan D. Crown, "New Light on the Inter-relationships of Samaritan Chronicles from Some Manuscripts in the John Rylands Library," *BJRL* 54 (1972): 282–305; "A Critical Re-evaluation of the Samaritan Sepher Yehoshua" (PhD diss., University of Sydney, 1966).

[9] See, e.g., ch. 40, which uses Arabic titles but at the same time may have relied on an early Hebrew predecessor of the LXX.

in the same manner as chapter 1 of Isaiah serves as an introduction to the sixty-six chapters of that book. The opening chapter of the SJ is a summary of the movement of the whole story. The writer of this chapter begins with the miracles experienced in the time of Moses, then traces the nation's history during the time of divine favor, when the kings ruled, and finally alludes to the experience of divine disfavor and the oppression by foreign empires. The recollection of the events is quite uneven. The beginning of the story is summarized in detail. Many miracles are recounted from the time of Moses whereas the end of the story is summarized much more generally. The impression is given that when the introduction was written, the early chapters of the SJ were well defined and established but the ending of the work was still fluid and open-ended. The story was meant to continue, and the author of the introduction in chapter 1 understood that he could not be specific about the concluding events, for the ending had not yet been written. Indeed, he implies as much when, at the end of chapter 1, he appeals to the hoped-for positive response that the children of Israel will give to God in prayer and obedience. An interesting feature marking the writing style of the SJ is the manner in which traditions, allusions, and quotations taken from the pentateuchal text are conflated and intermixed to form the narrative or theological description. For example, chapter 38 gives a description of life among the Israelites during the period of divine favor. As part of the description, the narrator describes the sabbatical year and jubilee by patching together, in quick succession, pertinent material from Numbers, Deuteronomy, and Leviticus. In chapters 3 and 4, SJ begins the story of Balaam and, in weaving the story, draws together texts from Num 2, 22, and 23; Deut 2; and later Num 25 and 31. This conflating stylistic devise is not at all uncommon in Samaritan texts and is amply attested in the Samaritan Pentateuch, as seen in the Decalogue texts of Exod 20 and Deut 5. The writers of the SJ are thoroughly immersed in pentateuchal texts and aware of biblical Joshua, Judges, portions of 1 Kings and Ezra, and traditions given expression in Josephus's *Antiquities*. When it suits their purposes, the writers of SJ make use of these other texts and traditions, in sometimes creative fashion, in order to compose their story and thereby create their own Samaritan identity.

BENEDICTIONS

Twenty six of the fifty chapters in the SJ end with a benediction inserted by the editor or author of the chapter.[10] Of these twenty-six, one (at the end

---

[10] The twenty-six benedictions appear at the conclusion of chs. 1, 2, 4, 5, 6, 8, 11, 15, 16, 17, 18, 21, 23, 25, 32, 34, 35, 37, 38, 40, 41, 42, 43, 44, 45, 46.

of ch. 34) is noticeably longer than the others and of a different style. In addition to these twenty six, two benedictions appear in Joshua's letter to Shaubak of chapter 29 (one appearing at the conclusion of the praise paragraph that begins the letter and the other appearing as a benediction attached to the end of the letter) that are very similar to other benedictions found in the book (chs. 6, 11, 37, 38). An examination of these twenty-eight benedictions yields several interesting observations that may be useful in reconstructing the editing of the book.

A Benediction Is Lacking in Chapters 47–50

There are no benedictions found in chapters 47–50. Although it may be said that the subject matter of these chapters did not warrant an editorial benediction, given the frequency of the benedictions throughout the SJ, these chapters are conspicuous for the absence of benedictions, and their absence may provide additional evidence of a separate author at work in these chapters.

The Benedictions in Chapters 1–25 Emphasize Praise

The word "praise" is dominant in the benedictions up through chapter 25 (appearing in seven of the fourteen benedictions in these chapters whereas "praise" appears in only two of the twelve editorial benedictions that follow),[11] and appeals for "mercy" frequent the benedictions in chapters 38–46 (in chs. 38, 43, 45, 46). It should be remembered that chapters 1–25 concern the period of divine favor whereas the next set of benedictions, chapters 38–46, concern the Shaubak affair and the introduction of the period of divine disfavor. "Praise" is mentioned in the benediction of chapter 46, which at one time may have represented the end of the book and been intended as a fit conclusion to the whole.

The Benediction in Chapter 1 Supports Its Function as a Summary

There are several reasons to think that chapter 1 of the SJ was written late and was constructed to function as a summary of the whole—at least up to chapter 46. The benediction appearing in chapter 1 may support this hypothesis. Mention of "mercy" is found in the benedictions only here in

---

[11] One of these two appearances is in the benediction found in ch. 34. That benediction is quite different from the others and may not be appropriately included in this comparison.

chapter 1 and in chapters 38–46. Just as the benediction of chapter 46 brings an element from the first part of the book to the conclusion, the benediction of chapter 1 brings forward an element found in the last part of the book. Also it appears as if the editor writing the benediction of chapter 1 has borrowed a phrase from the benediction of chapter 42 or the letter of Joshua in chapter 29. Chapter 1 ends with "Certainly, he is a hearer and answerer." The benediction of chapter 42 ends the same way: "Certainly, he is a hearer and answerer." Chapter 29 contains the phrase as well except for "Certainly." Only here, in these two benedictions and one letter, does the appellation appear in the SJ. The phrase is a fitting conclusion to the account of prayerful sorrow and repentance in chapter 42 and seems at home in Joshua's letter, but it seems to be unconnected to its context in chapter 1.

The Benediction in Chapter 34 Is Unique

The benediction of chapter 34 is unlike the other benedictions found in the book. Composed of three sentences, this benediction is relatively lengthy compared with the other benedictions, except those in character speeches (i.e., the Levitical speeches of chs. 14 and 15) and Joshua's letter (ch. 29).

The Benediction in Chapter 38 Reveals the Editorial Process

The benediction of chapter 38 may provide valuable information regarding the editorial process at work in the book. This benediction is linked to other benedictions in a two-staged way. First, it should be noted that the first half of the editorial comment in chapter 38 is quite similar to those appearing in 43, 45, and 46.

> ch. 38a: And the children of Israel were continually addressing and consulting God, *who guides with His mercy.*

> ch. 43: And blessed be God who does not punish the rebellious except after long delay and *showing mercy unto them.*

> ch. 45: And of God do we ask assistance because of what He has benevolently *bestowed through His mercy,* and upon Him be the trust put.

> ch. 46: And unto God be praise and thanksgiving for His kindness, of Whom *we ask mercy and pardon.*

The similarity in terms used in these benedictions, which are dissimilar to the other benedictions found in the book, points to the conclusion that they were authored by one editor. Only these benedictions (except the benediction found in ch. 1, which seems to be a summary of the whole book) make an appeal to God's mercy. "Mercy" is the object of an appeal made in Joshua's letter of chapter 29, but this appeal may well be an addition to the letter made by the same editor responsible for the benedictions of 38–46.

> ch. 29: Of this Lord do I ask assistance, and upon Him do I place my trust, and in Him do I grow strong, and Him do I fear, and *His mercy is a shield unto me,* and unto my children, and He is my sufficiency and excellent Protector.

Chapter 38, however, points to a second linkage. The last half of the editorial benediction in this chapter is similar to the benedictions found in chapters 6, 11, and 37.[12] All of them refer to God as "sufficiency" and as either "bountiful" or "illustrious Protector." The only other place this appellation of God appears is Joshua's letter to Shaubak, and there it is quite conceivable that it was an editorial addition made by the same writer of the benedictions in chapters 6, 11, and 37 and the second half of chapter 38.

> ch. 6: And of God do we beg that He would unite us to him through His mercy. Behold, He is over all things powerful, and *He is my sufficiency and illustrious Protector.*

> ch. 11: And God is the witness over us in this, and *He is our sufficiency and bountiful Protector.*

> ch. 37: And God is the Victor, the Protector, the Guardian, and *He is our sufficiency and illustrious Protector.*

> ch. 38: And the children of Israel were continually addressing and consulting God, who guides with His mercy. *And He is our sufficiency and illustrious Protector.*

> ch. 29: Of this Lord do I ask assistance, and upon Him do I place my trust, and in Him do I grow strong, and Him do I fear, and His mercy is a shield unto me, and unto my children, and *He is my sufficiency and excellent Protector.*

If this series of observations is correct, the following four hypotheses regarding the editorial activity present in SJ can be proposed: (1) Chapter 1 of the SJ was written after, and functions as a summary of, chapters 2–46. (2) Chapters 38–46 form a subunit, the writer of which also edited the letter

---

[12] The benedictions of chs. 6 and 11 do not include the "praise" motif, so common in the other benedictions from the first half of the book.

of Joshua in chapter 29 and inserted benedictions in chapters 6 and 11. (3) Chapters 47–50 were composed after the work of the editors of chapter 1–46 was complete. (4) The editorial benediction of chapter 34 is quite distinct and appears to be from a hand different from that of the composer of the other benedictions.

While there are many other evidences of editorial work in the SJ, these benedictions are perhaps the most obvious. Not only do the benedictions provide data by which to investigate the editorial processes and the layers within the work; the benedictions provide a glimpse of the editors' theology. An editor makes an appeal to God or offers praise to God according to his own set of values or felt needs. Some of this theology is discussed in the next section.

THEMES

Scholars have been divided over the proper way to characterize the SJ and other Samaritan chronicles. Is the book a midrash, or is it a chronicle with ample expansions?[13] Perhaps the question is best answered by considering what the SJ accomplishes. It gives to the Samaritan community a sense of their identity by describing their origin, the importance of the SP and Gerizim, and the nature of the Samaritans' relationship to God, their Jewish kinsmen, and the nations around. The present experience of weal and woe is contrasted to an ideal past wherein was experienced God's unmitigated blessing and to a hope for the same in the future. In short, the SJ helps provide the Samaritan community with a philosophy of history by which to understand their own existence.[14]

The Philosophy of History

In broad strokes, there are several epochs or eras that figure into Samaritan reckoning as described in the SJ. In chapter 6, Moses is presented as informing the children of Israel about what would happen to every tribe unto the "days of final perfection and completion." Here Moses speaks to the

---

[13] James A. Montgomery, *The Samaritans, the Earliest Jewish Sect: Their History, Theology, and Literature* (Philadelphia: Winston, 1907; repr., New York: KTAV, 1968), 301

[14] Alan Crown ("New Light," 284) speaks of the foundational quality of at least part of the SJ: "The Joshua portion of the manuscript is the earliest part of any Samaritan chronicle and . . . all Samaritan chronicles ultimately derive from the Samaritan Joshua tradition." The SJ begins a trajectory that will be followed by others.

Israelites about the period of divine favor, the wrath and error, the deluge of fire, the day of vengeance and reward, and the day of his return. Of these major historical epochs and events, the two periods that occupy the attention of the SJ are the period of divine favor and the period of divine disfavor.

The period of divine favor began when the Israelites conquered the promised land (ch. 28) and lasted for 260 years (ch. 38).[15] These years were characterized by peace and prosperity for land and people. It was a time of faithfulness, when sacrifices were made and both land and slaves were treated with respect and care. Peace and justice were the norm. All of this was the doing of God, who subdues enemies and keeps the land in happiness while removing disasters and multiplying Israel (as promised in ch. 10). Indeed, as summarized in chapter 38, the period of divine favor was a time when "Grace was full and Mercy all embracing," for the union between the people and their Lord "was close." But even as Joshua warns as early as chapter 10, divine favor should not be taken for granted.

This time of divine favor did not last. Again, in chapter 10, Joshua warns that a period of divine disfavor is looming on the horizon and indeed is upon the Samaritan community. It was on the first day of the 361st year of divine favor that the period of divine disfavor began (ch. 42).[16] So momentous was this event that the onslaught of the period of divine disfavor can only be compared to the expulsion of Adam from the garden of Eden (ch. 42). The day was marked by a darkness within the "holy house" (the tabernacle) that spread for five consecutive days. Sensing the dreadfulness of what was taking place, Uzi the imam took the implements of the temple and sought to hide them away safely in a cave where they could be retrieved after the danger had passed. This cave, however, was sealed and hidden by God and to this day conceals the temple vestments and vessels.

Since that day, the Samaritan community has continued under the divine disfavor of God. Schism and discord (ch. 43) have since marked the community, for early in the period of divine disfavor Eli "the Insidious" led many of the Israelites into error by establishing a rival place of worship at Shiloh and constructing a counterfeit ark of the covenant and eventually, as in the encounter with Zerubbabel, there came "books written after the days of Moses" (ch. 45).

The Samaritans commemorate sorrow and remorse in their rituals and vows. For through His "greatness and compassion" God will certainly restore

---

[15] A discrepancy appears between chs. 38 and 39, both of which read 260 years of divine favor, and ch. 42, which reads 360 years of divine favor.

[16] Crane (*Samaritan Chronicle,* 167) believes that this number is in error and should read 261st, consistent with chs. 38 and 39.

his favor to the Samaritans, although God alone knows the time. Until then prayer is offered, for, despite all else, this much is known, that God is a "hearer and answerer of prayer" (ch. 42).

Gerizim

The reader of the SJ will be struck by the relatively few references to Mount Gerizim. It is not until chapter 19 that the "Blessed Mount" is first mentioned. And it is by this name that Gerizim is known throughout the SJ.[17] The Blessed Mount hosted fortunate visitors three times a year (ch. 25). The honored status given to Gerizim understandably led to the designation "Excellent Mount," used twice in the SJ (ch. 24). The Blessed Mount was the site on which Joshua built a synagogue in which was housed the tabernacle of the Lord (ch. 24).

The designation Blessed Mount resulted in an interesting self-designation of the Samaritans. In chapter 45, the children of Israel (Samaritan sect) are labeled "Friends of the Blessed Mount." This chapter provides key determinatives of the Samaritan community. The Friends of the Blessed Mount gather to worship on Gerizim and assemble with the book of Moses (SP) whereas those who prefer Jerusalem as the proper place of worship must refer to books written "after the days of Moses." The Blessed Mount is the sole place for sacrifice, and from there a trumpet signal can be passed through all the land, informing the faithful when the sacrifices are performed (ch. 38).

A related designation for Gerizim, but with a very different emphasis, is "Mount of Blessing." Friend and foe alike use this term. Even Shaubak, the deadly enemy of the children of Israel, recognizes that Gerizim is a Mount of Blessing (ch. 27). Joshua is quick to announce the peculiar properties of Gerizim, for, as he puts it, the "Mount of Blessings" (ch. 29) is "the holy spot," the "House of our Lord," and the "place of our God."[18] Later in the SJ, Alexander acknowledges the Mount of Blessing as the noblest and grandest place on earth (ch. 46). And it is to the Mount of Blessing that the Samaritans retreat for prayer and fasting in order to receive from God a plan that will ward off a threat from Alexander without, at the same time, violating the commands from God found in the book of Moses (ch. 46).

The holiness of Gerizim is acknowledged specifically in chapter 45 when the returning exiles explain that worship on the "Holy Mount" must be resumed if the current agricultural blight is to be halted. There are two other

---

[17] See chs. 24, 25, 38, 41, 45.
[18] "Mount of Blessings" in ch. 29 is the only instance in which the plural "Blessings" is used.

instances when the holiness of the site is paramount. In chapter 42, the author appears to have Gerizim in mind when he refers to the "Gates of Paradise." Finally—and it is significant that this is the last reference to Gerizim in the SJ—in chapter 50, Bethel ("House of God") is the name given to the Blessed Mount.[19]

For whatever reason, three times in chapters 48–50 (most scholars recognize these chapters as from a separate authorial hand) Gerizim is known simply as the "Mount," with no adjective or qualifier attached. Nowhere else in the SJ is this simple reference given to Gerizim. The only honorific qualifier given to Gerizim in these chapters is the coded designation Bethel, mentioned in chapter 50.

The Nature of God

The SJ provides important insights into the Samaritan view of God. Besides references to God found throughout the narratives, divine descriptions are given in doxologies, benedictions, speeches, and letters. Often appeal is made to the faithful community for a specific action or decision based upon a perception of the nature of God and the character of God's actions. In this manner, God becomes for the Samaritan faithful the standard for proper conduct and belief. Following are some of the more prominent observations that can be made about God on the basis of material taken from the SJ.

Creator

One of the first descriptions of God to meet the reader of the SJ is the frequent appellation "Creator." Chapter 1 provides a litany of the miraculous acts of God on behalf of the Israelites. Miracles of deliverance associated with the exodus, the overthrow of Israel's enemies, and the giving of the law are depicted as expressions of the Creator. As Creator, God is unique, not able to be represented in any likeness (ch. 16), and not limited by anything in creation. By virtue of creation, God is able to do what he pleases, and so is the appropriate object of faith and prayer (ch. 5). God is sovereign over all humanity and, as such, set apart from the false gods and idols worshiped by the nations round about. Even though the schemes of Israel's enemies might include military might and reliance upon the powers of secret knowledge and sorcery, these are no match for the decisive and overwhelming intervention of

---

[19] It is interesting to speculate that perhaps the author here had in mind the story of Jacob and his dream of the grand stairway to heaven, for there two names are given, "Gates of Heaven" and "Bethel" (Gen 28:17, 19). The title "Bethel" will be used frequently to refer to Gerizim in the later chronicles. See the *New Chronicle* excerpts in ch. 4, below.

the Creator (ch. 3). Even the adversaries of the Creator are sustained by him
and subject to his command every bit as much as were the waters that "stood
still by the power of the Creator" (ch. 15). Shaubak's messenger is distraught
after witnessing the powers of the Creator worshiped by Joshua and the
children of Israel (ch. 28).

The Creator is Lord of both heaven and earth, and law comes from
God's eternal voice (ch. 1). Punishment for breaking the law is also perceived
to originate from the Creator (ch. 4). It is before the "temple of the Creator"
that the elders brought Zarah, who stole the forbidden things from Jericho,
in order to administer his punishment (ch. 18). The most rueful expression
of divine punishment administered by the Creator is the advent of the period
of divine disfavor that began during the time of Uzi. Darkness replaced the
presence of the Creator on the Blessed Mount (ch. 41), and so began the
period of divine disfavor.

The Command of God

The Samaritan view of God as Creator results in a tendency to shy away
from any hint of an anthropomorphic description of God. As alluded to earlier, the fact that God is Creator means that

> there is no likeness like unto your likeness, for You are the origin of ac-
> tions and likenesses and bodies, and forms, and shapes, and spiritual things,
> which are endowed with the attributes of Your nature. (ch. 16)

Consequently, for the Samaritans, it would be inappropriate to employ
anthropomorphic techniques when speaking of God. Occasionally, however,
the story presented in the SJ requires that God be present in some form of
agency. When divine agency is required, this presence is signified by the use
of the "Command of God," which is introduced in chapter 3. The manner of
this introduction is instructive.

> God then desired to make a manifestation of His mysteries: now behold
> He could not do this Himself, nor could He do it through one who wor-
> shiped Him after the manner of anyone of the children of Israel, nor could
> He do it by writing, or by the agency of any of His angels, but only by send-
> ing unto him His very Command. (ch. 3)

The Command of God confronts Baalam. Having frightened off
Baalam's companion, the Command of God becomes the "visible form of
the agent of the Creator" in order to communicate with Baalam (ch. 3).
Heedless of this first confrontation, Baalam continues on his journey until
now the "Agency of the Creator" and again the "Agency of God" intervene,
appearing first to Baalam's donkey and later to Baalam himself. The Com-

mand of God appears again in chapter 7, which recounts the momentous occasion of Moses' departure and his separation from Joshua and the rest of his companions.

Chapter 7 also includes a very interesting description of Moses that takes its importance from the Samaritan notion of the uniqueness of the Creator. In this chapter, Moses is being lamented and Joshua recounts the remarkable deeds of Moses performed by the power of God. In the middle of this description, Moses is commemorated as

> one who went out from the boundaries of humanity and human power into the Divine power!

Just as there can be no comparison to God, there can be no pretender to the status of Moses.

When on other occasions God communicates to an individual or group, it is customary for God to simply "make a revelation" (ch. 9) or a manifestation of Divine power (ch. 8); in this way the author avoids the temptation to anthropomorphize God.

Extended Descriptions

The Samaritans love to compose lists in their literature. The SJ is no exception, and some of its lists are helpful in learning about the Samaritan view of God. Chapters 29 and 37 both contain extended descriptions of God.

Chapter 29

> In the name of God, the Supreme King, the God of worlds, the Compassionate, the Merciful, the God of gods and the Lord of lords, the King of kings, the Knower of secrets, the One resolute in wars, the God of Abraham and Isaac and Jacob, the Destroyer of infidels, the Annihilator of tyrants, the Destroyer of the obstinate, the Abolisher of intriguers, the Collector of the dispersed, the Scatterer of the confederates, the One who brings the dead to life, the One who puts to death the living: His hand is above the highest of the highest, and under His outstretched arms is eternity, the heavens and the earth are in His grasp, the holy angels in all their numbers and the whole creation He did create by His omnipotent power, and the spheres and the heavenly bodies moved under His guardian chariot, their rapid course He stopped by His mere word, and put in motion moving bodies by His divine authority. Of this Lord do I ask assistance, and upon Him do I place my trust, and in Him do I grow strong, and Him do I fear, and His mercy is a shield unto me, and unto my children, and He is my sufficiency and excellent Protector.

With this extended description of God, Joshua begins his reply to the letter sent by Shaubak. The letter has two effects. Israelites, in whose hearing it is read (ch. 30), immediately respond by bowing down in worship to God and thanks for his provision to Joshua. The Israelite community claims that the description of God and the rest of the letter "consoled our souls, having strengthened our hearts." It "nerved our loins and lifted our heads." For the camp of Shaubak, the letter has just the opposite effect. Those who would do Israel harm, upon hearing of Israel's God, weep "until their eyes flowed blood." They "beat their faces and wailed to excess" (ch. 32). Worship and dread are paradigmatic of the proper ways to respond to God. For those seeking security in God, worship is the proper response, but for those who seek to oppose God, only dread can fill their minds.

The names of God listed in the beginning of Joshua's letter provide a composite portrait of the Samaritan view of God. Many of the characteristic names and the descriptions of God's power that follow are consistent with the prominence given to God as Creator. The whole universe, including the human realm and the divine, is subject to the will and power of the Creator. Even life and death obey God's commands. This God is not a distant force only casually interested in the affairs of humanity. God is personally involved with his creation, protecting and shielding those who place their trust in him and destroying, abolishing, and annihilating those who would threaten harm. At one and the same time, God is described as universal over all and yet particularly related to those God calls his own.

Chapter 37

> "God is the one who acts as the Hero for us in the wars, God is His name."[20] And the children of Israel followed him, while all of them were saying, "Who is like unto You, perfect in holiness? O, One who inspires terror![21] O, Revealer of secret things! O, Doer of wonders! O, One who protects His servants and those who love Him, in every place wherein they dwell!

> "And God is the Victor, the Protector, the Guardian, and He is our sufficiency and illustrious Protector."

In chapter 37, the threat posed by Shaubak is over. His army is routed and the magical entrapments set against the Israelites are broken. Shaubak himself is killed in spectacular fashion. This dramatic rescue is occasion for

---

[20] Exod 15:3.
[21] Exod 15:11.

praise of God. Part of the first paragraph is taken from "one of the paragraphs of our master Moses in his hymn of praise at the sea" (Exod 15). In both of these two quotations, taken from the end of chapter 37, the concepts of universal and particular inform the appellations given to God, just as in chapter 29. God is sovereign over all creation and as such has the ability and the right to intervene on behalf of those who love him, regardless of where they are located. Given this stature, God is to be relied upon for protection, guardianship, and victory.

One of the interesting titles given to God in this chapter is "Revealer of secret things." Knowledge, secret and mysterious, plays a significant role in the SJ, and it is not without significance that God is perceived as sovereign over this part of creation as well.

Secret Knowledge

Knowledge is a fascinating theme in the SJ. Secret knowledge is something that is both feared and held in respect. And as noted above, it is significant that God is sovereign even over knowledge and mysteries. The same sentiment that gave to God the title "Revealer of secret things" in chapter 29 claims that God "knows secret things" in chapter 18 and issues a doxology of praise to the "God who knows secret things" in chapter 17. God is sovereign over the realm of secret knowledge.

Secret knowledge is a power to be admired and feared. At the very beginning of the SJ, following the introductory chapter 1, the reader encounters an episode in which Moses passes to Joshua "knowledge of the profound secret" (ch. 2). This knowledge sets Joshua apart and prepares him for the difficult task of leading the Israelites as Moses' successor. The knowledge of the profound secret either is accompanied by or includes the vision of a dream, knowledge of science, and information of the Name. Together these constitute the tools available to Joshua by which to lead the people and accomplish God's good will for them. In this context, secret knowledge is a valuable treasure by which positive things can be accomplished. It is not always the case.

In the very next chapter (ch. 3), we find that men "unsurpassed in sorcery and wisdom" were sent to Baalam in order to do harm to the Israelites. Baalam, too, is known by his efficacious invocations and so is sought out. Yet he confesses that it is God who is the source of his wisdom and ability to bless and curse. Even though Baalam is prevented from cursing the Israelites, he is able to develop a strategy (ch. 5) that threatens the people of Israel with defilement and pollution.

Although the use of this secret knowledge is something to be feared, the Israelites are not left without protection. In the book of Moses, the Israelites have a resource to protect them from spirits, witchery, and the evil eye (ch. 23). God can give knowledge in other ways also. In chapter 28, God is praised and thanks are given for the "light of God" that was bestowed on Joshua, giving him the wisdom by which to compose a letter as fit response to Shaubak and his colleagues.

During the period of divine disfavor, however, the resources given by God for the protection of his people are ignored, and the children of Israel find themselves tempted by magic work and "secret doctrine," so that the land becomes polluted (ch. 41). As a result, "decline was perfected in them and disaster came upon them; for their sight was blinded" (ch. 41).

Two of the most notorious examples of unwholesome participation in secret knowledge are found in chapter 43. Eli (the Insidious), through knowledge of magic, obtains "riches, proud rank, and wealth" and is success-ful in "diverting the people by magic." It is this same Eli who creates an alter-nate site of worship at Shiloh, builds an altar there, and presumably also has constructed a counterfeit ark of the covenant. Samuel, too, has forever been awarded the infamous distinction of "magician and infidel," for it is Samuel whom Eli instructed, who "revealed to him the hidden things." Samuel "grew to be as potent in the working of magic" as Eli himself (ch. 43).

With only a few bright exceptions, this unfortunate state is continued to the very end of the SJ. Chapter 48 summarizes the condition of the Israelites:

> In that day the instruction of Israel was like as dust; there was no imam among them, nor wisdom, nor teaching of the Law, nor was anyone able in the days of these kings to give instruction in the Pentateuch; except one in a thousand and two in a myriad. And the children of Israel continued in this calamitous state until Baba Rabba arose.

And so, at the end of the SJ, the focus of hope for the future is Baba Rabba. His story begins in the SJ and must wait for a second chronicle before it is finished.

THE BOOK OF JOSHUA THE SON OF NUN

A word about the text of the SJ that follows is in order. The English text presented here is essentially that prepared by Oliver Crane in 1890. Crane's translation is very good and the one most often used. On occasion, however, the authors of this study have felt it necessary to deviate from Crane's work. Sometimes a different English word now seems more appropriate than that chosen by Crane. On some occasions, we have altered the sentence structure in order to provide a more readable translation. At times, Crane added ma-

terial in parenthesis in order to provide clarification for an unfamiliar identification. We have retained this approach. The reader should keep in mind
that material appearing between parentheses was added either by Crane or by
the present authors and is not found in the Arabic or Hebrew manuscripts.
Similar editorial additions were made by the Samaritan scribes, and these
have become incorporated into the various Arabic manuscripts of the SJ.
Such editorial additions are noted by brackets. At times, more familiar forms
of names or common nouns are used instead of the unfamiliar Arabic
form used in the SJ. Consequently, the edition presented here will not do as
the basis for a text-critical investigation but is intended simply as a doorway
to acquaintance with the Samaritan version of "Joshua the son of Nun."[22]
When necessary, an accompanying footnote gives the explanation of a term.

Samaritan Joshua may be outlined as follows.

I. The period of divine favor (chs. 1–37)
  A. Transition from Moses to Joshua (chs. 1–8)
    i. Introduction (1)
    ii. Appointment of Joshua by Moses (2)
    iii. Balaam and the Moabites (3–4)
    iv. Joshua and Phinehas sent by Moses against the Midianites (5)
    v. Death of Moses (6–8)
  B. Beginning of the book of Joshua the son of Nun (chs. 9–24)
    i. Organization of the nation and the covenant with Joshua (9–12)
    ii. Spies sent to Jericho (13)
    iii. Fall of Jericho (14–17)
    iv. Sin of Achan (18)
    v. A Gibionite ruse (19)
    vi. Conquest and division of the land of Canaan (20–23)
    vii. Joshua's assignment of tribal portions and building of a temple at
        Gerizim (24)
  C. Summary: Israelites' enjoyment of twenty years of peace and
      prosperity (ch. 25)
  D. War between Joshua and Shaubak (chs. 26–37)
    i. Shaubak's gathering revenge (26)
    ii. Shaubak's letter sent to Joshua (27)
    iii. Letter's effect and Joshua's reply (28–30)
    iv. Return of the messengers to Shaubak (31–32)
    v. Joshua and his army trapped in the seven magic walls (33–36)
    vi. Rescue of Joshua and his army by Nobah (37)

---

[22] A discussion of text-critical issues appears in Crown, "New Light," 282–305.

II. Death of Joshua and the end of the period of divine favor (chs. 38–44)
  A. Death of Joshua and his successors (chs. 38–41)
    i. Death of Joshua (39)
    ii. Vice-regents from Eleazar to Uzi (40)
    iii. Samson, the last king (41)
  B. End of the period of divine favor, the troubles that follow (chs. 42–44)
    i. End of the period of divine favor (42)
      1. Disappearance of the tabernacle
      2. Temple vessels hidden by Uzi
    ii. Disputes between the descendants of Phinehas and Eli (43)
      1. Building of a tabernacle by Eli in Shiloh
      2. Samuel critiqued
    iii. Eli's counterfeit ark captured from Shiloh (44)

III. The Ages and Period of divine disfavor (chs. 45–50)
  A. Under the Persians (ch. 45)
    i. Nebuchadnezzar and the fall of Israel
    ii. Resettlement of three hundred thousand because of blight
    iii. Conflict over rebuilding the temple on Gerizim
    iv. Sanballat and Zerubbabel in conflict over the correct version of the Law
    v. Worship resumed on Gerizim
  B. Under Alexander (ch. 46)
    i. Sparing of Shechem
    ii. Alexander's journey to the land of darkness
    iii. Alexander's flying chariot
    iv. Circumvention of the order to build images of Alexander by naming the boys "Alexander"
  C. Under the Romans (chs. 47–50)
    i. Betrayal of Jerusalem by two Samaritan brothers to Hadrian and the Romans (47)
    ii. Samaritan high priest ꜣAqbun, his son Nathaniel, and his grandson Baba Rabba (48–50)
      1. Death of ꜣAqbun's sons and the hanging of Samaritans on the walls of Nablus (48)
      2. Nathaniel and how he managed to circumcise his son despite the Roman interdiction, with the help of the Roman bishop Germanus (49)
      3. Samaritans forbidden by the Romans to ascend Gerizim; the posting of the mechanical bird to guard the way; Baba Rabba's plan to defeat the bird through his nephew Levi (50)

First Chapter

This is the book narrating the chronicles of the children of Israel, from the time that our ruler Moses, the prophet—peace be upon him—the son of Amram, invested Joshua the son of Nun with the Califate over his people. All of this is translated from the Hebrew language into the Arabic language,[23] after the manner of a rapid translation by word of mouth, and giving only the statement of the narrative and nothing more: even what God—Powerful and Glorious—showed forth of signs and miracles and wonders, which man is too weak to adequately specify and describe, such as what happened at the Jordan, and also at the time when the giants were humbled, and with what victory and power and might and authority God came to his (Joshua's) assistance; also what they (the children of Israel) witnessed at the time of their entering the land, besides what they witnessed in Wady el-Mujib,[24] and on mount Sinai[25] and its awesomeness, with the essential incidents of this event which God showed, even the quaking of its mountains, together with what there was of thunders and lightnings connected with this, and joining the fires to the very heaven, and made them hear the code of their laws from the overpowering and eternal voice; from whom shone forth flashes of light, representing the form of its writer, even the Creator,[26] after what happened to them at the Great Sea,[27] not to mention what their adversaries witnessed in Greater Egypt, and what calamities overtook their enemies, such as Pharaoh and his army, and 'Amlaq (the Amalekites) and its host,[28] and Sihon and his kingdom,[29] and Og the father of Anak with his sorcery,[30] and kings of Moab with their greatness.[31] Also what happened unto Korah[32] the son of the uncle of Aaron and to the company who were with him, namely, that some of them the earth opened its mouth and swallowed, and they went down alive to the deepest depths, while as to others of them the divine

---

[23] The oldest manuscripts of the SJ are in Arabic, and the text does at times suggest familiarity with a Hebrew *Vorlage* of the LXX. See, e.g., footnotes 110 and 180 later in this chapter. Later chapters of the work give no hint of a Hebrew original. Certainly several hands and editorial layers are present in the work.

[24] A tenth-century designation for the Arnon River.

[25] Exod 19–20.

[26] This is similar to the recitation of the mighty acts of God in Deut 4:32–37.

[27] Exod 14–15.

[28] Exod 17.

[29] Num 21:21.

[30] Josh 14:15; 15:13; 21:11; Deut 2:11; 3:11; Num 22.

[31] Num 22.

[32] Num 16.

fire came forth and consumed their bodies.[33] And also what happened to the people while they were in the wilderness forty years, suffering want, without a guide and with no provisions or clothing, and barely living and existing; whom the cloud overshadowed by day and the pillar of fire protected from cold by night,[34] and whose food was the manna from heaven;[35] and when there was need of water, our ruler Moses—peace be upon him—the son of Amram, brought it forth for them from the rock[36] and from the parched ground and stone,[37] until they themselves had drank, and all that were in the company both living souls and animals. And it shall come to pass that when they who are possessed of intelligence, but are yet unbelieving, shall have heard of what God did bountifully bestow upon them (the children of Israel), and with what happiness He did surround them, and how He lifted off of them all calamities, whether heavenly or earthly, and also what new things He revealed unto them, then they will know that there is no Lord but their (the children of Israel) Lord and no prophet, but their prophet, and no book but their Book, and no true religion but their religion; and (they shall also understand) the excellency of the perfect creed, and the certainty of its validity, and that it is greatest in rendering praise to the Creator Mighty and Glorious the One who is omnipotent to do whatever He please. And when one shall hear of the decline of the kingdom of the children of Israel, and what calamities and misfortunes and exiles and dispersions overtook them by reason of their disobedient doings and their rebellious actions, his fear will be increased for Him from Whom nothing escapes and of Whose kingdom nothing is destroyed—Blessed be He and exalted! And now of Him do we implore complete right guidance and all embracing favor in His mercy. Certainly, He is a hearer and answerer (of prayer).[38]

---

[33] Num 11:1–3.

[34] Exod 13:21–22.

[35] Exod 16; Num 11.

[36] Perhaps a reference to the rock said to have followed the Israelites through the wilderness, rolling along on the ground and providing water for the Israelites when needed, for which see Yehoshua Rawnitsky and Hayyim Bialik, *Sefer ha-agadah* [2 vols. in 1; Tel-Aviv: Devir, ca. 1966], 76. For an English translation, see Hayim Nahman Bialik and Yehoshua Hana Ravnitzky, eds., *The Book of Legends: Legends from the Talmud and Midrash* (trans. William G. Braude; New York, N.Y.: Schocken Books, 1992). See also 1 Cor 10:4.

[37] Exod 17; Num 20.

[38] This introductory chapter is quite explicit in its summary of the opening events but is much less exact in describing the ending events.

Second Chapter

At the completion of the one hundred and nineteenth year, on the first day of the eleventh month,[39] of the life of our master Moses the prophet—peace be upon him—God revealed unto him in the plain of Moab that he should lay his hand upon the head of Joshua the son of Nun, the spiritual man;[40] meaning by this that he (Moses) should give him (Joshua) knowledge of the profound secret and reveal to him the vision of his dream and the science of knowledge, as much as he was capable of bearing; by which his heart would be strengthened and his spirit perfected and his soul elevated, and the rule over the creatures (the children of Israel) be rendered easy unto him; and that he should also inform him of the Name, by which he should put to flight hostile armies and by which a nation that no land could contain and whose numbers were countless might be confounded. And He ordered him (Moses) to set him (Joshua) before Eleazar the imam—peace be upon him—and to assemble unto him (Joshua) the people of learning and knowledge with the nobles and rulers, and ratify a compact with him, and make a new covenant with him, and invest him with the kingly authority, and install him in the rule over all the children of Israel. Thereupon the Prophet laid on Eleazar the imam—peace be upon him—the command, which rested on him, to superintend the affair with completeness and splendor and not to enter upon any affair or turn aside under any circumstance except after he had seen to this. And at the completion of his inauguration, the priests sounded with trumpets, and the heralds made proclamation for his standard, and the banners and flags were unfurled to his reign. Our master, the prophet Moses—peace be upon him—had seen that he (Joshua) was desirous to go forth in the front line of battle during his (Moses') days in order that he might by actual trial gain experience of what he knew and had observed. And immediately he (Moses) gave command that there should be selected out from the children of Israel, meaning by this that there should be chosen from among them, twelve thousand men; from each tribe one thousand men; and thereupon he would with these make an attack upon the Midianites to take satisfaction for Israel out of them and their country. Now, before mention is made of the cause of this retaliation, we would remark that the children of Israel had been restrained from intermeddling in any way with the affairs of the Ammonites and Moabites and were under orders not to appropriate to themselves any

---

[39] Josephus, *Ant.* 4.8.49.
[40] Num 27:18; Deut 34:9.

of their territory;[41] and they did do only what necessity compelled them to do with them. Hereafter we will explain and elucidate this by the will of God and his assistance, and the goodness of his guidance and favor.

Third Chapter

When the children of Israel went down into the plain of Moab, God revealed unto our master Moses, the Prophet—upon him be the most excellent peace—that he should not have anything to do with the Ammonites and Moabites nor should he wage war with them; "Because I," said God, "will not appropriate any of their lands to the children of Israel."[42] And he (Moses) obeyed this and did accordingly. Now when it reached the ears of the kings of Moab and Ammon and Midian what had happened unto Sihon and Og, of destruction and ruin and the taking captive of people and the talking of cities, they were sore distressed and feared exceedingly because of this; and they sent messages unto Balaam, the son of Beor, by men unsurpassed in sorcery and wisdom—for all the solders knew of him by reason of his invocations.[43] And the delegates came into his presence and said unto him:

"The five kings of Moab and Ammon send unto you their salutations and say to you: O, our master and our chief, we know that circumstances are brought about by you, a knowledge of which the people of learning fall short of attaining unto, and that whatsoever you bless is blessed, and whomever you curse is cursed; and that you can put to flight all armies by your invocations and words. Now perhaps there has already reached you what has happened in Egypt through the children of Israel, and in the sea and in the wilderness, and what happened unto 'Amlaq, the chief of tribes, by reason of them, and what they did with Sihon and Og, and what they have resolved upon in reference to their permanent dwelling-places. And now their army has descended upon our border, and they are working for our destruction, and already they cover the face of the land; and we have come unto you and hope to obtain relief of you and security from them through your own free blessing and propitious aid, and also through what we have decided upon of happiness for you, and the rendering of your will absolute. Perhaps now our condition will be improved through your agency, and you will curse this people, and will prevail over them and effect a change in present circumstances through your renown which is spread

---

[41] Deut 2:9, 19.
[42] Deut 2:9, 19.
[43] Num 22, 23; Josephus, *Ant.* 4.6.2.

abroad and the dignity of your authority in consequence of your circumstances, riches, and servants; and there will be glory to us and to you
among all kings, in addition to what reward will be added unto this, in consideration for your grand beneficence toward a people whom no country
can obtain and whose numbers are countless and beyond reckoning; for
you will have prevented a multitude from being murdered by fire (i.e., war).
For the character and manner of this army is that it is not restrained by a
feeling of shame for an old man, nor does it accord protection to a woman,
or have pity on a child, or show compassion toward an animal; for they do
nothing else but murder with the sword, and stone to death with stones,
and crucify, and burn with fire: yes, this is its custom, and it does not allow
any mercy to be shown, or protection to be granted, unto any, and it
spares not even a leafless palm branch in its annihilating and destroying. By
God, O our master, hasten unto us, bringing with you whatever is necessary, and be not wanting unto us in this matter which involves the preservation of life, and we will reward a good deed with its like, and an evil deed
with its like. And now, peace."

And when Balaam heard this message, he made reply to the company of
wise and trained men and said unto them: "I will treat with due respect
your rights, and the rights of those who urge you on in this message; but
my action is controlled by the One whom I serve, if He gives me permission to go with you, I will accomplish your desire and the desire of those
who urge you on in the message, and I will accomplish their (the children of
Israel's) destruction, and in the end complete their annihilation, and will
leave unto you a memory, for which you will praise me to the end of the
ages. And now decide to lodge with me this night, and I will hear what shall
be addressed unto me, and we will wholly act in accordance therewith,
whether it be of good or evil." And the people consented and lodged with
him. And he began to offer worship to the One whom he was accustomed
to serve, and it was said unto him: "Do not you go with the people, nor
curse Israel, for they are blessed." And he came to them with these words;
thereupon they returned to the kings and informed them of what had happened; but this only increased the more their desire after them, and this
was high honor to him. And now there rode unto Balaam more illustrious
delegates than those who had gone before, and greater by far than they;
yet they made less promises to him and said in the second message: "Now
see to it that you come unto us; for we are able to honor you and to give
bountifully unto you." Thereupon the people came unto him with this message; and Balaam answered the messengers and said: "It is necessary that
you understand that if the kings should give unto me their houses full of

silver and gold, I cannot transgress what my Lord commands;[44] but now abide this night with me, and I will hear what communication shall be addressed to me, and I will act in accordance with it, whether it be favorable or unfavorable." So the people lodged with him; and the man started in on the beginning of his performance and service and worship. God then desired to make a manifestation of His mysteries: now behold He could not do this Himself, nor could He do it through one who worshiped Him after the manner of anyone of the children of Israel, nor could He do it by writing or by the agency of any of His angels, but only by sending unto him His very Command. And the companion of Balaam, upon beholding the specter of the Command of God, fled away from it, and he became the visible form of the agent of the Creator who addressed Balaam; for this was the device employed to communicate with him. And the Command of God said to him: "Did not I say unto you, O Balaam, when the people came unto you, 'Go with them'?" making inquiry to see what craving Balaam had for the journey. But he answered him not a syllable, though his usual custom was to say: "Not so; for without my God I give ear to nothing." And he did not fully believe that he had heard the correct interpretation of the speech until He commanded him to mount and ride, and then he was made to saddle his ass and went along with the wise men of Moab. And the anger of the Creator was aroused because of his starting out on the journey before he had sought instruction (of God), and He placed Himself in the way to make an attack upon him. Now he (Balaam) was riding upon his she-ass, and boasting of her before the people of learning, that he had no need of a guide when with her and that he had no necessity ever to beat her. But when she saw the Agency of the Creator—Mighty and Glorious—standing in the way, with His drawn sword in His hand, she swerved aside out of the way through fear of Him; and this was the first of the putting to shame of Balaam and of his remorse; and he beat her with his staff. And the Agency of the Creator removed to a place between walls in a field and stood still; and when the ass beheld Him, she shied into one of the walls and injured Balaam's foot, and he beat her more violently. And when the learned and wise men beheld this, they said unto him: "O our master, it cannot be that there is a cause for her opposition to the execution of this mandate of the Divine Word?" And he answered and said unto them: "It was desired that this mandate should be carried out." And the Agency of God again passed on until He stopped in a narrow place where there was no turning out either to the right or to the left; and when the ass beheld Him, she lay down under him (Balaam), and he again beat her violently. And God put speech

---

[44] Num 22:18.

on the tongue of the animal, and thereupon she said to Balaam: "What have I done unto you that you should beat me these three times? Am not I your ass upon whom you have ridden since you were created up till now? Have I ever acted badly toward you like this time?" And he said: "No." Then God opened the eyes of Balaam, so that he saw the Agency of God, even an angel standing in the way with His drawn sword in His hand, and he threw himself down before Him; and He said unto him: "Why have you beaten your ass three times? If you had got right in front of me, I would have killed you and saved her alive; for I have seen the wickedness of your inclination. Now, however, go along with the people, but keep carefully to what I shall say unto you, and do not overstep it."

After this Balaam journeyed on; and when the kings heard of his journeying, they came out to meet him, and they found him perplexed in his affair, and he informed them as to what had happened and that in accordance with it he could not do anything except by the command of God—Mighty and Glorious. And the people took him to the cliff that is described in the holy Pentateuch,[45] that he might behold all the children of Israel. Now, after the man had been thus met and honored and made much of, his zeal was increased to obtain to the uttermost degree the love of the people. Thereupon he built on the cliff that has been described seven altars, and offered up on every altar a calf and a ram, and began to worship that he might hear what would be addressed unto him.[46] And he heard what did not please him, and he announced what he had heard to the company of the kings; and they said to him: "Remove unto another place, and perhaps there the cursing of this place will be easier." And he obeyed them, and he did as he had done the first time, and he heard greater things than the first communication; and he began to go to the extreme in glorifying the children of Israel and honoring them. And the king of Moab said to him: "If you can not curse them, do not bless them." Then he asked them that he might remove unto another place, and he went and did as he had done the second time.[47] And his eyes fell upon the desert, and he saw the tribes of Israel, and divine spirits were guarding them, that is, the angels were protecting them, every soul; and he turned away the evil eye from them and hastened to glorify and bless them until he said concerning them: "O Israel, cursed be he who curses you, and blessed be he who blesses you."[48] And the anger of the king was aroused against him; but Balaam said unto

---

[45] Num 22:41.
[46] Num 22:14.
[47] Num 22:27.
[48] Num 24:9.

him: "Let not your anger be aroused against me; did I not say unto you that I could not act contrary to what I am commanded? But now assemble the kings with you that I may inform them, your company, of what will happen unto you and others besides you of the people, and I will give you information about a device, which, if carried out, will occasion their annihilation. Thereupon the kings assembled, and he made known unto them marvelous news, the explanation of which would be long; and he said to them: "Round about these people the holy angels keep guard, and the King of the heavens and the earth is with them, and it is not allowable to make use of sorcery against them, nor the science of astrology;[49] nor will His heart repudiate them, except when they give themselves over to unbelief or are led to do so by some stratagem; then the Creator will become angry with them and they will perish, and not a single one of them will survive."

Fourth Chapter

When the kings heard him relate what has preceded, they said to him: "What is the way to accomplish what you have mentioned concerning their destruction?" And he looked up the last resource of infidelity and pollution, and made it known unto them, and said to them:[50] "Select of the most beautiful and fair women as many as you can, and the king shall be the first to send forth his daughter with them; thereupon give unto each one of them an idol which she may worship, and an ornament which she may look at, and perfume which she may inhale, and food and drink; and the daughter of the king should be in a chariot which is wafted along with the wind, and it should be enjoined upon her that she make it her aim to go to the tabernacle and pay her respects to no one except to their chief unto whom the crowd shows deference, for he is their chief. And if in this she meets his approval, then she shall say unto him: 'Will you not receive me, or eat of my food and drink of my drink and offer sacrifices unto my god?[51] For after this I will be yours, and with you will do whatsoever you desire.' For know, O king, that by the chief of this people being polluted, both he and his company will perish, and of them there will not remain a survivor." And the kings did what he recommended unto them; and there were collected to them twenty-four thousand girls, and they sent them away on the Sabbath day. And as they descended opposite the tabernacle, the chief of the tribe

---

[49] Num 23:21, 23.
[50] Num 25; in Numbers, however, the women are identified as the daughters of Moab, and Balaam is not part of the account. See also Josephus, *Ant.* 4.6.6.
[51] The Baal of Peor in Num 25:1–5.

of Simeon rose up; for he was the chief of fifty-nine thousand men[52] and was in the advance. And the daughter of the king advanced unto him,[53] for she, on beholding the great deference shown to him by his companions, supposed him to be the prophet Moses—peace be upon him—and he ate of her food and drank of her drink and worshiped the idol which was in her hand, and after this she was submissive to him in his desire. Thereupon everyone of them, I mean this particular tribe, took one girl for himself; and the Creator became angry at the people and destroyed of them in the wink of an eye four thousand men together with four thousand girls.[54] And had not Phinehas the imam—peace be upon him—rushed from the presence of Moses, the Prophet—peace be upon him—while he and his assembly were weeping at the door of the tabernacle, and seized in his hand a lance and bursting in upon them thrust through the man and girl, I mean the daughter of the king, and dispatched them,[55] assuredly would the wrath of the Creator have destroyed the whole people; but by this action he removed and warded off the Divine anger from the children of Israel. And to Phinehas—peace be upon him—there resulted from this noble fame and an excellent remembrance, and a covenant to the end of the ages.[56] And praise be to God the Creator without cessation!

Fifth Chapter

When the stratagem of Balaam against the children of Israel was accomplished and there had perished of them this great number and they had been overtaken by this calamity, God revealed to the prophet Moses—peace be upon him—that he should take vengeance for the children of Israel upon the people of Midian[57] before he should return to his elements (meaning, by this, before his death). So he commanded Joshua the son of Nun, at the time of his investing him with his succession, that he should go forth with the company which he specially mentioned, and with him Phinehas the imam, for he had gained the victory and a name, and he it was who had averted the Divine anger, and not anyone else, for he had hastened to obey his Lord. Now Balaam had returned unto the king of Moab to congratulate him over the calamity of the children of Israel, and he

[52] Num 2:12, 13.
[53] Num 25:15.
[54] Did "twenty" drop from the text, reducing the number to four thousand? 1 Cor 10:8 reads twenty-three thousand, and Josephus, *Ant.* 4.6.12, reads fourteen thousand.
[55] Num 25:7–9.
[56] Num 25:11–13.
[57] Num 31:1–2.

found the kings collected together and indulging in joy and merriment, and before they were aware, twelve thousand men had surrounded their city, whereupon they made haste in sending out the harlots with ornaments and censers and perfumes, taking for granted that what they had made a successful beginning in would be carried out to a perfect completion. But they (i.e., the Israelites) slaughtered these (the women) with the sword. Then Phinehas—peace be upon him—with his cousin went in advance and sounded with the trumpets, and the walls of the fortress fell down in ruins,[58] and the army entered into Midian, and they killed simultaneously the five kings and every man whom they found in it. And they began to make inquires about Balaam, and they found him in a house of worship, and lo, he was engaged in worship and was performing service. And they brought him out, and he was talking in speech that was unintelligible and could not be understood, because of the greatness of his confusion and bewilderment and the aberration of his mental faculties. And Joshua the son of Nun exerted himself to preserve him alive that our master Moses—the peace of God be upon him—might behold him; but they of the tribe of Simeon who beheld him were not obedient, nay, even, they cried out the Law against him[59] and put him to death. And Joshua said: "Who killed him? Why have you done this, seeing we had taken him under our protection?" And they said unto him: "O our master, there should be no protection granted to an infidel, nor security to a sorcerer; had we not killed him, he might have effected the accomplishment of a stratagem against you and against your people. And we have dared to go contrary to you in killing him, because of what was in our hearts concerning his deed, and if there be sin in our action in violating the protection accorded to him, lo, we assume it; but to our master belongs such exalted sentiments that he will look with liberality upon our excuse." And he approved of what they said and justified their action. And the people plundered Midian and drove away its cattle and took captive its women and children; and not a thing remained in it but they took it. And they returned laden with booty, victorious and safe; not a single man of them was missing. And our master Moses, the Prophet—peace be upon him—with Eleazar the imam, the son of Aaron, and a crowd of chiefs went out to meet them. And when they beheld what there was among their number of captive women, our master Moses, the Prophet—upon him be the most excellent peace—became angry at them and said to them: "This crowd has

---

[58] The reader will recognize similarities to the Jericho story in Josh 5 and later in SJ 17.

[59] Deut 18:10–12; *Tg. Ps.-J.* Num 33:8.

been the cause of your destruction."[60] Thereupon he commanded them to kill every woman who had known a man, and every boy child, and that none should remain except female children who had not known a man, and that they, together with the company that was with them, should separate themselves seven days for the purpose of purification. And they did so. And the number of the female captives who remained over after those who were killed was thirty-two thousand girls; and of sheep there was 675,000 head; and of cattle there was seventy-two thousand head; and of horses and mules and camels sixty-one thousand head;[61] and of gold and silver and vessels and general goods, such a quantity as is impossible to define and describe. But more wonderful than this was the unharmed condition of the twelve thousand men who entered a province such as this was, without the loss of a single man of them, or even one of them being overtaken by the bow of a sword or hit with a stone.[62] Blessed be God, the One who is able to do whatsoever He please, and of Him do I ask assistance, and unto Him do I put my trust, and unto Him do I return penitently.

Sixth Chapter

When God informed our master Moses, the Prophet, of the time when he could no longer remain alive,[63] He commanded him to go up unto the mountain known as Nebo.[64] And he (Moses) proceeded to give instructions to Joshua the son of Nun, and to the children of his brother, and to the assembly of the leaders, with regard to all necessary matters. And they remained with him some time, along will all the officers of the army and the people of wisdom; and he put them under a covenant that they would go with the children of Israel in the way which he had commanded them and not swerve from it either to the right or to the left; and he ordered the priests to sound upon the trumpets and send forth heralds who should proclaim throughout the congregation of the children of Israel: "Whoever desires to see our master Moses, the Prophet—the most excellent, peace be upon him—let him come that he may hear his blessing and whatever he shall reveal, and look upon him and bid him farewell before he goes to the place which God has chosen for him." Thereafter he entered into the tabernacle and offered on the brazen altar the sacrifices,

---

[60] Num 31:14–18.
[61] Num 31:32–34.
[62] Num 31:49.
[63] Num 27:12–23.
[64] Deut 32:44–52.

and lifted up the veil, even the veil of the holy house, and cast incense upon the golden altar, and worshiped his Lord; and then he bid farewell to the temple and what there was in it of omnipotence and divine majesty, and went out. And all the children of Israel according to their ranks were gathered together unto him, and he sat down upon an exalted seat, as was his custom, whereon he was elevated above the people and the light of his countenance shone as the rays of the sun. And he began to deliver an address unto the congregation of the children of Israel, in which he gathered together just as many as a servant of God could of passages of praise to God, whose names are holy; and in it he expounded intelligence of the Divine Favor which was to come, and the cause of Wrath and Error. And he informed the children of Israel concerning the deluge of fire and the day of vengeance and reward, and defined the time of his return unto them.[65] Then he announced unto them what should happen unto every tribe, and that would marshal them complete in the days of final perfection and completion. And he blessed them altogether, and they listened unto him. And when the time came to bid farewell to each individual army, they began to cry aloud and wail and weep; and after a space of time he commanded them to be quiet and to sit down. Then he departed, walking slowly up the ascent of the mountain unto which God had ordered him to ascend, and with him were Joshua the son of Nun, and Eleazar the imam, and the assembly of the leaders who were bidding him farewell and weeping at the approach of his separation from them and clinging to him. And when the farewells were prolonged with them, and night drew near, a pillar of divine fire descended[66] and separated between them and their master—peace be upon him—and no one knows what happened to him after this,[67] even unto this time. His allotted period of life had reached its limit, and the term of his existence among men—peace be unto him—and now his dealings were directly with his Lord and His angels. And of God do we beg that He would unite us to him through His mercy.[68] Behold He is over all things powerful, and He is my sufficiency and illustrious Protector.

Seventh Chapter

When the master Moses, the Prophet—peace be upon him—disappeared from him and from the congregation of the children of Israel, and the

---

[65] 2 Pet 3:6–7.

[66] Josephus, *Ant.* 4.8.49.

[67] Num 34:6.

[68] Deut 34:10. The description follows the typical Samaritan aversion to anthropomorphism when describing God.

COMMAND separated him from them, which event he was unable to avert from himself, and there passed away from them the sight of him, and when all had completely despaired of his return, Joshua the son of Nun wept for him and proclaimed with his loudest voice, saying: "O Master! The death of every one of the children of Adam, from the first to last, was witnessed, and his grave seen; but you! Who has seen your grave? What prophet of the prophet can attain unto your glory, or prolong his memory unto the extent your memory is prolonged? Where is one who has brought to life the dead and caused the living to die, through the permission of his Lord, besides you? Unto what prophet do the infidels bear testimony as to his prophetic office, except you? What prophet, in the ages past or yet to come, did cause his congregation to hear the voice of the Creator from the regions of the heavens, except you? Where is one who shall arise, and his words ascend on high and ward off the Divine anger, and bring down Divine mercy, except you? What prophet fasted before his Lord until he fasted one hundred and twenty days including the nights, except you? What prophet boasted of his being the one who held conversation with God without anything intervening between them, except you?[69] Where is one who has trodden the fire, and cleft the darkness, and rent the clouds, and reached unto the curtain of omnipotence, besides you? What book ascribed to any prophet has in it the teaching of the worship of the Creator, and of how access may be had to Him, except your book? O one who killed the Nile with his rod![70] O one who did reveal new things! O one who showed forth wonders! O one who manifested signs! O one who lit up the darkness![71] O one who cleft the sea with his rod![72] O one who put to rout armies with his hand! O one who warded off the Divine anger by his petitions![73] O one who brought down Divine mercy by his intercessions! O one whose very sustenance was the worship of his Lord! O one who went out from the boundaries of humanity and human power into the Divine power! O one who understood the past and knew what was to come! O one who ruled his enemies by his invocation! O my master and my lord! How can I exist and how can your people exist, now that you are gone? After this his weeping increased as did also the weeping of the congregation that was with him, and when the grief and wailing had been long indulged in, with submission and humility, it was announced to Joshua the

---

[69] Exod 32:30, 31; Deut 9:9, 18, 25.

[70] Exod 7:20.

[71] Exod 13:21.

[72] Exod 14.

[73] Exod 32:11; Num 14:11–17.

son of Nun, saying: "Return you and those that are with you of the army, and do not oppose the Command of God"—May His name be glorious.

Eighth Chapter

When Joshua and the priests returned after bidding farewell to the prophet—peace be upon him—the congregation of the children of Israel met them, and they commenced weeping for their master, yea, every company by company, and they continued weeping for him thirty days and nights.[74] And the nations heard their clamor and wailing and crying, and they assembled together in confederation on the borders and were extremely happy when they were informed of the death of the prophet— peace be upon him—and they resolved to encounter the children of Israel. But when God—Powerful and Mighty—perceived the conspiracy of the Canaanites, of those who were assembled unto them, He made a manifestation of Divine power and revealed unto Joshua the son of Nun that he should strengthen his own and the people's courage by saying unto them that "as He had been with them in the past, so would He be with them in the future so long as they continued in worshipful submission." Praise be unto Him to Whom belong the kingdom and the majesty and the power and eternal existence.[75] There is no God but He, and no kingdom but His kingdom.

Ninth Chapter

After the death of Moses, Kalimu'l-Iah,[76] God made a revelation unto Joshua the son of Nun, the disciple of Moses, the servant of God, saying unto him: "O Joshua, arise, start out, and with your people pass over the Jordan unto the land which I am about to give unto the children of Israel; all the places which your feet shall tread shall belong to you.[77] Your boundary shall be from the wilderness to el-Ludnan (Lebanon), and from the river el-Farah (Euphrates) unto the uttermost sea; and no enemy shall stand before you. O Joshua, do not abolish the reading of what Moses the prophet inscribed and wrote, with what is entrusted unto the Levites in the place in the holy house, and learn from it night and day, even all the days of your life, that you may be instructed; for if you observe the same and do not

---

[74] Deut 34:8.
[75] This brings to mind the long ending of the prayer found in Matt 6:13.
[76] An Islamic title used for Moses, "Speaker with God."
[77] Josh 1:2–5.

swerve from what is commanded you to the right or to the left, you will succeed and prosper, and your enemies will be put to rout by you, and you shall tread upon their necks."[78] And at this time the communication ended.

Tenth Chapter

After Joshua had heard what God had revealed unto him, he joined unto himself Eleazar the imam—peace be upon him—and he sat down upon his sacred chair while Joshua sat upon his royal chair. And there gathered unto them the holy priests, and the Levites who offered the sacrifices, and the twelve chiefs who always attended them, and the chief judges, and the seventy chosen wise men, and the officers over the thousands, and hundreds, and fifties, and tens. And with the assembling of this congress, the trumpets sounded and the heralds went forth proclaiming a general assembling of the children of Israel. And it was not but an hour before there were gathered unto them the old men and the young, with many of the women and children and all the army. And then Joshua began to enumerate to them the things that God—Powerful and Mighty—had manifested by the hand of our master Moses, the Prophet—peace be upon him—on their behalf and that of their predecessors. Next he recalled to them wherein they had acted contrary to Him, and tried Him, and rebelled against Him. And he said unto them: "O assembled men, I am going to bind you to the covenant and compact which existed before the death of the Prophet—peace be upon him— that you will not associate others with God, and that you will see to the promulgation of the laws upon which this covenant is founded, and it is, namely, the explanation of the law and the explanation of what the obedient will receive and what shall befall the disobedient. And now this covenant in which I do confirm you is not with you and you alone but includes you and those whom you shall beget unto the end of the ages." And he told them what the other nations were wedded to, concerning the worship of idols, and informed them that God was with them as long as they remained in obedience but that He would remove His favor from them upon their acting disobediently and that then their ways would not prosper nor would there be a united nation. Then he proclaimed in his loudest voice: "Assembled men, let there not be among you a disseminator of corrupt designs, spikes of corn and wormwood,[79] [meaning by this, one who associates others with God and unites the worship of others with His worship]; nor let there be among you one who cogitates in his heart wicked

---

[78] This is similar to Josh 1:7–8.
[79] Deut 29:18.

doctrines or opposition to the command of God—Powerful and Mighty—lest there be a destruction of his mighty, holy nation and all its greatness, and separation from the Creator—may His name be holy—and your enemies attain unto their desires and plunder you of your cattle, and wives, and children. For whoever adopts these views or any part of them, there shall fall upon him all the calamities which were written in the Holy Law, and God will blot out the remembrance of him under heaven and will make him distinguished by reason of his calamities, apart from all the tribes of Israel. And so, be sincere with your souls and your conscience that I may renew the covenant with you in accordance with what you may say; and God and His heavens and His earth and His angels shall bear witness against you in what happens between us and you; may the sentence be in your favor and not against you. And now if you continue in keeping what has been commanded you, God—may He be blessed and exalted—will bless you and keep you and protect you and lead you to victory and will subdue your enemies and give the land concerning which He swore, by His own omnipotence, unto your ancestors, Abraham and Isaac and Jacob—peace be upon them. And He will keep you, and will keep the land in all happiness, and He will remove calamities and all disasters and multiply you; but when you shall have been disobedient and rebellious, the Divine Favor will be removed from you; and the Divine power from your side, and from your support, and the angels will be removed from your side, and the name of the greatest King depart from giving you assistance, and there shall fall upon you those things which are written in the book of Wrath and Curse, and He will scatter your troops and forget your affairs, and the enemies will take possession of you, and there will remain no longer to you a king, or shrine, or possessions, or men, and God will disperse you throughout the regions of the earth from one extremity of it to the other, and He will make you servants and subjects. So now, whatever you say and believe and covenant, let it be the real covenant binding upon you, and let this second covenant be added unto that which He covenanted with you through our master Moses, the Prophet—peace be upon him. Therefore act sincere from your souls, and the secret thoughts of your hearts.[80]

Eleventh Chapter

The congregation of the children of Israel answered him, while crying out, weeping, and humbling themselves before God, and casting their souls into His hands, saying: "O our master and our lord, we hear and will obey the

---

[80] This is reminiscent of Josh 24:14–24.

command of God—Mighty and Powerful—and of His true and faithful Prophet, and also your command, O king, and the command of our imam and our rulers, and there will be no opposition to what you order, and no deviation from what you say either to the right or to the left, nor from whatever our master Moses, the Prophet—peace be upon him—has ordained, and there shall be no rejection of a single part of it;[81] and whoever shall rebel and deviate, and act treacherously, let upon him be the Curse and Wrath, for after this manner did our master Moses, the Prophet—peace be upon him—agree with us and impose conditions upon us, and put us under oath, and covenant with us, and offer up for us the sacrifices, and we answered him as we have answered you. And God is the witness over us in this, and He is our sufficiency and bountiful Protector."

Twelfth Chapter

When Joshua beheld the zeal of the people, he said: "The One who has insight into you and your purposes is God." And he renewed with them the covenant and compact, and offered for them the offerings, and the imam blessed them. Thereupon he and the imam, each of them, sat down on his throne; and he summoned the leaders and demanded of them that they should make out a census of the children of Israel, tribe by tribe, and that the enumeration throughout the congregation should embrace all men from the age of twenty years up to the age of fifty years, excepting the tribe of Levi. And he ordered that this tribe should be enumerated, from the boy of a month old upwards: for so had our master Moses, the Prophet—peace be upon him—given orders before his death.[82] But such as were under age twenty and over fifty years of age were not to be included in the enumeration. And the leaders made out the census, and the whole amounted to 601,730 men,[83] although of this number the tribe of Reuben, and the tribe of Gad, and the half tribe of Manasseh had their landed possessions behind the Jordan,[84] even nine cities with their districts, which had belonged to Sihon and Og, the sons of Anaq, three cities and their provinces had been conquered by Nabih[85] and his cousin of the tribe of Manasseh. For it did come to pass that when our master Moses, the Prophet—peace be upon him—conquered these cities and destroyed their

---

[81] Josh 1:16–17.
[82] Num 26:4.
[83] Num 26:51.
[84] Num 32:1–5.
[85] The Nobah of Num 32:42.

inhabitants, there gathered unto him the leaders of these two tribes and a half, and they said unto him: "O our master and our lord, these cities suit us, for we have many animals and cattle, even though they be approximately less than one-sixth of the assigned lands while the whole number of the census of our men comes close on to one-fifth of the army of the children of Israel." And he rebuked them, supposing that they preferred settling apart from their brethren. But they answered: "Behold we will leave our luggage and our cattle in these cities, and we will march forward under one enrollment, thrusting aside every pretext, and we will not return to our assigned lands until our brethren have got possession of all their assigned lands, and after that we will return unto our assigned lands and to our own places."[86] And our master Moses, the Prophet—the most excellent, peace be upon him—answered them favorably in reply to what they had asked of him, and assigned to them while he was alive this region. And the first of those whom Joshua the son of Nun enrolled in his army were the two and a half tribes, and the whole number of their enrollment was 110,580 men; and according to these figures, the chiefs apportioned out the land from the Jordan to the sea. And this is the enrollment, based on the census, of the prosperous, victorious, holy, triumphant, and blessed army. And the census of the tribe of Levi was apart from the company of which mention has been made before; for the members of this tribe did not engage in the wars, nor did they separate from the service of their Lord; and the whole of their census, from a boy one month old and upwards, was 23,000 men.[87] And when the leaders came with the enrollment of the census, Joshua the son of Nun made them appear before him, and he announced good tidings unto them, namely, that God would bless them so as that there would result from one a thousand, as our master Moses, the Prophet—peace be upon him—promised them from God—may His name be blessed.[88]

Thirteenth Chapter

When Joshua the son of Nun heard about the mustering of the Canaanites and the assembling of the giants, he sent out spies from the men of experience, intelligence, prudence, and piety to see the army of the enemies and make an investigation and to proceed to Jericho and make an investigation as to the number of its men and of those who were collected unto them,

---

[86] Num 32:16–19.
[87] Num 26:57–62.
[88] Josh 23:10; Deut 32:30.

and then returning make it known to him.[89] So the spies bid the army farewell, and invoked God's favor, and started out on their journey, having changed their outward appearance to the condition of ones who had come from far distant places. Now the spies knew all the languages spoken in the army of the enemies. And when they arrived at it, they began to weep, and the enemy asked them what news they had, and they said: "We are men from the people of the east, our companions have heard tidings of this great nation, which was for forty years in the wilderness without a guide or provisions, and the report reached our company that they have a Lord whom they speak of as 'The King of the heavens and earth' and that He has appropriated unto them both our country and your country, and so our companions have sent us out that we may find out the truth of what has been reported unto us and make it known to them. And we have journeyed and already passed by you a long time ago, while you were busily engrossed in your occupations, and we did come to the army of that nation and found them perplexed, wandering round and round in the wilderness, and the secret among them was that their God had become angry at them and would not bring any of them into the land except two men; so we have returned with this good news, gladdened and rejoicing.

"Now when, at that time, we learned what this nation had done with Sihon and Og, and with their lands and territories, and also what they did with the kings of Midian and Moab and the taking of their women and children, and that this nation was bent upon entering your country and then our country, we made haste that we might make known to our companions the truth of this. And we journeyed unto them from the mountains, and we had but just reached the vicinity of the camps when there came forth unto us three or four men, and each of them took hold of one of us, and brought us into the presence of the new king, who had been invested with the kingdom as successor to Moses, the Prophet—the best of peace be upon him. Now his companion was merciful who lifted not up his glance to any one; but this one was as a giant man, whose conversation broke souls, and whose speech split hearts, and whose reproach struck astonishment into minds. And we had but just stood in his presence when he knew our name and our origin and our country, and when we started out, and the places at which we had encamped, and in all that he mentioned unto us he was correct. And we at once believed in him and his Lord, through fear of him, but he answered us: 'This faith is not a faith to be accepted when you do so through fear; yet there is no fear for you; go, return and say to all whom

---

[89] Josh 2:1.

you meet and to your companions: Look out for your own welfare, and whoever flees away is safe, but whoever remains shall perish. For after the space of a week, the water of the Jordan will stand still for me by the command of our Lord, the Highest, until His people shall cross over; and not a fortress shall be shut in their faces when they shall have gone around it seven circuits, for its walls will fall, and all they who remain, who are found inside, will perish: and the city and territory will be our territory, and the assigned lands shall become ours, assigned unto us by the King of the heavens and earth, whose creatures and servants all kings are.' And this is the whole of what we heard from him, and we know that his name is Joshua the son of Nun and that he is the one who put to route the Amalekites and is the slayer of Sihon, and the destroyer of Og, and the one who ruined the kings of Midian and Moab. O woe to us and woe to you, and whatever is attached unto our country and your country; for they are a people who have no pity, nor do they leave survivors or show compassion, nor do they make a truce, except with those who are outside of us and you, for we stand, in their estimation, in the character of infidels and pagans and as a haughty and rebellious people; and the one who is lucky among us and among you is he who takes his own people between his hands and flees away with all speed until he shall have got out beyond all their assigned lands, before he feels regret where regret will profit him nothing." And the men rode on and pursued their journey, and after this manner did they speak with all whom they met until they returned to Jericho, and here it became known about them, and they were sought after to be destroyed, and they begged protection of a woman who was called Rahab the innkeeper, whose house was beside the walls of the city, and she took them out and concealed them, and gave excuse unto those who sought them, saying that they had already returned.[90] Then she made a covenant with them and they with her that if God Mighty and Powerful should vanquish for them this city, they would spare her and spare whatever souls were in her courtyard, of her own people.[91] And the spies enjoined upon her to fix upon the roof of her house a sign which they should know, so that when she knew they were drawing nigh unto the city, she should display it; but they stipulated with her that they would be innocent of the blood of all such as were found, of her own people, outside of the courtyard. And she brought them out by night, and God willed their safe escape, and they returned to the army. And they told the king and the imam and their congregation what they witnessed and what had happened to them, and what

[90] Josh 2:8–14.
[91] Josh 2:13.

favor the woman had done in their behalf. And the congregation answered them that they would spare the woman, in accordance with what they had covenanted with her. And the report of her spread abroad throughout the army, and the whole congregation of them knew her.

Fourteenth Chapter

When Joshua the king heard the statement of the spies, he sent forth the leaders to proclaim throughout the army that they should proceed in the journey, having with them provisions for three days, and also to say in the proclamation: "O assemblies of men! Fear not, nor be dismayed, for God, your God, is about to journey with you that He may show forth with you a miracle at this time, to make you successful over your enemies; and as to the miracle which God will show you at the Jordan, the like of it has not been heard of in the ages past, nor shall the like of it be heard of in the ages yet to come.[92] And it is the first terror of you that shall fall upon the hearts of your enemies. Therefore, know that the holy priests shall carry the golden ark, which is the ark of the covenant, which covenant is celestial substance, for it is the tablets whose writings were of Divine light: behold they are celestial substance; and when the priests with the ark shall enter the water of the Jordan, the water will stand still and subside by the power of the ALMIGHTY until the water below flows away, while the water above shall mount up and increase upon itself until all the children of Israel, and those who are in their company, shall pass over in absolute dryness."[93]

Then Joshua the son of Nun himself called out and said: "O assemblies of men! God commands you that there should be between you and the priests who carry the ark an extent of equal space to two thousand yards, so do not approach unto it within this distance, that God may complete His work with you."[94] Then he ordered the twelve chiefs to take from under the feet of the priests twelve stones after the children of Israel had finished the passage over the Jordan, and that each one of them should write his name upon his stone in order that what had happened might be preserved and perpetuated through the eternity of the ages to come,[95] even the miracle which God—may His name be glorious—would show on the Jordan.[96] And the Levites proclaimed with loudest voice: "Praise be to

---

[92] Josh 3:1–6.
[93] Josh 3:12–13.
[94] Josh 3:7.
[95] Josh 3:4.
[96] Josh 4:3. Only the SJ records the inscription on the stones.

the God of Gods, and Lord of Lords, to Whose commandments animate and inanimate things are obedient, and the heavens and the earth and the seas and the rivers and all that therein is. There is no God but He, and no kingdom lasts but His kingdom, nor any power but His power, nor any sovereign except under His sovereignty. Perish whoever deny Him and believe in another than He, for He is God."

Fifteenth Chapter

And the children of Israel did as the king commanded them. And the cloud was lifted up on the first (day) of the first month, of the first year of the first period of seven years of the Jubilee even from the beginning of the entering in of the children of Israel within the boundaries of the assigned lands.[97] And up to this time there had elapsed, of the days of the world as established by the law, two thousand seven hundred and ninety-four complete years, and this reckoning of time is correct, which the learned know by chronological computations based on the era of the flood. And the priests proceeded forward when the cloud was lifted up, and attained to the distance from the army that he prescribed unto them. And when the priests with the ark approached the water of the Jordan, the Levites shouted aloud, and the congregation of the children of Israel joined in with them, saying with one voice: "There is no power or strength in the presence of Your power, O Lord of worlds!" And the water stood still, and rose up in accumulation, by the power of its Creator: He who is almighty over whatever He wills, the Worker of miracles and wonders. And continued to be heaped up, wave upon wave, until it became like unto huge mountains, while the priests stood praising God and shouting halleluiahs and saying: "Praise be unto Him, in obedience to whom everything exists." And they stood, with the ark, on the dry ground in the midst of the Jordan until all the children of Israel, with their large throng and their cattle, had passed over on the dry ground through the midst of the Jordan, on its bottom, and it was dry like as in the days of harvest. And the Levites were praising and shouting halleluiahs, and saying: "Praise be unto Him in obedience to whom everything exists. Praise be unto Him by whose will this is come to pass." And when the people came out of the Jordan, they observed the commandment and took the twelve stones from under the feet of the priests, and each man wrote his name upon his stone, and the king also took a similar stone. And when the priests with the ark came up out, the waters rushed down with great tumult, and winds blew violently with

---

[97] Lev 25:2.

the rushing down of the waters. And the nations heard about this great miracle, and their hearts were broken up, and their confederated troops were scattered.[98] And the water of the Jordan destroyed at that time many places that were near it, by reason of the great violence of the wind that accompanied it. And God does whatever He wishes—Glorious be His name. And of Him do I ask assistance, and upon Him do I put my trust, and unto Him be the praise for what He has bestowed.

Sixteenth Chapter

Then Joshua the son of Nun and the children of Israel offered up the hymn of praise, which our master Moses, the Prophet—peace be upon him— offered up at the sea of el-Qulzum[99] (Red Sea), and they added thereunto praises and halleluiahs, and rendered praise and thanksgiving for what God had generously bestowed upon them. And among the number of the hymns of praise which they offered up, they said: "Who is like unto You, O You who are perfect in holiness! O You who inspire terror! O You who reveal secret things! O You who perform new things! O You worker of miracles! O You displayer of wonders! How, O our Lord, shall we address You? O You revealer of signs! O You who make light the darkness! Who is like unto You? There is no likeness like unto your likeness, for You are the origin of actions, and likenesses, and bodies, and forms, and shapes, and spiritual things, which are endowed with the attributes of Your nature." On that day Joshua the son of Nun was magnified in honor among the children of Israel, and they feared him as they had feared Moses, the Prophet—peace be upon him—and they knew that God was with him. And Joshua the son of Nun set up twelve stones as a monument rising up in the Jordan.[100] And the chiefs erected the twelve stones in a place called Gilgal that the generations to come might behold them, and remember the drying up of the Jordan, and so give praise to the Doer of miracles; and that fathers might tell sons of this deed and that kings and nations might hear that our God is the one conquering God.[101] And when the kings of Syria heard of the children of Israel's crossing over into the land appointed unto them and about the stoppage of the water of the Jordan and its drying up, they arrayed themselves in funeral robes and were smitten with fear, and some of them died through fear of the children of Israel, on account of the

[98] Josh 2:11.
[99] The common Arabic name for the Red Sea.
[100] Josh 4:20–5:1.
[101] Josh 4:19–24.

greatness of the awe which they inspired.[102] And God made a revelation to
Joshua the son of Nun, saying: "Today have I spread awe of you and your
people over these nations, and I have lifted off from you, and from your
people, every impurity and infirmity." And Joshua named the place Gilgal,
and it is its name unto the end of the ages. And praise be unto God, the
One who endures without cessation.

Seventeenth Chapter

Upon the departure of the king from the place that he had named Gilgal,
they encamped in the district of Jericho, on the first day (of the feast of unleavened bread), the fourteenth day (of the first month).[103] And they kept
the Passover at this time and ate unleavened bread from the new crops.
And the manna ceased with their entrance into the land and their eating of
its crops and of the fruit of its trees.[104] And when the army had drawn near
round about the city, Joshua the son of Nun retired apart from the camps
that he might worship his Lord by night, and when he had finished his devo-
tions, he lifted up his eyes, and behold, the figure of a man standing, with his
sword drawn in his hand,[105] and he called out to him: "Joshua!" Thereupon
he (Joshua) replied: "Are you of us or of our adversaries?" And he answered him and said: "I am one of the messengers of God, who rule over
punishments." And he (Joshua) cast himself before him on the ground because of his majesty. Then he rose up and said to him: "Lay upon your servant the command which has been brought unto him." And he said unto
him: "King, take off your shoes from off your feet; for the place whereon
you stand is a holy place.[106] God—Powerful and Mighty—says unto you: O
Joshua, look before you, behold I am about to place in your hand this disobedient city, even Jericho, with its king and its people; now therefore
choose for yourself from among every tribe a thousand men.[107] And they
shall go round about the city, six circuits in six days, with the golden ark,
the ark of the covenant,[108] before them; and they shall not talk in conversation or be intent upon anything except offering up praises and halleluiahs,
nor shall they make an intermission in this or raise any great tumult during
the space of six days; yet the two priests shall be along with the two clam-

---

[102] Josh 5:1.
[103] Josh 5:10.
[104] Josh 5:12.
[105] Josh 5:13–15.
[106] Josh 5:15.
[107] Cf. the MT Joshua account, which has this speech directly from God.
[108] Josh 6:2–5.

orous trumpets. But on the seventh day they shall go round about the city the seventh time, and the two priests shall sound with the two trumpets, and when the company hear the sound of the trumpets, then let them shout with a loud voice, three times, saying: 'God is omnipotent in battles. God is His name.' And at the completion of this act, the wall of the city will be demolished, and the fortresses will fall down before the people, and the army shall enter the city and destroy it." And Joshua returned and assembled the leaders of his people, and commanded that they should select twelve thousand men. And when they came unto him, he gave orders to them to march, and with them should be the saintly priests, bearing the ark and two trumpets. And he gave instructions unto the company that they should offer up halleluiahs and praises during the six days in a low tone of voice but on the seventh day they should go round about the city six times, "And on the seventh time around, the priests shall sound the trumpets, and upon their hearing the trumpets, the whole army shall shout with a loud voice and instantly advance; and then the fortifications will be demolished, and God will put the city in your hands. And when this has been successfully accomplished by you and you have attained the city, you shall put to death every breathing thing which you find in it, whether of men or animals.[109] And you shall destroy it and burn it, and shall not leave in it any, except the woman who is known as Rahab the innkeeper; her you shall spare and also those souls that are in her courtyard, according as the spies made covenant with her. O assemblies of men! Be watchful of yourselves; do not take anything from the city; burn its gold and silver and brass and iron, and all its trappings, and do not meddle with anything that is devoted; for then would you and the army perish."[110] And the people did as he instructed them. And on the seventh circuit the priests sounded with the two trumpets, and they cried out with a great shout; and at that, the walls of the city fell down, and the army entered in and put to death every breathing thing in it, from man even to animals.[111] And they collected all the furniture that was in it, and placed it in the middle of the city, and burned it, and it became a mound never to be rebuilt. And Joshua proclaimed in the loudest voice: "O assemblies of men! It is forbidden unto you, and unto those who shall rise up of your seed, to build up in this city one single stone." And it is the first of the rebellious cities, known as Ancient Jericho; and this city was devoted, destroyed, burned, and converted into a mound, never to be built

---

[109] Josh 5:21.
[110] Josh 5:18.
[111] Josh 6:15–21.

up or restored throughout eternal ages.[112] And this was done after the spies had entered the courtyard of the woman, and brought out her and every soul that was in her courtyard, and preserved them from death. And the name of Joshua, by this act of his, was spread abroad unto the different regions of the earth.[113] And a man of the children of Israel committed a trespass and entered into the temple of the idols of this city, and he found therein a goodly thing of gold and tongue of gold, their weight was two thousand two hundred and fifty mithqals, and he took them and concealed them in his tent;[114] now it had been forbidden him to even touch it, not to mention his taking it in theft and hiding it in his place of abode. And the Lord became angry with the children of Israel on account of him.[115] And neither the leaders nor the king knew about this deed. But praise be unto Him who knows secrets and who shows forth miracles. Blessed be His name, and exalted be His fame.

Eighteenth Chapter

When it was morning of the day of which mention has already been made, Joshua the king and all the army came before the temple, and he made chiefs present themselves before Eleazar the imam—peace be upon him—and upon him were the jewels.[116] And the jewel which was inscribed with the name of Judah grew black; and he, in succession, presented the tribe of Judah, in its companies, name by name, before the jewel; and it grew black at the family of Zarah, the son of Judah. And the man at once presented himself and stood before Joshua the king. And the king said unto him: "O man! Lift up your face to the King of the heavens and earth, and know that He knows secrets, and O woe be to the one who imagines that he can conceal from Him anything or cover up from Him a matter. So now confess as to how you have sinned and what you have taken of the devoted thing; for God has become angry with His people on your account." And the man answered him and said: "I know, O king, that I have committed a great sin before God, Who knows what is secret and concealed, and I have been a traitor to the covenant of God, and of His messenger; for I entered the temple of the chief idol of Jericho and there found a goodly thing of gold, and tongue of gold, and their weight was two thousand and fifty mithqals,

---

[112] Deut 13:16; Josh 6:26.
[113] Josh 6:27.
[114] Cf. the theft of a mantle, silver coins, and a bar of gold in Josh 7:21.
[115] Josh 7:1.
[116] The reference is to the Urim and Thummim or the stones on the robe of the high priest, Exod 39:6.

and my soul became greedy for this, and I took it and buried it in my tent.[117] And now if a crime like mine can be pardoned, well and good, seeing that God is merciful and compassionate; but if there is no pardon for it, then let there be executed what you shall command in my affair." Then the king sent immediately trustworthy people, and they brought what the man had mentioned he had felt greedy after and so had taken it. And the governor and his associates, the chiefs, brought him before the temple of the Creator, and command was given that he should be burned outside the camp. And he took the man and burned both him and whatever children he had, and cattle, and all that he possessed, and he placed all in a deep valley and commanded the whole army to stone it with stones.[118] And he named the valley the valley of Achor. And after this God removed His anger from the children of Israel; for what they did appeased Him. And unto Him be praise for His bounty and the excellency of His favor and goodness.

Nineteenth Chapter

After the capture of the city, the king and his people returned unto the place that was named Gilgal. And they took no notice until there came unto them a company of men, whose faces were blackened, and their garments and shoes worn out, and with them was bread that had become putrid.[119] And they approached unto the king and unto the chiefs of the children of Israel in this place and saluted them as the like of them were accustomed to salute, and they prostrated themselves before the assembly; then they said to the king: "We seek protection of you and of your people that we may exist in your company; for we are of those who choose for ourselves God your Lord." And he answered them: "Verily I will not grant protection unto you unless you inform me who you are and from what place you come." And they answered him: "We are people from a far distance, we have heard of your fame, and what signs and wonders God— Powerful and Mighty—has revealed to the children of Israel, even in the sea, and in the desert, and in Wady el-Mujib (Arnon), and what has happened unto the kings through you. And now, O king, we have come unto you that we might be in the company of those who beg protection with you; for we believe in your Lord, and we will not resist whatever you shall prescribe unto us, be it small or great. And behold, you see our blackened faces, and our worn-out clothes, and our dried-out food; for we did not

---

[117] This weight is less by two hundred from that mentioned in ch. 17.
[118] Josh 7:22–26.
[119] Josh 9:5.

start out from our places to come here in garments of old clothes, but this is the necessary result after the long journey. And now trust us with protection that we may exist in the company of this great, blessed, holy people."[120] And Joshua bid some of his people advance unto them, and he entered into a covenant with them and swore unto them by the God of Israel that they would not kill them nor those who were members of their company. And when it was after three days, the king found out that they were of his enemies, from three towns near him, on the south of the Blessed Mountain,[121] and they were Jaba'un (Gibeon) and Qiryah (Kirjath-jearim), and Birut (Beeroth).[122] And no one of the army was able to go to this place because of the protection granted, and the oath, and covenant. Thereupon the king summoned the men and said unto them: "Why did you conceal from me, and say that you were from a distance, while you were neighbors?" And they answered him and said: "We knew that the God of the children of Israel had commanded you to destroy these places and not to spare the sword in any place in which a soul was, and we feared for ourselves and did what we did; and now we are in your hands, O king, do with us whatever you decide upon." And he set them at liberty and made proclamation throughout the children of Israel, saying: "Do not kill them; but they shall become among the class of those cutting wood and drawing water for the beasts."[123] And they did this with them, according to what he commanded.

Twentieth Chapter

Some of the Canaanites, when they heard of the children of Israel's passing over the Jordan, had fled to one people and another; but when they had been informed of what had befallen Jericho and its people, all those who were dwelling around Jordan and the Great Sea gathered themselves together, and entered into an agreement, and made preparation to meet the children of Israel, and join in battle with them. And they sent five of their chiefs, with the majority of the army with them; and they were bidden to advance and make an attack upon the three towns which had sued for themselves protection with the children of Israel.[124] And they began with Gibeon and put its people to great straits. And the inhabitants of Gibeon

---

[120] Josh 9:9–11.
[121] Gerizim.
[122] Josh 9:17. Chephirah is not found in the Samaritan version.
[123] Josh 9:21.
[124] Josh 10:5.

sent unto Joshua the king to inform him of the truth concerning the intentions of the kings, and that they had already commenced by destroying them, and that they were now in a state of severe siege and extreme distress; and they pled their cause with him with the greatest emphasis and begged him to deliver them from this enemy, who was carrying out the designs against them.[125] And while they proceeded on their journey, the king collected his assembly, and God made a revelation to him in that night, saying: "Do not fear, O Joshua, behold I am about to give over into your hands these five chiefs; do not let a single man of them, or of their soldiers, escape safe."[126] So he marched forward and surprised the army of the enemies by night, and the watchword of the children of Israel was GOD THE OMNIPOTENT IN BATTLES, GOD IS HIS NAME. And the five kings were driven in flight before them unto Kasahah (Azekah), and unto Makkedah.[127] And when the children of Israel came up with them, they conquered them and did not spare in killing them.[128] And Joshua spoke unto the day to stand still,[129] and it stood still; and the day was great, for God heard the voice of the children of Israel and sent forth the angels with them. And the five kings, the chiefs already mentioned, fled and found a cave in Makkedah.[130] Then the king ordered to place great stones on the mouth of the cave that he might keep them under guard until they (the children of Israel) should return when they have made an end of destroying the rest of the army. And he killed the multitude of the people, and not a single man of them did escape safe. Then they returned to the cave, and the king gave command to bring them (the five kings) out and to throw them down upon their faces and ordered the prominent leaders of the army to tread with the soles of their shoes upon their necks; and he said to the children of Israel: "Be strong and of good courage, and fear not, nor be dismayed, for thus shall God do with your enemies."[131] Then he gave command that the kings should be killed and be crucified until the setting of the sun; and after sunset he gave orders that they should be placed in the cave to which they fled, along with the wood upon which they had been crucified, and also that there should be placed over the mouth of the cave a mound of stones to perpetuate the knowledge of this unto the end of ages. And they did what he ordered, and they, being gladdened, assembled together.

---

[125] Josh 10:6.
[126] Josh 10:8.
[127] Josh 10:16–27.
[128] Josh 10:28.
[129] Josh 10:12–14.
[130] Josh 10:16.
[131] Josh 10:25.

Twenty-first Chapter

When it was the beginning of the eighth month [now this is the time of the journeying of this army], the king divided the infantry and cavalry into three bands and sent each band in a different direction while he and they who were with him journeyed along in the highway, tending towards the hostile people; and he first alone was the one who surprised the enemies' camp, and he held them for a considerable time in an engagement, and they were not as yet recovered from the surprise when there arose a cloud of dust, and the army approached from every side. And when the children of Israel saw one another, they shouted out with loudest voice: "God is our Lord, who wages instead of us the war." And God on that day showed miracles with the enemy, for it came to pass that every one who would flee, fire met him and burned him up. And a specter appeared among them, so that the horses did stampede with them upon hearing the shouts of the children of Israel and carried them down to death; and the hours of the day were lengthened out for them, as God had promised them, until they had accomplished in it the results of a whole year, and not a remnant of the enemies was left after this battle. And the king from Mahzun[132] wrote a letter unto Eleazar the imam, binding it on the wing of a bird, telling him in it the good news about what God had bestowed upon them and what He had shown forth among them of miracles and signs, which should be eulogized. And he also informed him that he would not return until he should have taken possession of the remaining territorial districts for the children of Israel. And he set the bird at liberty on the morning of the fifth day, and it immediately proceeded on its journey under the blessing of God and the goodness of His guidance and grace.

And he (Joshua) continued descending upon one city after another, and taking possession of them, and doing with the rebellious like unto what we have already mentioned, until he had completed the subjugation of the territories, and then he returned in the first month of the second year. And it resulted that he in one year took possession of all their territories, and this was the region of the seven Canaanites, whose fame is enduring, well known, and spread abroad. Then he and all who were with him removed apart for purification. Now there descended from the Blessed Mountain a great river that watered the lowlands, and to it the king went down with all his army. And when he had completed his purification, Eleazar the imam of-

---

[132] Josh 11:8. Perhaps a variant of LXX Maseron in place of the MT Misrephoth-maim.

fered up for the sacrifices, and they celebrated a grand feast, the carrying out of which was complete and consummate. Never was there witnessed a better feast than it; for the people were united, not having as yet dispersed throughout their territorial sections, and when they did shout and praise and exult with halleluiahs, they were heard in the most distant and remote places. And when the feast was over, the king and his assembly gathered together and began to arrange the distribution of the territories among their people; and they asked God, Mighty and Powerful, for His favor and guidance.

Twenty-second Chapter

The king selected men from the geometricians and their associates, and from the land surveyors, and those who were well skilled in matters pertaining to lands, and from those who were accomplished in surveying, and those who were expert in estimating. And he gave instructions that they should divide it into ten parts; and he himself set about equitably distributing the nine and one half tribes over the ten sections. Thereupon he defined unto them the boundaries of the lands according to what our master Moses, the Prophet—peace be upon him—explained in the chapter of the boundaries, which is mentioned in the Law,[133] where he says: "When you come into the land of Canaan (and this is the land that shall fall unto you for an inheritance according to the boundaries thereof), then your south quarter shall be from the wilderness of Zin along by the places of Edom."[134] And this is the boundary of the lands of the two and one half tribes. And then he again says: "And your boundary on the south shall be from the furthest eastern part of the Salt Sea unto the side of Egypt; and the goings forth of this boundary shall be at the gulf."[135] That is, from the isthmus of the wilderness; by which is meant the land of el-Hejaz (Arabia), and Syria, and the pass of Haljat (?), a narrow place which reaches to the sea (the Arabah). "And the going forth thereof shall be southward of Quds-er-Raqim"; meaning thereby to the south of a place called Quds-barna (Kadesh-barnea), upon the borders of Syria and el-Hejaz; for the idea held by the people of that time was to the effect that it came unto el-Khaq (?) until it reached unto the Nile of Egypt, which is the valley whose going forth is to the sea, the coast line of which extents from Egypt to Palestine and to Greece. "And your western boundary shall be the last sea." And the

---

[133] Num 34.
[134] Num 34:2–3.
[135] Num 34:4–5.

last sea is from Egypt unto Syria. "And the border towards Syria extends from the great sea to the mountain el-Jabal (Mount Hor) and to Ainan of Hums (Hazar-enan)." The king here means the bend in the mountain el-Libnan (Lebanon) as far as the limit of its land in the district of Damascus, until coming eastward it goes around it and returns sloping downwards unto the Jordan, and its goings forth are unto the Salt Sea, which is the final point designated in the beginning of the chapter.[136] "And this," (said Joshua) "is the smaller part of the assigned land, but they (the surveyors) shall make a return on the half of the greater assigned territories according to the sum of the census of the nine and one half tribes." Then he instructed them that they should set apart forty-eight cities, out of all the territories of the children of Israel, unto the Levites, taken out from the divisions;[137] and from their total number there should be six cities of them [even three cities from the whole number of the cities of the two and one half tribes, and three cities from the whole of the assigned lands of the nine and one half tribes], concerning which cities God—Mighty and Powerful—gave command that they should be set apart, and he named them "Cities of repulse"; that is, of refuge to the one who flees thereunto, even to the one who should kill his companion inadvertently, that is, by accident, or through carelessness, without intention, or malice aforethought; so would these cities be a repulse to the avenger.[138] And the slayer shall not be killed until he shall have stood before the judge and the assembly of the leaders; and now if he did kill intentionally, he shall himself be killed; but if it was through carelessness, then he shall flee unto some one of these cities, and he shall not go forth from it until the chief imam dies; and if he do go forth outside of the boundary of this city and the avenger meet him and slay him, then shall he be innocent of his blood.[139] And the men [that is, the geometricians and the estimators and they who were skilled in matters pertaining to lands] started out on their journey according as they had been commanded.

Twenty-third Chapter

After this the king assembled the two and one half tribes before Eleazar the imam—peace be upon him—and the leaders; and they thanked them for their deeds and the help and assistance they had rendered, and said unto

---

[136] Num 35:12.
[137] Num 35:7.
[138] Josh 20:1–6; Num 35:15.
[139] Num 35:26–27.

them: "You have zealously observed the covenant of God and the covenant of our master Moses—the best of peace be upon him—and there now no longer remains to us an argument against you; for verily, you have acted kindly, and have preserved life and borne hardships, and have been patient in abstaining from visiting those whom you have left behind, until your brothers have gained their goal in taking possession of their assigned lands. And now your standing is exalted, and your deeds grow before God your Lord, who is the rewarder of good deeds, with their like a thousandfold; and you have got possession of your assigned lands, which are most excellent for your people, and in them you have no opponent or oppressor.[140] And these are our wishes of good fortune to you in it: may God multiply unto you more of the same in addition to it." Then he gathered together their prominent men, and invested them with robes of honor, and gave presents unto them. And he commanded them and enjoined upon them to go over the list of the census; and they did this, and not a single man of them was missing. And they did eat and drink together and renewed the covenant between them that they would remain in obedience unto God always and in the love of His Prophet and keep His commandments and that they would come to the support of one another whenever any tidings should reach them, whether by night or by day, in ease or in distress, in joy or in sorrow; nor would they have a falling out with each other, nor pretend to be asleep but, on the contrary, would vie with one another in showing haste and speed. And they proceeded to bind themselves unto this with a great oath. And Eleazar the imam—peace be upon him—offered up for them the sacrifices, and then the leaders of the congregation of the children of Israel gathered together to bid them farewell. Thereupon the king appointed as king over the 110,580 men (which was the number of the two and one half tribes) Nabih the son of Jil'ad (Gilead),[141] of the tribe of Manasseh, and invested him with the royal robe, and placed upon him a crown, and had him ride one of his chosen horses, and sent forth before him a herald proclaiming: "This is the king of the two and one half tribes, who is invested with their judicial matters, who shall oversee their affairs, the chief leader of their army, the chief orator among them, the one who shall be asked concerning their affairs, and every judgment of his shall be carried out, and in whatever matter of judgment to Eleazar the imam—peace be upon him. O assembled men! Whosoever shall oppose his decree or withdraw from obedience to him, the blood of this one can be shed, and all the people shall be innocent of his crime."

---

[140] Josh 22:1–6.
[141] Num 32:42.

Then he delivered unto him a copy of the book of our master Moses, the son of Amram the Prophet—peace be upon him—and he enjoined him to read it night and day and informed him that in it were marvelous indicatory signs showing how life may be prolonged in this present fleeting world and in the world to come and also that in its reading was protection from spirits, and the evil eye, and calamities, and witchery, and the skill of the enemy. And he gave over to him twelve tribes, whom he commanded to adhere unto him and not leave him, until he should have corresponded with every chief of a tribe resident at the court of the king and the saint of God; and he also selected for him men from the learned, who might ease him in the administration of the government and whom he might consult in important matters which unexpectedly arose to him. And, moreover, he gave over to him two thousand men of the Levites, who should take up their residence in the cities that had been set apart unto them among these tribes, and these should receive the portion of God and the portion of His saints, tithes and votive offerings, and should perform whatsoever sacrifices were incumbent upon them in every month, and should execute the judicial sentences in the presence of their leaders, and should establish prayers for them and oversee the matters which it is unlawful for anybody else but them to do. Thereupon the banners were unfurled before him (Nabih) and the trumpets sounded, and the saint of God and the king (Joshua) rode out with their assembly to bid them farewell; and it was a great day, the like of which it was not possible to have existed in the world. And they proceeded on their journey under the protection of God, victorious, triumphant, happy, and rejoicing. And when the news reached their friends who were watching over their affairs on the other side of the Jordan, their assembly came out to meet them. And Nabih divided out that region according to the sum of the number of his companions. And the Levites entered into their places and attended to the offering of praises and halleluiahs. And glory be to God for His bountiful favors unto them.

Twenty-fourth Chapter

After the return of the geometricians and those who were trained in surveying the land out into fields and equitably proportioning them and in rendering correct judgments as to their trees and everything that would hinder their cultivation, the king and the twelve chiefs assembled together. Now these were they to whom our master Moses, the Prophet—peace be upon him—had given instructions that they should unite with him in dividing out the land, with the restriction, however, that no one should obstinately oppose him nor should any quarrel or dispute occur between them;

and they began to arrange the division of it into ten parts and distributed the tribes over the ten parts according to the greater or lesser numbers a tribe had, until they had equalized all this. And when they did come to an agreement with regard to it, they permanently settled it and perfected it, and clearly set forth; and when the opinion of the assembly was agreed as to the rectitude of this, they brought up the lists unto the saint of God, the imam Eleazar—peace be upon him—and when he had carefully perused it, he wrote it. He wrote with his own hand a copy of the distribution and divisions of the tribes. Thereupon he wrote ten tickets, inscribed on which were the parts of the distributions and of the assigned lands, and he wrote the name of each one of the parts of the tribes upon a ticket and gave unto each several chief his ticket. And then each chief went apart with his people, and assembled the leaders of his followers, and divided out every part, according to the sum of the census, to every man according to the size of his family. And with every one (of the chiefs) there went forth some of the geometricians and surveyors to equitably arrange matters among them. And the district embracing the Excellent Mountain fell among the assigned lands of Joshua the king, the son of Nun, and of his comrade Caleb, the leader of the whole tribe,[142] and with which he had started out on the journey (from Egypt) in company with him (Joshua). Thus was every one permanently located in his place. And he (Joshua) distributed some of the Levites, every one in the place that had been set apart for him out of the whole of the assigned lands, over and above the division, that they might administer the affairs of the people in reference to prayers and judicial matters and also receive the tithes and perform the sacrifices. And he assigned unto each tribe chief justices who should correspond with the imam and give him information of what happened in their districts. Then Joshua the king built a fortress on the mountain to the north of the Blessed Mount, which (fortress) is known as Samaria. And his habit was to visit with Eleazar one day in each week; and one day with the learned, that he might take counsel with them; and one day with the chiefs, that he might inquire into their affairs; and one day he spent in attending to his own business and matters; and on three days he left not the Book of God during night and day. And this was his method in his administration of government, when he was not out waging war; for he did not hold himself aloof from them. And he built a synagogue on the summit of the Blessed Mount and collected and kept in it the tabernacle of the Lord, and no one after him did hold it, except the priests and the Levites.

---

[142] Yet Josh 14:14 assigns Hebron to Caleb.

Twenty-fifth Chapter

Then the children of Israel began to inhabit their assigned lands and to put them under perfect cultivation, and to worship their Lord with acceptable service, and to fulfill on each day whatsoever sacrifices were incumbent upon them. And God favored them with blessings and watchful care, so that calamities were removed away from them; and not a single one of the kings of the enemies did have power to do any violence unto them. So that there was a multitude of their own travelers journeying from every province unto the Blessed Mount three times a year, along with various kings, with wealth and joy and gladness; and not one of the enemies dared even to look towards them or stand up in opposition to them. And the king and the leaders and the whole army continued in rest and tranquility for a period of twenty years. There was no molestation or insurrection, since now their surrounding enemies were far removed from them and dispersed throughout the regions of the earth; and they who were near them had made peace with them, so no one was stirring up a commotion, nor was there a kingdom spreading itself abroad except their kingdom, or any hand outstretched except their hands. And not a single day did pass but that they heard news of all their companions; and thus did they continue to have communication with them until this period came to a close. Then after this there happened those things which, by the will of God and His assistance, we will narrate and explain. [To Him be the praise.]

Twenty-sixth Chapter

Haman, the son of R'awan, king of the Persians, had been put to death along with all the kings whom Joshua had killed. Then his child grew up who was known by the name of Shaubak, and he was eminent in attainments and in the acquisition of wealth. And he began corresponding with kings throughout all the regions, puffing some of them up, and stirring up others of them to anger, and influencing some of them by promises, and conciliating others of them with gifts of riches. Thereupon he said that he wished to take revenge for the murder of his father. And he also corresponded with the survivors of the Canaanites and recalled to their memory what the children of Israel had done with their children, their wives, their cities, and their possessions. Then he sent also unto the king of Arminiyouh (Armenia) the Greater, and Rumiyouh the Less (Asia Minor). And he joined unto himself the son of Japheth the giant,[143] and also sent unto the king of Sidon

---

[143] Gen 10:2.

and of el-Qaimun[144] and to the king of Syria, making known unto them what army had been assembled together unto him, and agreed with them that they should assemble together at el-Qaimun. And the opinion of the chiefs of the army and its leaders were agreed that they should send (as spy) a clothing-merchant who should count the men and inform himself as to the army [one who was clever in prudent management] in order that he might make known to them the condition of the children of Israel and how was the way to them and the means of getting at them. And they resolved to write and forward by his hand a letter from their company to Joshua the king so that they might obtain security from him, seeing he acted as a messenger, for upon a messenger rests no crime and hence no fear.

Twenty-seventh Chapter

The letter began:

"From the assembly of the giants, the confederated, well known, far-famed, victorious, triumphant, mighty in courage, protected from armor, and the foremost of all mortals, to Joshua the shepherd, the son of Nun, and his people. Peace from us unto you.

"We know, O murdering wolf, what you have done in the cities of our associates and that you have in murder destroyed all of their leaders and sent them down to the bottom of the lowest depths, and have demolished the places in which there was for us aid, and have put down the provinces which were our supports and from which our helpers were ever providing themselves with food, and have destroyed for us thirty cities,[145] besides residences and small towns, and that you did not reverence old men nor have compassion upon little infants, nor did you give ear unto them and grant them protection nor leave a place unto those begging safety of you. Nor grant time for good action. And the reason of this (your success) was that then we were distracted by discords and dissensions and a lack of unity in our counsels; but now understand, O murdering wolf, that we are coming unto you with all the kings in harmonious agreement, with spirits in concord, and tongues that have pledged mutual covenants, and hands that have been struck together. With conditions all-perfected, and souls full (of wrath) and accumulated complaints, and livers, as it were, cut asunder, whom no stampede can ever overcome nor a great fire (war) put to fright.

---

[144] Yokneam?

[145] MT Josh 12:24 reads thirty-one cities, and LXX Josh 12:24 reads twenty-nine.

"And now after thirty days we will bring on the battle between us and you in Merj Balata,[146] in front of the mountain upon which you worship your Lord, which is referred to as the Mount of Blessing. And there will be no delay on our part or on the part of any one of us; so be prepared for those whom you shall meet, and make no excuse for yourself by saying that you are taken by surprise or that the enemy came against you by night. And, moreover, know that in our company there are thirty-six kings, and in the army of each king sixty thousand knights, besides foot-soldiers innumerable and countless, who ridicule armaments; and there is also with us the son of Japheth the giant, who has with him a thunderbolt of steel, and when he hurls it, and it is granted full success, it kills a thousand men, and when full success is not granted, it kills five hundred men; and they who are with him are kings, and with them are instruments and implements of war that they have inherited from their grandfather Noah—peace be upon him. Therefore take knowledge of this and act in accordance with it, and look out for yourself, for you are about to be brought to account for what you have done. And now peace."

And the messenger took the letter and proceeded on his journey at once. And they began to draw up the army and arrange it in order, and set out upon the journey to el-Qaimun that they might unite with their confederates whom they had summoned by letter to be present.

Twenty-eighth Chapter

The messenger executed his orders on the tenth day of the second month of the twenty-first year of the reign of the children of Israel after their entrance into this territory; and he arrived on the fifth day (of the week), the morrow being the day el-Miqra (the Convocation), that is, the feast of weeks. And he handed his letter unto the king as he was sitting upon his royal throne pronouncing sentences upon such of them as were worthy of death, and such of them as deserved to be burned, and such of them as deserved to be stoned, and such of them as deserved to be imprisoned; for important cases were referred up to him at the time of the feasts, and then judgment was passed upon these in accordance with the light of God and the command of His saint. And he (Joshua) did not turn towards the messenger until he had concluded his judgments and had finished rendering his judicial decisions at the end of the day; then he took the letter and read it at his home, and not a single person knew about it until his feast had passed

---

[146] The plain to the east of Mount Gerizim.

by, and so the people did rejoice during their feast; but he himself was distracted in mind. Meanwhile the messenger was beholding the greatness of the army, and its good qualities, and the circumstances of the king and his prudent management, and the affairs of his Creator and His power, and the descending column of fire with its majesty, and he likewise saw the saint of God and the terror which hedged him about, the like of which had never been seen or the like of it heard of in preceding ages. And when the children of Israel had celebrated the feast, the king gathered together his assembly, and had proclamation made throughout his army, and sent word to his chief commanders to assemble in their presence, but placed the messenger in confinement in a certain place so that he might not witness their agitation or change of countenance. And when the leaders of the people were assembled, he read unto them the letter of the giants and said to them: "Certainly, never have I been overtaken by anything similar to this letter; and though I have waged wars for sixty years, yet never have I heard its like nor anything approaching unto it." And when they heard the letter, their color changed and their heads hung down, and they said: "Never have we heard the like of this performance, nor have we ever encountered anything similar to it, or waged war with an army such as this is; but this war is one for God, and for us and for our children, and for you, O king, overseer and master; and now manage us in accordance with the guidance and grace of God, and we will be obedient to your supreme authority."

Then he brought out to them a reply which he had dictated, and he had dictated that which he had composed in accordance with the light of God—may His name be Mighty—and he said to them: "This I lay before you as a reply that I have written and as an address that I have drawn up, and if it seem to you to be the proper thing, I will send it; but if your opinion be that it should be abandoned, I will disregard it."

Twenty-ninth Chapter

It began, saying:

"In the name of God, the Supreme King, the God of worlds, the Compassionate, the Merciful, the God of gods and the Lord of lords, the King of kings, the Knower of secrets, the One resolute in wars, the God of Abraham and Isaac and Jacob, the Destroyer of infidels, the Annihilator of tyrants, the Destroyer of the obstinate, the Abolisher of intriguers, the Collector of the dispersed, the Scatterer of the confederates, the One who brings the dead to life, the One who puts to death the living: His hand is above the highest of the highest, and under His outstretched arms is eternity, the heavens and the earth are in His grasp, the holy angels in all their numbers and the whole creation He did create by His omnipotent power; and the spheres and the heavenly bodies moved under His guardian chariot, their rapid course He stopped by His mere word and put in motion, moving bodies by His divine authority. Of this Lord do I ask assistance, and upon Him do I place my trust, and in Him do I grow strong, and Him do I fear, and His mercy is a shield unto me and unto my children, and He is my sufficiency and excellent Protector.

"But now to proceed to what follows: I am Joshua the son of Nun, the mortal and spiritual, the disciple of Kalimu'l-lah (Moses), a child of Khalilu'l-lah[147] (Abraham); upon me and my people be peace, mercy, and success. But as for you, O you people of unbelief and false religion and licentiousness and given over unto the curse, corrupters throughout the land, destroyers of the servants of God, worshipers of idols, who kneel down unto images, who bow down unto the celestial bodies, who are subservient unto spirits, who are slaves unto matter; let not the peace of God rest upon you or upon your people, and may He not make your way successful or your circumstances prosperous, and may He not have pity upon your young or feel compassion for your aged, may He make your condition ruinous and scatter your confederation; and this He will do by the terror of His power and the omnipotence of His will; for He is a hearer and answerer (of prayer). You have mentioned [may God not let the remembrance of you remain, may He not make you successful in a single thing, may He not bring to completion anything that you have begun, may He not leave any life unto you] that you are reinforced, joyful with good news, irresistible in power, and fully able to undertake the expedition towards me and engage in battle with me around the place on which I worship my Lord, which is the Mount of Blessings and the holy spot, even the house of our Lord and the place of our God. May you have no life and may that not come to pass, and may you not behold my place with your eyes, and may the hallowed plain not be polluted with your armaments, and may you never boast that you have trodden my soil, nor of even having approached unto my soil, nor of having got into my vicinity through any way whatever. But now as to your granting a delay: God does not grant unto you a delay in undertaking the journey until after the expiration of thirty days, and therefore I will not put off the journey unto you, nor will I grant you any delay except only for seven days, and then I will make the attack and with me will be the troops

---

[147] Khalilu'l-lah, "friend of God," an ancient designation awarded to Abraham. See also 2 Chr 20:7; Isa 41:8.

that I will select; and they who have been tyrannical will then find out with what overthrow they shall be overthrown. Therefore know for a certainty and consider and understand and be aware that I shall bring on the battle between me and you in the place known as el-Qaimun, and it is verily the place in which you shall not get away from me, nor depart from it, nor flee unto another place, but there be destroyed by the slaughter of the sword, and put to death by strangling, and burned with fire, and annihilated in vengeance; it shall not be unto you, O deluded ones, as you now boast it shall. And I do not say as you say, that there will march with me six hundred thousand men who did wage war with Greater Egypt and did eat the sacrifices of the Passover, and around whom the angels kept guard, and who crossed the sea in dryness and journeyed through the wilderness without any guide, the pillar of fire sheltered them from the cold by night and the pillar of cloud sheltering them from the heat by day, and whose food was the manna from heaven during forty years, and for whose sake the bitter water became sweet, and for whose sake the water was brought forth from the rock, and who heard the voice of the Creator—His mention be honored and His name glorious—and who beheld the quaking of the mountain at his command and the destruction of Sihon and Og and their people, and who inhabited their cities, and for whose sake the water of the Jordan was stayed until they passed through it, and who fought with Jericho and with the cities that you well know. I do not boast that there march with me giants, as you boast; but there march with me twelve thousand young men who entered Midian in safety, fought with it, and came out safely from there. There is with me no thunderbolt such as you mention; but with me is the Lord of thunderbolts and the Controller of the blowing winds; yes, with me is the One who takes away spirits and who hears the voices of prayer, the Creator of the whole creation and the Distributor of gifts, whose greatness is glorious; He is the God whose creation is all gods and whose servants all kings are—blessed be He and exalted—in His company are three angels of His, of whom one brought the water of the flood upon the world to destroy corrupt transgressors,[148] and another scattered the king of Babil (Babel, Babylon) and his host[149] and demolished their fortress and changed their languages, and another lifted up his five fingers against five kings of cities, even Sodom and its buildings and riches and animals and plants, and rained down upon it sulphur and fire and salt;[150] He who has in His company thousands and myriads of thousands of angels

---

[149] Gen 6–9.
[150] Gen 11.
[150] Gen 19:15–29.

similar unto these. What king then shall boast that he can stand before this King, whose rank and dignity is so great, whose position is so exalted, by whose mighty power the kings were destroyed and in obedience to whom the true believers believe? What army can stand before Him? What giant can march out against Him? What great commander can escape from Him? Unto what place can any flee from Him? Have you not heard of our poems wherein we say: "There is no power or might except in God,[151] the Exalted, the Great; if it (the power of God) came to the water, it (the water) stood still. The idols heard it and fell down one after another"? Know that you are the ones to be consumed, taken and killed; you shall not find a place unto which to flee, nor a refuge on which you may rely; you are ruined, you are discomfited, you are destroyed, yes, your people and your men and yourselves, and you have made your wives widows and have rendered your children orphans; you have made your enemies to rejoice, and you have cut off your purpose before its allotted season and have made weak your power before its time; you were ungrateful with the Divine mercy, and God took it away from you; you have been rebellious against the Divine compassion, and God has ceased to bestow it unto you. The earth was broad for you and not narrow for you either in condition or riches, but now there is no place or locality for you, seeing you have opposed the One to whom belongs the great and high dominion and have become subservient unto a decaying image and your intentions are bent upon the destruction of the holy, favorite people, who are the guardians of the children of the prophets of God and of His apostles. Who did swear unto them by His Name—mighty and glorious—that He would apportion unto them this territory, and now this Lord—blessed be He and exalted—says unto His people that He will guard them as a man guards his eye. O ones whose hearts God has obscured, and whose understanding He has bewildered, and whose spirits He has extinguished, and the light of whose eyes He has darkened! Have you not heard what happened through our friends unto your friends, when our ancestor Abraham, el-Khalil—peace be upon him—marched against your friends, and in his company there were only three hundred and eighteen men; yet he did destroy of them five kings, the like of which was never heard of, nor did their fight cease short of Damascus?[152] Have you not heard what befell the people of Egypt and what signs and wonders God—may He be exalted—showed because of their abusive reveling? Have you not heard how my comrade did kill the Nile with his

---

[152] Exod 15:2–3.
[153] Gen 14:1–2.

rod,[153] and crush the sea by his prayer, and stop the water through the reverence and respect that he inspired,[154] and turn back the Divine wrath by his intercession,[155] and cause the Divine compassion to descend by his words, and put to rout armies with his hand,[156] and how the earth swallowed up those who opposed him?[157] Have you not heard what happened unto us in the wilderness and what befell Sihon and his kingdom,[158] and Og and his pride,[159] and Balaam and his sorcery,[160] and the kings of Midian and their host,[161] and the kings of Syria and their pomp? Have you not heard what happened unto us at the Jordan[162] and what happened unto us with the kings who joined in a confederation and assembled together to attack us?[163] Have you not heard how I called upon my Lord to prolong the day, and the day did return after its setting, and the day stood still for me like as if it had been a whole year?[164] And it will thus stand still for me a second time during your destruction. I do not boast that I am a giant, or the disciple of a giant, or the child of a giant. I boast that I am the disciple of Kalimu'l-lah (Moses), the mortal and spiritual; and a child of Khalilu'l-lah (Abraham), the foundation of the prophets and the top branch of the pious; I boast in the myriads of the holy who march around my army. I am no giant, but the Lord of the giants is with me; and yet my stature from the ground up is five royal cubits. I do not dress in armor even, and in coats of mail and helmets; but my clothing is tunics of dark blue and purple and variegated crimson, and the royal crown is on my head with the name of my Lord inscribed upon the crown. I ride upon a white colt whose saddle-cloth is of purple and its saddle of pure gold: these are my distinguishing characteristics and these are my boastings. Aided by the prophets, surrounded by the holy, the Lord of creation is my armament, and His angels my triumph, and His omnipotent power my reliance. And He is the beholder of your affairs as well as the affairs of me and my people. We believe in no lord but Him, and no king besides Him; and He is our sufficiency and excellent Protector."

---

[154] Exod 7:20–25.
[155] Exod 14:26–31.
[156] Exod 32:7–14.
[157] Exod 17:8–13.
[158] Num 16:1–35.
[159] Num 21:21–30.
[160] Num 21:31–35.
[161] Num 22:24.
[162] Num 31:1–20.
[163] Josh 3.
[164] Josh 9.
[164] Josh 9:12–14.

Thirtieth Chapter

When the children of Israel heard this address and this reply, bowing down, they prostrated themselves before God and spoke, saying: "How adorable is He who has guided you! How adorable is He who has enlightened your heart! How adorable is He who has illuminated the light of your intellect! How adorable is He who has ennobled your soul! How adorable is He who has sanctified your spirit! How adorable is He! You have consoled our souls and have strengthened our hearts, you have nerved our loins, you have lifted up our heads, you have exalted our renown, you have spread abroad our glory; yes our friends do exalt, for you have destroyed our enemies and have annihilated their host. And now we are swift and zealous subjects in your presence, ready to go unto the horizon of the seas and to the abyss of darkness and unto the burnings of fire. And this is the approval and opinion we express to our master the king and let him carry it out by transmitting this letter; for in it lies the destruction of our enemies and their ruin, and the breaking up of their hearts and their purposes, through the power of God and his omnipotent might." And the king gave immediate direction that they should make known to him the list of the enumeration of those who had been chosen from the army and that they make proclamation for them to mount at once. And scarce an hour passed before three hundred thousand men had mounted, every one of whom was renowned for manly qualities and skill, chosen men they were, the like of whom or better rank and file than theirs had never been seen. And the officers returned and said unto him: "O our master and our lord, there have assembled for you three hundred thousand chosen men, and if you were to command that there should be chosen as many more as they, we would be prompt to do the same, for in our lists there are other three hundred thousand men, but they are separated from us, and the mustering of them will be accomplished in the course of a week." And Joshua the king answered them, saying: "If He would destroy our enemies with six hundred thousand men, He is able to destroy them with three hundred thousand men." And he commanded that the messenger should be brought, for he knew that he was possessed of wisdom; and he read the letter to the multitude in his presence. Thereupon he said unto him: "Look at and behold what I have collected unto me in one single hour, with regard to whom I do not need to bother myself about their provisions or look after their condition, and in three days there will gather unto me a number equal to them through the power of God and His omnipotent might; so now make known to your companions what you have witnessed of the affairs of God—Mighty and Powerful—even the power of His people. And behold! I am about to march right on the tracks of my letter with the help of God and his power and strength."

Thirty-first Chapter

When the messenger had heard the king, and his speech, and the reading of the letter and its words and perceived the discipline of the army and its staunch condition, he took the letter and immediately started out on his journey with head downcast and heart torn asunder and color changed and eyes weeping. And when he arrived at the army of the enemy, he found them assembled together in el-Qaimun. And when he saw them, he wept with great weeping and cried with a loud voice, and said to them: "O woe unto me for you, and sad am I for your sakes. Where are you marching? Is it unto the sea of darkness? Unto him who does not listen to a word of yours nor sends back peace to you? Unto those you have no stability or durability or permanency; every affair of theirs is in earnest, no jesting or secret backbiting exists among them. Therefore give attention unto the reply to the letter; that you may know that God is over all things, powerful, therefore I explain unto you what I have witnessed, and inform you of what I have seen; for if I should continue for one year explaining and expounding about Him, I should not make known His substance or make known any of His attributes."

Thirty-second Chapter

He then took the letter and read it unto the company of the kings. Now the inscription written upon it was:

"To the company of reprobates, rebels, libertines, infidels: the conniving, rebellious, polluted, and cowardly people; the filthy, self-disgraced, whose destruction is near at hand and whose ruin is just impending:

"From the excellent, the faithful, the associates of purity, light, glory, firmness, and victory and possessed of authority and influence, the celebrated, far-famed, set-apart, chosen, protected by God, assisted unto victory by His power, sheltered under His mercy and compassion; and He is their sufficiency, and upon Him is their reliance."

Upon the reading of this inscription they wept until their eyes flowed blood, then they opened the letter, and a man read it in a plaintive voice while they began beating their faces and wailing over themselves to greatest excess until they had finished its reading. And the letter was not completed before their stomachs were in knots, and their heads bent down, and their hearts broken, and their tears poured out, and their intellects bewildered; and they were neither able to arise from their places nor rest in quiet in them, for dementia and agitation had seized them. Then they cried out while weeping and said: "Woe unto us and unto our children, we have destroyed ourselves, we have brought about the violation of our women, we have waked up the sleeping lioness,[165] we have stirred up the crouching lion, we have let loose the elephant that was tied, we have roused the bull that was tethered." And now their tongues jabbered on in their mouths, stuttering exceedingly as if tongue-tied, and they neither understood what they said nor what was said to them; yes, they were deaf, they were dumfounded, they were stunned, they were bewildered, the hair on their heads stood on end and they tore their garments. Then there came unto them the sheikh of the magicians, and with him was the mother of Shaubak the son of Hamam, who was skilled in magic and who worshiped the great luminary and the seven stars, and along with her was a crowd of the magicians and wizards and conjurers, and these calmed them, saying unto them: "O you who turn back! You have wrecked your army before you have seen the enemy, and you have killed yourselves before your time; the leaders of the army should not do this among the flock, you have unnerved the men with fear, you have slaughtered them without a sword being used. Sit down with us and listen with reason unto what we say, and bring here the messenger whom you sent, and consider what he shall describe unto you." So they brought the messenger, and he began to describe the king (Joshua) and the feeling of awe that he carried away with him, and he described the army tribe by tribe, and the Divine ordinances that he had witnessed, and the grand condition of affairs that he had seen. Then the messenger said to them: "O assembled men, accept my counsel, and do not yield yourselves unto any other; for I have seen what you have not seen; therefore know what shall overtake you by surprise, for after three days will come the heavy rush and flight, and the abandonment of our baggage, and the saving of ourselves and our possessions; for, truly, he (Joshua) is a magnificent commander, he is not to be held as contemptible and insignificant; and against this people neither sorcery nor stratagem is possible. Every god whom you worship and serve will flee away from before their God whom they worship. Have you not heard what happened unto our master and chief Balaam?" Thereupon the band of magicians went apart by themselves and the mother of Shaubak with them, and they agreed in opinion that they would work out for them his (Joshua) loss of

---

[165] Num 23:24.

composure so as that he should not come unto them. And they began op-
erations and built their altars and offered up their sacrifices, and they were
answered in what they requested, and they sat down in order that they
might deliver their mandate with power and force. But God delayed this
unto them according as He willed. Blessed be He and exalted, for the con-
summation that He brought about.

Thirty-third Chapter

When Joshua the king desired to start out on the journey, he met with the
saint of God, Eleazar the imam—peace be upon him—and said unto him:
"Go ahead, invoke a blessing upon your people and bless them, and when
we have proceeded on our journey, continue repeating it, and do not
cease standing before your Lord humbly beseeching Him, until you hear
tidings of us." And Eleazar the imam went to the tabernacle, and blessed
the people, and invoked a blessing upon them, and then he proceeded to
bid farewell to the king and to weep while the priests invoked upon him
safety and success and prosperity and good fortune. Then he commanded
the Levites to make proclamation throughout the army in accordance with
what our master Moses, the Prophet—the most excellent peace be upon
Him—had enjoined upon them in the Holy Law at the command of God,
where he says: "When you go out in battle against your enemies and see
horses and footmen and a people more than you, be not afraid of them; for
God your God is with you, which brought you up out of the land of
Egypt"[166]—and so on to the end of the chapter. And this having been executed, at close of the proclamation, Phinehas, the son of the imam—peace
be upon him—his cousin sounded on the two trumpets of clamor,[167] and
the congregation of the children of Israel shouted with one voice, and the
angels in heaven and on earth did tremble by reason of their shout. And
having knelt and bowed down, they then mounted and journeyed forward
until they arrived in the vicinity of el-Lejjun.[168]

Thirty-fourth Chapter

When the children of Israel arrived at el-Lejjun, before they were aware of
it, Joshua and those who were with him had got inside of seven walls of
iron, and the device of the magicians against them was completed in order

---

[166] Deut 20:1.
[167] Num 10:9.
[168] On the Plain of Esdraelon (Megiddo?).

that the decree of God—may He be exalted—might be accomplished with regard to exalting the renown of Nabih, the king of the two and a half tribes, who was beyond the Jordan; for not a thing of this work had been effected but for the sole purpose that the renown of Nabih might be glorified and his name spread abroad. And one object of this was that if the giants were put to rout, they would cross over with them and, while they were fatigued, follow hard after them; and it was in their purpose so (to do). And another object of this was to show up the result of the counsel of the deities of the giants; for Phinehas alone did blow on the trumpet and dissolved every perplexing machination that the magicians had wrought. And another object of it was that Joshua the king's loss of composure might continue until the souls of the giants had become strong and their hearts elated and they settled down at ease, that the army of Nabih might cross over east; then would the magic from the west be dissolved, and the army issue forth and close upon the enemy from all directions until not one of them should escape. Now this war was the last war that Joshua the king witnessed; for the time of his death had drawn near. And we will recount what happened, so that even a hearer shall be as if he had been a witness of it; and he will be astonished at this great stratagem and will praise Him who is powerful over all circumstances and spirits. Blessed and exalted and glorious be He above all that the ignorant heathen mention. Mighty be his name; and He it is from whom help is to be sought and in whom trust is to be placed.

Thirty-fifth Chapter

When Joshua saw what had come to pass unto him, he remained in great perplexity and tremendous fear and began to desire of his Lord that a dove might alight upon him from the doves of Nabih, his cousin; and he had not finished expressing his desire before the dove alighted in the room, and he praised God—Mighty and Powerful; then he looked at it and knew that deliverance was certain. And he began and wrote a letter unto Nabih, his cousin, which I am about to make mention of, by the will of God and His assistance.

Thirty-sixth Chapter

"I write unto you, O my cousin, may God protect you and take care of you, while I am sad of heart, weak in strength, with weeping eyes, humbled in soul, on the very verge of destruction, and three hundred thousand men along with me; for the stratagem of the magicians has been accomplished upon us, and I and my people are imprisoned and perplexed inside seven walls of iron, and In front of us are thirty-six kings in complete joy and universal exultation while we are in sadness and weeping and fear thereby. And now such affair as this had not been completed against us except only that there might be accomplished what God—may He be exalted—desires with reference to the exaltation of your renown and the spreading abroad of your authority; and God, God is the One, O my cousin, Who makes weak and makes strong. And truly you know what covenants and compacts exist between me and you, so rise up immediately and do not sleep; and if you are asleep, awake; and if you are awake, run; for I and the company of your brethren, who are looking for deliverance from God—exalted be He—and you, are imprisoned inside seven walls of iron at el-Lejjun, and the host of the enemies are in el-Qaimun; so let not slackness nor rest nor laziness nor hesitation overtake you, but outstrip the blowing winds and make manifest that by which you shall be remembered unto the end of the gliding ages, by the will of God and His assistance."

And when Joshua had finished folding the letter, the dove did not wait until it had been tied on to its wings, but snatched it in its bill and flapped its wings and soared aloft.

Thirty-seventh Chapter

Now Nabih was sitting upon his judgment throne, his waist bound up and on him a green robe and a green turban, and he was engaged in looking into the judicial affairs when the dove threw the note into the room, and he opened it and read it, and his eyes gushed forth with tears and he cried aloud, at which the court became agitated. And he himself then cried out at the top of his voice: "Assembly of my brothers and my cousins and my comrades! Follow me and reach your brethren; for they are imprisoned by magic inside seven walls of iron at el-Lejjun. Assembly of Men! Haste! Haste!!" And they that were around him shouted out with a mighty shout, the sound of which was heard unto the horizon of heaven and to the regions of the earth, which were their assigned lands. And now the shout increased and voices were intermingled, and there mustered immediately, as though they had been for a long time and period prepared and equipped, six thousand men whose garments were white and their horses red, and six thousand men whose garments were red and their horses white, and six thousand men whose garments were green and their horses black, and six thousand men whose garments were black and their horses piebald; not to mention the various colored and renowned ones who were many and without number. And the women and children joined in rendering aid. And there went forth of the men an innumerable multitude; and Nabih went forth, riding upon a celebrated colt that was spotted like a leopard and was fleet as the winds, and behind him was his army and he was saying: "Fire! Fire!![169] No rest and no repose!" And the shout rode up on high, and a wonderful warning presented itself in the sky, so that the birds dropped down one after another and fled away from the great wind into the desert, and wild animals did not remain quiet in their dens, and from these was witnessed (an omen) the like of which had never been seen in the past. And when Nabih drew near to the great meadow, he halted until his army had collected together. And it came to pass that the mother of Shaubak went up to a lookout she had in el-Qaumun to worship the great luminary according to her custom, and when she beheld the luminous star—that is to say Nabih—rising up out of the east, she made haste to descend unto her son, and she said to him: "Lo! A luminous moon is rising up out of the east, and about him are brilliant stars," meaning Nabih and his soldiers, "and if he be of our enemies, O woe unto you and woe unto me; but if he be for our assistance, then it is well with you and well with me." And he became enraged at her because she had hastened unto him with woe, and he killed her—may God have mercy on her. And he put on his armor and took his bow and arrows studded with pearls and corals, and he made proclamation throughout his army and advanced alone against Nabih; and when he drew near him and saw him, he said unto him: "O Nabih, what is the matter with you that you bark?" And he answered him: "Yes, my name is Nabih, the son of Jil'ad, the son of Makir, the son of Manasseh, the son of Joseph, to whom was given the kingdom of Jacob the son of Isaac the son of Abraham, who killed the kings of Syria; and my lord has sent me to curse you and destroy you, and as my father killed your father, so will my father's son kill your father's son; and now, O you cursed! O you unclean one! Who art you?" And he said to him: "I am Shaubak, the son of Hamam, the son of Fut (Phut), the son of Ham, the son of Noah, whom God did bless at the time he came out of the ark. Stand for me until I shoot first, and then I next will receive (your shot)." And Nabih said unto him: "Of God I ask assistance because you shall shoot first and kill first. Let drive, O cursed, O unclean one!" So he (Shaubak) let drive at him with the first arrow; now he was— God curse him—a man shooting with determination and confidence, who never missed the mark. But Nabih dodged his head, and it passed by him and did not hit him. Thereupon he shot at him a second arrow; but Nabih lifted himself into the air, and it passed between him and his saddle. And he

---

[169] "War! War!!"

shot a third arrow; and he (Nabih) deflected it with his right hand. And Shaubak the son of Hamam began to desire to flee away, and Nabih said unto him: "Where do you flee, O cursed, O unclean one? I have received from you three witnesses (of your skill), now receive of its kind one witness from me: take this from my right hand, which God has blessed—and to Him belongs the mighty power." Then Nabih shot it, and the arrow rose up to heaven and reversing came down into the head of the man, and penetrated to his belly and to the belly of his horse, and plunged into the earth to a depth of five royal cubits, which is twelve cubits according to this cubit, and in that place immediately a fountain gushed forth, which is called 'Ain en-Nushshabeh (the Fountain of the Arrow) unto this time. And when the children of Israel witnessed this miracle, they shouted out in honor of God—Glorious and Mighty—saying: "There is no power or might except in God." And when Joshua and they who were imprisoned with him heard them, God made a revelation unto him, saying: "Speak unto the priests that they sound with the two trumpets."[170] And when they had done so, the walls crumbled and fell down; and the army closed in upon the enemies, and the trumpets of the angels were heard from heaven. And Joshua said to the day: "Stand still for me," and it stood still, and to the winds: "Assist me," and they assisted him. And while the enemies were hurling from the east, the west wind was returning each missile unto its hurler, and thus so it happened from all directions. And as to the man who had the thunderbolt with him, when he hurled it, it leaped back upon the enemies and killed of them one thousand men; and the sword continued doing its work among the rest of them until the horses plunged in blood up to their nostrils.[171] Then said Joshua to his people: "This day has annihilated the power of the confederates and of the allies of the confederates. All the children of Israel should offer praises and halleluiahs to the King of kings and Lord of lords, who has rescued them, and preserved them, and protected them, and delivered them, and uprooted their enemies." And the king was offering praise and saying: "God is the one who acts as the Hero for us in the wars, God is His name."[172] And the children of Israel followed him while all of them were saying: "Who is like unto You, perfect in holiness? O One who inspires terror![173] O Revealer of secret things! O Doer of wonders! O One who protects His servants and those who love Him, in every place wherein they dwell!" Now, this is one of the paragraphs of our master

[170] Num 10:9.
[171] Rev 14:20.
[172] Exod 15:3.
[173] Exod 15:11.

Moses, the Prophet—peace be upon him—in his hymn of praise at the sea. And Joshua moreover said: "God shall fight for you, and you shall hold your peace."[174] And this also is one of the sayings of Moses, the Prophet—peace be upon him. And they lodged on the field of battle and rested that night; and they ceased not to commemorate God the whole night long with hymns of praise and halleluiahs until the rising of the sun, secure from any attack, amid great noise and merriment and gladness and booty, now that their enemies were destroyed and the remembrance of them blotted out. And God is the Victor, the Protector, the Guardian, and He is our sufficiency and illustrious Protector.

Thirty-eighth Chapter

Now the length of this period was two hundred and sixty years. And the well-ordered arrangement of the days of Divine Favor existed during the days of Joshua the king, and after him until the termination of this period, as I am about to mention and set forth. And they (the children of Israel) continued keeping the Sabbaths and the solemn assemblies—I mean the new moons and the feasts—and from the era of the king they continued giving the land rest, one year in every seven years;[175] in this year there was neither sowing nor cultivation, but yet every one had what was needed. And the children of Israel were delivering over to the Levites the tenth of all that came to them,[176] and they possessed of every seed, sowing and fruit, and animal and other things. And the Levite was delivering over the tenth of this unto the high priest. And the children of Israel had another tenth,[177] which before God they were disposing of, for themselves and for the imams and the infirm. And when they planted in the ground a new plant, its fruit was not eaten except when in the fourth year the imam ate it,[178] and then in the fifth it became released and made free to everyone. And the Hebrew slave who had served seven years was emancipated, and dominion over him was taken away.[179] And when an Israelite, driven by want, sold his child and himself, there was always to him a right of ransom, and his account was settled, with reference to his years of service to come, on a basis of wages. And if there was not found for the Hebrew slave either

---

[174] Exod 14:14.
[175] Lev 25; Exod 23:10.
[176] Num 18:24.
[177] Deut 14:22–29.
[178] Lev 19:23–24.
[179] Exod 21:1–2.

a near or distant relative who would ransom him,[180] he was set free in the year of Jubilee;[181] and so like was it with their lands which had been sold. And there was in every seven years a division of the land among the tribes with reference to overplus and deficiency. And they always had chiefs whose duty it was to write up the calendars and keep record of the things that were brought to the treasury. And the firstlings of animals and seeds and fruits were carried unto the minister;[182] and not a single ram or sheep or ox was sacrificed except upon the altar on the Blessed Mount, unless it was defective[183] and was of the seven species, such as the deer[184] and the roebuck and the buffalo and the gazelle and the antelope and the giraffe. And they had judges who gave decisions for them as to the commands and prohibitions (to be observed) at all times, so that they might keep them with right observance.[185] And no one of them was able to commit an abomination, such as infidelity[186] and other things of magic, but that it was brought to light, and the doer of the shameful thing, before he was aware, would be apprehended even though he was in the most remote parts of the assigned lands, for this was revealed by the jewels which were on the minister.[187] And this minister would make a woman drink of the water of the temple when her husband had suspicions against her; and if she had indeed been unfaithful to him and had become defiled with some one else, he would curse her; for if she was innocent in this regard, then she would return unharmed; but if she was guilty, she was detected and immediately destroyed.[188] And likewise it was that no one did kill an innocent person but that his murderer was made known by circumstances that were brought about and the truth came to light.[189] And there were transgressions and shortcomings and brutal deeds which the slaves did without due consideration. These did the minister, the imam, assume upon himself on every fast day,[190] which is the tenth day of the seventh month wherein expiation is made for souls and spirits, such as for the raising of leavened bread during

---

[180] Exod 21:2; Deut 15:12; Lev 25:39.

[181] Lev 25:40.

[182] Deut 18:1, 4.

[183] Lev 22:22–25.

[184] Deut 14:5.

[185] Exod 18:21–22; Deut 1:13–17.

[186] Exod 20:3.

[187] The Urim and Thummim (Exod 28:30) or the jewels in the breastplate of the Ephod (Exod 25:7).

[188] Num 5:16–22.

[189] Num 35:13, 24–25.

[190] Lev 23:27–30.

the feast of unleavened bread.[191] And there were orders of the Levites; some of them wrote the Law; and some of them wrote hymns of praise and the genealogies; and some of them watched over the treasury of the children of Israel; and some of them had charge over the constant, perpetual burnt offering, and the continual ceremony in the temple; and some of them had charge over the anointing ointment, and the aromatic incense, and the perfume of the sacrifice, and the flour and the oil, and the candlesticks; and some of them had charge over the vessels of the temple and their arrangement, and the duty of looking after their condition; and some of them selected the animals (for sacrifice) out from the doubtful ones; and some of them did the sacrificing; and some of them sprinkled the blood upon the altar; and others of them did place in position the victims; yea, every company was organized for its special official work and did not leave what had been prescribed unto it.[192] And the continual burnt offering was offered up before the rising of the sun[193] and after the going down of the same; and at the time when the blood of the burnt-offering was shed upon the altar, the priests sounded the trumpet on the summit of the Blessed Mount, and then the imams sounded in every district, and it was but the wink of an eye before all the children of Israel knew that the sacrifices had been offered up on the altar, and they rose up to pray; and the prayer was accepted, and the blessings were simultaneously bestowed, and Grace was full and Mercy all embracing; yes, circumstances were well ordered, and affairs were known and understood through the Divine light and auspicious favor; for the union between them and their Lord was close. Now this is an epitome of the whole. And the children of Israel were continually addressing and consulting God, who guides with His mercy. And He is our sufficiency and illustrious Protector.

Thirty-ninth Chapter

Joshua the son of Nun, reigned forty-five years,[194] and at the approach of his death, he assembled the children of Israel, and put them under covenant, and bound them to an obligation that they would carefully keep what the Prophet Moses—peace be upon him—did, when he bid farewell.[195] And he selected twelve chiefs from the congregation of the nine and a half

---

[191] Lev 23:6.
[192] Num 1:50–51.
[193] Num 28:4.
[194] Josephus, *Ant.* 5.1.29, reads twenty-five years.
[195] Josh 24:1.

tribes, and when he had tested them as to their knowledge and aptitude for administration, he cast lots over them in the presence of the congregation of the children of Israel at Merj el-Baha (Meadow of Beauty);[196] and the lot of king fell upon a man whose name was Abil,[197] the son of the brother of Calab, of the Judaic tribe. And he invested him with the royal authority and jurisdiction, and placed on him the crown, and had proclamation made throughout the congregation that they should be obedient to his commands. And he commanded him to be obedient unto the minister of God, and allow him an inspection into all his circumstances, and not carry out a matter before he had made it known to him. And Joshua the son of Nun, peace be upon him, died, and they buried him in Kefr Ghuweirah;[198] and Caleb his comrade died, and they buried him near him. And this new king entered upon administering the government of the people, and he walked with them in perfect ways. And the report of the death of Joshua reached the king of Moab, and he sent and collected troops and advanced against his territory; and this king (Abil) mustered his people, and God assisted him to gain the victory over them, and awe of him fell upon the remainder of his enemies, and he conquered territories and added them unto the assigned lands. And he reigned nine years, and then he died. And after him, Tarfi'a of the tribe of Ephraim was appointed successor, and when he was invested with the kingship, the king of Ammon marched against him; but God assisted him to gain the victory over him, and he continued in rule during the period that God had decreed to him, and then he died. Thereupon after him, up to the end of the space of time which has been previously mentioned—and it is two hundred and sixty years—there were nine kings appointed to the office, who succeeded one another from all the tribes and continued in their ruling two hundred and fifteen years; for Joshua the son of Nun had reigned for the rest of the years. And the last of them was Samson the king, who was unique among them: no one was seen as handsome as he, and he obtained greater victories over his enemies. Yet nevertheless, strength and beauty and success and perfection shall be ad judged unto those who follow after them in the footsteps of those who have preceded them, and who act in accordance with their deeds and offer sacrifices similar to their sacrifices.

---

[196] See Gen 12:6. SP Gen 12:6 reads "Plain of Seeing," located east of Nablus.

[197] The biblical Othniel (?), Judg 3:9–11.

[198] MT Josh 24:30 indicates that Joshua was buried at Timnath-serah, but Judg 2:9 identifies the spot as Timnath-heres. LXX Josh 24:30 adds a reference to the flint knives used in the circumcision mentioned in Josh 5:2–4.

Fortieth Chapter

When the death of Eleazar the imam—peace be upon him—drew near,[199] he did as Joshua the son of Nun had done, and collected the leaders of the children of Israel, and put them under a covenant and bound them to an obligation of obedience, and bid them farewell, and then bid the temple farewell, and worshiped his Lord; and when he came walking out, the holy odors were fragrant on the borders of his garments. And having gone to Kefr Ghuweirah, he stripped off the holy garments that were on him and placed them upon his son Phineas—peace be upon him—and he died and was buried in Kefr Ghuweirah;[200] and all the children of Israel wept for him, after the custom of their fathers. And after him his son was installed, and he did as his father had done. And when his death approached, he also bound them to a covenant, and offered up sacrifices, and bid farewell, and, having gone to Kefr Ghuweirah, stripped off the holy garments that were on him, and put them upon one of his offspring who was to succeed him, and then he died and was buried in that place. And after him there were installed five ministers for the Lord, and they served Him with acceptable service and did as they who had gone before them had done, even up to the period that has been mentioned; and its days were well managed, adorned with the Light and with celestial and terrestrial happiness, up to the installment of Uzi,[201] the last of the vicegerents of the Lord in the days of Divine Favor, and he was a young man. And the king of that time died, and another king was not appointed. Now the number of the years of the earth, from the time of Adam up to this time, was three thousand and fifty-four years. And there was gathered unto them, before the death of Samson, a great multitude, so that if it was spread over the earth it would have filled the world by reason of the abundance with which God had blessed them and multiplied their possessions. But now there came to pass that which Moses, the Prophet—peace be upon him—had spoken of in the address that he delivered: "Jacob shall eat, and be satisfied; Israel shall wax fat"; and let it be looked up to the end of the chapter in that great song.[202] For then they did go astray from the way that he had prescribed unto them, that they should keep to and do. And the Omnipotent is our sufficiency, the Most Glorious, the One who is slow to chastise the rebellious.

---

[199] Josh 24:33.

[200] MT Josh 24:33 reads Gibeah.

[201] See 1 Chr 6:5–6, 51.

[202] Deut 32:15. The SP and the LXX read "Jacob ate his fill," but the MT does not include the phrase. The SP reads "Jeshurun" not "Israel."

Forty-first Chapter

Now he was the ruling judge over the children of Israel, and took great revenge upon the nations, and destroyed a multitude of them. And when
they were informed of his death, they assembled and bound themselves together by oath, and great zeal took possession of them. And when they
read in the books of Balaam that these people could never be destroyed
except by unbelief and pollution, they began to have recourse to devices to
obtain a knowledge of how to work magic, and they did not leave a place,
however remote in distance, which was prescribed for this profession but
that they sent messengers in search of it; and they obtained from there an
ample share of the appearance of miracles, the like of which dupe the common people. And they sent some of the learned doctors from among their
companions, and with them this knowledge; and they arrived in the neighborhood of the house of God. Now there was at this time no king administering the government, nor saint overlooking the holy matters. And the
doctors entered into dealings with a company of the children of Israel who
were people of pride, and expounded unto them the secret doctrine, and
instructed for them one hundred men of the people, and wrought it out
through their agency. And they inaugurated this audacious procedure and
action on a hill to the south of the Blessed Mount, and the place, from the
sum of their number, received the name el-Miat.[203] Thereupon they set to
building up the place and offering sacrifices to idols, which produce no
profit either in the present or in the future. Then the company removed,
through fear of the children of Israel, to the west of the Blessed Mount;
and on their going, their like followed after them, and they settled in a village on the slope of a mountain, and the place, from the number of their
company, received the name el-Miatai,[204] and in it they resided a brief time.
Afterwards they removed from it, for they had multiplied in numbers and
increased and branched out, and the place, on account of their great number,[205] received the name Fer'ata.[206] And God did not manifest His rebuke
nor anger until the affair of these infidels had reached unto all the leaders
of the children of Israel throughout all their assigned lands. And when they
became careless and negligent about rising up against them and had turned
aside and became polluted, for some of them were overcome with cowardice and laziness and others of them were engrossed, each one, in his

---

[203] "One hundred."
[204] "Two hundred."
[205] Judg 12:15.
[206] "Branching out."

own possessions and wealth and riches and pride and supposed that poverty would not overtake him though he might override the world; and others of them were jealous, and the greater part of their will was bent towards waywardness. And the saints of God were overcome with blindness and confusion and cowardice; for envy was rife in the tribe of Phineas, and discord reigned among them. Now when these infamous deeds and brutal affairs were carried out, the angels shrunk away from them, and the Creator became angry at them and took away His presence from them and from the Blessed Mount; and the light that had shone forth in the temple departed, and the Divine fire that had not been separated from the offerings upon the two altars was taken away; and decline was perfected in them, and disaster came upon them, for their sight was blinded. And we take refuge in God from misfortune, and of Him—mighty be His name—do we ask assistance.

Forty-second Chapter

When it was the morning of the second day (of the week), the first (day) of the year 361[207] of the reign of Divine Favor—which day is known for greatest calamity and mightiest disaster and long-lasting sorrow and widespread grief, which is like unto the day on which our father Adam was expelled from the garden, even the day in which was announced his death and the death of his seed—Uzi the imam, the saint of God whose greatness was spoiled and whose glory was ruined and whose holiness was destroyed and whose light was extinguished, passed, in the morning of this day, the calamities of which have been mentioned, to the temple and lifted up the veil of the inner holy house, and he beheld none of the signs of Divine Favor. And he looked, and lo! dense darkness, and a black cloud spread abroad within the house, and he remained performing alternate service during the third day and the fourth; and when it was the morning of the fifth day, he looked at this darkness, and lo! it had spread and enveloped the foundations of the house; and then he knew that God—Mighty and Powerful—had become angry at them and had taken away the light of His omnipotence and mercy and compassion from the place and from the children of Israel. And he began to gather up the vestments of the temple and the vessels of gold and silver, which had been from the days of the Prophet—peace be upon him—and went out from the tabernacle. And God revealed unto him in the Blessed Mount an open cave, which no one had noticed in that place before that day, and he took all that he found in

---

[207] See, however, the number 261 in chs. 38 and 39.

the temple and placed them in that cave.[208] And when he came out of it, he wrote upon its mouth an inscription in his own handwriting, and made a list of what he had placed in it, and distinguished it with signs; then he turned to look again and could find neither cave nor sign nor writing. At this, he lifted up his voice in weeping and wailing and lamentation, and there gathered unto him the company of the Levites, and the twelve chiefs who acted with him, and likewise the seventy wise men, and they made inquiry of him as to his weeping and crying, and he informed them of what had been revealed to him. And when he explained unto them and their people, they tore their garments and beat their faces and bowed down their heads, and assembled their company and began enumerating what things God—Mighty and Powerful—had bountifully bestowed upon them and what they now saw of punishment and banishment and sorrow and calamity, and they did say: "Woe unto us and to our children after us, and how great is the exultation of the enemies over our misfortune! How great is the joy of the confederates over you, O Israel! Your guardian is taken away, and who will now look after you? Your prop is taken away, and who will now support you? Your king is taken away, and who will now help you? Your power is taken away, and who will now strengthen you? The Compassionate has become angry with you, and who will now show pity? Signs were shown for your sake, Egypt was devastated for you, the Divine power appeared on your behalf, the sea was divided that you might cross, Pharaoh and his people perished that you might be preserved, manna descended for your sustenance, bitter water became sweet to satisfy your thirst,[209] the voice of the Creator was heard for your instruction, the rock brought forth water to test you, 'Amlaq was put to flight at your desire, the Creator let the Divine power dwell round about you for your protection, and His name alighted upon you that your enemies might have fear of you. He placed the pillar of cloud as a sign of His tender compassion for you. He closed up the two mountains of the valley el-Mujib (Arnon) that you might pass over safely. He destroyed Sihon and Og that you might inherit their cities and possessions. He struck with terror the kings of Ammon and Moab and Midian that you might plunder their cattle. He stopped the water of the Jordan that He might display your power and make prominent your glory and exalt your fame. He killed the seven tyrant kings that He might give to you their land and their cities and their

---

[208] See traditions of the hiding of the temple vessels in 2 Macc 2 and Josephus, *Ant.* 18.4.1.

[209] Exod 15:22–25. The episodes describing water from the rock have been mentioned before, but here only is the miracle of turning the bitter water sweet.

kingdoms. He gave over to destruction those who assembled together for your slaughter. He abolished Shaubak the son of Hamam and those kings who were assembled with him to slay you. He commanded the heavens and the earth to guard you and protect you. He removed the calamities of the skies and stars from you and from your country. He surrounded you with the greatest prosperity and the largest blessing. He assigned unto you the most exalted places, and the most glorious of which is the Gate of Paradise.[210] He gave unto you a kingdom in which no one boasts besides yourself. He bestowed abundantly upon you His grace, the like of which was never heard of in former ages. He assisted you with His angels and His omnipotence. He enveloped you with His mercy and surrounded you with His compassion. He took you into His keeping with joy on His part and took you under His protection among his own. But you have forsaken His worship and renounced belief in His name, which should be exalted, and you have worshiped one that has not the power to remove calamity even from himself. You have not regarded those who became infidels, and your Lord has disregarded you. You did cover up from Him, and He covered up His face from you. Our master Moses, the Prophet—the most excellent, peace be upon him—led you aright, but you did not believe him. He informed you, but you did not listen to him. He instructed you, but you did not obey him. Joshua, his disciple, made covenant with you, but you disregarded him. Where does your flight tend? Who will find refuge for you? From where will you find help for yourselves? Who will rescue you from your enemies? You supposed that your victory resulted from the multitude of men when, lo, the victory was the result of good behavior. Where are those who know our leaders? Where is the One who has pity on our infants? Where is the One who hears our voices? Where is the One who makes atonement for our sins and transgressions? Where is the One who makes manifest our power? Where is the One who renders our glory conspicuous here?" And they now felt remorse where remorse profited them nothing, while their weeping became great and their grieving violent. Thereupon they took vows upon themselves that they would commemorate this sorrow on the second and fifth days (of the week) always, until the favor of God—glorious be His might—should return unto them. And He is the one who knows when it will return; and we pray Him to remove His anger and let fall the veil of His protection over us through His greatness and compassion. Certainly, He is a hearer and answerer (of prayer).

---

[210] Mount Gerizim?

Forty-third Chapter

Discord had arisen between the descendant of Phinehas (Uzi) and his cousin Eli, whose name being interpreted means "The Insidious." This erring man was of the tribe of Ithamar,[211] the brother of Eleazar the imam. Now the right of administration belonged to the tribe of Phinehas, and it was this tribe that was offering up the sacrifices upon the brazen altar and stone altar.[212] And this man—The Insidious—was fifty years old and, being great in riches, had obtained for himself the lordship over the treasure house of the children of Israel; and he had obtained, through the knowledge of magic, what he had acquired of riches, proud rank, and wealth. And his self-importance being great in his own estimation, he gathered to himself a company and said unto them: "I am one to whom to serve a boy is impossible, and I will not reconcile myself to this, and I hope that you will not be content to have me do this." And the company answered him: "We are under your command, and under obedience to you; command us in whatever you will." And he put them under covenant that they would follow him unto the place where they purposed going on the morning of the second day (of the week). And he offered up offering on the altar without salt,[213] as if he was ignorant, and immediately started out on the journey with his outfit and company, and cattle, and everything that he possessed, and settled in Shiloh. And he gathered the children of Israel into a factional sect, and held correspondence with their leaders, and said unto them: "Whoever desires to behold miracles, let him come unto me." And there was collected to him a multitude in Shiloh, and he built for himself a shrine there, and organized matters for himself in it on the model of the temple, and erected in it one altar,[214] on which he might sacrifice and offer up offerings. And he had two sons, who used to gather the women into the temple in the morning and lie with them[215] and would eat up all that was present of the offerings of wine and other things.[216] And this man continued diverting the people by magic for the space of forty years; for God—exalted be He; glorious be His might—delayed this unto him. And there was Samuel of the

---

[211] See 1 Kgs 2:27; 1 Chr 24:3, 6; 2 Sam 8:17, Josephus, *Ant.* 5.11.5.
[212] Deut 27:5 See also SP Exod 20:17.
[213] Lev 2:13.
[214] Contra the Mosaic instruction to build two altars, an altar of incense (Exod 37:25) and an altar of burnt offering (Exod 38:1).
[215] 1 Sam 2:22.
[216] 1 Sam 2:12–17.

tribe of Aaron, the Levite,[217] the magician, and the infidel; for his father had delivered him over to him (Eli) when he was four years old, saying unto him: "This is a son whom I have received in fulfillment of a desire, and it occurred suddenly to my mind that this boy ought to serve in this temple throughout the days of his life."[218] So the erring man received him, and instructed him, and revealed unto him hidden things; and he grew to be as potent in the working of magic as he himself was. And blessed be God, who does not punish the rebellious except after long delay and showing mercy unto them.

Forty-fourth Chapter

When the nations heard of the schism among the children of Israel, there gathered together of them a multitude of those who were inhabiting Yufa (Joppa) and Lydda (Lod) and Beit Jibril and Gaza and other places, and they carried out the plan of making an attack upon the company that was in Shiloh. And the army of the erring man went forth to meet them, but it was overthrown and put to flight, and there were killed of his companions four thousand men.[219] And the troops returned to their friends and said unto him (Eli): "Behold, the cause of our defeat is that the ark of gold was not with us"; so he delivered unto them the ark and sent forth his two sons with them, and the flower of his army, in place of the first (army). Now they of the nations who had assembled had arranged an ambush, and upon the sallying forth of his army, the army of the nations closed in upon them, and the sword did its work among them; and the ark was taken,[220] and the two sons were slain. And one of those that had escaped safe stained his garments with their blood, and came to their father while he was sitting upon his seat, and said to him: "Disastrous news for you; for your two sons are killed, and my garments are even stained with their blood, and the ark of gold has been taken, and the sword has annihilated your people." And when he heard tidings such as this, he threw himself backwards off his seat, and his neck was broken and he died.[221] And when his daughter-in-law heard of this calamity—now she was pregnant and near giving birth—the pains of childbirth grew violent in her, and she died.[222] And so this man

---

[217] 1 Sam 1:1. Samuel's father was an Ephraimite. 1 Chr 6:28 indicates Samuel was from the house of Levi.

[218] 1 Sam 1:26–28.

[219] Cf. the story of the defeat by the Philistines in 1 Sam 4.

[220] A counterfeit ark from the perspective of the Samaritans.

[221] 1 Sam 4:18.

[222] 1 Sam 4:20.

received reward for his action in this world, and he shall also be brought to account in the next. Blessed be He, Whom no affair escapes, and from Whom nothing is hidden. Blessed be He and exalted.

Forty-fifth Chapter

He was one of the kings of the Persians, who had conquered the countries and subdued the people, and the kings obeyed him. And he restored the authority of all the kings of Syria, and they went to the king of Jerusalem and entered into agreement with him that they would come under the rule of Nebuchadnezzar and become submissive to his decrees.[223] And they continued in this manner twelve years; but when it was the thirteenth year, they broke the compact and revolted, and he pardoned them. And when he warned them and they were not affected with fear, he marched against them in the fourteenth year and destroyed any of them he met. And he directed his march toward Jerusalem and besieged it till he captured it, and he killed in it with great slaughter, and took its king and put out his eyes and sent him to Beit-A . . . ,[224] and burned all the buildings and the edifice which Solomon the son of David had constructed. Then he turned aside towards our country, that is, this country, and made proclamation therein that whoever was found remaining in it after seven days, the shedding of his blood would be permissible. Thereupon he took to goading the people and driving them out unto every country, and brought people from el-Furs (Persia) and settled them in this country, the home of the children of Israel, who now fled to the most remote parts of the world, scattered and dispersed throughout the regions east and west. And the word of the Holy Law came true: "And God shall scatter you among all people, from the one end of the earth even unto the other end of the earth."[225] And after a certain time had passed by, letters were brought back from Persians who were dwelling in their (the children of Israel's) territory in Syria, regarding the earth's refusing her crops and fruits; for when the fruit promised well, the destroying blight would waste it.[226] And the letters in regard to this reached the king, and he had the leaders of the children of Israel brought before him, and made inquiry of them about this state of affairs, and they said: "The cause of this is our

---

[223] In the SJ there is only one conquest. No mention is made of a civil war or of an Assyrian conquest of the northern kingdom.
[224] Text is missing at this point. 2 Kgs 25:6 reads Riblah.
[225] Deut 28:64.
[226] 2 Kgs 17:25–26 has an attack by lions instead of blight. Josephus, *Ant.* 9.14.3, has a plague for which there was no cure.

removal from the land and the abandonment in it of the service of our Lord; and we do praise God for its disorder, so that we may return unto it, and serve our Lord upon the Holy Mount, and offer up offerings as He commanded us in His Book by the hand of His Prophet—peace be upon him." And the king replied to them: "Go and build the house of your Lord and offer up the offerings, and serve your Lord as was your custom, and I will assist you."[227] And they said to him: "Give unto us a writing by your own hand unto all our brethren, who are scattered abroad throughout all the regions; for we cannot return except we all go together." And the king gave them a writing in his hand, permitting them to journey to Syria. And they departed from his presence, glad and rejoicing for what God had kindly bestowed upon them. And the imam and the king sent letters to every place, saying: "Know that the king—may God make him powerful— has granted us permission to go up to the holy place and build it up, and offer up the offerings upon it with the service that is acceptable. And now it is necessary that you make haste, you and your harem and your children and all that you posses, that we may assemble and go, and carry out the orders which he has commanded unto us concerning the service of our Lord—Mighty and Powerful." And the people all came together, and the offspring of Judah said to them: "We will unite all of us, and go to Jerusalem and build it up, and we will be one word and one soul." But the offspring of Aaron and Joseph said to them: "No, but on the contrary, we will go up to the Mount of Blessing and build up the holy place, and we will be one soul and one word." And they persisted in the dispute until it became necessary that they should come together into the presence of the king. And he decided in favor of them (the descendants of Aaron and Joseph) after this manner: the children of Israel, the Friends of the Blessed Mount, assembled with the Book of Moses, the Prophet—peace be upon him— and relied upon what it is said in designating the Blessed Mount, and no place else, as the proper place; and the offspring of Judah assembled, relying upon what certain books written after the days of Moses, the Prophet—peace be upon him—designated with reference to Jerusalem being the place. And the books were brought and read in the presence of the king; and when he had carefully considered this matter, he saw that the intention of all was the Blessed Mount. But Zerubbabel answered and said unto him: "O king, the book which I have furnishes me with arguments in favor of Jerusalem and the offering up of offerings therein; would you then compel me to go up and offer up offerings upon the Blessed Mount?" And Sanballat the Levite answered him, saying unto the king:

---

[227] Ezra 4 provides an interesting contrast to the version recorded here.

"The books which Zerubbabel has are a lie and a fraud. Permit me to throw them into the fire; and this, my book, if he is able, let him take it and throw it." And the king gave permission unto Sanballat to throw the books of Zerubbabel into the fire, and he did this, and they were burned up. Thereupon he gave permission unto Zerubbabel to throw the book of Sanballat, and he took it and said: "My books are mine alone, but the Holy Book belongs both to him and to me." And the king answered, saying unto Zerubbabel: "I see that your books are false; why did you abstain from throwing his book?" Thereupon he (Zerubbabel) feared lest he be put to death, and he took the Law and cast it into the fire; and it jumped out of it. And he asked permission of him to throw it in a second time; and it was not affected by the fire in the least. Thereupon he humbled himself before the king, beseeching him that he might throw the book a third time; and he granted him permission, and he took it and spat upon a paragraph, and cast it into the fire, and the place that had been spit upon burned, and then it sprang out into the bosom of the king. And the king immediately became angry at the children of Judah and put to death immediately of them thirty-six souls of those who were present. But Sanballat, he and his company, obtained great honor with the king; for the king gave him gifts and presents and chain necklaces and bracelets, and invested him with the silk robe of honor, and promoted their leaders, and sent them away with the whole multitude of Israel who returned from the first exile, and their number was three hundred thousand men. And thereafter they followed the true religion, after having been unbelieving, and pursued right guidance, after having wandered into error. And God accepted them and broke the chains of their captivity through the mercy He had for them, and the compassion He felt, and the remembrance He had for the covenant with Abraham and Isaac and Jacob— peace be upon them. And the king sent unto all the Persians who had taken up residence in their assigned land and removed them from it to their own country; and the people (of Israel) entered into their assigned land, which is their holy place. And they made the sacred equipment similar unto that which was in the (former) temple, and they offered up a multitude of offerings; and the earth gave forth its good things and returned unto its former beauty and splendor; and with the carrying out of this act (on God's part), nothing was withheld from them, nor did He veil to them what of Divine power He veiled from their ancestors. And to every circumstance there is a cause, and to every fate there is a final limit. And of God do we ask assistance because of what He has benevolently bestowed through His mercy, and upon Him be the trust put.

Forty-sixth Chapter

The whole number of the years from Adam up to the time of King Alexander was three thousand nine hundred and thirty years. And when Alexander undertook the war against Darius the Persian, he saw in his sleep an angel descending from heaven in the form of an imam and clad in his robes, who said unto him: "Fear not, O hero, you shall conquer Persia; for I am about to deliver him (Darius) into your hand: behold God is with you." So he (Alexander) attacked him (Darius) and killed him. And when each nation was subdued, its imams were brought unto him in the hope that he might see one like unto that form; but he saw none. And when he came to Sur (Tyre) to conquer it, there were dwelling in its neighborhood some of the Samaritans, and these Alexander summoned that he might win them over to his side; but they would not consent, for they had bound themselves by an oath to this people.[228] And he blamed them and directed his march towards the region of Nablus; and its people came out to meet him, and when he saw the form of the chief imam, he hastily descended from his animal and prostrated himself before him. And when his attendants saw what he did, they also hastily dismounted and prostrated themselves while all the retinue wondered why he had been bent upon their destruction; and his companions said to him: "Truly, these people have bewitched you." But he said to them: "They have exercised no power; by God, I am not bewitched, but only seized with great emotion; for, truly, at the time of my going forth against Darius, there met me a man similar to this individual and like unto him in form, who said to me: 'Go forth against Darius, and fear not; for, lo, you shall kill him,' and thus it did come to pass." And Alexander was moved with love for the Samaritans, and acted kindly toward them, and said unto them: "Verily, your God is the God of gods and Lord of lords." And Alexander conquered all the country of India and Persia and Greece and other places. Then an impulse led him to desire to see the whole earth, whereupon it was planned for him to make a journey into the land of Shades upon she-asses that had colts, and he carried it out. And when they had tied the colts in the light, they entered upon a journey of three days into the darkness. Thereupon they took of the dust that was upon the ground, and then came out and examined it when they were in the light, and they found that the dust which they had with them was rubies and pearls, whereupon he regretted that he had not taken more of it than he had; for who would not take what someone has abandoned? And he

---

[228] A very similar story is told by Josephus, except that he reads "Jews" for "Samaritans," in *Ant.* 11.8.5.

said to his companions and his wise men: "In how much time can I see rapidly and quickly all the regions of the world?" And his wise men and companions said unto him: "If you desire to see the world in one moment and in the briefest space of time, summon the skilled carpenters and command them to construct a chariot with screws and apparatus, which will rapidly ascend and descend, then take four of your trained eagles and tie them to the four corners of the chariot, and hang meat to the top part of the chariot so that the eagles cannot reach it; for if the eagles crave the meat, they will ascend towards it, and the chariot will then be borne aloft through the air until it be lifted up on high, and you shall see the buildings and what is round about them. And when you have the desire, the screws shall be put in rapid motion, and you shall have the meat changed about and hung below, and the eagles will go downwards in a desire to get at it, and will descend with the chariot to the earth unto the level spot which you desire." And Alexander did just so and ascended into the air until he had seen the earth; then the eagles reversed and descended with him until he alighted on the spot which Alexander built up and called its name Alexandria. Thereupon he came to the Mount of Blessing and acknowledged it to be the noblest of places and the grandest, in praise to God—Mighty and Powerful. Then he proceeded to invest his companions with the authority over the territories until he had gone over all the earth.[229] And when his companions beheld his liberality to the children of Israel and his compassion upon them, and that he did not rebuke them for anything, whether it was a grave affair or a trifling action, they became envious of them; and his companions said to him: "Why does this nation transgress every religious ordinance in neglecting to comply with the established statute? Why do you not summon it and make instant demand of them concerning the establishment of idols and images?" And so he at this time commanded the imam—I mean the chief imam—and the chiefs of the children of Israel that they should set up to him in all their habitations statues and images; and then said to them: "I am about to go unto Egypt, and upon my return let me find what I have commanded." Then Alexander set out on his journey. And the chief imam assembled all the leaders of the children of Israel, and they went up to the Mount of Blessing and fasted and prayed and offered praise, and humiliated themselves unto God—Mighty and Powerful—and He disclosed to them an excellent idea, that they should name their boys with the name of the king Alexander. And they sent unto every place, ordering them to name every boy that should be born unto them with the name of the king Alexander; and they did this. And when three years had passed, the

---

[229] 1 Macc 1:6.

king Alexander returned and came up from Egypt, and when he came to the lands of the children of Israel, he saw in them neither statue nor image, and he was troubled by this, and summoned the leaders of the people and demanded of them the reason. And they replied that they established unto him images who were endowed with rational speech, and moved like paragons of obedience, and were quick to obey. Thereupon they brought forward immediately their children, of whom there had been gathered unto them a great number; and he said unto them: "What are your names?" And they said: "We are servants of the king Alexander, who are named with his name." And the king and his disciples were pleased and approved of what they had done. And when the imam saw the satisfaction of the king in what had happened, he threw aside his restraint and said to him: "The reason of our neglecting the setting-up of idols is fear of our Lord—Mighty and Powerful—who has prohibited us from doing this, and when He—exalted be His fame and mighty be His name—saw the purity of the purpose, He made known unto us that we should substitute our children in place of idols. And the king approved of this on their part and said unto them: "I know that your God is the God of gods and Lord of lords." Thereupon the king bestowed upon them gifts and spread abroad the praise of their deed. And unto God be praise and thanksgiving for His kindness, of Whom we ask mercy and pardon.

Forty-seventh Chapter

When this king, whose name was Hadrian, came to reign after Alexander, he went down to Egypt and killed a multitude of the Nasara (Christians), those who believed in the Messiah; and when he had built a city in el-Hajar,[230] he went down and besieged Jerusalem. Now, prior to this, there was a city there called Yasuf, and in it were two brothers, Ephraim and Manasseh, who were Samaritans. And a certain Jew had gone up with some young doves, desiring to enter with them and make an offering in Jerusalem for his sins; and he passed the night in Yasuf, and the two brothers took the pair of young doves and slew them, and substituted in their place two big mice. And the man arose in the night and went unto the priest who was installed in the temple and said to him: "Offer up for me this pair of young birds." And when the priest opened the basket, the cheat of the two mice was discovered, and he laid hold of the man to kill him; but he said: "A trick has been played upon me. I passed the night at a lodging place in Yasuf, and there were none there except two Samaritan boys, and I took up my jour-

---

[230] Petra?

ney in the night, out of my fear lest the offering which I was to offer for my sins might escape from me, and I knew not that this trick had been perpetrated upon it." And they sent unto the innkeeper and arrested the two brothers to punish them; and when they confessed that they had done this, they gave orders that they should be put to death, but certain of them said: "If we kill them, their services are lost; rather let them be among the servants of the temple serving all their life long, eating the thorn which is the food of birds and drinking water, and sleeping upon the ground." And after this Hadrian came down to Jerusalem and besieged it; but the Jews used to go out of the tunnels which Solomon the son of David had constructed (one of which led) to Jericho and another to Lydda, and (the inhabitants of these towns) were giving unto them whatever they could eat and furnishing them with everything. And they (the inhabitants of Jerusalem) would go up on top of the walls and say to them (the besiegers): "See what our Lord does for us, He sends down upon us food; as He did with us in the wilderness, thus now again does He do." And they used to throw to them from above the wall fruit, both fresh and dried, and other things, and would say to them: "Eat such as our Lord sends down upon us." And they would also say: "Take unto you of what we have as sacrifices to the king; for behold our Lord, as much as we are in need of, the same He sends down upon us; as He did with us in the wilderness, thus does He with us now." And Hadrian had given credence to them, in as much as the war had become fatiguing, and did reckon their statements to be true. Now when this affair came to pass, the two brothers Ephraim and Manasseh came together, and wrote a note, and worked it up in clay, and threw it from above the wall to Hadrian the king, and it reached the king and he opened it and read it, and there was written in it this: "Do not deem their statements to be true; and if you desire that we should inform you how you may conquer the country—well and good; but, verily in consideration for that which shall enable you to be victorious in the war, save our souls from death. Now if you do desire to get possession of the country, send unto Jericho and unto Lydda and seize the mouths of the tunnels, and let not anything enter into them nor anyone go into them; and also seize Bethlehem, and demolish the duct through which there comes in unto them oil and water and sesame-oil and honey." And the king did according to what they said unto him, and he also sent and had brought into his presence the Samaritans Ephraim and Manasseh, and they were present with him in besieging Jerusalem. And he reduced them (the inhabitants of Jerusalem) to such sore straits that women ate their daughters and men their sons. And he rose in attack against them while they were observing the requirements of the law, and when they beheld themselves spoiled of everything, they sued for protection. And when they (the Romans) took possession, Hadrian gave orders that they should not molest the temple until he went in, and when he entered, he took the priest who belonged to the temple and said to him: "For whose name was this dwelling built?" The priest said unto him: "It was built for the name of the Creator of creatures." And when he had entered into the place, he saw a painted picture and by its side an idol, and when he saw them, he said to the priest: "This place was built for the name of the Creator of creatures, and is this done in it?" And he seized hold of him to punish him; but he (the priest) informed him that it was a deceit which the Jews who served the idol had made, notwithstanding Aaron had commanded that they should worship the Creator of creatures. And this wicked king saved Ephraim and Manasseh from being killed; and Hadrian set up in the city an image upon a pillar in accordance with the will of Ephraim and Manasseh, for the purpose of showing unto them (the inhabitants of the city) his rank, and it is there unto this day; and he also erected two images and named the first image after the name of Ephraim and the second image after the name of Manasseh; and he gave orders to the leaders of the Jews that no one should pass by in front of them but only behind them; and they are obliged to do this even unto this day. And Hadrian went out from there unto Qiryat el-'Arba (Kirjath-Arba), which is Hebron, and did like as he had done in Jerusalem. And Manasseh said unto Hadrian: "Make a bell in honor of my name, and let the bell be rung for my name." And he did so. And he went from there to Nablus, for he desired to destroy it, but while he was in Merj el-Baha and was elated upon his passing through it, they (the companions of the king) said: "If this is carried out, it (the Samaritan nation) will instigate a heroic revolt, and whoever sees this in Nablus will be inflamed with the zeal of a hero." So they collected together and said unto him: "As far as it is possible unto you, spare (the place)." And God moved his heart to pity, and he dealt kindly with it and with those who led the troops in Nablus; and he built there a town on Mount Gerizim and called it Saqarus after the name of his father. And the doors that were on Jerusalem were of yellow brass, plated with silver and ornamented with gold, which Solomon had made, the like of which no one, though strong of hand, could ever make, and he (Hadrian) carried these away and placed them on the door of the dome which he had built on the ridge of the mountain that is over against Nablus. And after this Hadrian went to Rome, and the Samaritans came together and purified the places wherein Hadrian had been; and the Jews plotted a wicked thought against them, and went unto the king, and said to him: "Behold how you are aiding the Samaritans and yet they are wishing your destruction. Make investigation and see how they have burned with fire every place wherein you were." And when Hadrian heard their words, he said: "We will kill every circumcised one." And he pronounced judgment of death upon the villages and upon every city, and prohibited baptism, and interdicted (the observance of) the Sabbath and feasts, wishing to ruin Nablus and destroy it, like a field laid waste. And when the Samaritans heard of this mighty calamity, they fled away, and were stricken with terror, and hid themselves from the presence of his great wrath, and they did not enter into a house nor reside under a roof, and there remained for them no shelter except the deserts and forests and caves. And he came and burned the houses, and crucified the teachers (of the people), and put to death its judges, and they did die in prisons by starvation, and their dead bodies were thrown out and not buried, and rights were infringed both as to themselves and their dead bodies, and they were persecuted in castles and on the roads. And when he came to destroy Nablus, he began from the city gate on the west until he arrived at the four pillars that were above the declivity at the base of the mountain. And they captured there a man who was fleeing that he might not be killed, and he fled into the presence of Hadrian, and entreated him, and said unto him: "I beg of you, by the honor of the One whom you dost worship, O king of the age, hear of me one word, and after that do with this nation what you wish." And when he had bound himself by oath, he listened to him, and the captive said: "Send and make investigation into the conduct of the Samaritans, for though they do burn every place wherein a foreigner has been that they may purify it from his tracks, yet we have not done this out of malignity or hostility to you. And the Jews have spoken unto you only deceitfully because we did render aid to you in reducing them to straitened circumstances and also because we did at once furnish you with provisions." So he (Hadrian) said that he would no longer put to death anyone, and he showed favor to the city and did not destroy it. And he set up three images after his likeness, in the city on top of pillars, on the spot where the man fled away from being killed, and also two images on the aqueduct. And after this Hadrian died—may God have no mercy upon him—and he died in woe and every kind of affliction, and his reign had lasted twenty-one years—may God crush his bones. And the space of time from Adam up to his death was four thousand five hundred and thirteen years and seven months. And in those days the Book of Choice Selections was taken away, which had been in their hands since the days of Divine Favor; and there was also taken away the Songs and Praises, which they were accustomed to utter over the offerings, each offering according to its merits; and also the Hymns, which they used to sing in the days of Divine Favor. Now all these constituted a library which had been preserved with greatest care generation after generation, through the time of the prophets unto that day, by the hands of the chief imams. And there was also taken away the Book of the Imams, which they had, wherein their genealogy was traced back to Phineas; and there was also destroyed the Annals, wherein was recorded their birthdays and the years of their lives, and of these not one ancient book or chronicle was found except the Law and a book containing their lives. But we have written up the years of the life of the chief imam and a genealogy from the chief imam ʾAqbun; and this comes (in the next chapter).

Forty-eighth Chapter

Now it was once said to him: "Brother of the king! Everything in your house belongs unto the king," and ʾAqbun said: "The whole of it belongs unto God, and I have given over my spirit unto God and I will not renounce my Lord." And they[231] went and seized two men of the children of the imams, and said unto them: "Seek refuge in our gods, and you can depart to your houses unharmed." But they utterly refused and said: "We will not do that." So they killed them in punishment and threw their corpses outside the wall—that is, the wall of Sebustieh—and they crucified of the wise men of Israel a company of thirty-six men on the gate of Nablus. In that day the instruction of Israel was like as dust; there was no imam among them, nor wisdom, nor teaching of the Law, nor was anyone able in the days of these kings to give instruction in the Pentateuch except one in a thousand and two in a myriad. And the children of Israel continued in this calamitous state until Baba Rabba arose.

In those days ʾAqbun knew his wife, and she conceived and gave birth to a son, and he named him Nathaniel, and this Nathaniel was the father of Baba Rabba, who broke the brazen bird that was on the Mount preventing them from ascending it; for this the Romans and (their) magicians had done. After this the chief imam ʾAqbun died; but before he died, he said at this time to his son Nathaniel: "O my child, be not troubled with regard to these times, or these calamities, or the power of the enemies; know that in a short time these distresses will disappear, for these calamities are tests sent by God upon us that He may prove whether we ourselves are faithful and are not forsaking the worship of God our God. O my child, these calamities and straits will vanish away; for God—may He be exalted—is able to cause them to disappear from us." And the imam ʾAqbun proceeded to make a revelation unto his son in accord with this, and invoked blessing on

---

[231] Romans?

him, and said unto him: "O my child, be on your guard against worshiping any other than God; for even if you were to be crushed under stones, God would give you strength to worship Him. And God will raise up from you one who will get the ascendancy over this infidel oppressing nation." And the prayer of the Rabbi ꞌAqbun was granted at that time with regard to all that he invoked for his son. For, from his son, there arose Baba Rabba, and he brought about that which happened to the Romans. And at that the imam ꞌAqbun died and was removed to his people: may God benefit us with his blessings. And all Israel mourned for him, and wept for him thirty days.

Forty-ninth Chapter

When the Rabbi ꞌAqbun died and was translated to his people, Nathaniel took the office of imam in place of his father.[232] And he knew his wife, and she conceived and gave birth to children, and he was granted of her three children; his first born was Baba Rabba, his second was ꞌAqbun, and the third after these two was Phineas. Now when the imam Nathaniel was granted his first born, he was for some time perplexed with regard to him, as to how he should circumcise him; for the Romans at that time forcibly prevented them from performing circumcision and set over them curators that they might not circumcise their children, and there was stationed at the door of the residence of the imam Nathaniel a deputy of the king, named Germanus the Roman. And when the Rabbi was granted this child, he took it on the day of circumcision, and placed it in a basket. and put wool on top of it and under it, and said unto the maidservant that was with him: "Take this boy and go in advance of us into the field to the cave, and we will follow after and overtake you that we may circumcise him; but let no one know what you have. Take him and go out from the door of the house while we will go out from the rear of the house." And the maid took it and went out; and when he issued forth from the door of the house, Germanus the deputy said to her: "Perform, girl, what you have in mind, and fear not." And the maid went with the infant to the cave and repeated unto the Rabbi Nathaniel the speech of Germanus; and he in fear said: "The affair is God's." And they circumcised the little one, and the maidservant returned with it just as it was; and when she came to the door, Germanus said unto her: "Rear him in peace, O my child." And when she had passed, she repeated to the Rabbi the speech of Germanus, and he was smitten

---

[232] Ch. 49 also appears in the *Annals* of Abu'l Fath, who probably borrowed the material from the SJ.

with great fear and said: "Who has informed Germanus of our business? I cannot mollify his anger except with great riches." And the Rabbi was worried and went forth to Germanus, the deputy over his house, with his hands full of gold. And Germanus said unto the Rabbis: "I will have nothing to do with this, except only will take of this just three dinars so that you may not say that I am laying a plot for you; for, truly, I will not make this known unto the king." And when Germanus had bound himself by oath unto the Rabbi, his heart became good, and the Rabbi made it to be remembered of Germanus; and it came to pass that whenever they circumcised any of their children in a cave, they would invoke a blessing on Germanus, saying in the Roman language: "May God be merciful unto Germanus the Roman priest"; and unto this our day, they invoke a blessing on him immediately after every circumcision. And the Romans did mix hogs' lard in every thing that was eaten and drunken, so that they (the Samaritans) might be afflicted with bodily infirmity. And the houses of prayer that we had were shut up, and they prevented us from going up on to the Mount, by means of a talisman that they fixed above it. And we continued in this strait and great calamity for the space of twenty years until God comforted us and saved us from the power of the infidels, and this was brought about by the hand of Baba Rabba.

Fiftieth Chapter

When the kingdom passed away from the children of Israel and the Romans ruled, they gave over to judgment and crushed under the stones of torture many of the Samaritans until they should renounce their faith and bow down unto idols; and many of the Samaritans perished through this cause. And the Romans did not allow one of the Samaritans to circumcise his child, but stationed trustworthy men of the Romans over the houses of the Samaritans to prevent them from performing circumcision. And the Samaritans were in the habit at that time, when a child was born unto them, to place it in a basket and cover it with wool and go with it to the cave and circumcise it underground by the light of candles. And also then the Romans prevented the Samaritans from ascending the Mount; for they said: "Whoever goes up on this Mount shall be put to death." And the Romans placed upon the summit of the Mount a talisman, and this was a brazen bird, and it used to turn round with the sun, following its circuit, and it was so that if a Samaritan did go up, the bird would screech out: "Hebraeus" (Hebrew), and they would know then that there was a Samaritan on the Mount, and would issue forth against him and kill him. And the children of Israel continued in this distress until Baba Rabba arose; and in him there was a spirit of resolution and zealous patriotism. And Baba Rabba assembled the Israelite community and said:

"How long shall this polluted nation go on dominating over you? Arise, let us lift up the children of Israel from this oppression, and let us be zealous for God—may He be exalted—as our father Phineas was zealous, and there remains to him a goodly remembrance unto the end of the ages. And now know that I have resolved upon the destruction of the Romans, and I will purify Mount Gerizim of them, but not a thing can be accomplished for us except by the destruction of this bird that is stationed over the temple, and this cannot be accomplished for us except by a stratagem that God has revealed unto me. Now you know that this is a time of infidelity, and they have many kings, and my plan is to send Levi, the son of my brother, to Constantinople, the city of the Romans, that they may learn what they talk about, what it is that makes them powerful, and may gain knowledge of their religious sects. And he shall go in the garb of a Christian Monk (or) priest, and no one will know him, and the Romans will not know who he is; and he will come back to Mount Gerizim and will go up to the church and make use of a stratagem to smash the bird; and when they (the Roman guards) attempt to repel him, he will employ stratagem and get the power to ascend the Mount, and will supplicate God upon it, and He will then give us the victory over our enemies."

And all the people said: "O our master, do what seems good in your sight." And he said: "Give unto me your own handwritings that after his coming back your souls will stand by him." And they did this, and Baba Rabba led forth the son of his brother to Bethel[233] in the presence of the people and said unto him: "Be attentive however you may be, and set your mind upon learning everything, and be on your guard that you cease not to read the Pentateuch night and day, and God shall help you in all your doings." And he sent away Levi, the son of his brother; and he pursued his journey, seeking Constantinople. Now Levi was an intelligent, knowing, acute, and pure man, yes, in him was found every virtue; and he arrived at Constantinople, and sought after learning, and diligently applied himself, and he obtained what he sought for; and with his keenness of intellect he continued reading for the space of two years, and there remained no one among all the Romans more learned than he. And he arose to such eminence in learning that the Romans used repeatedly to come to do him reverence, and by reason of his eloquent attainments in learning they made him Archbishop, and he was elevated to the highest rank among them until kings used to

---

[233] Mount Gerizim, the Samaritan "house of God."

come to his door, and no king could assume the kingly authority without his orders nor put on a crown except by his command. And it came to pass at the end of thirteen years that he said unto the king: "I have a desire to visit the church which is on the Mountain of Nablus." And the whole army assembled, and the king and the legions marched in his service. And when they encamped at Nablus, the king sent for all the people who were in Nablus to come out to meet the Archbishop. And when the Samaritans heard this, they were struck with a great fear, and all the people assembled and said: "We have lost hope in the opinion we had with regard to Levi, whom we sent away on his journey; for no tidings have come back from him, and without doubt he has perished, and as to this Bishop who has now arrived, we have heard that he is the head of the nation of the Romans, and they proclaim of him that he is profoundly versed in infidelity, and the Romans call him . . ."

Chapter 3

Kitab al-Tarikh (The *Annals* of Abu'l Fath)

INTRODUCTION

Written by Abu'l Fath in 1355, the *Annals* is a narrative of the Samaritan story that begins with Adam and ends with Muhammad. Certainly, the *Annals* is history from a certain point of view and can be criticized, according to modern canons of historicity, for a lack of scientific inquiry. But this was not Abu'l Fath's purpose. Writing during a very dark and difficult period of Samaritan history, when the community was only a "shadow of its former self,"[1] Abu'l Fath was motivated by a desire to preserve Samaritan traditions and a certain pride in the past. He indicates in his introduction that the *Annals* was commissioned by the Samaritan high priest Pinhas but was also written to satisfy the curiosity of the ruler of a country in which Abu'l Fath had traveled. Three years transpired from the time of the original request by Pinhas and the commissioning of the work. During that time, presumably, Abu'l Fath gathered materials useful for his compilation (including materials provided by the high priest), so that, sifting through all that was available, he could say, "I have aimed at what was true and sincere, and endeavored to compile an authentic narrative." As we will see, modern scholars have often disputed Abu'l Fath's claim, but regardless of those scholarly assessments, the *Annals* has assumed a place of importance in the Samaritan story.

The *Annals* is first mentioned in Western scholarship by Abraham Ecchellensis in 1653. Eduard Bernard produced a brief summary of the work in 1691, and several sections were translated a century later, in 1790 and 1792 (Christian Friedrich Schnurrer). Several additional partial publications of the *Annals* appeared during the nineteenth century,[2] as did a complete text

---

[1] John Bowman, *Samaritan Documents Relating to Their History, Religion, and Life* (Pittsburgh: Pickwick, 1977), 114.

[2] Silvestre de Sacy, *Chrestomathie arabe* (Paris: Imprimerie Impériale, 1806); J. M. Jost, *Geschichte des Judenthums und seiner Secten* (3 vols.; Leipzig: Dörffling & Franke, 1857–1859); R. Payne-Smith, "The Samaritan Chronicle of Abu'l Fath, the

in Arabic with a Latin introduction by Eduardus Vilmar in 1865.[3] Vilmar concluded the *Annals* to be an example of Samaritan apologetic literature and offered mixed evaluations on its worth as a chronicle with historical value.[4] Some following Vilmar were less appreciative. John Nutt, who wrote in 1874, identified what he called "historical blunders" and concluded, "It is unwise to accept anything as genuine which comes to us recommended only by Samaritan authority."[5] At the turn of the century, James Montgomery, too, expressed skepticism over the historical value of Samaritan chronicles.[6]

This negativity began to be tempered somewhat in the first quarter of the twentieth century as some scholars began to realize the sociological value of the Samaritan chronicles. In the Schweich Lectures of 1923, Moses Gaster expressed appreciation for the *Annals,* commenting on its value for understanding the Samaritan community.[7] More recently, in 1977, Simeon Lowy, who thinks the *Annals* are based upon very old sources, also has attempted to see the literature from within and has shown a deep appreciation for the stated purpose of the Samaritan authors.[8]

Paul Stenhouse represents the high-water mark of scholarly investigation into the *Annals* of Abu'l Fath during the last half of the twentieth century. His translation of the *Annals,* published in 1985 and based upon the manuscript Huntington 350 in Oxford's Bodleian Library, has been exceptionally helpful.[9] The translations of Stenhouse and of John Bowman are used for the excerpts appearing in this study. Minor alterations have been made to those translations to make the text more readable.

Arabic Text from the MS in the Bodleian Library," *Deutsche Vierteljahrsschrift für englisch-theologische Forschung und Kritik* 2 (1863): 304–35, 430–59.

[3] E. Vilmar, *Abulfathi Annales samaritani* (Gotha, Germany: F. A. Perthes, 1865).

[4] Ibid., xxxi.

[5] John Nutt, *Fragments of a Samaritan Targum, Edited from a Bodleian MS, with an Introduction Containing a Sketch of Samaritan History, Dogma, and Literature* (London: Trübner, 1874), 131. Silvestre de Sacy (*Notices et extraits de divers manuscrits arabes et autres* [Paris: Imprimerie Royale, 1829], 242) may represent the extreme of this position, characterizing Abu'l Fath as containing ridiculous anachronisms.

[6] James Montgomery, *The Samaritans, the Earliest Jewish Sect: Their History, Theology, and Literature* (Philadelphia: Winston, 1907; repr., New York: KTAV, 1968), 90.

[7] Moses Gaster, *The Samaritans: Their History, Doctrines, and Literature* (London: Oxford University Press, 1925).

[8] Simeon Lowy, *Principles of Samaritan Bible Exegesis* (Leiden: Brill, 1977).

[9] Paul Stenhouse, ed., *The Kitab al-Tarikh of Abu'l-Fath, Translated with Notes* (Sydney: Mandelbaum Trust, University of Sidney, 1985).

Stenhouse took seriously the conditions that led to the creation of Abu'l Fath's work. The Samaritan community in Syria and Palestine was scattered and drastically reduced by the prolonged conflicts in the region, first by the Crusades and then by the invading Mongol armies of the khan. The effects of plague in the first half of the fourteenth century and the social upheaval caused by the dissolving Mamluk Empire in the middle of the fourteenth century added to the Samaritans' woes. As if all this were not enough, Abu'l Fath himself mentions that general knowledge of the history of the community was fading, that there had not been any recent records of events, and that the records that had been written were in disarray.[10] Combined with all this, the high priest's interest in the *Annals* and his part in the discovery and public showing of the Abisha Scroll (months before the completion of the *Annals* by Abu'l Fath) make it plausible that the *Annals* filled a specific social function.

> We suggest that the Chronicle of AF *[Annals]*, like the newly found scroll (the Abisha Scroll) was intended by the High Priest to prepare the Samaritan people for the *mirabilia Dei* which it was believed would soon be revealed to them; to bring the Samaritans back to study of and love for their religion and traditions; and last but not least, to bring some grounds for pride and hope to a people oppressed not only by recent events but by a long history of persecution and frustration of national and religious ideals.[11]

Abu'l Fath's *Annals* is an important work for understanding the Samaritan worldview. Stenhouse shows his high esteem for the *Annals* when he states that Abu'l Fath's work is "rightly regarded as the 'key' to unlock Samaritan self understanding in areas of social history, theology, sectarianism, and chronology."[12] In a sense, the work has both a "descriptive" and a "proscriptive" function. The *Annals* describes the world from the Samaritan point of view. It gives ample demonstration of how the Samaritans in the past related to the world around them, sometimes experiencing the blessing of God and other times the divine disfavor. The *Annals* sets boundaries. It describes the appropriate limits of what it means to be "true Israel," and in this way the *Annals* is proscriptive as well. By appreciating the nature of the Samaritan community of the past, the Samaritan community of the present is prepared for an anticipated future of promise.

---

[10] *Annals*, 2.

[11] Paul Stenhouse, "Samaritan Chronicles," in *The Samaritans* (ed. Alan Crown; Tübingen: J. C. B. Mohr, 1989) 221.

[12] Ibid., 264.

Abu'l Fath indicates that he had several sources available to him when writing the *Annals*.[13] These sources are (1) the Book of the Allotment of the Regions, (2) the Chronicle of the Book of the Allotment of the Regions, (3) the Samaritan book of Joshua (SJ), along with additional material, (4) an assortment of three partial (defective) chronicles from his personal collection, (5) a genealogy (procured from the high priest Eleazar), and (6) some pamphlets.

Stenhouse has investigated the interrelationship of the sources.[14] As the reader will observe by simply glancing through the following excerpts, Abu'l Fath made extensive use of SJ. The *Annals* also borrows broadly from the genealogy as well.[15] Abu'l Fath seems genuinely intent on preserving the past—at least as he sees it—and so uses the resources at hand to represent that past. This preservation even includes easily recognizable inconsistencies in the account (i.e., the account of the Dustan heresy). But Abu'l Fath's work is not complete. In a sense, the *Annals* is open-ended. It tells the Samaritan story until the time of Muhammad but does not write the last chapter. Indeed, some manuscripts of the *Annals* go further, adding material to that written by Abu'l Fath and continuing the story from the 750s up till modern times. The *Annals* of Abu'l Fath is one part of the ongoing Samaritan story.

THE *ANNALS* OF ABU'L FATH: EXCERPTS

The following excerpts depend heavily upon the text prepared by E. Vilmar and the translations of John Bowman and Paul Stenhouse. The text presented here has been divided into different paragraphs from those presented by Stenhouse and more excerpts than those given by Bowman. Additional headings are provided to identify more easily the subject matter of the text. Occasionally, vocabulary and syntax have been altered from the Bowman and Stenhouse texts in order to produce a more readable presentation. The short descriptions or identifications of items of interest before the excerpts are not present in the original manuscript but are the present authors' additions.

---

[13] Abu'l Fath also mentions one source that he did not use because he judged it untrustworthy: the "Chronicle of Sadaqah." He also appears to draw upon accounts written by Josephus, e.g., the account of Darius (Josephus, *Ant.* 11.3, 8).

[14] Stenhouse, "Samaritan Chronicles," 240–60.

[15] A. Neubauer, "Chronique samaritaine, suivie d'un appendice contenant de courtes notices sur quelques autres ouvrages samaritains," *JA* 14 (1869): 385–470.

First Excerpt: The introduction to the chronicle.

In the name of God the merciful, the compassionate, in whom I place my trust. Praise be to God the eternal, the living, who by his divine power created what exists—the means whereby one arrives at knowledge of him—and (who) made this knowledge an elevation and a dignity for faithful people who are pure-minded in (their) obedience to him. He shed upon his prophets and upon sincere people a light which exceeds the bounds and degrees of understanding. He sent forth our lord, Moses son of Amram, abundant peace be upon him, who by his miracles was a dazzling vision for the elect among his creatures who were (thereby) disposed to accept his law. He made them recognize those things that are permitted and (those things which are) forbidden, the place of their Qibla,[16] the place of his angels, the source of his mercy. He imposed upon them the observance of the Sabbath, which is the shield of Israel and the lock of his domain. May God grant us (the privilege of) death during its observance, and the love of this mighty prophet! May he add us to the number of his people and not make us like those turned out of his house: those who are denied his intercession in the life to come. He inspired us with perfect observance of the law, and the Qibla, and the priestly office that comes down to us through the descendants of Phinehas, who was solicitous for the affairs of God by his zeal.

May perfect peace be upon all his prophets who forbade (all forms of) defilement and commanded the fear and love of God. Thus speaks the slave who is poor in the sight of Almighty God, Abu'l-Fath bin Abi al-Hasan, the Samaritan, the Danafite, after praising and thanking Almighty God: that when he was in the presence of our lord, our High Priest, our foundation and guide, the mighty priest, the great, the active, the learned, the ascetic, the God-fearing, the pious, endowed with a pleasant and gentle disposition, the joy of (our) days, the refuge for the human race, the blessing for the (Samaritan) communities, the Sibyl of the Israelite nation, noblest of nobles of the line of Aaron, quintessence of High Priests of the line of Phinehas his exalted ancestor, master of the trustworthy covenant, Phinehas, may God send his blessing upon him and upon all the community, and lengthen the days of his life in the city of Nablus, which is under God's protection; that during certain months of the year 753[17] the slave complained to him about

---

[16] A term designating the direction to face during prayer. For Samaritans, prayer is to be made facing Mount Gerizim.

[17] 1352 C.E.

the lack of any familiarity with the affairs of past generations, may Almighty God have mercy upon them, to say nothing of (the lack of) any recent presentations of what took place after the death of the Messenger of God, upon whom be peace. And (he further complained) that vast numbers of them and their community were in scattered and dispersed circumstances and that their Chronicles were in a similar state of disarray. So he (Phinehas) gave the slave the task of compiling a Chronicle of all the records of events that involved the Fathers—may God Have mercy upon them—in full, from the beginning of the world when God created Adam, upon whom be peace, up to recent times.

The upshot of this was that the slave took the request (too) lightly and allowed himself to become preoccupied with concerns of a worldly nature until Almighty God brought it about that he again met Phinehas in Nablus, which is under God's protection, during the month of Ramadan in the year 756.[18] The slave recalled what he had been commanded to do, and saw that he had a duty to obey the command. Accordingly, he asked Phinehas, by reason of his friendship, to ask help for him in this from the Almighty and Glorious God. This he promised to do and brought out what he possessed of old Chronicles and (copies of) the Sayings, in Hebrew and Arabic; and these form part of the present compilation. I put my trust in God and have striven hard in the exposition, with genuine dedication to the work. I have extracted the cream and cut down on such Greek expressions as I considered, on the whole, to be not worth including—as I feared the (possible) tedium—but without, however, spoiling the meaning or embellishing it in any way. Rather I have aimed at (presenting) the unblemished truth and (what is) the authentic tradition and have transmitted only what I found to be agreed upon in the Chronicles.

If there should be anything in this which is not true, then let God seek revenge for it from whoever is responsible. Mercy and forgiveness must be begged from God for any defects that may have occurred as a result of carelessness or misunderstanding. The sources from which I have compiled this Chronicle are as follows: (1) the Chronicle Qit al-Baladi in the Arabic script and language, belonging to our lord, the above-mentioned High Priest; (2) a(nother) Chronicle (containing) the Qit al-Baladi in Hebrew script and the Arabic language—an incomplete copy belonging to the above-mentioned; (3) a Chronicle within which was bound the Book of Joshua, and other things besides, in the Arabic script and language, (also) belonging to the above-mentioned; (4) three incomplete Chronicles in He-

---

18 1355 C.E.

brew script and language which belong to me and which I got from the seat of Government in Damascus, which is protected by God; (5) a (copy of) the Chain[19] transcribed in the hand of our lord the above-mentioned High Priest, from (a copy) in the handwriting of Eleazer the Great High Priest, may the Radwan[20] of God be upon him, containing the antecedents of the Samaritans, may God have mercy upon them; (6) a few sheets in the handwriting of the above-mentioned. As for the Chronicle of the wise and distinguished Sadaqa, the slave took nothing from this because the priests whose names and pontificates he recorded don't agree with the other Chronicles. He was, however, particularly skillful in making up the opinions which he attributed to them, in setting out questions and answers, in smoothness of style and excellent rhymes—were it not for the fact that in the Chronicles one looks for the exact truth and sets out to transcribe what is authentic, without any additions or omissions. As to why the slave undertook this task—the reason is that he found himself in a particular country and its ruler asked him about their Chronicles and sought them from him; so he compiled the above-mentioned Chronicle for him and presented it to him. [21]

Second Excerpt: The period of divine favor, an idealized view of the past[22]

They began the inhabiting of their allotment, and it was a perfect and contented habitation. God manifested blessings to them, as well as protection, so that misfortunes were averted and not a single enemy prevailed over them nor stood in their path (to obstruct them) when they came from every city three times a year to the illustrious Mountain.[23] With them would be livestock, wealth, and goods without number, (making) a great joyous and happy tumult; yet none of their enemies took advantage of them nor opposed them. They used to let the land lie fallow for one year in every seven, neither sowing in it nor tilling. The sons of Israel would give to the Levites the tithes collected for them from what was sown of fruit and animals, and so on.[24] The Levites then paid a tenth of this to the High Priest. The sons of Israel had a second tithe which they distributed as they saw fit, on the House of God, on the priests, and on the infirm. When

---

[19] The *Tulida* or "Genealogy."
[20] "Divine favor," referring to the period of God's blessing prior to the sin of Eli.
[21] Stenhouse, *The Kitab al-Tarikh*, 1–3. Used by permission.
[22] Stenhouse, *The Kitab al-Tarikh*, 38–41. Used by permission.
[23] Exod 23:17; 34:22; Deut 16:16.
[24] Lev 25:1–7.

they planted a new plant in the ground, its fruit was eaten only in the fourth year, when the High Priest ate it. In the fifth year it was unrestricted—permitted to everyone.

The servitude of the Hebrew slave ceased for him every seven years. When a needy Israelite sold himself or his son, he remained like a hired laborer, and his ransom was determined according to the (number of) years (he had worked) and how close or distant it (the year of his redemption) was from the Jubilee year. If none—near or far—could be found to redeem him, then he went out a free man in the year of Jubilee. In the same way properties were sold in the Jubilee year.[25] Every seventh year the land was (re)divided among the tribes according to their increase or decrease (in numbers). The first fruits of animals and things sown, and fruit, were taken to the High Priest. No lambs or goats or cattle were sacrificed except on the illustrious Mountain provided they were not blemished or from one of the seven categories of stag, gazelle, roe animals that lie on their breast, wild goat, or giraffe. They also had judges (Hakam) to whom they referred on every occasion.

Whenever one of them committed a serious offense like heresy or sorcery, and so on, there was no way he could escape; he would be taken (prisoner) even if he were at the remotest frontier of the territory; and the "give-away" was the jewelry which the High Priest wore. If a woman was suspected by her husband (of adultery), she was made to drink sweetened water. If she became sick, then she was discovered, her guilt was manifest, and she perished forthwith. But if she were guiltless, then she became pregnant and blessed with children.

When an innocent man was killed, his murderer became known from the circumstances that worked together to reveal the truth. There were lesser, inadvertent sins which anyone could commit without meaning to. These were atoned for by the High Priest on the Day of Atonement, that is, the tenth day of the seventh month. It is called the Day of Fasting, and on it took place the purification of body and soul. Some of the Levites on the illustrious Mountain copied down the Torah while others wrote hymns and genealogies and Chronicles and other things. The sons of Gershon selected the beasts (separating them) from those which were blemished, and used to take them to their brethren to be offered as sacrifices on the altar. They separated the offerings into sections, and whatever they were told to do, they did. The sons of Merari placed the sacrifices on the altar, and the

---

[25] Lev 25; Deut 15:12–17.

free-will offerings and the wine to be spilt, and the oil for the anointing. The following were the sons of Kohath: Eleazer, upon whom be God's peace, who bore the office of High Priest and was clad in the sacred vestments and attended to the blessing of the people and atonement in the temple, and Ithamar, and his sons Asur and Alkanah and Abisaf, who attended to slaughtering and sprinkling the blood, skinning the animals, sounding the trumpet, and the trusteeship of redeemed goods and expiatory offerings.

The ministry of the sons of Kohath went to Eleazer and Phinehas, and the ministry of the sons of Gershon and the sons of Merari went to Ithamar and his sons.[26]

These were the servants of the High Priests who stayed on the illustrious Mountain. The rest (of the Levites) dwelt in their hamlets and were dispersed among the Israelite tribes to instruct and to lead the prayers. They were the ones who took a special share (of the produce) of the land and the trees, of things succulent and things dried, of the specially set-aside portion of the dough, of the corners of the fields, of the fruit of the trees in the fourth year. From the sacrifices of the sons of Israel they took the forearm, the jaw, the head, the choice portions of sheep among other choice offerings that the people of Israel offered year after year. The offering of the everlasting sacrifice was made before the rising of the sun, and (again) before it set, immediately the trumpets were sounded so that they would know that the sacrifice was being offered then; and they would stand and pray. Their prayer was accepted, mercy dwelt with them, blessings were multiplied, prosperity was widespread, their affairs prospered, and their deeds were renowned. They were on intimate terms with their Lord, and he granted their requests and their prayers.

Third Excerpt: The Abisha Scroll[27]

Phinehas his son and successor was a strong ruler, widely esteemed and very distinguished. He it was who worked out the calculation of the dimensions of the latitude of Mount Gerizim, namely, fourteen hours and five-ninths of an hour, in the days of his father in the thirteenth year of the kingdom of Israel in the land of Canaan.

---

[26] Num 26:57; 1 Chron 6.

[27] Stenhouse, *The Kitab al-Tarikh*, 44–45. Used by permission. The Abisha Scroll is the venerated copy of the SP housed in Nablus.

It was in the above-mentioned year that Abisha son of Phinehas wrote out the Holy Book which is now to be found in Nablus, under God's protection, in the safekeeping of our lord the High Priest Phinehas, may God repeatedly bless him and lengthen the number of his days, by whose means God made known its whereabouts after its disappearance and its being hidden from his predecessors in the High Priesthood.

This is the good news—if God so wills it—which will reveal the return of the Radwan[28] in his day and in the days of his children who are steadfast in the service of this Book, which is the consolation of souls, the assurer of hearts, and the certainty of truth handed down by means of the Samaritan community—may Almighty God give them increase. In this year, it was again uncovered on the Sabbath of the feast of Tabernacles. This was a marvelous occasion. All the assembly present witnessed to the Tashqil that it contained.

It commences at "and it will be (that the Lord your God) will bring you,"[29] which follows "Hear O Israel,"[30] and is as follows: "I, Abisha, son of Phinehas son of Eleazer, son of Aaron the priest upon whom be the Radwan of the Lord and his Glory: I wrote out the Book of Holiness at the entrance to the Tent of Meeting on Mount Gerizim in the thirteenth year of the dominion of the sons of Israel over the land of Canaan, to its borders around it. I give praise to the Lord."

This illustrious Book represents the Radwan. Whoever is sincere in seeking something in its presence or, if absent from it, asks its help with heart and soul, he will be heard, and his needs will be satisfied. We beseech Almighty God to help us through its special dignity, its blessing, and the blessing of its ministers and their noble descendants.

Fourth Excerpt: The end of the divine favor[31]

The total from Adam, upon whom be peace, to the death of Samson, who was the last of the kings of the Radwan, was 3,054 years. When Samson died, there was a sign in it, and mighty signs among the pagan nations, many of whom he had destroyed.

When news of his death reached them, they unsuccessfully sought some means of taking their revenge.

---

[28] The period of divine favor.
[29] Deut 6:10.
[30] Deut 6:4.
[31] Stenhouse, *The Kitab al-Tarikh,* 46–50. Used by permission.

They had read in the Book of Balaam that these people could be destroyed only by magic, moral depravity, and unbelief.[32]

So they learnt how to concoct it from a group that was practiced in it, and they carried it on, even in Beth El. There was no king at this time to lead the people, so they trusted a group of the sons of Israel (who came) from a people wanton and destructive of the circumstances of this life. These showed them magical arts, and they took part in them.

At first, 100 men came together on the southern (slope) of Mount Gerizim and offered sacrifices to foreign gods. The name of this place was called, after them, "The Place of the One Hundred." Then, out of fear of the sons of Israel, they went to another place and offered sacrifice to strange gods (there); as they had grown to 200 men, the place was named after them "The Two Hundred." From "The Two Hundred" they went up to another place. They increased in numbers and offered sacrifice to other gods. As they branched out from there, the place was called "Farata." Their altars are there to this day. Nevertheless, God was patient with them, and his anger did not fall upon them, nor did he hide the Radwan from them. It happened that at the time of the death of Samson, what was hidden in souls was made plain.

A terrible civil war broke out between Eli son of Yafni, of the line of Ithamar, and the sons of Phinehas because Eli son of Yafni resolved to usurp the High Priesthood from the descendants of Phinehas. He used to offer sacrifice on the altar of stones. He was 50 years old, endowed with wealth and in charge of the treasury of the children of Israel. He continued for a time, gathering a group around him to whom he said, "I am one to whom it is anathema to serve a child. I do not wish (to do) this myself, and I hope that you will not consent to it."

They answered as a group and said, "We are at your command and under your obedience: order us as you see fit, and we will not disobey."

Accordingly, he made them swear that they would follow him in all his purposes. He offered a sacrifice on the altar, but without salt, as if he were inattentive. When the Great High Priest Ozzi learnt of this and found out that the sacrifice was not accepted, he thoroughly disowned him; and it is (even) said that he rebuked him. Thereupon he and the group that sympathized with him rose in revolt, and at once he and his followers and his beasts set off for Shilo. Thus Israel was split into factions. He sent to their

---

[32] SJ 3.

leaders, saying to them, "Anyone who would like to see wonderful things, let him come to me." Then he assembled a large group around him in Shilo and built a Temple for himself there; he constructed for himself a place like the Temple. He built an altar, omitting no detail—it all corresponded to the original, piece by piece.

Now, he had two sons, Hophni and Phinehas, who rounded up young women of attractive appearance and brought them into the Tabernacle that had been built by their father. They let them savor the food of the sacrifices, and had intercourse with them inside the Tabernacle.[33] At this time the children of Israel became three factions: a (loyal) faction on Mount Gerizim; a heretical faction that followed false gods; and the faction that followed Eli son of Yafni in Shilo. When the people had become indifferent to rectifying excesses, pretending not to notice, when their eyesight had become dimmed and they were reluctant to show disapproval, then the angels fled from them. God became angry at them, his indignation fell upon them, and he took his patronage from them. The fire that was manifest by his divine power in the Tabernacle went out. The divine fire, which had not divided the sacrifices on the Monday, disappeared. That day is notorious as a day of terrible misfortune and great evil, of protracted affliction and widespread grief. It was like the day on which our father Adam emerged from the garden!

Ozzi the High Priest went in to conduct the service and raised the Veil of the Holy House. He witnessed none of the usual signs of the Favor. He looked, and behold: pitch black darkness was seen in the House. It happened that he went back again to serve on the Tuesday and the Wednesday. And when he went in on Thursday he noted that the blackness had intensified and (now) enveloped the whole House. He found that all that was within the Curtain had disappeared. It was then that he knew that God—powerful and glorious—was angry at them and had taken his power and mercy and benevolence away from them, away from the place and away from the sons of Israel. He looked, and behold, there was a cave in this place—Jabatha was gaping wide—something he had never seen before this day. He began to collect the sacred vestments and gold and silver vessels and put them in this cave. And when he had collected them all together in it and went out through the entrance, the cave was sealed. He wrote on the entrance, inscribed a mark upon it, but when he came back to the place on the Friday morning, he could find neither the cave, nor the writing, nor the inscription (that he had put) there.

---

[33] 1 Sam 2:12–25.

He then lifted up his voice in weeping and lamenting. He bewailed his lot
and what had come upon him and the sons of Israel in his days. The assembly of the Levites, and the 12 leaders who dwelt with him, and the 70
wise men gathered around him asked him what was the matter with him.
So he told them what had been revealed to him. And when he had made
plain to them that the anger (of God) was upon them and that the time of
Bliss and Favor was finished, they ripped their garments, uncovered their
heads, increased their groans and wailing, and began to recount all the favors that God—Glorious and Powerful—had shown them and how (now)
they could expect retribution and affliction.

Fifth Excerpt: About Saul, David, and Solomon[34]

But let us return now to the account of Eli son of Yafni. When he went to
Shilo and built a Tabernacle there, the one who erected the copy of
the Tabernacle from the time of the Radwan was called Tola son of
Iqwa. There was (also) a certain man called Elkana, from Sufin, a Levite
from among the sons of Kohath of the line of Abiaseph son of Korah
son of Izhar[35]—the one who rebelled against the lord Moses, upon whom
be peace, and who was burnt to death by fire—who had a son called
Samuel. He presented the above-mentioned son in the name of the House
which Eli had built, to serve in it. This is the genealogy of Samuel: son
of Elkana, son of Nawal, son of Azaria, son of Safania, son of Tahat, son of
Abiaseph, son of Korah, whom his father sent to Eli after he had been
weaned.[36]

Eli raised him and instructed him in the art of witchcraft and astrology that
he had acquired from Arhamis, who was foremost in the philosophy of
Greece. When he (Arhamis) heard about the disobedience of the sons of
Israel, he had come from Greece to Eli in Shilo and had prevailed on those
who were in Farata, worshiping idols, not to manifest the truth to Eli and
his followers.

Let us now return to the recollection of those who resided on the Holy
Mountain, to gain an accurate picture. When Samuel had learnt magic and
become proficient in it, he claimed to have the gift of prophecy, and they
believed him. The Creator—Powerful and Glorious—was very patient

---

[34] Stenhouse, *The Kitab al-Tarikh*, 52–64. Used by permission.
[35] Num 16:1.
[36] Cf. 1 Sam 1:1.

with the erroneous old man Eli, who ruled his domain and organized his people for 40 years.[37]

Then a very learned man from among the sons of Israel joined forces with him, to worsen his crime. The kings of the Philistines got the mastery over him, captured the Ark, and put it in the house of their idol.

Samuel went down to Shilo, he and his disciples with him, and continued sacrificing and making offerings wherever he saw fit. He changed the name of God Powerful and Glorious, went to Sufin, and built an altar for himself there, and offered sacrifices upon it. When he grew older, his disciples said to him, "Put a king over us!" So he took Saul son of Kish from the tribe of Benjamin and made him (their) king.[38]

Saul was a mighty king and deceived the sons of Israel, wise men included. Only the tribe of Phinehas and the tribe of Joseph, and with these a few others from among the tribes, remained on the Holy Mountain and preserved the faith. In the beginning of Saul's reign a(nother) difference of opinion broke out between the sons of Israel who were in error: some of them opted for Shilo while others preferred Mount Gerizim, and others again said, "Neither here nor there!"

A man was found who was to make holy a (certain) place: he was David son of Jesse from Bethlehem of the tribe of Judah. He was born in the year of Jubilee on the first day of the feast of Tabernacles. Jesse his father said, "Someone has been found who will make holy a (certain) place." The erroneous people all came together to celebrate his birth and agreed upon the Beit Maktesh Kifna,[39] which is al-Quds (Jerusalem). All of them were in agreement with this and pinned their hopes on it. Jesse went to Saul and counseled him to make war on the sons of Israel who were still living in the Beautiful Plain because they had not abandoned the illustrious Mountain nor followed their (Jessie and Saul's) whims, nor were they sacrificing wherever they sacrificed, and because they (the Samaritans) had the remnants of the Philistines fighting on their side. For when the sons of Israel who followed the truth had become weak and fewer in number, they had entered into a treaty with the (pagan) nations and sued for peace. Consequently, the hatred between them and the erroneous children of Israel intensified and hardened, and the latter became very angry.

---

[37] 1 Sam 4:18.
[38] 1 Sam 8–12.
[39] A Samaritan derogatory name given to the Temple Mount in Jerusalem.

Saul said to his people, "Victory has been revealed to me. These peoples don't bother me! Behold, I am going to empty out their holy places and rid their paths of whoever lives alongside them. Prepare provisions and arms. Let the men of Saul and the children of Jerusalem be summoned."

So they left his presence, and in the seventh hour of the day, with hearts brim full of arrogance, they encountered the sons of Israel in the Beautiful Plain on the Feast of Tabernacles. These latter were quite composed, little suspecting the (impending) disaster. They put to death all the Samaritans whom they found; and these became dispersed on the roads. They killed Shishi the Great High Priest in Greater Salem and took captive the women and children. They burnt the tabernacles, and going right up to the top of the Mountain, they took those who were hiding there and killed them like the priests and others besides. They demolished the stones of the altar and stayed for a few days on the Upper Mountain and in Luza, which was a city, wrecking havoc in it!

They pitched their tents in the Beautiful Meadow for thirty days and put to death all whom they found, until they had killed so many of them that their number couldn't be counted.

Nevertheless, the sons of Israel continued in obedience to God, and observance of the truth, for twenty-two years. They were unable to ascend the Holy Mountain, so they would kneel in worship in their places. The feasts were celebrated without joy and without bowers; the Synagogues were without congregations, and the Holy Place devoid of people praying. They (Saul and his men) sowed it, like all the (other) fields.

The Book of the Torah was the same for both groups, and they did not disagree over the Hebrew script. The Sabbaths and the Feasts and the Fallow years were the same, though the erroneous ones hold their heads up while the observant ones[40] have their heads bowed, and their speech is in an undertone. The ex-voto offerings and first fruits and tithes went to the Holy Place of the erroneous ones. Their priests served the erroneous ones[41] who went out on the feasts, an assembly too numerous to be counted, in great joy and tumult. As for the observant ones, Saul appointed persons to prevent them from going up to the Holy Mountain on their feasts. These used to go around, scouring the Mountain and all the roads leading up to it, killing whomsoever they found. They took possession of the villages and their wealth, and they settled some of their own people in

---

[40] The Samaritans.
[41] Those worshiping in Jerusalem.

them. They made life extremely burdensome for them. Because of the dreadful things that had happened to them, the Samaritans met in secret and decided to flee from before their enemies the erroneous ones, (thus) cutting themselves off from the illustrious Mountain. They said that when Almighty God restored his Favor to them and destroyed their enemies, they would return. They arrived at a decision in this matter and scattered to the four corners of the earth.

A group of them, however, decided to alter the feasts until God should bring them comfort: "Then we will return to the truth, and not follow the people of error." All their names were written in a Register, and they are as follows: Anis whose name was Antis, but they changed his name when they changed the feasts; Elishma' the Great, who was from among the Levites, together with his companions; and Kohath and his brethren from among the priestly dignitaries (who dwelt) in the Citadel; and Aisha son of Tola from the tribe of Asher, living in Hebron; and Machir from the tribe of Manasseh, who was living near Jerusalem; and Nahal from the tribe of Ephraim, who was living in Timna.

These were the leaders, and their brethren were those on Mount Gerizim. They agreed about changing the feasts and swore that when God restored the Radwan to them and they had the strength to return, they would abandon the changing of the feasts and revert to the truth. The total length of time from the taking away of the Radwan until the changing of the feasts was 90 years. The sons of Israel, the observant ones, dwelt with Sisir, king of Baisan. They made a covenant with him and he treated them well.

After this, the Philistines came together and did battle with the erroneous ones, Saul and his people, killing them. They crucified Saul and his three sons Jonathan, Aminadab, and Malchishua on the citadel of Baisan, and afterwards they were burnt.[42]

David son of Jesse of the blood line of Judah succeeded him as king when he was 18 years of age.[43] David had intercourse with a woman who was already married. Then he killed her husband.[44] He had married one of Saul's daughters, but he divorced her. She then married another man, whom David obliged to divorce her so that he could remarry her.[45] When he went out (on one occasion) with the Ark, which was in his possession, on a

---

[42] Cf. 1 Sam 31:2–7.
[43] Cf. 2 Sam 5:4.
[44] 2 Sam 11.
[45] 1 Sam 3:15–16.

wheeled cart to the Holy House, a priest had gone ahead to greet him from on top of the conveyance, but the cow which was under the cart (supporting it) gored him, and he died.[46] He then left the Ark in the house of one of his young servants.

He used to indulge in all sorts of irresponsible behavior and began offering sacrifice by his own hand wherever he pleased and blessing the people; he ate the bread that was made on the Sabbath altar. He also consecrated the threshing floor which he had bought for fifty gold shekels from Nabui. And he likewise consecrated the cow with the cart. From that time on he made the threshing floor their Qibla. David was (for all that) accustomed to go on pilgrimage to Mount Gerizim and upon it to offer tithes and sacrifices and ex-voto offerings and alms. It is recorded that David continued to act according to the mind of Samuel and Saul. Neither he nor his people had a Qibla until he reached the age of 70. Jerusalem was the Seat of his kingdom.

This is the genealogy of David: son of Salma, son of Tarah, son of Nahshon, son of Amminadab, son of Ram, son of Hezron, son of Perez, son of Juda. His father's mother was a Moabitess because they had intermarried with them at the time of the heresy.[47] Her name was Naomi.

David had a number of sons, among whom were Amnon, Absalom, and Shalima, that is, Solomon. He also had a daughter, Tamar.[48] Now Amnon, her brother, loved Tamar, and was stricken by a strong passion for her, and fell sick from it. One of his acquaintances could tell from his appearance and strange behavior that he was tormented. So he asked him about it, and he explained his difficulties and his love for his own sister. He (the acquaintance) suggested to him that he stay at home until David his father and all his family came to visit him. And when Tamar came in to see him, he should tell her that he was entranced and that the very sight of her restored him to health. After she had been put at her ease by this, he could satisfy his lust with her and have his way with her. So he did as he was advised, and when Tamar came in to him, he got up and raped her. No sooner had he done this to her than immediately he felt a loathing for her, threw her out, and she went away from him disheveled and bleeding. She was wearing a white, long-sleeved cotton garment.[49] She was sister to

---

[46] 2 Sam 6:6–8.
[47] Cf. 1 Chron 2:11, 12.
[48] 2 Sam 13.
[49] 2 Sam 13:18.

Amnon by his own father and mother. Absalom, her full brother, found her as she was coming out of Amnon's quarters, weeping and exhausted.

"What is the matter with you," he asked her.

She replied, "My brother Amnon has violated me and has done to me what you can see."

Absalom was angry enough to kill Amnon, but when David learned Absalom's hatred for his brother Amnon, he prevented his doing this. Two and a half years passed before it occurred to him to resort to subterfuge. He went to his father David and asked him if he could enjoy himself with his friends. David assumed that he had forgotten what Amnon had done to his sister Tamar, so he granted him the permission he sought. He was reclining with his company, and his brother Amnon with him; he instructed the cup bearer to make him drunk. When he was completely drunk, Absalom's young men took him away from the festivities and killed him, cutting off his head.

When David got to hear of this, he sought to kill Absalom, who fled to Hebron, where he stayed for a while.[50] A large number of his father's army joined him there. When David sought to review his troops and count his young men, he found that the greater number of them had sided with Absalom his son. Then David set out after him and joined battle with him at the Rock of Ephraim.[51] A terrible battle ensued between them, and the number of those who died on both sides was around 20,000 men. When the crowd was in the heat of battle, Absalom got hung up by the hair of his head, on the branch of an olive tree, and he remained hanging there, unable to free himself.[52]

One of his father's soldiers came upon him and informed one of his father's commanders about the matter. He ordered him to kill him, so he went back and killed him. When David learned of his being killed, he grieved over him bitterly. David grew old and was stricken by the palsy. So he summoned all his leaders to assemble, entered into a covenant with them, and they swore obedience to Solomon his son.

They accepted him, covenanting with him and swearing obedience to him, and (swearing) that they would enlist under his command. Treasures

---

[50] Cf. 2 Sam 13:37.
[51] Cf. 2 Sam 18:6–7.
[52] 2 Sam 18:9–15.

of gold and silver and bronze were given to him from what he (David) had looted from the Arameans and the Greeks, and so much else besides that it could not be counted nor estimated. David was king for 47 years, 7 of which were in Hebron and 40 in Jerusalem, and then David died.[53]

His son Solomon succeeded him as king. All the tribes obeyed him, and he was ambitious in the quest for learning in his day.[54] David had laid down the foundations of the Temple, but it was Solomon his son who completed it in (the first) four years of his reign. It was 60 cubits long and 20 cubits in breadth.[55] In it he put all the representations of the entire animal kingdom. He put a throne in it and plated it with gold. The roof was held up by 12 statues of oxen—three looking towards the north, three towards the south, three towards the west, and three towards the east. He had ornaments made for it, over 2,000 cups inlaid with flowers.[56] None of the kings of the earth had ever made a throne like it. He had two statues of angels made from olive wood that he plated with pure gold. He made them overshadow the four corners of the Temple with their wings, having their faces turned one towards the other. He made pillars of bronze adjacent to the Temple door: a column on the right and a column on the left.[57] On the two columns was copper filigree work the whole length of the columns, covering them like a curtain.

He made seven pulpits for the Temple: (in fact he made) seven of everything. And he wisely put whatever he made on rollers so that it could be moved by this means wherever he wished. Thus Solomon constructed the Temple—the aforementioned Temple renowned among men and angels. When he had finished making it, priests came from everywhere and offered sacrifices in it on the day of its inauguration, of a thousand head of cattle.[58] Mention is also made of a throne that he made of gold and silver (and put) at the gate of his Palace. He also made 300 shields of gold and silver that he hung on Mount Lebanon so that people could see that in his time there was no fear and no depravity.[59] He imposed taxes to be paid by each of the 12 tribes annually: each month by a different tribe. From this tax he received enormous revenues that could not be counted or calculated. And this did

---

[53] 1 Kgs 2:10.
[54] 1 Kgs 4:1–3.
[55] 1 Kgs 6:2.
[56] 1 Kgs 6:14–36.
[57] 1 Kgs 7:15, 2 Chron 3:17.
[58] Cf. 1 Kgs 8:5.
[59] 1 Kgs 10:17–18.

not include the wealth that came to him from (subject) kings and the commerce that he carried on. He had 700 wives and 300 concubines, to say nothing of women from the Amonites, Moabites, and Sidonites and one of Pharaoh's daughters.[60] They used to take the daughters of kings from all the nations (for him); he was in thrall to the excess of his passion (for them), built a temple for them, set up their idols in them, and allowed them to worship them. When daughters of kings came to him, they made him agree to allow them to practice their religions, and not to prevent them from worshiping idols.

The stories told about him are too long to be expounded here.

Sixth Excerpt: Of Elijah, prophets, and the Holy Scroll[61]

They claimed that they had prophets, but they attributed to God—Powerful and Glorious—what he had not said to them. They said that among them there were some who spoke the truth and others who did not speak the truth. In fact, there was none who spoke the truth among them. For truly, as they used to talk after the manner of sorcery and astrology. They used to manipulate the people and confuse their thinking; they used to lead them along the path of crime and lies and led them astray. At that time, Hanania was claiming to be a prophet, as was Elijah.

This Elijah drowned in the Jordan and died. They claimed that he had ascended into heaven after his death and that he had been given the keys of heaven, so that it would not rain unless he wished it to do so. They also claimed that he went to Sarafand and found a woman who was baking bread, and that he stayed there until she had locked up, and that he then stole the bread. The infant son of the woman then died of hunger, and the woman chased after him for her jar and informed him about her son's death. Thereupon he prayed for him and he came back to life.[62] They tell atrocious lies, which God forbid! A number passed themselves off as prophets, among them Eli son of Abikush, and Abdil (son of) Hanania, and Sadaqia and Alyishm and Ailusus, and others as well.[63]

The family of Phinehas and the family of Joseph from Mount Gerizim did not deviate. They served no strange gods, and they did not worship and

---

[60] 1 Kgs 11:1–3.
[61] Stenhouse, *The Kitab al-Tarikh*, 68–69. Used by permission.
[62] 1 Kgs 17.
[63] Are Eli and Alyishm references to Joel and Amos? Stenhouse asks the same question in *The Kitab al Tarikh*, xvii.

kneel to idolatrous images. They did not accept any prophet after Moses, nor did they believe in any book other than the Torah. They observed solely the Scroll of the Law. They added nothing to it, nor did they subtract anything from it.

Seventh Excerpt: The return to the land[64]

So Abdal, the Great High Priest, and his assembly wrote to all the cities in which the Samaritans were scattered among the nations, and said to them, "Brothers—may Almighty God strengthen you—know that our God, and the God of our fathers, has looked down upon us in his mercy and been gracious towards us in his compassion. He has come back to us and answered us; he has heard our voices. He has freely granted to us that our enemies (themselves) suggest to us that we should return to our places and go back to our homeland and that we should serve our Lord on the Mountain of his Holiness and in the Place of his angels. Now, we are delaying on your account and are waiting for you in the city of Haran. Let us all come together and return to God in good fortune and in peace."

The letters reached them, and after reading them, they sent back their reply to Abdal, the Great High Priest, and said to him, "We will not listen to you, nor will we return except under the leadership of a prophet like Moses, as happened to our fathers when they went out of Egypt."

Thereupon he wrote a second time to them and said to them, "O my brethren, rise and set out; otherwise we cannot be responsible for your blood or for the blood of your children. For there will never again rise up a prophet like Moses to lead you out; nor will there ever again be a king like Pharaoh to bar your way. Open up the Law and read it, and then you will understand that there will never again be a prophet after Moses. For were the (hypothetical) prophet who might come after him to do what Moses did, there would be no need for him. For it is said in the Law, 'I have bestowed upon you a perfect Law. Neither add to it, nor take away from it,'[65] throughout all your generations. It will remain valid for the generations of your children, and your children's children for as long as the wise, divine decree lasts. And this is so because the Almighty Creator knew through his foreknowledge how the rules of the world were to be established and how best to improve the lot of the human species, and so he made this Law to be in harmony with the condition of the human race and in conformity

---

[64] Stenhouse, *The Kitab al-Tarikh*, 81–84. Used by permission.
[65] Deut 4:2.

with the most perfect order: a surer way for man to perfect his condition in this world and in the world to come. This was to ensure the means of his arriving at an improvement in his circumstances and to ensure the means of his continuing in this perfected condition that will lead him (eventually) to salvation. And were the prophet who comes not to do what Moses, upon whom be peace, did, then he has already forbidden your accepting him or listening to him. For he also included in the Law that if it is good for this generation with their differences of character, status, and whims, then it will (remain) good for all future generations and for all persons growing up. Now it is for you to choose what you must do; and we will be innocent of your blood and of what will befall you."

Some of them accepted this while others of them rejected it. A great number remained on in exile and have never come back up to our own day, for, they reasoned, "surely there will be other exiles after this one, and of what advantage is it to us to return? It is better to stay here, where we are."

And these remained as they were, and have never returned up to our own day.

Eighth Excerpt: Concerning contention over the Torah[66]

When Zerubbabel and his assembly of Jews all came together in Haran and appeared before Surdi the king there, a debate took place between them and the Samaritans over the Qibla.[67] The Samaritans produced the Book of the Great Scroll from the Temple in Nineveh and read out the verses that show that Mount Gerizim is the Qibla. Zerubbabel then produced a Scroll that he maintained was the Scroll of David and which (he claimed) showed that David said that the threshing floor in Jerusalem was the Qibla.

A debate then ensued between them in the presence of the king. The Elders of the family of Ephraim and the family of Phinehas said, "The Almighty Creator forbade the offering of sacrifice after the entrance into Palestine except in the Chosen Place thus: 'See to it that you do not offer your whole offerings in any place at random,' to the end of the verse.[68] The sacrifice which he commanded to be offered on Mount Gerizim was after the entrance into Palestine, and this entails the necessity of the offering's being made in the Chosen Place, that is to say, upon Mount Gerizim, for 'it is the

---

[66] Stenhouse, *The Kitab al-Tarikh*, 85–93. Used by permission.
[67] The direction one should be facing during prayer.
[68] Deut 12:13.

Chosen Place and also the offering of Whole Offerings and Thank Offerings. These latter are two legal terms. Each of the two was to be offered in
the Tabernacle which is the dwelling Place of God's Angels, and the
Shekina, as is written, 'If his offering be a Whole Offering,'[69] to the end of
the passage at the words 'before the Lord.' Or again, 'If a man's offering be
a Thank Offering' up to the last words 'he shall present it before the
Lord'[70] and the saying 'he shall slaughter it before the Lord'[71] and 'he shall
slaughter it before the entrance to the Tabernacle.'[72] If this (interpretation) be correct, then the command about sacrificing Whole Offerings and
Thank Offerings on Mount Gerizim involves the erection of a Tabernacle
on it; otherwise the offering of the aforementioned sacrifice which had to
be correctly performed in it would not be valid. This is as much of obligation as the duty (to offer sacrifice). The text involves the building of (such)
a place and continuing to offer sacrifice in it. If it be necessary that sacrifice
be continually offered in it, then it is equally necessary that the Shekina
should dwell in the place. This is what was enjoined in the saying 'the place
which the Lord your God will choose as a dwelling for his name,'[73] as all
shades of opinion and belief will agree."

Then they put the question to them, "Is it necessary for the sons of Israel
to recite the Name of God on Mount Gerizim or not? If you say 'no,' then
you contradict the Torah, for the Almighty Creator commanded the recitation of the Chapter of Benedictions upon it. He commanded six of the
tribes to recite the Benediction over Israel upon it. But the Benediction requires an elucidation of his Mighty Name according to the saying 'You shall
pronounce the Blessing on Mount Gerizim.'[74] And this is to the point. As
for the recitation, and the detailing, and the point of (its being) here, that is,
the recitation mentioned in the saying 'You shall pronounce . . .'—the main
thing is the *doing* in the place (designated). And this is more properly so of
the Blessings. For the point of the Blessing is that prosperity be increased
and that its effects be obtained. And the point here is this prophetic statement about it, which has the force of a prayer and the same pattern. And
this can be brought home to you by the statement at the beginning of the
verse 'Understand that this day I offer you (the choice between) a Blessing

---

[69] Lev 1:3.
[70] Lev 3:1.
[71] Lev 1:5.
[72] Lev 3:2.
[73] Deut 12:11.
[74] Deut 11:29.

and a Curse.'[75] As is well known, what the Messenger (of God) promul-
gated before that day was the recitation of the section of the Blessings and
Curses over all the people, and he made a covenant about it with them according to the saying 'These are the words of the covenant which the Lord
made,' to the end of the verse.[76] He commanded him to read the Blessing
over Israel, in the saying 'Those who shall stand for the Blessing of the
people on Mount Gerizim.'[77] As regards the fact that both the passages we
have quoted require the explanation of the Attributes and the Illustrious
Names of God, this can be seen from the saying 'Then all the peoples of
the earth shall see that Yahweh is called (by this name) there, for you,'[78] to
the end. The reason for reading נקרא, that is, 'was called for your sakes,' is
so that when a people is powerful and capable, then its capability may be
recognized. And when the Almighty willed that the sons of Israel be (recognized as) under his dominion, he took this name. He ordered the Messenger (of God) to make it known that it was a sign of God's aid for them
and a symbol of the disenchantment of their enemies, and as a proof of
help—help for them. As he said in his speech (to the) Pharaoh, 'Yahweh
the God of the Hebrews met us,'[79] to the end of the verse. So this means
that if the Almighty wished to receive a name for our sakes, then he is
more than enough assistance for us while, on the contrary, for you he
is disappointment. You must obey him; we have to praise him. But this will
be authentic only if the Name is clearly pronounced and not just written
down. For this reason he prepared a reply for those whom he permitted to
elucidate his Name, saying to Aaron and to his house, 'They shall pronounce my name over the Israelites, and I shall bless them.'[80] Apart from
this instance, he forbade its utterance and threatened anyone who utters
it, in the verse 'Whoever utters the name of the Lord shall be put to
death.'[81] It is clearly intended, therefore, that his Mighty Name be manifested; and it is well known and incontrovertible that it was on Mount
Gerizim that the tribes were meant to utter the Mighty Name of God.
That is the sense of the word 'Chosen' for the uttering of his Name there,
as we maintain and as you deny. He said, 'But you (shall go) to the place
which the Lord your God will choose to receive his Name, that it may

---

[75] Deut 11:26.
[76] Deut 28:69.
[77] Deut 27:12.
[78] Deut 28:10.
[79] Exod 3:18.
[80] Num 6:27.
[81] Lev 24:16.

dwell there,'[82] to the end of the verse. In this passage, he enumerates all the acts of worship that the Holy One will make holy in the place where he wanted the tribes of Israel to manifest his Name forever and ever. And therefore it must be that it (Mount Gerizim) is the Holy One, the Place of the Tabernacle upon which the offices of worship are to be performed, and the designated place for the fulfillment of the duties of religion. All of this implies that God has manifested himself on Mount Gerizim. However, there is nothing of any of this in the passage on the Cursing. The Creator mentions this only in the context of the Blessing; it is not mentioned in the context of the Cursing. For Blessing is a kind of recompense, in that it is commensurate with the effort taken. Whereas the Cursing is a kind of punishment, which is not meant to be striven for. Thus the Place of Blessing is opposite the Place of Cursing. For the uttering of a curse dismays the soul, saddens the heart, and depresses the spirit while the Blessing is the contrary of this. Mount Gerizim is no Place for Cursing and in fact is quite unsuitable for it, and is a Place that is free of it. It follows, then, that this is the Place designated for the manifestation of his Name and the carrying out of the formalities of worship. Otherwise, talking about it would involve a contradiction, for, as is implied in the proverbial saying 'Can there be joy and happiness where cursing manifests itself?' this excludes Mount Ebal, as is obvious. The opposite occurs on Mount Gerizim on account of the Blessing, as in the passage 'Because the Lord your God has blessed you'[83]—something that is true of Mount Gerizim but altogether untrue of Mount Ebal. This is one of the proofs that it is the Chosen Place, as (can be seen from) the following verse, 'In the Place where I cause my Name to be invoked, I will come to you and bless you.'[84] The meaning of 'I will come' is really 'I shall have my angels dwell there.'"

They adduced proofs from many other texts as well and demonstrated that the Qibla, that is to say the Mountain designated by Almighty God in his Holy Law revealed by means of Moses son of Amram, upon whom be peace, can be none other than Mount Gerizim.

Surdi the king cross-examined them thoroughly. He and the learned men of his day pondered the subjects that had been debated, and weighed the proofs. When the Samaritans had finished presenting their proofs, he said to Zerubbabel and his companions, "Have you anything left to say?"

---

[82] Deut 12:5.
[83] Deut 12:7.
[84] Exod 20:24.

They answered, "Our tradition has it that David and Solomon both said that the Qibla is Jerusalem!"

Thereupon Sanballat the Levite said to them, "If, as you say, David and Solomon considered their Qibla to be *the* Qibla, where used the priests to go (before that) to present their offerings every year, as He says, 'year after year . . . in the place which the Lord God will choose'?[85] If you accept the Law, then accept (all) that is found in it."

Surdi the king then said, "Let us offer sacrifice on Mount Gerizim!"

Thereupon Zerubbabel became enraged in the presence of the king and said, "The writings which we possess prophesy that sacrifices will (only) be offered in Jerusalem." To this Sanballat retorted, saying to Surdi the king, "The books which are in the possession of Zerubbabel are forgeries, deceits, and lies. Order me to, and I will throw them into the fire. But as for this Scroll of the Torah (of ours), let him throw it if he can."

So, Surdi the king ordered Sanballat to throw the Books of David into the fire. He threw them into the fire, and they were burnt up. Then Surdi commanded Zerubbabel to throw the Book of the Torah (of the Samaritans). He took it, opened it, looked in it, and then said, "I can not throw it. For my Book was mine alone; but this Book is mine and his because the one who wrote it is the lord, the Messenger (of God) Moses, upon whom be perfect peace."

Surdi the king, in reply, said to Zerubbabel, "I consider your Books to be nothing but forgeries and lies. Why did Sanballat throw your Books into the fire while you do not throw his Books?"

Out of fear, Zerubbabel then took the Scroll of the Torah and threw it into the fire. It leapt into the air and came out of the fire. Then Zerubbabel asked permission to throw it a second time; so he ordered him to throw it. He threw it the second time, but it flew and came out of the fire again. So he asked permission to throw it a third time. He took hold of it, opened it, spat upon it, and then threw it into the fire. The place where he spat was burnt, but the Book leapt out of the fire and flew into the presence of Surdi the king. The king became very afraid, and Abdal and Sanballat rose in his esteem and were honored by him before all the people. The nations learned that the Book of the Torah that God had revealed by means of Moses, upon whom be peace, was the only perfect one.

---

[85] Deut 15:19–20.

Ninth Excerpt: Of Ezra[86]

He forbade the rebuilding of Jerusalem, and they demolished what had already been erected in it. (Consequently) bad feeling worsened between the Samaritans and the Jews, and their mutual loathing intensified. Because of what happened to the spirit of the Jews over all this, Ezra and Zerubbabel set about making up an alphabet of their own, different from the Hebrew alphabet; they made it of 27 characters.[87] They tampered with the Holy Law, copying it out of the alphabet they had newly created.

They cut out many passages of the Holy Law because of the fourth of the ten commandments and the references to Mount Gerizim and its boundaries. They added to it, cut things from it, changed it, and misconstrued it. May God oppose them! In the morning of the Day of Days, Ezra, may he be cursed,[88] called the Jews together and said to them, "God said to me yesterday when he gave me this Book, 'This is the Book of God, the authentic truth. Put your faith in it and make copies of this one alone.'"

Tenth Excerpt: A Samaritan Diaspora and the Dustan sect[89]

We shall now return to the topic of the high priests, the favor of God be upon them! We have already mentioned the rule of Hezekiah, what happened in his days and how long he held office. He thereupon died and passed to the mercy of God. Hananiah assumed office after him and continued in the high priesthood for twenty-four years; and after him reigned Amram, who held the priesthood for thirty-two years. This Amram is the one whose son King Darius took as a husband for his daughter. The reason for this being that Darius' daughter had seen in her sleep a boy, a handsome young man, standing before her while someone kept saying to her, "This shall be your husband." She awakened from her sleep with her mind agitated and her heart tormented, and when her father saw her, she was overcome with passionate love. Now since he loved her greatly, he said to her, "What is the matter, my little daughter?" So she told him the story and recounted her dream, whereupon he summoned painters who painted many pictures and brought them to her. And she said: "He resembles this

---

[86] Stenhouse, *The Kitab al-Tarikh*, 97–98. Used by permission.
[87] The additional letters being the *sofit* forms.
[88] Ezra, who in Jewish tradition is called Ezra the Blessed because of his role in preserving Torah, is called by the Samaritans Ezra the Cursed because of his role in perverting the Torah.
[89] Bowman, *Samaritan Documents,* 78–83. Used by permission.

picture." The King then supplied that picture to several men who were to go round to various countries searching for anyone who looked like it. And they went round until they came to Nablus. Now it happened that the son of Chief Priest Amram had just then come out, and they found that he resembled that picture, at which they seized him and took him to the king. And when the king's daughter saw him, she said, "This is the very person whom I saw in my dream." She soon was married to him and had three children by him, two sons and a daughter. Some time later he said to the king, "I have a longing to see my father, my mother, and my family," to which the king replied: "Go wherever you wish." So he departed, together with his wife and children, and reached Badhan. When the Samaritans heard of his coming, they were disturbed and said, "Why did he not expose himself to death by remaining steadfast in his faith? Instead, he has sinned and brought grievous shame upon himself and upon the nation." Some of them were of the opinion that he should be killed, while others thought otherwise. The final resolve was to kill him, and so they killed him, his wife, his children, and his accompanying servants. When King Darius heard about the killing of his daughter and her husband and children and those who were with them, it affected him tremendously, and he assembled troops in order to kill all the Samaritans. Now, those who had killed the king's daughter and her companions fled to Babel and lived in safety, while those who had been of the opinion that these persons should not be killed remained in Nablus, where a countless number of them were killed, and the rest were taken to be punished by the king. When they were asked, "Why have you done what you have done?" they replied: "We have done nothing. Those who did the killing told us that they had done it out of zeal for their faith. Now all of them have fled to Babel and are safe. Yet, it is we who are about to perish." So the king commanded that the sword be withdrawn from them and that no more be killed.

And the King, who loved the Jews, set up over them a king from among them named Simeon,[90] who commanded them to build the sanctuary. And when they had finished building it, they expressed joy and gladness, saying, "There is no sanctuary but ours, no priesthood but our priesthood, and no Levites except those who are around us." They prevailed over the Samaritans and forbade them to go up to Mount Gerizim; they demolished the altar and the Temple which 'Abdel had built; and they remained upon the mountain for forty days, laying it waste and defiling it. They set watchmen over the Samaritans to prevent them from worshiping towards Mount

---

[90] Simeon Maccabee.

Gerizim, observing their festivals and gathering in their holy places, and they severely oppressed them. When this became too much for the Samaritans, they wrote to those who had gone to Babel, and they came over, so that they all joined together to form an army and set out with raging fury in their hearts. First, they killed the Jewish watchmen that were placed over them, then they turned on the Jews and killed an incalculable number of them. Thereupon they went up to Jerusalem and killed all who were in it; but Simeon, the king of the Jews, fled, and they did not get hold of him. They demolished the structure which the Jews had constructed, and razed the wall of the sanctuary from its foundation. When King Darius heard of this, he stood by "Those Who Went Astray" (that is, the Jews) and helped them; he subdued the "Observant Ones" (that is, the Samaritans) and did not allow them to ascend the mountain; he rebuilt the wall of the sanctuary once again; and he gave the Jews authority over the Samaritans, so that they reduced them to nothing until the Samaritans could not bear to continue to remain under their rule. The Samaritans thereupon assembled in the Synagogue, and as they pondered over their plight, they found their spirits broken, overwhelmed, and subdued, and they themselves left with no strength or power; and they agreed to depart from under the rule of the Jews and to look for relief from them and their tyranny. They took out the Law of God and deposited it in a place that they knew, while they wept and wailed so bitterly that they were nearly undone because of the intensity of their tears and their moaning. Afterwards, they embarked in ships; some of them reached the outlying regions of the earth, some went to Babel, and some to Wadi al-Kutha. That is why the Jews call the Samaritans "Kutheans" and go so far as to deny them the name of Israel. Some of the Samaritans went toward the rising of the sun;[91] others remained in Nablus as they were and suffered such calamities and afflictions as cannot be described. Those who remained were not permitted to observe anything pertaining to their faith, either Sabbath, or festival, or New Moon's Day, or reading in the Law of Moses, the son of Amram—upon him be the most bountiful peace—until they forgot it. After this, Simeon, the king of the Jews, died—may God have no mercy upon him—and there reigned after him Arkiya, his son. In his reign there arose a quarrel between the house of Ithamar and the house of Manasseh. The latter said to the family of Ithamar, "Let us have a portion of the Meadow of al-Baha (Splendor)." An adjudicator then arose who thought that he could satisfy them, but he did not succeed at all, for he said, "Mount Gerizim belongs to you, and to them, and to all Israel; Nablus belongs to the house of Ephraim alone; the

---

[91] I.e., east.

Meadow of al-Baha belongs to all the tribes; and the Scroll of the Law belongs to all Israel."

And the Jews increased in unbelief and error, and the nations were troubled by their tyranny and their error. Thereupon the kings assembled against them, killed an incalculable number of them, and finally besieged them in Jerusalem until they perished. The kings then took possession of Jerusalem and laid it waste. Thus, the community of the Jews was scattered among the various countries, and trouble and disaster overtook them. At that time, the Samaritans were gathered together from beyond the sea, from Babel, from Wadi al-Kutha, and from every place, and they came back to Mount Gerizim, rejoicing in their return; this was done by command of the king. And the ten stones were returned to their places in the Mountain in order that the Scroll of the Law might be read there.

About that time, a sect split off from the community of the Samaritans and adopted a teaching of its own; they were called the Dustan because of their abolition of the legitimate festivals and of all that they had received by tradition from their fathers and their grandfathers. They differ from the Samaritans in some things; every water-spring in which is found a creeping thing they found unclean, and when a woman begins to menstruate, they do not commence counting (the period of her impurity) until the evening of that day, on the analogy of the festivals which run from sunset to sunset. They banned the eating of eggs except those found when birds are slaughtered. They likewise declared unclean the unborn fetus of animals after their death. They also declared that overshadowing of tombs causes uncleanness and that, consequently, anyone whose shadow fell on a tomb must remain unclean seven days. They banned the benediction "Blessed be our God for ever"; they forbade pronouncing the name *YHWH* as the Samaritans do and pronounced it instead *ELOHIM*. They claimed that in the book that they had and which was written by the children of the Messenger (of God), it was stated that God shall be worshiped in the land of Zawila until the time when He shall be worshiped on Mount Gerizim. They renounced the use of astronomical tables, and they made the number of days in every month thirty days, without exception. They abolished the true festivals, as well as the commandment of fasting and mortification; and they used to reckon the fifty days from the morrow of the Passover, as do the Jews. They allowed their priests to enter a house suspected of uncleanness, in order to see what was in it, but without saying anything, so that when they came back outside, they would be clean even though the house was suspected of uncleanness; this on the analogy of a house known to be clean. And when a house was attached to the unclean house and they wanted to know whether it was clean or unclean, a man would sit down facing it and watch it, and if a clean bird perched on it, they declared it clean, but if an unclean bird perched on it, they declared it unclean. On the Sabbath day they considered it unlawful to eat or drink from vessels made of copper or glass or of anything capable of becoming unclean and then being cleansed, but only from earthen vessels, which, if they became unclean, cannot be cleansed. They would not feed or water their cattle on the Sabbath day but would instead place before the cattle on Friday whatever was needed for them. They differed from the Samaritans also in many things other than matters of belief and law, and for this reason they separated from them and made for themselves synagogues and a priesthood of their own.

The son of the (Samaritan) High Priest became their spiritual leader, and this is how it happened: The (Samaritan) community brought irrefutable evidence against him to the effect that they had found him with a loose woman; they therefore shunned him and placed him under a ban. His name was Zura'ahu.[92] When he saw that there was no hope for him in the (Samaritan) community, he inclined to the Dustan, who accepted him and made him their High Priest. He composed a book in which he satirized all the (Samaritan) high priests, and he did it in a most skillful manner. There was no one in his time more learned than he, and that is why they called him Zura'ahu.

Eleventh Excerpt: Of Alexander and Darius[93]

Then, when Alexander saw how magnificent this place was, how nothing better or more honorable was to be found in all the world, he decided to erect a place of worship in it. He asked the High Priest about this, but the Great High Priest refused, and this request weighed heavily upon him and upon the Elders of Israel. The High Priest said to him, "O king, you manifest the way of your justice, and we have been impressed by the impartiality of your intelligence and favor: do not act in a way contrary to what you have desired; do not act except as you have indicated." So he forbore from this—afraid of the efficacy of their prayers against him. When he had decided to set out, he said to Hezeqia, the High Priest, "I have seen, under

---

[92] "He sowed"; perhaps this is an answer to the story of Neh 13:28, casting doubt on the priestly lineage associated with the Dustan.

[93] Stenhouse, *The Kitab al-Tarikh,* 116–20. Used by permission.

the circumstances, what your blessing has done for me; I should now like your advice about fighting my enemies."

So the High Priest said to him, "Be careful that your decisions don't pander to your passions, without satisfying your God and Creator. And take care that sound opinion doesn't desert you and that passion doesn't master you. Do not do what you do out of a desire for worldly achievement or the pleasure of victory. This world is a House of Deceits, and just as you have been given, so shall you be deprived. Let your biggest worry be to serve your Lord. And if it should happen that you have to kill your enemy, then do not kill him without some brake on your passions and your anger. For to be always angry and to go against sound opinion will lead one to pass over into the wilderness of deception and on into the pools of death, submerging one in the seas of destruction. Moderate your fiery anger with cool forbearance, and treat this passion with the medicine of good advice. Your aim must be to get the army of your enemy to fight among themselves; and then you will benefit from his surprise (at this tactic). And the way to do this is to have spies planted among those closest to your enemy, especially among those of them who are better informed but easily impressionable, and deceive those among them who may easily be taken in. Let your aim be that they (the spies) glean information for you from their slips of the tongue that will lead you to the secret of their king, which is better than having them deceive you. And if such a secret comes your way, broadcast it, make it known for your own ends. Write it on the tongues of his associates that he (the king) is suing for peace, and spread it secretly. Put in your letter what you consider to be the genuine secrets of your enemy, and spread them in your court so that the spies (of your enemy) who are amongst you may carry them to him, and thus lessen the numbers of those upon whom he can still rely in the event of war. This will be the cause of his spirit's drooping before you, and you will obtain what you desire. There is no doubt about it; put your trust in it."

When he heard this from him, he found it very agreeable, and he was guided by it, and he (accordingly) set off to do battle with Darius. Darius was a mighty and powerful king who had conquered all the kings of the Persians and the Greeks. Philip, who was king of Greece and father of this Alexander, paid tribute to him.

After he was killed and was succeeded by his son, Darius sent to him, asking him to pay what his father had customarily paid. He refused to do this. So he sent a second time to him to ask him, and with the envoy he sent a bag with poppy seeds in it. He (Alexander) asked his teacher Aristotle about the secret (meaning) of this, and he said to him, "By this he wants to say that the number of his soldiers is very great, and that the Persians are powerful."

So he summoned the envoy, and taking the poppy seeds, he ate them in his presence and sent off his answer to him, giving him a bag with mustard seeds in it to carry back with him, to symbolize large numbers and invincibility.

When Darius saw the message and the grains of mustard seeds, he became angry and incensed. He summoned his soldiers and his commanders and ordered them to set out with all his forces. News of this reached Alexander; he also learned that Darius had said in his Council, "This boy is pretentious, but my fame and my army are powerful. The way to defeat him is such and such."

The conversations of the Two-Horned One reached Darius, but (in fact) it was Alexander himself who had spread this around, and the spy of Darius reported it back to him. Then there arose a disagreement between him and his close associates, and he sought (to identify) the spy planted in their midst. They became afraid and decided to kill him. They took him unawares, and cut off his head, and came with it to Alexander to ingratiate themselves with him. His answer to them was, "Bury his head," and to issue a command to have them crucified. They were crucified, and above them they wrote, "This is the punishment of one who betrays his king and deceives the people of his faith and his country." The nations presented no difficulties for him after this, and mankind obeyed him. The total life span of Alexander was 36 years, and for 18 of these he ruled.

Twelfth Excerpt: Gives proverbial advice[94]

As for the High Priest Hezeqia, when news of Alexander's death reached him, he mourned him and feared for the Samaritans from his successor, for in his day he had been a benefactor of theirs.

The nephew of the High Priest Hezeqia was appointed Governor in the region around Nablus. His name was Simon, and he was a man who accumulated wealth and loved the world. When his uncle saw him preoccupied with the world and very industrious about possessing it, he rebuked him, but he refused to change. Then he (Simon) became seriously ill, and his

---

[94] Ibid., 124–26. Used by permission.

uncle looked after him, and (although) he saw what he should do to (help) him, he saw no interest (on the part of Simon). So he said to him, "O nephew, the condition that you are in is like that of a man who has drunk salt water; every time he drinks more of it, he becomes thirstier. And you, every time you gain a piece of this world, it is only for you an incentive to gain more: Death is closer than it may seem."

Then he said to him, "O uncle, I am industrious to possess what will be sufficient for me and what will make me independent of other men."

So he said to him, "O nephew, if you seek from the world what will be sufficient for you, then the smallest part will suffice for you. But if you seek from it what will make you (completely) independent, then not even all of it will make you such.

"O nephew, this world and the next one are two opposites for human beings. Whichever of the two prevails over him, he will identify with it.

"O nephew, the acquisition of habitual good deeds is better than the acquisition of divisive gold.

"O nephew, good deeds are the best mount for a man to ride upon in order to be saved.

"O nephew, the world is a sea; and the next life is the seashore; and good deeds are the best vessel for a slave to board, to arrive at it.

"O nephew, this world is transitory, and the next life is permanent. What is lasting is better than what disappears.

"O nephew, anyone who demands too much from this world is like the silkworm: every time it spins its cocoon around itself, its prison grows."

Thirteenth Excerpt: Translation of the Septuagint

This excerpt tells about the translation of the Septuagint and provides a lengthy explanation of the preference for the Samaritan Torah over the Jewish Torah. Following the discussion of the Torah is an explanation of the Samaritan relationship to the Sadducees, Pharisees, and Hasidim (Essenes?).[95]

---

[95] Bowman, *Samaritan Documents,* 126–35. Used by permission.

In the day of this above-mentioned (High) Priest, Dalyah, there arose a king whose name was Faltama (Ptolemy). He loved learning and wisdom, was diligent in gathering books containing learning and wisdom, eagerly occupied himself with them, and exerted himself in making himself familiar with them. Now, when the Egyptians saw that he pursued the way of justice and traveled in the path of truth, they chose him to be king over them; they thereupon sent a message to him asking him to come to them so that they might set him up to reign over them. So he went out and came to them, and they made him king over them; and when he learned that the cause of his election was his love of knowledge, his eagerness for it, and his traveling (in the way) of justice, his desire for wisdom increased all the more. He searched for it ever more diligently, and he intensified his efforts to gather books dealing with it. So he assembled books and searched for them in every country and place that he might become known for his learning.

Now, in the tenth year of his reign, he became acquainted with the disagreement that existed between the Samaritans and the Jews regarding the Torah and with the refusal of the Samaritans to accept any book other than the Torah that was reputedly handed down by a prophet. In his desire to become acquainted with this matter, he sent to the Jews, asking them for a number of their elders, and addressed a similar request to the Samaritans also. And so there came from the Samaritans a man called Aaron, and with him a company of Samaritans among whom was the scholar Symmachus, and Jahudta. From the Jews there came a man called Eleazar, and with him a company also. Now, when Ptolemy learned of their arrival at Alexandria, which at that time was a seat of knowledge, he commanded that lodgings be assigned to them according to their number in the place which is called al-Ruwak and that each one of them be kept separated from his companions. Then he commanded also that there should be with every one of them a Greek scribe to write down what every one of them translated. And so the Samaritans translated the Torah while the Jews translated both the Torah and the other books that they had; and it is said that the world was darkened for three days. When the king learned of this, he looked in the Torah which was in the hands of the Samaritans and saw there some things which were not in the Torah of the Jews;[96] and he found that, for the most part, the sacred text possessed by us was more perfect than that possessed by them.[97] He thereupon inquired about the cause of this disagreement, whether it

---

[96] The SP is often characterized as "expansionist." Is this the Samaritan rebuttal to that charge?

[97] The inclusion of "for the most part" is altogether unexpected here.

concerned things indispensable to the Law or whether the Law was perfect without them and could dispense with them.

To this the Samaritans replied: "The Qibla is one of the principles of the Law and one of its pillars. It is utterly impossible that Moses the Lawgiver should have died without informing the people of the Qibla. With us it (the Qibla) is the last of the Ten Commandments, for the first of them prohibits the worshiping of anyone other than God, this is followed by commands and prohibitions, and after this God concluded the Ten Commandments with the commandment appointing the Qibla (towards Mount Gerizim) because the marks of His majesty and dignity appear upon it. For this (that is, the Qibla) the Jews have no explicit commandment. Rather, according to them, Moses died without informing (the people) of the place, yet he has commanded both us and them to offer a sacrifice at that very place, as it is written, year by year; nor did the (High) Priest (Aaron) inquire where this sacrifice should be brought. Now in the past did the High Priests offer sacrifice, or did they not? If they did, it must have been in an accustomed place. And if they did not offer it, they transgressed the command of God Most High. This despite the fact that they agree that the Tabernacle stood on the Mount for many years and that the people every year offered what He had prescribed for them. Moreover, the Creator Most High has stringently commanded us in His Divine Scripture that we should not offer burnt sacrifices in any place that we may see but only in the place which God has chosen:[98] 'There thou shall offer Your burnt offerings. And there thou shall do all that I command thee today.'[99] He has thus prohibited us from offering sacrifices anywhere else, and ordered us to offer His burnt offerings in that specific place alone and to bring there the tokens of our worship for Him. Indeed, He (Himself) has mentioned, both in our text (of the Law) and in theirs, that this place is a high and lofty mountain (and not the low hills of Jerusalem), by saying upon one of the mountains, at the place where Isaac was offered as a sacrifice, in the mountain of Your inheritance,[100] the place which You have made for You to dwell in. Then He called it the ancient mountain, as He said in the Blessing of Joseph, "With the finest produce of the ancient mountains and the abundance of the everlasting hill(s).' And because of this, Joseph considered specially the dignity that is in it—this majestic mountain, the home of God's might; for Joseph, when he was the cause of the life of his ailing father, inherited the place

---

[98] The twenty-one occurrences of "have chosen" in the SP instead of the MT "will chose" are well recognized.

[99] Deut 12:14.

[100] Exod 15:17.

which was the place of everlasting life. And it belonged especially to him, and in the Torah there are many proofs of this. And it is the place of Return (to the life to come) also; and it is one of the great roots of religion and one of its supports because, if one does not know that there certainly is reckoning and requital, he would follow his own passion and go to extremes therein, and would be less interested in, and glad about, his religion and its works, and have neglected obedience if there is no promise of reward for obedience nor threat of retribution for disobedience; and one would also take the road of passion and neglect his obligations and duties. And it has come about in a number of places that we and they agree upon some of it and differ on others; but what we disagree about is the section which more rightly concerns the life to come, which says in our Book, 'To the Day of Vengeance and Recompense,'[101] but with them, 'Vengeance is Mine and recompense.' And the difference between His saying, 'Vengeance is Mine and recompense,' and His saying that their deeds are with Me and stored up in my storehouse until the Day of Vengeance is great. And there is a great distinction between them because, according to their wording, He could take vengeance at this hour, or tomorrow, before and after, and it might be in this world or it might be in the next world; but with us it is when He describes the multitude who have neglected to obey Him and have become accustomed to do and to praise what is not to be done, as the sting of snakes[102] and the poison of malevolent serpents. His saying is, 'Their grapes are grapes of poison,[103] their clusters are bitter.' But, of course, the grapes in this context were not poison, nor their clusters bitter, and by that He only meant to what evil he who used it wrongly would come in the next world. And so later on He said by the way of predestination, 'Is not this laid up in store with me, sealed up in my treasuries until the Day of Vengeance and Recompense?' And there is in this world no day of such description. Then He said in this section, 'I kill and I make alive.'[104] But He does not put any to death except one who is alive, and He does not make alive except one who is dead. Then He said at the end of the threat, 'Praise His people, O you nations.'[105] Tidings to His people who know His Law, that He avenges their blood for their oppression. And He said after this section, 'And I repay those who disobey Me with Vengeance,'[106]

---

[101] Deut 32:35. So reads both the SP and the LXX.

[102] Deut 32:33.

[103] Deut 32:32.

[104] Deut 32:39.

[105] Deut 32:43a. Strangely, the SP, the LXX, and the DSS read "heavens" whereas the MT reads "nations."

[106] Deut 32:43b. The MT lacks this line.

meaning He gives an excess of retribution to His opponents who forsook knowledge and the doing of what was laid down in His Law. And He said, 'Cleanse the land of My people,'[107] and the hidden meaning in it is that the Most High compelled one who touches a grave (to be unclean) seven days,[108] and one was not purified except after the making of atonement on the third day[109] and the seventh, and then one was completely free of uncleanness. Then one went to the ritual of cleansing, as the obedient do, for their obedience completely frees them from the impurities with which they were mixed and the touching of their tomb does not cause impurity because of them, for the world has become pure just as the tombs of the apostate are defiled. And there comes in one of our songs: 'People will leave this world with what they have obtained for the next world, or with what they have lost. And when Death comes to them, they go out of this world, and nothing followed them from it to the Next World except their deeds and what their souls had acquired. With good they are rewarded in it, or with bad they are requited therein. Of the things of this world we have not mentioned many and have not bothered with (them), since this is not the place for them.'"

And when the king reflected on what they had said, and meditated on their arguments, he knew that the truth was in their hands and that the complete, perfect Torah was that which they had, and he said to them: "What do you say about those whom the Jews call prophets and these books which they have?" And they said: "As to these, truly, we do not recognize their prophecy nor their books because they (the books), O King, either have come down by the hand of prophets or by other than prophets; and if they were by the hand of prophets, the Mosaic Law has forbidden that after Moses there should be a prophet, for He says: 'And there has not arisen a prophet since in Israel like Moses.'[110] If we demanded from them the substance of their claim, although that sort of thing is not accepted by us, then either it will bring something like what is in the Torah—either their argument is the same as the Torah—and in that case there is no need of it, or it falls short of what is in the Torah. Then to follow the more complete thing is more necessary, or their argument contains an increase on what is in the Torah, and in that case the religious law both with us and with them has prohibited the acceptance of that sort of thing, according to

---

[107] Deut 32:43c. The LXX and the SP read, "Cleanse his land (you) his people." The MT reads, "Cleanse his land for his people."

[108] Num 19:16.

[109] Num 19:19.

[110] Deut 34:10.

His saying "you shall not add to it or take from it"[111] meaning that the Law is complete, nor to annul what is in it, for that would be abrogation Abrogation is not allowed with us. And he said: "O he who is present with the king, the argument of the Greeks in favor of abrogation is that which was banned at a later time, and what was bad at one time may become acceptable at another time; and that follows the aim of the Lawgiver and the character of those on whom it was imposed. And these things are not of that which the law pertains to, in so much that the quality (ought to) adhere to it as long as that thing endures." And they said: "Consider this answer; had what you mentioned of characters and circumstances been right, considering these things, differences at the same time would have been possible, as the characters of people of one period are not equal nor similar throughout but are different and disagree. But as for your saying that it is not one of the things on which a judgment depends whereas the quality adheres to it as long as that particular thing endures; but our shortcoming and our inability would not realize its cause and its means, and it is not that if minds could not grasp the knowledge of something, that thing would be impossible in itself.[112] And when the Creator Most High knew, by His foreknowledge, of our inability and the shortcoming of our intelligences to comprehend the knowledge of the reasons of this and its causes, He disclosed it to us by religious law, and He indicated to us its rules and its qualities with a complete indication, and some He indicated in detail; but we must not assume that the rule follows the reform, as He forbade to us the camel, since it lacks certain of the marks of purity, and the pig as well, and others, even though these marks are there, and this is the cause of the rule; and the rule follows the cause, and the cause is lasting as long as the species endures, for the Law lasts as long as Creation lasts. And sufficient for us is what Tradition has to say about its being eternal, and the mention of its causes in general, such as the permitted animals and the forbidden animals similarly. And regarding the being eternal, we know that the necessity of rule(s) about it is everlasting, and that is that one should follow its prescriptions; and it is not right to follow the honor of the worshipers over dispositions nor their customs and only follow the substance of it, and the essence of it particularly, but the impressive prescriptions concerning the rule(s) and the exclusive adherence to rule always openly."

---

[111] Deut 12:32.

[112] This is undoubtedly a difficult sentence. The intent of the sentence is to affirm a universal constant, independent of historical circumstance, even if that universal constant is beyond human reasoning, but known through Divine Revelation.

As he was pleased with their answer and their arguments pleased him, so their status was raised in his eyes, and their persuasion became preponderant with him, and they continued like that. May God have mercy on them! They had clear arguments and eloquent and incisive proofs and sound and persuasive reasons. And he honored them and raised their names among men after Aaron came to King Ptolemy. And he (Aaron) said to him (King Ptolemy), "We have received from the seventy elders (God have mercy on them) who bear the marks of the prophet, and who receive this Law from him, that he prohibited them from accepting anything other than it because the Creator, Most High is He, when He taught by his foreknowledge how mankind can be reformed and its affairs be set aright, sent down by the hand of His prophet (the most trustworthy of His world) a Law comprising the manner of the road to righteousness for humanity and keeping to that righteousness, and humanity's following the Law in this world. If they do not approach in pilgrimage to a place in which He is, then He would grow anxious about their word; but the pilgrimage is made now by their command to the place in which He is, and whoever does not do that, He kills him; and the Jews prevented them from pilgrimage to the Blessed Mount, and when they prevented them, three sects branched off. One of them was called the Pharisees, and the meaning of that is 'Those who separate themselves'; and this priest was from this sect. And another sect was called the Sadducees, and they were only called by this name because they disliked to behave other than justly; and they quote only the Torah and what the Scriptures indicate by analogy, and they do not allow anything other than it of that which the Pharisees' sect allows of books, wishing to remain in accordance with the views of the ancestors. And their dwelling was in villages that are around Aelia.[113] The other sect was called the Hasidim, and the meaning of that is "The Righteous Ones,"[114] and this sect is the one that is nearest to the Samaritans; and they hold their belief and dwell in the villages that are in the neighborhood of the Blessed Mountain for the purpose of devoting themselves to worship.[115] And there was violent enmity between the Sadducees and the Pharisees. Each party allowed shedding the blood of the other. And the cause of that was the secession of the elders who separated in the time of John (Hyrcanus) that they might have a book

---

[113] Jerusalem, renamed Aelia Capitolina when rebuilt by Hadrian.

[114] Some scholars speculate that Abu'l Fath is dependant upon Josephus for his delineation of the three sects. If so, it may be that the Essenes are in mind instead of the Hasidim. The similarity to Samaritans is then found in the common veneration of Moses and perhaps in shared pentateuchal readings.

[115] Whether Essenes or Hasidim, neither group held any special allegiance to Gerizim.

of religious law, for it was agreed that a book of religious law would bring benefit on them. And his commander in chief and his chief men came, and the seceding elders were present with him; and they passed judgment on his intelligence and got the mastery over him; and when they ate and drank out of respect to him, and he said joyfully to them: 'Indeed I am a disciple of yours and shall have recourse, in what I do, to what you say and what you see fitting. And I have accepted what you have said, and I ask you if you have known sin and error in me; (if so) bring me back from that and prevent me from (committing) it.' And they said to him: 'May God bring you back from error and sin, and may you be virtuous and straightforward in all your doings.' But among them was a man called Eleazar, and he was great among them. He wanted to stop him (John Hyrcanus) from appointing to the priesthood any of his relatives. And he said to him: 'If you want to be virtuous and to give up sin as you have mentioned, then it is up to you to remove yourself from the priesthood and to be satisfied with kingship, because you are not fit for it (the priesthood); and that is because your mother was a prisoner in the days of Antiochus.' And he said to him: 'As for my mother, when she was captive, she and my father were routed and hid in a cave of the mountain. So what is the reason for depriving me of this right and handing over His (God's) service to the elders of the seceding group (the Pharisaic party)?' So he brought them and he said: 'What do you say about a man who reviles a man about something of which he was never guilty?' And the elders said: 'We want to know the sentence.' So he told it to them. And they said: 'He ought to seek pardon by an offering, or he should be struck forty (times).' He replied: 'Truly (I say) that he should make an offering and be struck forty (times).' Then from that time he (John Hyrcanus) transferred to the sect of the Sadducees. And he forsook the Pharisaic party and treated them as enemies. And he said: 'These truly are the Pharisees, that is, Seceders from the Law of God.' And he killed a great company of them, and he burnt their books and proclaimed in his kingdom that one should prevent people from teaching about Pharisaism, and he killed many of those who disobeyed him. The Sadducees and the Samaritans were permitted to kill them. And this king had before this come down to Sebaste, which is a town of the Samaritans, and had besieged it closely, and had conquered it and slaughtered many of the Samaritans. Then he came to Nablus, and waged a mighty battle, and killed a great number of the two parties, but was not able to enter it as he had been able to do at Sebaste. But when John (Hyrcanus) transferred to the Sadducees and did to the Pharisaic party what he did, and burnt their books, and prohibited the children from learning from them, (then) he returned to seek (to make) the pilgrimage to Nablus, to the Blessed Mountain, and confirmed that it was the House of God. But the Samaritans refused to make it possible for him to go (up) to it. And they were vigilant to prevent him and overcame his pride by the greatness of their God. So when he despaired of that, he began sending offerings and tithes, freewill offerings, and alms, and gifts to it, and he continued (doing) that, and the Jews who were called Pharisees went away to Aelia."

Fourteenth Excerpt: Of Jesus and his disciples[116]

After the High Priest Nathaniel, the High Priest Yehoqim occupied the Great High Priesthood for 32 years. In his days, the Messiah was born, son of Mary, son of the Rabbi—peace be upon him—Joseph, the Carpenter. All the days from the Fanuta until the birth of the Messiah were 1,300.

He was born in Bethlehem and claimed to be a prophet in Nazareth. He had followers and a sect. Among those whom he sent out among the nations were Peter, whom he sent to Rome; Andrew and Matthew, whom he sent to the Sudan; Thomas, to the land of Babylon; Philip, to al-Qarwan and Africa; James, to Jerusalem; and Simon, to the land of the Berbers.

Herod plotted to kill the Messiah, but he escaped from his clutches. The High Priest Yehoqim died in the mercy of Almighty God, and he was succeeded by Jonathan, who was High Priest for 27 years.

In the days of Jonathan, the Messiah was persecuted, and the Governor killed him in the days of Tiberius the king. He was crucified, he and the 12 persons of his company, in Jerusalem. All of them were placed in a sarcophagus. I have found in an old Hebrew Chronicle that two persons (only) were crucified with him. And that John the Baptist, the disciple of the Messiah, was beheaded in Sebastia. The reason for his being called The Baptist was that the Jews used to baptize all who wanted to become Jews. Out of hatred for the Messiah, they forbade him to be baptized in(to) it. However, the aforementioned John took him and baptized him in the Jordan, at Jericho. The Jews used to believe, whenever someone was baptized in(to) it, that whoever was baptized was cleansed from all impurity and all misdeeds. This is the baptism that the Christians still have today. When they were able to, they (in their turn) forbade the Jews to be baptized in(to) it!

---

[116] Stenhouse, *The Kitab al-Tarikh,* 147–48. Used by permission.

Fifteenth Excerpt: Concerning philosophical disputes[117]

After Eleazer, ᵓAqbun was High Priest for 23 years. In the days of this ᵓAqbun, terrible hardships fell upon the Samaritans from Commodus the king—worse than anything that had befallen them from Hadrian. He forbade them to read the Torah; he closed the schools of learning and (forbade) all instruction in the Law. He bolted shut the Synagogues. The High Priests fled, as did the wise men, from the tyranny of Commodus the king on account of the great number whom he killed and crucified in every place.

The reason for this (persecution) was a debate that took place in his presence between Levi and a man from his (Commodus') community called Alexander Aphridisias, from Aphridisias, concerning the coming-into-being of the world. Alexander said that its Substance and Prime Matter were eternal and that the Creator only provided the Form and Accidents. Levi replied that Substance and Matter need an originator, just as Form and Accidents do. To this, Alexander retorted, "This would lead to a situation where the world would not be possible and where God would have no power to bring it into being. For, if he had the power from the first, then before that it cannot have been possible. And yet, if before that it were impossible, this would be a restriction, and there can be no restriction on his power."

Levi said that the world was possible of existence *ab aeterno* and that no time could be conceived in which the coming-into-being of the world could not be conceived.

"If it were to be supposed that the world simply 'existed' without being created and it be tried to prove that this belongs to the realm of possibility, then this would be a figment of the imagination—an intellectual fiction—and the world would be insubstantial and immaterial. And if something were to exist such as Matter and Substance, then it would exist *de se*. This existence must be either possible or necessary. If it were possible, then the argument would be as before. If it were necessary, however, then it would share with the first Almighty One in eternal existence. And if it did thus share, it would not change either *in toto* or *in partibus,* for change is an effect and an effect presupposes an Agent. For the one thing cannot be both Matter and Agent under any aspect."

---

[117] Ibid., 163–65. Used by permission.

The debate between them dragged on, with argument and polemic. The situation reached the stage where the possibility of the Creator's "Speaking" was denied. And the Mission of the Messengers is (implicitly) denied by whoever denies that the trustworthy Message has been uttered. Perhaps more of the discourse of this question ought to have been given here.

But I have related it as I found it, and as much as I could cope with.

Sixteenth Excerpt: The story of ᶜAkbon[118]

Now, the High Priest ᶜAkbon was possessed of very great wealth, and they sought the High Priest ᶜAkbon, and he was afraid, and he concealed himself; and they searched for him in the mountains and the caves and in every place, but they did not find him. So the king said to his servants: "Plunder all his wealth and burn his house." And they did that and burned his house. And there were burned in it the prayers and ascriptions of praise and the songs which were said on Sabbaths and Festivals and which had been handed down from the days of Divine Grace. And it was said to the High Priest ᶜAkbon: "All that is yours has been taken, and your house is burnt down." And he answered and said: "All is from God and it belongs to God. If they have obtained mastery over me and my abode, I submit myself to affliction and destruction, but I will not disavow God nor Moses, His prophet, nor His Law." So they seized his two sons and the King said to them: "Worship idols." And they said: "We will die, but we will not worship other than God the Merciful." And they inserted sticks under their nails, and they flayed them alive, and they put them to death with all torture, and they cast their corpses to the dogs. They hanged on the walls of Nablus thirty-six priests, and they did not take down their corpses until they fell of themselves. And in the days of this king, Commodus (may God curse him), none taught his son the Torah except one out of a thousand and two out of a myriad secretly. And Commodus ruled thirty-two years and he died (may God not have mercy on him). And in the tenth year of his reign, the Persians appeared, and Ardashir the son of Babaka the son of Sasan was victorious over the Romans; and he was the first of the kings of the Persians in the second dynasty; and it is said that Ardashir means "with the long arms," but he was only nicknamed that because of his being a bold fighter (or treacherous murderer) and of the greatness of his rule. And his (Ardashir's) appearance was five hundred and forty-five years after Alexander. He was a violent killer. Now the High Priest ᶜAkbon feared for the Sa-

---

[118] Bowman, *Samaritan Documents,* 136–39. Used by permission.

maritans, so he sent to him (Ardashir) Ahirod and Joseph, who were possessed of learning and understanding. And they found him in Iraq, and went in to him and said: "O King, the king is a tree of which justice is its fruit, and if you do justly, God will establish the foundations of your glory, and He will be pleased with what you desire." So the king was pleased with their speech, and he showed good cheer in his face and kindness on his expression; and Joseph said to him: "O King, you know at this hour the nobility of yourself and the excellence of your power." And he said: "And how did you know?" So he said. "O King, the noble soul is known by its acceptance of the truth, and when it has accepted the truth, it reveals signs of its acceptance in the body." And he became more pleased at his speech, and he inferred from that the source of his excellence; and he asked him about himself, the object of his worship, and his religion. And he answered him regarding all that. And he approved of that in him and wrote for him protection for himself and the people of his religion and their pious foundations and their houses of worship. And the two of them bade the king farewell and returned thankful.

Now the High Priest ʿAkbon was blessed with a male child. And he said: "God has blessed me, compensating me for the loss of my wealth and my sons." So he called him Nathanel. And there remained to the High Priest ʿAkbon some of his wealth, and he built for himself a beautiful house in Namara; it is a village west of Nablus, and he dwelt in it. And Suyaris (that is, Severus) the king sent to the High Priest ʿAkbon, saying to him: "I desire that you go to worship the idols and the pictures as we do; I will make you my deputy in the Kingdom, and I will entrust you with all that is in my storehouses of treasures and clothes, and I will restore to you all your possessions." But he returned answer: "This is the thing which I will not do, and I will not deny God my God for the goods of this world, that has little to do with truth and much with falsehood." And the chiefs of his kingdom advised him to compel the Samaritans to worship their idols and, if they refused, to kill them. And Suyaris said to them: "What advantage will it be to our idols if we kill the people? And how is it lawful for us to kill him who chooses death rather than worship other than his God? And they say that the Lord whom they worship, He is the Lord of lords, and God of gods, and He is, so they pretend, Creator of the heavens and the earth; and how can we prevent them from worshiping Him if they do not admire our God? No, let us leave them in their error, and if they wish to worship our idols, let it be by their choice; but if they do not wish, we will not compel them." And his servants said to him: "If you do not kill them, act severely towards them and set watchmen over them to prevent them from practicing circumcision and purification; and we ourselves will make for our god altars in every place." So the king did that, and he imposed also a tax on the children of Israel for keeping the Sabbath. And when ᶜAkbon drew near to death—it was towards the beginning of the reign of King Alexander—he (ᶜAkbon) sought his boy, Nathanel, and gave him his last charge and said to him: "Pay no heed to these times and these calamities nor to the strength of the enemies of God, whereby in their rebellious conduct they have rebelled; but know and be sure in your heart, my boy, that these calamities are a trial from God to us to make clear that we should have afflicted our spirits and devoted ourselves to the service of God, exalted be He; be patient, my boy; the calamities and the difficulties will be altered and cease, and one will arise from us and save us and will remove from us this violent band and put it far from us." And his boy, Nathanel, and the company with him answered him and said to him: "May God your redemption act on our behalf." And the High Priest ᶜAkbon said to them: "This is not he who will arise from us to establish the age of Divine Grace in its entirety, but this violent hand he will break and make it cease from us by the power of God—exalted be He." So the High Priest ᶜAkbon died, and his period of office as High Priest was twenty-three years. And there reigned after him his son, Nathanel, thirty-two years; and there befell the Samaritans in his days calamities and distresses such as no tongue can describe.

Seventeenth Excerpt: The story of Baba Raba[119]

This was in the reign of Alexander (God curse him!), for he was more tyrannical than Commodus. And in his days there were calamities and excess. He killed and ordered that everyone in the neighborhood of any village not worshiping his god should be killed, and he who killed him have weighed out for himself a reward of twenty bronze coins. So it happened that every one of the people, when there was enmity in his heart for an Israelite, would sit in the neighborhood of the village until he met him, then he would kill him and have weighed out for him twenty bronze coins as the king ordered. And he killed many scholars, and he devastated synagogues and burnt teachers and imprisoned little children and crucified wise men and killed young men for no offense; and he burned them in caves and ruined many girls and thereby defiled their fathers, the priests, while they plundered them. And he set over them, in the villages, some Romans to prevent them circumcising. And they, when it was morning, would say: "Would that it were evening." And when it was evening, they would say:

---

[119] Ibid., 139–59. Used by permission.

"Would that it were morning." Out of doors the sword was bringing bereavement; within the house was dread and fear. And Nathanel begat three sons: Baba, the firstborn, ʿAkbon, the second, and Phinehas, the third. Now Phinehas' home was in Mahana, but Baba was a strong man of dignified and stern bearing, and he had zeal and sanctified spirituality. When he saw what had befallen his tribe and the people of his religion because of Rome, he reflected and thought earnestly and deeply about it, and said: "I want to be zealous for religion. Apostasy has become prevalent and certain truth is made void. Remind the body (of the people) of the word of 'sincerity and unity.'" And he said to his brothers and to the community: "How long will these uncircumcised nations, that be against God, treat us harshly? They intend to ruin us, and they prevent us from keeping God's way and commands. However, we of the children of Israel and we of the tribe of Levi, we are not like them in zeal. We will be zealous for the truth and bring up Israel from this affliction in which it stands because of the enemies of God. And has anyone been zealous for God with zeal like this and not succeeded in it? For Levi and Simeon were blessed; they had no anxiety or fear for the villages that were around them in the disaster that befell Nablus (Shechem). And the tribe of Levi, when they killed the worshipers of the calf,[120] how it resulted in blessing to them and dignity for them! And Phinehas, our Father, when he alone was zealous for God,[121] apart from the community, how it resulted in responsibility and steady dignity acquired for him alone of his tribe, and his offspring for ever. And now let us show courage for the sake of the nation and the commands of God our God; and nothing remains to us apart from crying to God and seeking His Gate[122] with prayer and fasting, and humility and repentance, and abasement and earnest prayer; so we will abase ourselves in obedience to Him and ask help of His power and His strength against our enemies; for He has assisted us by His Grace and His Bounty, and if He has withheld His mercy from us, then we will have to abase ourselves in pleasing Him and obeying Him and be zealous for the pure Law; and we should strive to renew the learning of the Law which has perished, and we should be eager to raise the standards of truth which have disappeared and been obliterated. And we should imitate our predecessors among those who longed to meet God, and seek His reward; and we should purify our hearts of the stains of sins, and we should banish them from evil inclination. And if we do, then God knows the sincerity of our intentions and the purity of our thoughts and

---

[120] Exod 32:26–29.
[121] Num 25:7–12.
[122] Mount Gerizim.

the sincerity of our hearts; He will help us and supply us with strength and success in repelling these uncircumcised impure ones; so we will drive them out from this pure holy land and set fire to their wily and filthy followers."

Then he arose and performed ablutions and prayed and fasted, and went up the Sacred Mountain and made supplication to God, and made humble entreaties to Him, and humbled himself and abased himself. And summing up his call for help, he said at the end of his prayers: "I beseech Thee, O He who by His power has created all that exists, O He who has set it in order by His wisdom, and O He who has made it move at His will and when He wishes make it rest. And O He who has chosen this people by His Grace and His Bounty to obey Him, so that He render victorious this nation, which does not flee for protection for itself except to You and not relying on nor trusting in any save Thee. Nor is there a helper for it save You, and You know what has befallen that nation from those kings who do not believe in You, who deny the need to obey You, who worship what Your Law has declared abominable, who stray from Your guidance, who are remote from Your Favor, who worship idols that are deaf and dumb, the work of their own hands, and make their fancies their God; and if our sins have made us deserving of destruction, You take our souls to Yourself, and if our misdemeanors preclude Your help and Your comfort to us, do not let our enemies get Your mercy, and if we deserve thereby the dominion of our enemies over us, do not charge us with what we are not able to do because of our enemies, at the pain of submitting to the worship of their idols and to rebel against You, and their preventing us from commemorating Your name and explaining Your attributes. And You have promised us that You will not cast us off from Your mercy if we were in the lands of our enemies. Our eye is upon what we resolved upon in pleasing You. And we have determined completely to follow the ways of Your Unity, and You are the Powerful, Victorious One; so accomplish for us what You swore to us in Your gracious Favor, and look upon us in Your mercy, and deal with us according to Your Favor and Your Liberality as You did with our Fathers in releasing them from the hand of the Egyptians, when You manifested Your miracles in the land of Egypt, and divided the sea that the Israelites might cross, and destroyed the unbelieving Pharaohs, and assisted Your people, and made them to reign in the land of the obstinate Giants."

When he had finished his supplication, he returned to his brethren and his congregation and said to them: "What do you think?" And they answered him and said: "Good is all that you have said. And right is it; wherever you command us to go, we will go." And Baba Raba went out and his brothers and his associates, and they passed through all the places of Israel. And they opened the synagogues that their enemies had shut up; and he and his brethren gathered in them first, and read the scroll of the Law in the hearing of all the people, and ascribed much praise and glory to God with uplifted voices. And Baba sent and brought all the scholars of the Law and the priests from every place; yet he could only find out few of the elders of Israel and Sages because they had perished in the period of Roman (domination), since they had not sacrificed to their gods. So Baba Raba said to them: "Go every man (of you) to his place, and persevere and reflect and strive to instruct all Israel, men, women, and children, in the Law of God that they may keep it, and follow the commandments and laws as did your fathers. And guard the reading of the Law, and see to the soundness of the Synagogues and the Blessing. And every man who does not keep and does not fulfill this charge wherewith I charge, I will kill him. Now it was a hard thing which was on Israel from Baba Raba, for he compelled young and old, and the elders to teach, and because of that it was difficult for them.

But the children of Israel removed their cares, and they drew a good omen for their freedom and rejoiced exceedingly at this speech. And Baba Raba took seven men from the best of Israel, men who were wealthy and experts in the Law, and he honored them by calling them Sages. For the priestly community were not called Sages. And of the seven above-mentioned Sages, three were priests and four were Israelites; and as to the priests, the one who was greatest in power among them was called in Israel the High Priest. Then Baba came and called the priesthood, Sages, for the sake of honoring those of them who were called thus, and the naming of the priests was their prerogative and for them to hand down after them, because, when he entered Beisan, the priests did not meet him and they did not do what they should by way of honoring him but, when he entered the city, they came greeting him according as their custom was. However, he removed them from their offices in which they were, and they did not meet him when he went out from the city; so he put Israelites in their places doing all their tasks except the carrying of the Sacred Book; and the children of Israel (that is, Israelites) were to perform the commandment of circumcision though it had not been theirs before that to do it; and they were saying in the synagogue: "Full of Glory" and "Full of Pardon."[123] And all the service of the synagogue they carry out until this day. And there the genealogy of the priesthood was missing. So he made them claim descent

---

[123] Apparently a liturgical response that before was mouthed only by the priests.

from them that preceded them, for none of them was any longer concerned to preserve his lineage, as Baba Raba would not confer the name
"Sages" except on honored scholars, whether they were priests or Israelites. And as for the body of the priests, he did not confer on them either
the name "Sage" or "priest." And Baba Raba honored the seven Sages, and
he clad them in a robe of honor, and he created for everyone of them a
special rank as an honor to him and his posterity after him, which should
not be annulled nor terminated; and he made them sit before him, every
man according to his rank, until every man knew his place. And the seven
above-mentioned were heads over all the people; every man was to keep
watch on his jurisdiction, and guide his people to the laws, and distinguish
for them between unclean and pure, and make them acquainted with the
reading of the Law; and the first Sage was Arub'l, a descendant of Ithamar,
and he was the Haftawi,[124] and his limit (of his jurisdiction) was from Beit
Kabiha in the great plain; and he had the first rank, so that he should inter-
pret before him first. The second was Jose, an Israelite from Kefar Sabla,
and he had the second position and the interpreting at the end; and the
third, Al-Yanah from Sarafin, had the second reading, while the fourth was
a Kahin Levi from Zaita, and he had the reading at the beginning and commemorated the names of those who were honored with dignities and gifts
at any time; the fifth was an Israelite from Kefar Maruth, interpreting fifth,
and the sixth was Amram Darir, a priest from Kefar Safasah, and he held
the place of giving the second interpretation. It is recorded that this is the
father of Markah (the Favor of God be upon him). And the seventh was an
Israelite. In this manner, Baba Raba organized the seven men, priests and
Israelites, and said to them: "You shall command and prohibit and shall be
set in precedence over all Israel great and small and be Sages over them;
and everyone who stands before you and who disobeys you in anything
which you command him, I will sue him." And among the body of seven
men, Baba set up four called "overseers."

Now this management and organization was not from the time of Divine
Grace; but there were, in the time of Divine Grace, seventy Elders chosen,
and of the multitude, Israelites, and twelve from them heads over all the
multitude of Israel. He was called along with the High Priest, but he did not
have full control over the priests and he was judged by them. But in the
tribe of Levi, for any offense, either the High Priest (judged) or one of the
[elders?] High Priesthood deputized for him (the High Priest) in the presence of the elders until it was said that they were too cautious in judgment;

---

[124] "Interpreter" or "translator."

and likewise (did) the elders in the presence of the priests. The office of elder was not inherited from father to his son nor from the son to his father, but if one of them died, another was put instead of him from among the scholars of the nation; then the choice was in the hand of the High Priest and in the hand of the Elders. This was the organization of the (period of) Divine Grace. However, the Sabu'ai did not obey Baba Raba and had not heard of the choice of him, and they did not accept the Sages whom he organized; but their priests were judging in their villages. And the seven Sages whom Baba Raba set over them were going round the rest of the villages, and they kept the Sabbath in them, making known and disclosing whether there was there any priest to whom unmindfulness[125] had happened in an injunction or in a law or judgment among the priesthood of the Sabu'ai; (then) they would raise their matter with the chief who was friendly to them. But in every way they would assist Baba Raba and show for him at all times concern and regard. And Baba Raba said to the Sages: "Consider and reflect on all you do, and beware of unmindfulness and mistake, and feel concern for the reading of the Law and the teachers." And Baba Raba built in the confines of the Sacred Mountain a cistern of water for purifying oneself therewith at the time of prayer, and it was before the rising of the sun and at sunset. And he built a house for prayer that the people might pray in it, facing the Sacred Mount; and they remained until the time of the Kingdom of the Franks (may God curse Them).[126] And the house of prayer which Baba Raba built was on the site of the house of prayer which was built in the eyes of all in the days of Divine Grace; and he made it resemble it and made its floor, a piece of land (such) as one could see clearly. And he took seven stones from the stones of the Temple that the men of Saul destroyed, and he made them benches for the seven Sages, and he took also a big stone, and he placed it for his own seat. And Baba Raba built eight synagogues in the villages with no wood in any of them; and there was the synagogue at 'Awarta; and the synagogue at Salem; and the synagogue at Namara, and the synagogue at Kirya Hajja, and the synagogue at Karawa, and the synagogue at Tira Luza, and the synagogue at Dabarin, and the synagogue at Beit Gan. And he built a place for the order of the reading and the interpretation, and the hearing of those with questions, before the house of prayer, so that every one in whose mind there was a question could ask the Sages about it and they might answer him rightly. And he who wanted to be called a "Sage" should present himself at the times of Festivals and New Moons and present himself before the High

---

[125] Errors.
[126] The Crusades.

Priest and the Sages; and if they found him sound, they called him "Sage." And Baba Raba said that the reason for the building of a house of prayer and a place of knowledge was so that the kings of the earth should not think that he showed regard to anything of the states of the kings and their countries which departed thereby from the worship of God and the doing of His commandments nor that they might think that he showed regard to anything frivolous, anything after the nature of jesting. And Baba Raba distributed the priests over the heads of the people as he found them, and he gave them an inheritance. And Baba Raba said to the Sages: "Depart in peace and be strong and be brave and be afraid of none and not in fear all the days of my life." So the Sages went from his presence with great strength and joy of heart, and there was great joy in all Israel. And when the Sages entered the villages, they manifested joy and praise to God and appeared in judgment, and the people did as the Sages did. But the overseers[127] arose, preventing them. So they killed them; they burnt them with fire on the eve of the beginning of the seventh month; and thereby came about the Samaritan custom now of the boys of the cities and villages burning the ones as a memorial of that night on which they burnt the overseers, who prevented Israel from serving God.[128] And when advisers to the king heard that the chief ones of Israel killed the overseers, they sent [messages] condemning the chief ones of Israel. And Baba Raba heard and went out to meet them, and put them to flight, and killed them; and they who had been put to flight returned in a very bad state. Now Baba Raba knew they would muster and come to him, so he chose for himself men from the best of Israel, men of war, and he prepared and gathered them also, a mighty company. And they came to Baba Raba with a strong hand, and Baba Raba went out to meet them, and God gave him strength and victory; and he killed them and obliterated them and filled Mount 'Askar with their corpses. But those who were safe fled to the king and informed him about what had happened to them, and the king magnified himself and acted insolently, and his power became strong against Baba Raba. And he gathered and mustered against him tens of thousands. Now when Baba Raba heard, he sent word to all the places of Israel that all the men of war should come to him; and they came from the coast of the sea and from the mountain and from the south and from meadowland and from the lowland, 10,000 men of them advancing, ready for war, and their warriors with swords and spears and the bow and arrows ready for their enemies. And

---

[127] Roman overseers, not Baba Raba's appointees.

[128] This custom is given a second origin several pages later in the episode of Baba Raba's victory on Mount Gerizim.

Baba Raba saw that the men were many and they needed much expense and provisions, so he went out with a strong hand and took all the villages which the unbelievers of the enemies had prepared against them and which they had taken from the children of Israel; and the men took food from them as would be enough for them day by day. And he ordered that no one should pay tax to the king nor carry provisions or food to his (the king's) army. Baba Raba loved the inhabitants of 'Awarta, since therein were buried the Fathers, the glorious and blameless High Priests; Eleazar and Ithamar and Phinehas—the peace of God, Most High is He, be upon them—and Baba Raba dwelt there. And he was informed that the enemy had arrived and were in great number and a numerous company. Then Baba Raba and the company stood before God, Blessed is He and Most High is He. And they presented themselves to Him in sincere worship, and the horns sounded, and they cried with a loud cry: "O God, look from Your Holy Dwelling from heaven and redeem Your people Israel from the hand of Your enemies, for the war is not ours but Yours, O our LORD." And Baba Raba went out to war with his enemies, and God saved Israel on that day with a mighty salvation, and they killed their enemies, and they fled from their presence. So Baba Raba pursued swiftly after them and overtook them and slaughtered many of them, and destroyed of them men and beasts in the mountain that is opposite Nablus, and the place is unclean because of their corpses until this day.[129] And God made Israel rejoice greatly, and they knew that it was the power of God, Most High is He, which delivered them.

And God put it in the soul of the king who was at Mosul that he should fight with Alexander and take the lands from him; and the war was great and violent with Alexander, and God put into the souls of the Arabs, the Ishmaelites, that they should come to the dwellings and plunder and smite them. And Baba Raba heard and went out to meet them and pursued after them swiftly to the valley of the Jordan, and smashed them and slaughtered many of them, and took great booty from them, sheep and cattle and camels and very many garments. And when the kings of the earth heard that Baba Raba had gone out and fought with them and smashed them, they sent food and provisions for men and sent to him wealth and robes of honor. And Baba Raba said after that: "God has been good to us and to all Israel and delivered us with this great deliverance and put our enemies into our hands, and we have taken their wealth; and these (enemies) are those who came to take us and to take our children captivity. God put them into

---

[129] Mount Ebal, the mount of cursing; Deut 27:13.

our hands, and it was a great deliverance for our other enemies; because of that they have this great generosity to us, and He has proved to us what God Most High has shown in the Holy Law,[130] that your enemies shall incite you but you shall tread on their skulls; now go in faith and of right, every man to his place, until I need you to come to me; but there shall remain with me 3,000 accompanying me always. And I shall put them in villages around the village of 'Awarta, in which I am dwelling, so that they may be near me."

So they did that, and Baba Raba called and blessed them, and every man returned peacefully to his place. And it happened that on every Saturday night the foremost of Israel, from every place, and the nobles of Nablus came to the priest, Baba Raba, with horses and men, greeting him. And the king would at no time take a place that was within his power, except when the priest ordered it in his own handwriting. Then Alexander died, and he had not been able to take tax from Israel. So when the kings were unable to take tax from the children of Israel, they said to the Jews: "If you are able to kill Baba Raba, you shall be enabled to build the sanctuary." And many Jews were dwelling in the village of Namara, and when Baba Raba went to keep the Sabbath there, the Jews determined that they should go in to Baba Raba and his brothers on the eve of the Sabbath to kill him, for they, at the standing for prayer, were unable to carry a sword. But that was not accomplished, for God in His mercy was kind and their affair was revealed on the Thursday, and that was because a Jewish woman learned of their plan.[131] She had a friend, a Samaritan woman to whom she had become attached, and she said to her: "I wish you not to enter the Samaritan synagogue on the eve of the Sabbath." And the Samaritan woman said to her. "Why is that?" And she said to her: "I fear that you will betray me." So she swore to her that she would not betray her. Then she said to her: "The Jews want to kill Baba in the synagogue on the eve of the Sabbath." So the woman came and informed Baba, and he made it clear on the Friday that he would keep the Sabbath in the synagogue. And he entered the synagogue clad in his clothes, but when it was dark, he changed his robe and he went out of the synagogue, and no one knew about his going out; and when night came on, the Jews gathered together, and they were many people. And they entered the synagogue searching for Baba Raba, and they held the doors and lit the fires in it, thinking that Baba Raba was inside. And when Baba Raba saw what they had done, he cried out against them, he and his

---

[130] Deut 33:29.

[131] Occasionally, Jewish neighbors of the Samaritans are treated with honor and appreciation. See also the story of the death of Baba Raba.

company. Then when they heard his voice, they threw down their weapons and came to him, and they said to him: "We are your servants. And we have sinned because we sought your blood." And he held them all, and he detained them until day appeared; then he killed them all, and burnt them, and took the fort that was opposite the castle, and drove them from it except the woman who had informed them; for her he took and was good to her and made her a Samaritan woman, for she remained afraid of the Jews. And a company of the Jews came and burnt many crops in the fields, and Baba went out and killed a numerous company of them. Then Gordianus the king ordered them to build a sanctuary, and they gathered material for the building and wanted to turn their hands to the building. But God manifested a wonder from heaven, and winds came and carried off all that had been gathered, and all was destroyed and the building stopped. So until now they have not proposed to build it.

Now I came across an ancient Hebrew history,[132] and in it was mentioned a story concerning Baba Raba, and I decided that I should set it down in this history so that no one who might happen to come across it would think that I had not observed it.

And it is that Baba Raba said to the congregation of the children of Israel: "It has seemed good to me that the son of my brother should journey to Rome[133] and busy himself in their law, then he will return in the garb of a monk, a priest; they will not know where he is, and he will go up to Gerizim and cross to the synagogue and by using guile break the bird Talisman; and when he has done that, we will be able to go up to Mount Gerizim and petition God on it. And He will give us victory over our enemies." And all the people said: "O our lord, do what seems good to you." So he said: "Give me your signature so that after he has gone, you will not change your mind." So they did so, and Baba Raba brought Levi his nephew before him in the presence of the company. And he said to him: "See how it will be and apply your mind to learning everything, and take care lest you stop reading the Torah night and day, and God aid you in all your deeds." So Baba Raba sent his nephew Levi, and he went traveling toward Constantinople. Now this Levi was a clever man, worthy, and expert in the Law, pious and chaste. In him was all excellence; and he spent seventeen years

---

[132] Perhaps the SJ, in which part of the following story is found. The fact that most manuscripts of the SJ are in Arabic and Abu'l Fath claims to have come across the story written in Hebrew may mean that Abu'l Fath knew of a version of the legend separate from Joshua or that he was aware of a Hebrew version of the SJ.

[133] "Rome" here is an Arabic reference to Constantinople.

on his travels, and when he came to Constantinople, he sought instruction, and strove successfully to obtain what he sought, and remained occupied ten years. And there was not in all Rome one more knowledgeable than he. And he increased in knowledge until the Romans, all of them, would come to serve him; and because of the greatness of his knowledge, they made him the greatest bishop. And he was exalted to highest position with them until all the kings began coming to his door. At that time the king could not rule except by his command, and he directed the king's crown itself. However, when the thirteen years for his journeying were completed, he said to the king: "I wish to visit the churches which are at Nablus." So all the troops were brought forth, and the king went and the forces in his service; and when they came near Nablus, the command of the king was conveyed to all the peoples that they should come out to meet the great archbishop. And when Baba Raba heard about that, he was greatly afraid and gathered all the people and said to them: "We are deeply worried about Levi; we sent him off, but no news of him has arrived, and there is no doubt that he has perished; and this great archbishop who is coming, I have heard, is the chief of the nation of Rome and their model, and I have heard that he is far gone in misbelief.[134] So we can be certain of our complete destruction if we do not go out to meet him, and we shall not be safe from him if he is displeased with us. And all the troops of Rome are before him, and he may command them to kill us, so what can we do to him without enmity and without war in the face of their multitude."

And when they heard that, they were greatly afraid, and they said: "We rely on God, and Him do we obey." After that, he arrived at Nablus and the entire crowd went out. And Baba Raba and his people went out, and when they drew near the great Archbishop, he lifted up his eyes and saw his uncle. And all the body of Israel, the Samaritans, were great in fear and were calling out to him with a very great din, and with that, tears appeared in his eyes. But his uncle and the Samaritans did not know him, for they had sent him off when he was a beardless youth and now he returned thirty years old, fully bearded, and in this great majesty. And Levi turned to the king, and he said to him: "These people, what are they?" And the king said to him: "O our lord and our master, these are infidels who are called the Samaritans," and "What do they know and worship?" And he said: "They worship a god who is not seen, and who has no form." And he said: "How do they not worship idols and images?" and the king said to him: "We are wearied with these, but they have done so." And he said: "If

---

[134] At this point the SJ suddenly breaks off.

they do not, then they shall not be allowed to live." And the news of the speech of the Archbishop spread abroad regarding the duty of the Samaritans, and their fear increased. Then Levi, and the king in his attendance, went up to Mount Gerizim, and when he was on top of the Mountain, the bronze bird cried out "Ebraios."[135] And he said: "What is this?" And he said: "This Talisman does not let a Samaritan come up the mountain without this bird calling out 'Ebraios.'" And he said to them: "I perceive it cries out, but see if there is a Samaritan upon the mountain and kill him." So they went round upon the mountain, and they did not meet any. So Levi went over to the church, and he sat down and all the kings before him, and the brazen bird was calling out and would not cease screeching. And Levi said: "What is the matter with that bird? It has wearied us with its crying, and yet there is no Samaritan on the mountain, and without doubt it has become weak-minded, and there is no need for us to have a headache by its remaining." And the king said: "You have said rightly, O my Lord; what do you want us to do with it?" And he said: "Smash it." So they smashed it and threw it down, and that was the eve of the beginning of the seventh month. And when four hours had passed of the night, while all the kings and the priests and the monks were asleep, Levi arose, took his sword in his hand, and went down to his uncle, Baba Raba. And it happened on that night that the Samaritans had assembled with him and they were afraid, perplexed as to what they should do about this great Archbishop who had ordered their killing. And while they were thus, suddenly there was a light knocking at the door, and they were afraid. And Baba Raba arose and the heads of the people looked at who was knocking at the door, and when they opened the door, they saw. And behold it was the great Archbishop, and they were surprised to see him; and Levi prostrated himself before his uncle Baba Raba, and embraced him and fell on his neck and wept and said: "Now let me die, since I have seen your face and know that you are still alive."[136] So Baba Raba knew that he was Levi, his nephew, and never was greater joy in the heart of Baba Raba and his community; and Levi began describing to his uncle and to the people all that had happened to him, and they were rejoicing and joyful about him and at what he was saying. And he said to his uncle: "When tomorrow night is a thing of the past, we shall describe that night as the unsheathing by young warriors of their swords, and they shall be with me; and while the people are sleeping, I will get up and smite their watchmen, and will apply the sword among them and wipe them out." And when they were

---

[135] "Hebrew."
[136] Gen 46:30.

agreed on that, Levi arose, went up to his place, and found them all sleeping. And they did not know of his having gone down or of his coming up. And when the beginning of the seventh month was drawing to a close, Baba Raba sent to all the villages in which were the Samaritans, and he said to them: "Be ready for the coming of the night, and when you see fire on a dome,[137] at the right moment, kill the supervisors who are over you, and do not spare of those around you a single man of the Romans, but kill and strike out with the sword until you all meet together in the meadow of Baha." And when the night came, all the people were mustered and ascended Mount Gerizim, and Baba Raba was in the forward ranks of the troops; and Levi arose with the might and power of God Most High, and smote the guards of the king, and the monks, and the priests, and cried out in a loud voice: "The LORD is a Man of war; the LORD is His name."[138] And when Baba Raba heard the voice of Levi his nephew, they all raised their voices, saying as he had said, and they unsheathed swords and killed many of the Romans. And they did not cease until they had wiped out everyone who was on Mount Gerizim. Then they kindled the fire on the top of the Dome, and all the Samaritans arose and killed all the overseers who were over them, and there did not remain one of them. And they continued throughout the whole night burning the churches of the Romans, destroying them until they had effaced their name from Mount Gerizim and round about. There has remained a memorial of that to our own day, for at the beginning of the seventh month the children of the Samaritans gather together wood, and they burn it on the night of the outgoing[139] of the beginning of the seventh month.

When the Romans who were on the coastal areas heard what had befallen their companions at the hands of Baba Raba, they gathered together a very large body of men and came seeking Baba Raba until they came near Nablus. Then Baba came out to them and smashed them and killed most of them. The news reached King Alexander[140] at Rome; now he was the king, and he gathered many troops, men of war, and he sent them against Baba Raba. But God helped Baba Raba against them, and he smashed them; and the war between them was over by the village of 'Askar, and

---

[137] Undoubtedly a structure, used for signal fires, on the peak of the mount.
[138] Exod 15:3 in the MT tradition. The SP, avoiding anthropomorphism, reads, "God is a hero of war."
[139] The same custom is said to originate during the rebellion against the overseers who hindered the work of the newly appointed sages.
[140] Certainly a misidentification, as Severus Alexander was much earlier than the time of this story.

he killed them, leaving only a few of them, so they asked for reinforcements of troops against Baba Raba, and he equipped tens of thousands against him. When Baba Raba heard of that, he wrote letters to all the Samaritans to present themselves. And they presented themselves to him from every place, ten thousand horsemen, warlike youths with their weapons and their military equipment. And Baba Raba delivered to them the villages in fee; and the news came to Baba Raba that his enemies were coming in number like the sand of the seashore. Baba Raba stood before God Most High, and prostrated himself, and sought help from God. And he spent a long time praising and glorifying God, and he made for himself ambushes in burial grounds, and he said to them: "When you see battle has taken place between us and when I cry out at the top of my voice, 'O people of the graves, assist me,' then emerge from the graves." And the number of the ambushes was five thousand, and when Baba Raba drew near his enemies, the priests sounded the trumpets, and all the people lifted up their voices, saying: "God is a mighty man in war, God is His name."[141] And the earth was rent by their voices, and the battle was joined between them. No battle in this world was ever like it, and Baba Raba cried out in the middle of the battle and said: "O people of the graves, aid me against the enemies of God." And the soldiers of Rome were astonished. When he spoke thus, the men who were lurking came out saying: "Fear not! Fear not! All of us will strengthen you, and the rest of the dead are coming after us; on every side they will strengthen you." And when the Romans saw that, they thought that it was genuine, and their hearts were broken, and they lost courage, and they turned back fleeing, and some of them fell over others. And God came to Israel on that day with a mighty victory.

This is what I found in the copy that I have described, and God knows best about the unseen; but there remains information about Baba Raba in the copies (of the manuscripts), and even if it occurs later, it will be given, for it deals with the same topic.[142]

And after all that, Philippus sent messengers to Baba Raba with a letter in his own handwriting, saying to him: "It is desired by our ruler and our lord the great king that he may grant a favor to the slave, that he should come to him at Constantinople, where he will stay with him a few days.

---

[141] See Exod 15:3.

[142] This editorial remark, which appears to be Abu'l Fath's recognition of inconsistencies in the account, at the same time expresses his commitment to recount all available to him.

And when we are satisfied at having seen him, then he will return here."
Baba Raba gathered together his people, and his son, and his family, and
informed them that he must go on the journey. And his father and the
heads of his people said to him: "How is your cheerfulness possible, seeing
that the people will be left alone and we would have found comfort at
your hand? So do not do that lest we return to humiliation and degrada-
tion and be reduced to nothing, for your enemies were extremely disappointed at your victories." And he said to them: "Know that I have
submitted my command to God, Mighty and Glorious, and perhaps this
enmity will cease and this fire be extinguished which is between us and the
nations. And if God will, I shall not delay, but soon I shall return to you;
and if it be not so, then the matter is finished as far I am concerned, and I
bequeath you my son, Levi."

Now this Levi was his son, and not his brother's son. And they said to him:
"Let a company of us go with you; they will serve you." He said: "I will not
have that, but I charge you not to turn aside from keeping the commands
of God and His ways. And fear not nor grow anxious, but be strong and be
of good courage, for God is with you and will not forsake you." Then he
took the hand of his son Levi and delivered him to Nathanel, his father,
and said: "This is my charge to you, and my command to you is that you
will keep him in it; may your happiness continue and the trust of all the
people likewise." And he went in company with the messenger of the king,
and when he drew near, King Philip summoned the crowd to go out to
meet Baba Raba; and all the people went out with crosses and images in
prayer. All the kings walked alongside Baba Raba's camel, and he alone
continued riding. And it was a great day for him when he entered Constantinople with great pomp. No king had so entered. And when he was in
the fortress, the King said to the great ones of his kingdom: "Baba has
come into our power, so what do you think we should do with him?" And
some of them who were there said: "Have him killed." Others said: "That
is not possible, for he is a great king and we have sworn to him that we
shall not harm him; if then we were to do so, it would cause the destruction of all Rome and of their survival." So the king said: "Truly have you
spoken. It is our duty that we serve him, and we should consider his opinion, but we shall not let him again go from this country all his life." Now
formerly he had had gold and silver, so the king ordered its return to him,
and he charged all the watchmen of the gates about him. But Baba said to
the king: "I want to return to my family." And he said to him: "Stay with us
some time and be at ease." And he knew that he had got hold of him. So

when the father of Baba saw that his son did not come, he married his son Levi to Rebecca, daughter of his uncle ʿAkbon.

Then Nathanel, the father of Baba Raba, died. And after his death, Levi went to be with his father at Constantinople, and he stayed with his father a few days. And Baba Raba was sick with a mortal sickness; and when the sickness increased in him, he sought a man, a Jew, a true friend of his, and he handed over to him his son Levi and said to him: "I want you to bring him to his people and his relatives, but do not hand him over to uncleanness, but guard him like your son." And he bound him by oath to that. And Baba Raba died in Constantinople by the mercy of God Most High, and the day of his death was a momentous day; and he was buried in a beautiful tomb, and the Romans built a beautiful church over it. And after his death, the king brought his son Levi and released him and restored to him all that had been his father's, of gold, silver, and raiment, and sent him off. And he sent in his service on the journey men to bring him to his people; and the Jewish man went with him and did as Baba Raba had charged him, and he served him until he brought him to his relatives. When the people heard of the arrival of Levi the son of Baba Raba, they rejoiced greatly for him, and all the community of Israel came to Namara. They greeted him, and they filled the earth and the wadis and the riverbeds and the fields. And they brought their companions, many and good, and they made for him a festival with the ceremony of eating in the wadis and the mountains and meadows and fields. And all the people wanted Levi to come and go and bless them; so throughout the length of that day he remained, mingling with the Samaritans, and would go round among them. And all the Samaritans were rejoicing and being happy with him until the evening came, the time of prayer. He crossed to his house; he prayed and laid down his head to take rest. Now no food had entered his mouth that day; and they brought to him food, but they thought that he was sleeping, and they would have roused him. But he could not be roused, and they drew near him and discovered what was the matter with him, for they found that he was dead (God Most High have mercy on him). And joy was turned to violent grief; the like of it there had never been; and they buried him in the grave which his uncle ʿAkbon had prepared for himself in the village of Namara, and he was first to be buried in it. And when Rebecca his wife saw her cousin was dead, she swore by her soul not to eat or drink until she died; and she died on the seventh day after the death of her cousin, and she was buried beside him in the above-mentioned tomb.

Eighteenth Excerpt: The priest ᶜAkbon and of Dusis and his followers[143]

So the priest ᶜAkbon was invested with the high priesthood after the death of his nephew. But there were men powerful, stern in judgment, vigorous in affairs, who all spoke against him and said that the (High) Priest ᶜAkbon was acting unfairly in judging and that he was speedy in carrying out a judgment if it affected those not related to him but if it affected his relatives, he did not do that. And some of them agreed they should testify against the daughter of the priest ᶜAkbon, whose name was Maryam, that they found her with a Samaritan man. And those who cast suspicion on her agreed together that he should flee until the priest had decided what should happen in the case of his own daughter; and thus he would make it plain whether he was acting wrongfully in judgment or not. So they came before him, and they testified with false testimony against his daughter to the effect that they had found her with a certain person (and) not on the road.[144] So he sent seeking that person, and he found he had fled, and the affair seemed to him to be certain by the flight of the accused; so he took his daughter and burnt her as God said, in passing sentence in His revelation:[145] "And the daughter of any priest, if she profanes herself by playing the harlot, profanes her father, she shall be burned with fire." But in that night he saw her likeness in a dream saying to him: "In the place where you burned me, O my Father, kill not until you have examined and searched out; for me you killed unjustly." And on the second night and on the third he saw this dream exactly the same; and he arose on the morning of the fourth day for judgment, and he brought the witnesses, and he disputed with them. Then they acknowledged that they had wronged his daughter and had witnessed falsely to test the High Priest's judging of his relatives. So he burned them as God said: "Then you shall do to him as he had meant to do to his brother."[146]

And at that time, Philippus the king took from ᶜAkbon all the wealth which Baba Raba had left, in the presence of the companions of Levi his son.[147]

---

[143] Bowman, *Samaritan Documents,* 159–67. Used by permission.

[144] Single women were permitted, when occasion demanded, to travel on the road with a man (i.e., in a public place), but to be found off the road (in a private spot) was incriminating.

[145] Lev 21:9.

[146] Deut 19:19.

[147] Philippus is also identified in this story by *Chronicle Adler.*

And there reigned after him Dahikhus,[148] and he was worse than Alexander at his worst; and he sent to the land men and among them a wicked man called Rakas. Now it came to pass during his term in Caesarea that he found a woman praying and her son with her in her room. He visited it frequently for one year and two months, then he commanded his servant to bring her to him. When she came before him, he said to her: "To whom are you praying?" She said: "I am praying to the God of the Heavens and the Earth." He said to her: "Do you see him when you pray to him?" And she said to him: "I do not see Him, nor can any see Him."[149] And he said to her: "Why do you not pray to one you can see?" And she said to him: "That is hateful to us." So he said: "Punish her so that she will worship the idols." So his youths took her and beat her, but she could not be made to worship. So he said: "Bring fire and burn her." So they brought fire and he said to her: "If you do not worship the idols, I will burn you and your son in fire." But she refused to worship, so they took her son and threw him into the middle of the fire. And when she saw her son in the fire, she hurled herself into the fire upon him. The two of them were burnt completely. When Dahikhus the king heard, that seemed good to him, and he said: "The like of this should be done in every place." But God did not spare him, and he was killed (may God not have mercy on him). And there reigned after him Tahus, and he ill-treated the Samaritans, and he set over them agents to prevent them from saying prayers and sacred readings and from doing the commandments.[150] And the name of the agent who was over the house of the High Priest was Germon, and he sat at the door of the High Priest night and day. Now he was possessed of great dignity, and they feared him greatly. Then the High Priest ʿAkbon was blessed with a male child, and he and his family and the heads the Samaritans were gathered together, and he said: "How can the act of circumcision of the child take place?" And he (Germon) remained with him and with them continuously. When it was the morning of the eighth day, the High Priest took a basket and wrapped up the little one in wool and put him in it (the basket) and covered him with wool, and he said to the woman: "Take this basket and go out. Wait for me at Ras al-'Ain. And the woman took the basket out, and Germon was at the door. When Germon saw the basket, he knew that the baby was in it, and he said to the woman: "Do your business joyfully." So she went with ʿAkbon, and she told him the saying of Germon,

---

[148] Decius.

[149] See SJ 16.

[150] *Chronicle Adler* does not include Tahus and assigns the story of Germanus to Decius.

and he was violently afraid, but he said: "The affair belongs to God. Let Him do as He thinks best." So he entered the cave, and circumcised the boy, and handed him in the basket to the woman as he was, with the wool over him. And after a short time, ᶜAkbon went home, and Germon stood up and said in Hebrew (for he knew Hebrew better than ten Samaritans) *Rabbi, rabbi hadi,* which being explained is "O my master, rejoice greatly." Now when the High Priest heard that, he was violently afraid and went into the house and said: "Who gave Germon information about us?" And he filled his hand with gold and said to Germon: "Take this little in exchange for much." But he said: "Far be it from me that I should sell my obedience to God today for the lucre of this world." And the High Priest's fear increased when he refused to take the gold. But when Germon saw the High Priest's fear, he said to him: "Your heart is good. Do not fear, for I, for the sake of God, have treated you proudly. But for the sake of your good pleasure, I will take from all this three dinars, and it will be as if I had taken it all. So rejoice in your son. May God spare him to you." So in that hour did the joy of the High Priest ᶜAkbon increase in his son, and the community was gathered with him, and they greatly praised and glorified God (praise be to Him the Most High). And ᶜAkbon said to the community: "This event shall be commemorated by us forever, and we shall implore mercy on this overseer, Germon, at the times of festivals and holy convocations (as follows), *Dekir letob ad leolam Germon 'Asora Rom'a,* that is, 'May Germon the Roman overseer be remembered for good forever.'"

After that came Dusis the son of Fufali.[151] Now he had committed adultery with the wife of one of the chief ones of the Jews in one of the villages of the Jews; and the leaders of the Jews sought to kill him. But he said: "Do not kill me, and I will go to Nablus, and I will restore in the house of Ephraim the two golden (bulls),[152] and I will make them causes of dissension, and I will compensate you for all the shedding of blood they have caused you." So they let him live because of that. And this is written among the Jews,[153] that they released him from condemnation because of what he would do in Nablus. Now the origin of Dusis was from the mixed rabble who went out with the children of Israel from the land of Egypt to Nablus. And Dusis went to the village of Askar. And there was there a person called Yahdu, a very learned man, who was unique in his time in knowledge and in law. And Dusis followed him closely and gave him generous alms, and he went into him one day and found him eating firstlings. So Dusis

---

[151] *Chronicle Adler* places the rise of Dusis in the high priesthood of ᶜAkbon.
[152] 1 Kgs 12:28.
[153] The source to which Abu'l Fath is referring is unknown.

said to him: "Is it lawful for you to eat firstlings when its blood has been sprinkled on the altar, as it says, 'You shall sprinkle their blood upon the altar,'[154] and so on." Yahdu said him: "And it is like the bread of which God said: 'And you shall eat neither bread nor grain, parched or fresh,'[155] and so on." And they stopped eating bread and firstlings for a period two years; when they had finished being ascetic, after two years they entered Nablus and ate and drank and got drunk. Now Yahdu got drunk and slept in his place; so Dusis took Yahdu's mantle and went and gave it to a prostitute and said to her: "Take this mantle, and when it is the day after tomorrow, go up the mountain, and all the Samaritans will be on it. And seize hold of the elder who will be next to the High Priest; his name is Yahdu. And say that he has committed adultery with you and he left his mantle in pledge with you in lieu of your payment; and that you need not fear, for you are known for this. So take this, your reward: six dinars."

Now when Yahdu awoke and sought his mantle, he could not find it. So he went to the people of the town, asking them about it. And they swore to him they had not taken it. So he sought Dusis and he could not find him. And when it was the third day—now it was the Day of Atonement—the prostitute went up to the mountain and found the elder whom Dusis had described to her beside the High Priest; she accosted him and asked for help and said: "O my lord High Priest, take my payment from the elder who stands beside you." He said: "What have you to do with him?" She said: "He spent the night with me and gave me this mantle in pledge, and I lost him until today." And they said to Yahdu: "Is this your mantle?" He said: "Yes, this mantle is mine." And the High Priest said: "Take him to be burned." But Yahdu said: "Do not act hastily as to my case. Those with whom Dusis and I were drinking know it, so let them and Dusis be bound by oath as to it, as to what opinion is to be held; but if you neither hold me nor them trustworthy, then burn me, me and this whore." Then the High Priest ᶜAkbon called the whore and said: "Tell me the truth, and if not, I will burn you, and I will burn this man with you." So she confessed the truth and said: "Oh my Lord, Dusis gave me six dinars and this mantle and said to me: 'Do this deed.'"

And the High Priest ᶜAkbon searched for Dusis but could not find him. For Dusis, because of his fear of the High Priest ᶜAkbon and the violence of his strength and the swiftness of his resolve, fled to Suwaika, and lodged with a woman whose name was Amantu the widow, and said to her: "I am the son

---

[154] Num 18:17.
[155] Lev 23:14.

of the High Priest." So she served him, and he spent many days with her writing. And when he had finished his task, he knew that the High Priest ᶜAkbon would not pardon him but sought him; so he arose and departed from that place to another, and he charged the woman and said to her: "I know that behind me is one who seeks me and wants to kill me, so I asked of you the right of entry to your lodging. You shall say to him who comes seeking me that he stayed with me a short space of time writing on these pieces of paper and went out and departed but I do not know where he has gone. However, he charged me that no one was to come near these pieces of paper until after that person had gone down into this pool and dipped himself in it and that nothing should soil you after you have cleansed yourself of the stains of the road."

Dusis went to Anbata and went up the mountain and concealed himself in a cave and died in it from hunger, and dogs came in and ate him. This is what happened to Dusis, cursed be his name. And as for the High Priest ᶜAkbon, he did not cease pursuing until he heard that he had come to Suwaika and that for a space of time he had been with Amantu the widow. So he sent Levi, the son of Phinehas his brother. Now he was a man bold in religion. And he sent along with him seven men to bring in Dusis and to kill him as he had intended to do to Yahdu. So Levi went, accompanied by the men, and they came to Suwaika and entered the house of Amantu the widow and said to her: "Is not my friend Dusis with you who deserves to be killed?" And she said: "I know not that he deserves to be killed, but I was exceedingly generous to him when he said to me: 'I am the son of the High Priest.' And I found him continually busy and writing on pieces of paper, and when he wanted to set off on a journey, he said to me: 'No one is allowed to approach them until he has dipped himself in this pool.' And he went away from me, and I know not where he has gone."

Then Levi said to the company: "What is against our dipping in this pool and purifying ourselves from the stains of the road before we venture to read names of God, Most High is He?" So one of the men who accompanied Levi went down to the pool and dipped and came up and said: "My faith is in Thee, LORD, and in Dusis Your servant and his prophecy." Levi called out against him and struck him and said to another: "Go down." And he went down, dipped, and said the same as had the one who had preceded him. And they went on dipping until not one of them remained undipped. And they were repeating this saying and testifying regarding Dusis in prophecy. Levi was perplexed in his mind and said: "By God, now I will dip and see the wickedness of these men and their blasphemy, and I will oppose them if God, Most High is He, wills." Then Levi went down and dipped and came up and said: "My faith is in Thee, LORD, and in Dusis Your prophet. Woe to us who pursue after the prophet of God, Dusis." They took the books of Dusis, and they found that he had altered much of the Law, for example, punishment (prescribed) and more. But they all preserved what he had written and altered. Then they returned to Nablus, and they said to the High Priest that they had not found him and that he had gone from the woman and she did not know where he had gone. Now when it was the first Festival Day of the Feast of the Passover, the Samaritans were gathered together, and the High Priest ⁢Akbon said to the son of his brother, Levi, the son of Phinehas: "Rise. Read:[156] 'Then Moses called all the elders of Israel.'" And Levi arose and read until he reached "Take a bunch of hyssop."[157] He read, instead of "hyssop," "thyme," as Dusis had altered it, and the Samaritans refuted him. But Levi said: "No, the correct (reading) is what God said by the hand of Dusis (upon him be peace), 'thyme,' and truely you, all of you, are shamelessly ignorant of the prophecy of Dusis; you alter the festivals and make a substitute for the greatest name, Yahweh, and send chasing after the second prophet whom God had first signified from Mount Sinai. Woe to you from God."

Thereupon they said: "The scholar has blasphemed." And his uncle, the High Priest, cried out against him and said: "Kill him!" And Levi fled, and the Samaritans followed him to a point near the field of Joseph, and they vied with one another as to the number of stones they threw at him. And they went on stoning him until he died; and they made a cairn of stones over him, and it is called Levi's monument until this our day. And when the men who were with Levi saw what happened to Levi, they concealed their affair and led astray along with them a company of people who believed in Dusis; and when they became numerous, they turned towards a village beside Jerusalem out of fear of the Samaritans. When Levi had been stoned, these took palm leaves and smeared them with Levi's blood and said: "This is he concerning whom God said: 'Lest blood be shed in your land.'[158] And what was the sin of Levi that he was stoned? When he testified that Dusis was a prophet (saying he was a prophet), he was killed." They took the books and put in them the palm leaves, and agreed among themselves that whoever wanted to see the palm leaves of Levi and read Dusis' own writing should fast seven days during the nights thereof before he should see them. They said that the dead would rise soon, also that Dusis had prophesied that he would die aged twenty-eight of hunger and thirst and dogs

---

[156] Exod 12:21.
[157] Exod 12:22.
[158] Deut 19:10.

would eat him after his death. So Levi, his first martyr, was stoned in the field of Joseph. They cut their hair and made all their prayers while in water; and when they bathed in the water, they used to cover their bodies when they went down into it. And they did not go out on the Sabbath day from house to house. They kept no Festival but the Sabbath day, and if it were shifted from its proper time to another time, they would not put out their hands from their sleeves. Also, when one of them died, they would gird him with a strong girdle and put in his hand a staff, and on his feet sandals, and they would say: "When we arise from the graves, we will arise in readiness." It is said that they believed firmly that as soon as the dead were buried, he would rise from the grave and go away to Paradise. All these rulings were drawn up by Dusis (may God curse him). And these followers continued in hiding until the Samaritans left off trying to kill them.

Nineteenth Excerpt: Simon and his controversy with the sect of the Messiah[159]

Then the High Priest ʿAkbon died (God Most High have mercy on him), and his son succeeded him in office, and he continued in the Priesthood thirty-one years. Now Nathanel had a son whose name was Yah'am, who had a serving girl called Sul. She was enamored of the already mentioned Yah'am and fell more and more in love with him and became obsessed with him, but he would not devote himself to her. But when she knew that he would not fall in with her and that she would not get any response from him, no, that he would not heed her nor give heed to anything but prayer and worship and occupying himself with learning, she despaired of him, but the passion kept working in her. She went to Simon, the wizard from 'Alin, and said to him: "My lord the High Priest salutes you and desires that you kill his son, for he is disobedient to him and has disappointed his parents. He desires that he be killed in secret, and these twelve dinars he has furnished for you." Simon thought that her words were true,[160] so he said to her: "Whatever he has commanded us, we will do." And he said to the greatest of the Jinn: "Go to the son of the High Priest and take his soul, but do not cause his spirit to pass until his father regrets his killing and wishes the keeping of our power over his life." So the Jinn went immediately to the son of the High Priest, but he was not able to have power over him because he was eating firstlings.[161] He returned and said to Simon: "I have no

---

[159] Bowman, *Samaritan Documents,* 167–74. Used by permission.
[160] In *Chronicle Adler,* Simon does not believe the girl.
[161] I.e., he was in a state of ritual purity.

power over him because he has sanctified himself and is eating holy things." Simon said to him: "Go to him, and when he has finished the food, seize him." So he went, and he returned to him the next day and said: "I have no power over him because, when he finished the food, he prayed again until morning." Simon said to him: "Follow him until the rule of the night[162] overtakes him and you have power over him." And he continued with him until the rule of the night befell him. And he became impure, and he was nearby him and seized his soul until he swooned and became like one dead. Then his father and mother and his relatives arose and cried for help, and much was their crying and much their uproar; and the Samaritans came and wept mightily, and the father was unable to bear his grief for him. The Samaritans tried to console him, but he refused to be consoled, and he lost composure. Now Simon was present in the assembled company of the mourners, and when he saw the High Priest in great grief and sorrow over his son, he was astonished at him, came to his side, and said: "I see you in this great grief, yet you sent your serving girl to me in order to have him killed. But if you want him to live, let me know." And he to him: "Earn the reward from God, Mighty and Glorious." Simon drew near to him and exorcised him, and he arose at once but knew nothing of what his condition had been. Then the Priest brought his serving girl and tortured her; and she confessed that she had done that because she had not obtained what she longed for from him. So he put her to death in the sight of the people. Simon was confounded before the High Priest, and went away immediately, and traveled to 'Armiya. And he and the disciples of the Messiah competed in witchcraft, but he gained the mastery over them.[163] Then he found a Jewish philosopher whose name was Philo from Alexandria, and he (Simon) said: "Strengthen me, and I will stop the sect of the Messiah." Philo said to him: "Rest your soul, for if this matter is from God, no one has power to stop it."[164] So Simon returned and came to Beit 'Alin, and died and was buried in the wadi that is situated opposite the house of the disciple who testified to the Messiah first, and his name was Saftanah.[165] The disciples of the Messiah were fifteen persons,[166] the last of whom became a Jew, and to

---

[162] I.e., a seminal emission.

[163] I.e., Jesus. In *Chronicle Adler,* Jesus is not called the Messiah but simply the son of Mary of Nazareth. See Acts 8:24 for a different version of the contest between Simon and the disciples of the Messiah.

[164] In Acts 5:39 this statement is placed in the mouth of Gamaliel.

[165] According to Mark 8:29, this confession is first made by Simon Peter. That Peter's house can be identified and serve as a landmark for Simon's grave is remarkable.

[166] It is unclear why Abu'l Fath numbers fifteen instead of the more normal twelve.

him were attached the circumcised disciples.[167] And after that, they did not accept the circumcised, but all of them were uncircumcised.[168] And men called Ba'unai (Ebionites) seceded according to the opinion of Dusis and his disciples. And they came to Beisan, and they made for themselves a place in the market of the beasts of burden; but the seven men who were disciples of Dusis all perished.

Then arose one called Ansma, who began leading men astray and attempting to annul the festivals. Now a man of the Samaritans saw in his sleep Abraham, Isaac, and Jacob. They were saying to him: "Go to Ansma and say to him: 'Refrain from causing our children to err and destroying them; and if you refrain not, then you shall perish and everyone who listens to you.'" But when it was told him, he increased more in rebellion and began to make them err more than before. And he said, "You do not know the festivals except in dreams." And on a certain Sabbath night he was at a house and the seven with him, and in the house an accident occurred, and they perished to the last of them. So none remained of the Ba'unai except one man.

And another sect arose from them whom they called Kiltai (but I found a Hebrew version Katitai), and they said: "Do not keep any commandments, for all commandments are annulled." And they went up to Mount Gerizim and said before God: "Oh God, what Dusis Your prophet said we will do here; we have annulled all the commandments, and You are the One who is able to reveal the Tabernacle." And God afflicted them, and they went down from the mountain barking like dogs, and they continued like that till they died. When men saw what had happened to them, they turned from believing firmly in them.

And there arose another sect from these, the company of the Ba'unai, who caused to sin by their saying that the world shall endure because Dusis had died his shameful death, and Levi was stoned because Dusis had died and all the righteousness of the world had died. These believed firmly that the winged dragon would rule the creatures till the day of resurrection. And they bound men to silence, and the inner secret of their way of acting they did not disclose to anyone. They used to practice in a village whose name is Maluf; they were called Sadukai. They lasted seven years, and when their

---

[167] Perhaps Abu'l Fath has in mind Peter, who is remembered for advocating circumcision in his confrontation with Paul. Or perhaps Abu'l Fath has in mind someone added as in the manner of Acts 1, for whom there is no mention in the New Testament literature.

[168] A reference to the Jerusalem council of Acts 15?

secret was revealed, the place where they were fell upon them, and they perished to the last of them

And there arose after this the Abiya and Dusa. One hundred and twenty persons inclined towards them and said: "All the commandments have not been annulled, so let us go out to the wilderness as Dusis said, for what we experience is neither security nor Divine Grace." So they went out from Nablus on a Sabbath day, and passed the graves and crossed the Jordan on the Sabbath day, and went out to the wilderness. And snakes set on them and killed them, and only two of them were saved. And they narrated how they met their death, and this sect passed away also.

And there arose an insolent man called Salyah the son of Tairun the son of Nin, and he sought advancement in the synagogue. The people of the city did not enable him to do so, so he went out and came to the Samaritans and began making them err and said: "Come up with me and see how the Tabernacle will appear." And they made for him a large tent, and he began teaching in it; and he said from this tent: "Let us go up to Mount Gerizim." And a hundred and eighteen men were gathered to him. Now he stipulated for them asceticism for each one, and no woman should come to them, nor a boy, as Dusis said. And Baunai came back and they said, "Bad is what they said, that the dead will shortly arise and no one need fast if he wants to see the palm leaves of Levi and the handwriting of Dusis, nor need one pray in water." So he began changing festivals and making this error among the Samaritans; he called Mount Gerizim a substitute, similar to the everlasting mountain. Further, he said that he who prays towards Mount Gerizim is like one who prays toward a grave. He divided the unclean practices into two: one was called primary and the other intermediate. He declared permitted marriage with the Gentiles and the touching of woman in menses. He said that there is no uncleanness in dead animals except that which is prohibited for eating. As for all the pearls which they used, and the clothing which they wore, and the rest of the fine garments which are the root of it, it is the business of the Gentiles, not the business of Israel; it does not make unclean. He permitted also the touching of the dead and said: "Wherever he wished, he might pass provided it is not contiguous to it ; and it is not incumbent on him to be purified except the first day only." He said that a child acquires what his mother acquires of uncleanness. And he said: "There is no holiness in the time of error," and he prohibited the continuous immersing of oneself and baptizing on the Sabbath day. And he called the name of his soul "The Measurer." He made the prayer, like the reading, be from a sitting position. He said that the synagogues were like houses of idols, so he who paid anything to the Synagogue, it was as if he paid (it) to the house of idols. And he made vessels, in which were the (manuscript) scrolls in the synagogue like the prostitute when she passes with pomp. He made every man, when he read or prayed, cover his head; and he who did not do what he said deserved the curse. He ordained that the teachers of the Samaritans should be those concerning whom God said: "You shall make for yourselves no idols."[169] And he it is who established the reading Qinah. He said, concerning himself, that he was the father of all who listened to him, and they were the Dustan (that is, Friends) calling him: "Oh our father," while his disciples were saying: "May God cause the spirit of our father Salyah to pour forth, but grant that he die not on the Sabbath." And he changed the reading of the greatest Name, and he said one should only read "Blessed is He." He put a stop to the ascending of the noble mountain and said that one does not fling away what one visits frequently, following the words of Dusis (God curse him). And he made women read with the men in the meeting place. Then he died (may God not have mercy on him) on the Sabbath day. Now he had never gone up Mount Gerizim in his life.

Five brothers arose from Taira Luza. They were called the sons of Josadak; and another was called Sadok the Great from Bait Fara. And they differed from Salyah and his companions, for they said that Mount Gerizim was sanctified as was the House on it and that it was incumbent that one do what is written and one should not do what is not allowed upon it. Anyone who came near to a dead man should bathe, and on the first day he should cleanse himself before touching anything. But they called him by the above-mentioned name "the Measurer" and agreed with him on annulling "And Blessed is His Name for Ever." They organized the making of a distinction in relation to all Sabbaths and annulled the saying of "Moses commanded us a law."[170] After that Ulianah went out who was living in Alexandria, and there was gathered together to him a company, and he said: "Receive from me the Divine Grace; it will appear, and we have no power to act straight, since we read all together; but let the men be set apart from the women and the women from the men, and the sons be set apart along with their fathers, and let none take anything from anyone; but he who wants to have a measure of anything in itself, let him say: 'Holiness belongs to God.'" So he removed the men from the women, and the sons from their mothers, and the men divorced their wives and left their possessions. And Bustunus went out against them from the sea, and destroyed of them many people,

---

[169] Lev 26:1.
[170] Deut 33:4.

and threw a company of them into ships. And Ulianah died; and he died an unclean death. Those who remained of his sect thought they were under Divine Grace, but they were mistaken, for a number of trials befell them; yet they did not change nor take warning; and there arose after that others who were called Faskutai, and they said: "Here there is no Garden and no Resurrection, but there is only trial, and the woman is the strength of the trial." So they said: "A man ought to sleep with a different woman six nights, and they should be clothed." But when it was the seventh night, they discarded the clothes, for they were now free from whoring and they had reached the limit of temptation. And when they had done that, all of them had contaminated themselves by whoring. So they arose and castrated themselves and said: "He who has castrated himself, filthiness has passed away from him."[171] All those divisions came from the books of Dusis; and there came upon the Samaritans because of them great error and great sin and vice and enmities from which no profit came; but God is the Rewarder of every man according to his act.

Twentieth Excerpt: The Samaritans, Christians, and Muhammad[172]

Then the Christian champion took the field, a powerful and huge man. The Christians said to him, "We are all relying upon you." They also had a dog with them, which was like a lion and could swallow two cats. Taking the field for the Samaritans was a man (called) Bustiya from Kfr Aqr, his dwelling. He was like a devouring whirlwind of fire. (The Samaritan warrior) knelt in the presence of Almighty God, the Giant of Giants, and set out to do battle with a sincere heart and a pure intention. Then the dog leapt at him at the outset; and he dealt it a blow that broke its legs. God gave the victory to Bustiya, who killed his opponent. The Christians then fled, as did all who were with them. After this contest no one (ever) returned to demand their tombs.

After Eleazer came Nathaniel for 31 years. In the 13th year of his pontificate, Zaitun king of Byzantium came to Nablus and oppressed the Samaritans and obliged them to embrace the religion of the Christians under pain of being burnt to death, or pressed to death, or tortured by fire. He began looking for the important men of the community, and the Hukama, and the priests.

Zaitun said to them, "If you will not kneel before this cross, then you will all be killed!"

---

[171] The filthiness is not in the lust but in the physical act.
[172] Stenhouse, *The Kitab al-Tarikh*, 239–49. Used by permission.

They said, "We surrender our lives to death, for the sake of our Lord; but we will kneel to no one but God."

So he killed them. He then took seventy Hukama and tried to force them to kneel to idols. They also refused, so he had them executed in the middle of the market place near the standing columns. And the Samaritans used not to walk in front of these columns—only behind them. Then Zaitun, may God curse him, took the Synagogue which ʾAqbun had built, and put a throne in it, and made in front of it a place of sacrilege. Then he went out and came to the Synagogue of Baba Raba and asked, "To whom does this place belong?"

They said to him, "This place (belongs) to the Samaritans. They pray in it to God their Lord, before this Mountain."

He said, "But it does not have an image on top of it!"

They told him that they prayed to a being who was unseen and immaterial. Zaitun had Nathaniel the Great High Priest brought, and assembled the leaders of Israel, and said to them, "Sell me the Mountain of your Qibla!"

They answered him, "We and all we possess are at the disposal of the king."

He did not stop until he had taken the Temple and all around about it, the water pool and the cistern of water to the north.

He added buildings to the Temple and surroundings; and to the cistern of water (he added) buildings similar to the Temple. He built a Church inside the Temple which he painted white and from which lamps were hung to glow in the night to let those in Constantinople and Rome see. And he built a tomb on Mount Gerizim to the south of the Temple.

When a son of his died, he buried him in it, and Zaitun said, "This will be for the Samaritans, for them to reverence. Let a cross be made and put on top of the tomb, and let the people be told, 'Kneel before it,' and whoever will not kneel, let them be killed by the sword or crucified or crushed to death or blinded by fire."

Large numbers of houses were emptied, and villages were ruined by the oppression of Zaitun, may God curse him. Adultery was a byword in his day. Many girls and wives of Samaritan men became defiled in the days of the Byzantines, and according to them, adultery was not a grave sin. Indescribable distress and disgrace came upon the Samaritans in his days. Then Zaitun came back again and built a tomb for himself at the limits of the mountain, near the Royal Canal, which ran over the road. He commanded that he should be placed in it when he died so that the Samaritans would do him reverence when he was dead. But when he did die, may God show him no mercy, he was buried in the tomb in which his son had been buried facing the citadel near Jabatha. He was the last of the kings of Byzantium in this land. But they remained and used to form into numerous gangs that would plunder the villages and pillage them. Whenever someone heard that a person was wealthy, they would torture him until he handed his wealth over to them. And if they heard of a pretty woman, they would come in their hundreds and two-hundreds and would rape her until she died. The more powerful would take advantage of their neighbor and devour him. The people were decimated and the towns destroyed.

Nathaniel was succeeded by the High Priest Eleazer, who was great High Priest for 25 years. At the end of the High Priesthood of this Eleazer, Muhammad came. All the years from the disappearance of the Radwan to the coming of Muhammad were 1,993 years. And the total from Adam, upon whom be peace, to the coming of the above-mentioned was 5,047 years. At this time there were three men, astrologers very skilled in their profession. The first was a Samaritan called Sarmasa from Askr. The second was a Jew whose name was Ka'ab al-Ahbar. And the third was a Christian, a monk called Abd al-Salam. They knew from their craft and from their astrology that the Byzantium kingdom was gone and that the king(dom) of Islam had begun in the person of a man from the sons of Ishmael, from the Beni Hashim, with a characteristic mark on his back, between his shoulder blades—a white birthmark the shape of the palm of one's hand. Some say that it was yellow. When they heard that he had been seen, the three of them came together and said, "Let us set off and see if the man is he about whose appearance we foretold; and (let us confide) our secret to him concerning Masters of the Books and the sects so that we won't suffer at his hands what we suffered from those who went before him."

So the three set out and came to the city in which he was. They asked one another, "Who will go in first?" Ka'ab al-Ahbar said, "I (will) go," and he went into him (first) and greeted him.

He returned the greeting and asked him, "Who are you—a Jew?"

He said, "I am one of the leaders (of the Jews), and I found in my Torah that a king would arise from the stock of Ishmael to rule the world and that no one could prevent him."

Abd al-Salam then went in after him and said, "That is what I found in the Gospel"—although in fact all that they knew came from astrology!

Then Sarmasa went in and said to him, "You have a magnanimous religion and rule over the necks of the world. There is a sign for us on you—it is between your shoulder blades."

Muhammad was delighted at their words. He undressed, and behold: there was a big white birthmark between his shoulder blades. Then Ka'ab al-Ahbar and Abd al-Salam became Moslems. He rejoiced exceedingly at the two of them and sat them both by him and said to Sarmasa, "Why do you not do as they have done?" He permitted him (to approach closer), but Sarmasa was not able to approach closer to him.

He said to him, "I have what I regard as necessary for me—namely, the Law and (my) Faith. I am happy in my Faith and cannot come over to you. I cannot forsake my Faith."

Muhammad was ill-pleased at him and asked him, "What do you want, O Samaritan?"

Sarmasa said to him, "O my master, I have come to you to get a covenant and a treaty that we can rely upon, I and the people of my faith and my religion: a covenant of peace and security, as a protection for persons and families and property and religious endowments and for freedom to erect houses of worship."

So Muhammad instructed a scribe to draw up a covenant for them, of peace and security according to what he had requested. The Scribe entered his presence (and wrote), "I, Muhammad bin Muttalib, have commanded that a treaty of peace and security be written down for the Samaritans concerning themselves and their families and their property and houses of worship and religious endowments throughout all my realm and in all their territories. And that this be effective for them and as a covenant of peace among the people of Palestine and as a safe conduct."

Then Sarmasa took it and left his presence.

But Umar bin Rabia and Abdulla bin Jahash advised him to get the covenant endorsed by Ali bin Abi Talib. So he went back to Muhammad and stood before him and said, "O my master, I have come to you from an extensive, vast, and distant land and from a religious group that is weak and which the polytheists have persecuted and which the idol worshippers have overcome. We look for deliverance to God by means of you. I have been advised to obtain the endorsement of Ali bin Abi Talib for this covenant."

So he instructed Ali to sign the document, and he wrote for them from him (as follows): "I append to this covenant of peace for the Samaritans a guarantee for themselves, their families, their belongings, their houses of worship, and their religious endowments throughout all my lands, in every place and throughout all my possessions—that it be for them a safe conduct."

This was written down on a piece of leather, and he (Ali) gave it to him. Sarmasa kissed the ground from a respectful distance and said farewell.

Muhammad said, "O Samaritan, depart! In your lifetime you can indeed say, 'Let no one touch me.' You have a pledge. Do not violate it. Look to your God, whom you are still loyally following."

"Let us burn it, and then let us tear it up and throw (the pieces) into the sea."[173]

Sarmasa then returned to Palestine and announced the good news to the Samaritans about what God had done to make his path successful.

May God have mercy and compassion on this man, Ka'ab al-Ahbar, and Abd al-Salam stayed with him (Muhammad), and Ka'ab al-Ahbar became his secretary and organized what was organized and advised him on all problems.

The total number of years from Adam to the appearance of Muhammad was 5,047. This is the detailed list as I have described it in the Chronicle: from Adam to the end of the Radwan, 3,054 years.

The breakdown is as follows: Adam, 130 years; Seth, 105 years; Enosh, 90 years; Cain, 70 years; Mahallel, 65 years; Jared, 62 years; Enoch, 65 years; Methusaleh, 67 years; Lamech, 53 years; Noah, 600 years up until the Flood and 2 years from the Flood to the birth of Arphaxad; Arphaxad, 135 years; Shelah, 130 years; Eber, 134 years; Peleg, 130 years; Reu, 132 years; Sereg, 130 years; Nahor, 79 years; Terah, 70 years; Abram, upon whom be peace, 100 years; Isaac, upon whom be peace, 60 years; Jacob, upon whom be peace, 87 years; Levi, 52 years; Kohath, 71 years; Amram, 55 years; Moses, upon whom be peace, to the Entrance into Palestine, 120 years; Eleazer, upon whom be peace: the length of his leadership in the Radwan was 50 years; Phinehas, upon whom be peace, 60 years; Abisha, 40 years; Shishi, 50 years; Bohqi, 35 years; Ozzi, 25 years, the end of the Radwan and the disappearance of the Tabernacle; Ozzi lived 1 year after this. From Ozzi to the appearance of Muhammad was 1993 years.

---

[173] This comment indeed seems out of place. Is it a mischievous plan devised by Sarmasa's two companions?

The breakdown is as follows: Shishi, 39 years; Bohqi, 23 years; Shafat, 28 years; Shallum, 25 years; Hezeqia, 20 years; Jonathan, 28 years; Ya'ir, 21 years; Sadaqia, 28 years; Ahiyud, 20 years; Majar, 21 years; Yusaduq, 25 years; Dalia, 25 years; Ya'ir, 19 years; Jonathan, 28 years; Yishma'al, 26 years; Tobia, 28 years; Saduq, 20 years; Amram, 28 years; Khalifa, 24 years; Amram, 38 years; 'Aqbun, 36 years; Aqbia, 39 years; Halal, 45 years; Saria, 40 years; Levi, 50 years; Nathaniel, 52 years; Azria, 35 years; 'Abdal, 40 years; Hezeqia, 40 years; Hanania, 24 years; 'Amram, 32 years; Hanan, 25 years; Hezeqia, 21 years; Dalia, 41 years; 'Aqbun, 40 years; 'Aqia, 35 years; Levi, 41 years; Eleazer, 44 years; Manasseh, 36 years; Ya'ir, 39 years; Nathaniel, 41 years; Yehoqim, 32 years; Jonathan, 27 years; Elyishma, 33 years; Shamia, 10 years; Tobia, 8 years; Amram, 11 years; Aqub, 9 years; Amram, 9 years; 'Aqbun, 30 years; Phinehas, 40 years; Levi, 25 years; Eleazer, 32 years; Tobia, 28 years; Eleazer, 41 years; 'Aqbun, 23 years; Nathaniel the father of Baba Rabba, 32 years; Baba Rabba's High Priesthood is not counted, for he was High Priest during the lifetime of his father; 'Aqbun, 26 years; Nathaniel, 41 years; 'Aqbun, 20 years; Eleazer, 25 years; 'Aqbun, 24 years; Eleazer, 17 years; 'Aqbun, 30 years; Eleazer, 40 years; Nathaniel, 31 years; Eleazer, 25 years; Nathaniel, 20 years; Eleazer, 28 years. It was in his 12th year that Muhammad came.

The total from the creation of the world to the writing of this Chronicle that was in the year 756, according to the figure we referred to above, is 5,803 years.

Let us now return to a recollection of what is found in the Chronicle of the Fathers. We had reached (the point) where Sarmasa went to Muhammad and received treaties of peace and protection. After this the Ishmaelites went out against the Byzantines and utterly routed them, so that they fled from before them. The Samaritans who lived along the coast fled together with the Byzantines from before the sons of Ishmael. But Muhammad (himself) never mistreated any of the followers of the Law.

I have heard a saying from al-Hakim, who had it on the authority of the writer of the tradition, namely, the most learned Fadal al-Wajud al-Shaikh Nafis al-Din Abi al-Mufarraj bin Kitar, that it was said in a tradition of the ancestors concerning Muhammad, "Muhammad was a good and mighty person because he made a treaty of friendship with the Hebrew People."

This is what I have found in this Chronicle.

God knows best.

Chapter 4

Additional Samaritan Chronicles:
The *New Chronicle* (Chronicle Adler) and
Chronicle II

INTRODUCTION

In addition to the *Annals* of Abu'l Fath, two other Samaritan chronicles play prominent roles in telling the Samaritan story. The *New Chronicle* and *Chronicle II* extend the story of the Samaritan community up to the beginning of the twentieth century. Both of the chronicles are eclectic in nature, borrowing from earlier sources and molding them into the story and point of view that dominates each.

In addition to providing insight into the Samaritan self-understanding, which includes a Samaritan perspective on key social events, both chronicles contain interesting commentary about the communities and groups with whom the Samaritans had reason to interact. For example, the *New Chronicle* contains interesting comments concerning some of the Hebrew prophets and the books that bear their names as well as an account of events that led to the fracturing of the Israelite nation. Likewise, *Chronicle II* contains narratives concerning the pivotal moments in the history of ancient Israel (the division of the kingdom, the unfortunate construction of a temple in Jerusalem, Hezekiah's career). In addition, *Chronicle II* contains a fascinating narrative concerning the career of Jesus of Nazareth and the early history of the "kingdom of the Nazarenes" (Christianity), including a list of the books commonly used by the Nazarenes.

THE *NEW CHRONICLE (CHRONICLE ADLER)*

The Samaritan story is continued to the very beginning of the twentieth century by a work now commonly known as *Chronicle Adler*. It takes its name from E. N. Adler, who, along with M. Séligsohn, published a French translation of the chronicle in 1902–1903.[1] Adler admits that he was never permitted to view the original manuscripts but obtained a text from a German Jew living in Jerusalem who had transcribed a copy from the original in Nablus. The chronicle, although completed in 1900, as noted by the scribe's colophon, is not entirely of recent origin, as Samaritan chronicles grew over time, with succeeding generations adding to and modifying existing material as they saw fit.[2]

Besides an awareness and sometimes use of Jewish biblical materials, *Chronicle Adler* makes extensive use of other sources, two of which can be readily identified: the *Tulida (Tolidah)* and Abu'l Fath's *Annals*.[3] As does Abu'l Fath, *Chronicle Adler* uses for a structural skeleton the genealogy of high priests provided by the *Tulida*.[4] Chapter headings, if that is what they can be called, are simply the name of the priest and the number of years that he served (e.g., Uzzi the son of Buhki, twenty-five years; Sisi the son of Uzzi, thirty-seven years). Around this central thread, notes are added concerning items of interest both within and outside the Samaritan community. Soon after its publication, Adler conjectured that *Chronicle Adler* was nothing other than the "Chronicle of Sadaqah," rejected for use by Abu'l Fath but preserved and supplemented to form *Chronicle Adler*. Interesting as Adler's hypothesis may be, it has never won wide support.

Fruitful observations can be made by comparing *Chronicle Adler* with the *Annals*. *Chronicle Adler* at times changes the record found in the *Annals*, eliminating some of the more glaring inconsistencies and abridging some of the blatantly unhistorical sections of the *Annals*. Finding these changes still inadequate, Bowman makes a harsh judgment when he states, "Chronicle Adler shows that the Samaritans have learned nothing more about historiography since the fourteenth century."[5] This sentiment, though perhaps accu-

---

[1] E. N. Adler and M. Séligsohn, "Une nouvelle chronique samaritaine," *REJ* 44 (1902): 118–222; 45 (1902): 70–98, 160, 223–54; 46 (1903): 123–46.

[2] Colophons, as noted in the discussion of the SP, are not infrequent in Samaritan manuscripts. They often identify the date and place of the manuscript production and the identity of the scribe, in this case Ab Sakhwah ben 'As'ad ben Yishma'el ben Abraham ha-Danafi.

[3] For the awareness of Jewish biblical materials, see, e.g., the sections "Abdiel, the son of Azaraih, 40 years" and "Hezekiah, the son of Abdiel, 30 years"; for their use, see the quotations discussed in footnotes under the sections "'Akabyah, 39 years" and "Nathanel, 52 years."

[4] Séligsohn (Adler and Séligsohn, "Nouvelle chronique," 190) suggests reliance upon a third source: "ספר דברי הימים." But others think this simply another reference for Abu'l Fath's work (Paul Stenhouse, "Samaritan Chronicles," in *The Samaritans* [ed. Alan D. Crown; Tübingen: J. C. B. Mohr, 1989], 230).

[5] John Bowman, *Samaritan Documents Relating to Their History, Religion, and Life* (Pittsburgh: Pickwick, 1977), 88.

rate when compared with the historiography of the modern West, does not seem to appreciate the patterns of historical consciousness embedded in Samaritan chronicles. The view of history begun by the SJ and refined in the *Annals* is present in *Chronicle Adler* as well. These chronicles are written by the Samaritan community for the Samaritan community and are intended to tell the Samaritan story.

The following excerpts of *Chronicle Adler* are taken from Bowman's translation of the French version of Adler and Séligsohn.[6] Vocabulary, punctuation, capitalization, and syntax have been changed at times to make these excerpts more readable. Introductory comments preface each section in order to provide a brief description of the section or to point out to the reader something of interest in the section. This material, added by the present authors, is not found in the original manuscripts.

THE *NEW CHRONICLE (CHRONICLE ADLER)*: EXCERPTS

First Excerpt (Adler): The story of Eli and his apostasy

This excerpt also addresses the beginning of the period of divine disfavor and identifies groups within Israel and their characteristics.

Uzzi the son of Buhki, 25 years

Now in those days the prince over Israel was Samson, of the tribe of Dan, who was a mighty man in the land; he was the last of the kings of the period of Divine Favor, for in his days the LORD hid the holy Tabernacle from the eyes of Israel.[7] And so at that time Eli the son of Yafni went and made for himself an ark of gold, wherein he placed the books written in the handwriting of his ancestor, our lord Ithamar. He also made for himself a tent and pitched it at Shilo, because the children of Israel who were at that time in Shechem and in other cities of Palestine had driven him from Mount Gerizim, together with those who joined him. There in Shiloh he built an altar and offered sacrifices upon it, and all the men of the tribe of Judah joined him, as well as many men from other tribes. And all the things that Eli had done, are they not written down in the Book of Chronicles?[8]

---

[6] See ibid., 87–114.

[7] The story is found in the SJ. Deut 32:20 uses the concept of "hiding my face from them" as a form of divine displeasure and punishment.

[8] Could this be a reference to the *Annals?*

And the children of Israel in his days were divided into three groups:[9] one did according to the abominations of the Gentiles who served other gods; another followed Eli the son of Yafni, although many of them turned away from him after he had revealed his intentions; and the third remained with the High Priest Uzzi the son of Buhki, in the chosen place, Mount Gerizim Bethel, in the holy city of Shechem, and in all the (other) cities. Then the LORD hid from the eyes of all Israel the holy Tabernacle that Moses had made by the command of the LORD in the wilderness. This happened at the end of the priesthood of the aforementioned Uzzi.

Second Excerpt (Adler): The story of Samuel

This excerpt also tells the story of the beginning of the monarchy with Saul and David, and the discord between the observant Israelites (Samaritans) and the new breakaway community in the south.

Sisi the son of Uzzi, 37 years

In the days of his priesthood, Eli the son of Yafni died, and Samuel the son of Elkanah arose in his stead to attend the Ark which Eli had made at Shiloh; it is said that he was of the sons of Korah the son of Izhar. He appointed as king over his community Saul the son of Kish, the son of Abiel, the son of Seror, the son of Bechorath, the son of Afiah, of the sons of Benjamin.[10] And there was great enmity between Saul and his community, on the one hand, and the community of the observant Israelites, on the other,[11] who were of the sons of Phinehas and of the sons of Joseph, with a few men from among the sons of Benjamin. And so there was a great war between them and the community of Saul and Samuel. . . .

Buhki the son of Sisi served for 23 years, Sabat the son of Buhki served for 28 years, Sallum the son of Sabat served for 25 years, Hezekiah the son of Sallum served for 20 years, and Jonathan the son of Hezekiah served for 28

---

[9] Later in the *New Chronicle* ("Jonathan, 28 years"), four groups will be identified. *Chronicle II* follows this designation, also delineating four groups, but goes further, specifically calling the fourth "the Rebellious" followers of Jereboam. The descriptions of these groups provide building material for the developing Samaritan self-identification.

[10] As recipient of the blessing of Samuel, the whole monarchic tradition that eventually settles in Jerusalem (Jebus) is due criticism from the Samaritan chronicler.

[11] The observant Israelites, the Samaritans, are caught up in the political struggles between Saul and those who oppose him.

years.[12] In the days of the latter's priesthood King Saul died, and the community of Shiloh[13] made David the son of Jesse king in his stead, he being thirty years old at the time when they made him king. Jair the son of Jonathan served for 25 years, and Delaiah the son of Jair served for 25 years. In the days of his priesthood King David the son of Jesse died. The duration of his reign was forty years seven in Hebron and thirty-three in the city of Jebus.

Third Excerpt (Adler): King Solomon

This excerpt also tells the story of the building of the temple in Jerusalem (Jebus), and the evil into which Solomon led the south.

Jair the son of Delaiah, 19 years

In the days of his priesthood, King Solomon the son of David built the Temple which his father had founded at the threshing-floor of the Jebusite;[14] he built it four hundred and eighty years after the crossing of the children of Israel into the land of Canaan, and two hundred and twenty years after the concealment of the holy Tabernacle which had been made by the command of the LORD in the wilderness.[15] Solomon reigned over all the tribes of Israel, even as David his father had done, for forty years in the city of Jebus.[16] He had many foreign wives, including the daughter of Pharaoh, as well as Moabite, Ammonite, Edomite, Sidonian, and Hittite women.[17] Moreover, he had seven hundred wives (who were) princesses, and three hundred concubines, and his wives turned his heart. And so it came to pass that in his old age his wives inclined his heart towards other gods, and he worshiped them, and thus did what was evil in the eyes of the LORD, and did not fear Him, nor keep His commandments and His statutes. The name of Solomon's viceroy was Abisaph the son of Berechiah,[18] who was born four hundred and ninety years after the crossing of the children of Israel into the land of Canaan.

---

[12] The *New Chronicle* uses the succession of priests as the skeleton upon which to build its history.

[13] That the community of Shiloh anoints David indicates that he will fare no better than Saul in Samaritan estimation.

[14] 2 Sam 24:24–25.

[15] The concealment of the tabernacle on Gerizim begins the period of divine disfavor, which will continue until the appearance of the Taheb.

[16] 1 Kgs 11:42.

[17] 1 Kgs 11:1–2.

[18] 1 Chr 15:17.

Fourth Excerpt (Adler): The prominence of Shechem and the Blessed Mount

This excerpt also identifies four groups, one of which is the "keepers" (Samaritans), within Israel.

Jonathan, 28 years

In the days of his priesthood, King Solomon the son of David died, and his son Rehoboam was made king in his stead. He was brought to the city of Shechem to be crowned there,[19] for it was the custom of the kings of Israel to be invested with the crown of the kingdom in Shechem, below the chosen place on Mount Gerizim Bethel, that is to say, the Sanctuary of the LORD. And at that time the tribes of Israel separated themselves from the jurisdiction of the kings of Judah, so that Rehoboam the son of Solomon ruled only over the tribe of Judah while Jeroboam the son of Nebat ruled over the rest of the tribes of Israel for twenty-two years; Rehoboam ruled over the tribe of Judah for eighteen years.[20] During that time the tribes of Israel were divided into four groups. The first was the community of the Keepers,[21] who remained true to the truth, and they were the sons of Joseph, the sons of Phinehas, and a few of the sons of Levi and Benjamin, who maintained the sanctity of Mount Gerizim Bethel. The second group consisted of the sons of Judah and the sons of Benjamin, who maintained the sanctity of the city of Jebus. The third group belonged to one of the tribes dwelling in the town of Faratha who worshiped Baal. And the fourth group were those who followed Jeroboam the son of Nebat.[22] And Jeroboam removed to the city of Samaria and dwelt there.

Fifth Excerpt (Adler): The purchase of Samaria and the name "Samaritan"

Notice that "Samaritan" is not the preferred Samaritan self-identification.

Ishmael, 26 years

In the days of his priesthood, Jeroboam, the son of Nebat died, and Nadab reigned in his stead for two years; then he too died and was succeeded by

---

[19] 1 Kgs 12:1.
[20] 1 Kgs 15:1. Abu'l Fath claims that the rule lasted seventeen years.
[21] The self-identification of the Samaritans.
[22] Abu'l Fath calls these the "Rebellious."

Baasha[23] the son of Ahijah. And likewise in the days of his priesthood, Rehoboam the son of Solomon died, and there reigned in his stead over the tribe of Judah Abijam, his son,[24] for two years. His son Asa, who ruled over the tribe of Judah for forty-one years,[25] succeeded him. And in those days a man[26] from the sons of Ephraim the son of Joseph went and bought the (site of the) city of Samaria from a man whose name was Shomer; and it and the cities which were round about it were called the cities of Samaria, and those of the children of Israel who dwelt in it were called Samaritans down to this day.

Sixth Excerpt (Adler): The purchase of Samaria and persecution in the time of Tobiah

Tobiah, the son of Ishmael, 28 years

In the days of his priesthood, Baasha the son of Ahijah died; and Elah his son reigned in his stead for two years.[27] His successor Zimri reigned for only seven days,[28] whereupon Omri became king in his place. It is said that it was Omri who bought the hill of Samaria from Shomer for two talents of silver.[29] And in the final year of the priesthood of Tobiah, the Ishmaelites came and waged war against the children of Israel who were Keepers, and slew the High Priest Tobiah on Mount Gerizim. From that time and for a long period thereafter no high priest was able to dwell on Mount Gerizim.

Zadok, the son of Tobiah, 20 years

Amram, the son of Zadok, 28 years

Hilkiah, 24 years

Amram, 38 years

Seventh Excerpt (Adler): The kings of Judah and Israel

Note the differences with the biblical account.

---

[23] 1 Kgs 14:20.
[24] 1 Kgs 15:1.
[25] 1 Kgs 15:8.
[26] 1 Kgs 16:24 identifies this man as Omri.
[27] 1 Kgs 16:6.
[28] 1 Kgs 16:9–15.
[29] 1 Kgs 16:24.

Amram, 38 years

In the days of his priesthood, Jehoahaz the king of Israel died, and his son Joash[30] reigned in his stead for sixteen years. Jehoash the king of Judah likewise died and was succeeded by his son Amaziah, who reigned for twenty-nine years.[31]

Eighth Excerpt (Adler): Pretenders

This excerpt identifies as "pretenders" the prophets honored in the Jewish Bible. It also tells the story of the founding of Rome.

'Akkub, 36 years

In the days of his priesthood, Joash the king of Israel died,[32] and there reigned in his stead his son Jeroboam for forty-one years.[33] In those days appeared Hosea, Joel, and Amos, who called themselves prophets, but the community of the Keepers did not hearken unto them,[34] in obedience to the command of the LORD in the Torah, "You shall not utter a false report."[35] After Jeroboam died, his son Zechariah reigned in his stead for six months,[36] being succeeded by Sallum the son of Jabesh, who reigned for one month.[37] Amaziah the king of Judah likewise died,[38] and Uzziah[39] reigned in his stead for fifty-two years.[40] And in those days also there appeared a man of the sons of Edom[41] whose name was Romulus; he founded the city of Rome, and reigned in it for thirty-seven years. At that time, Romulus made a census of his men, and their number came to three thou-

---

[30] 2 Kgs 10:35.

[31] 2 Kgs 14:2.

[32] 2 Kgs 14:16.

[33] 2 Kgs 14:23.

[34] Our chronicler mentions prophets such as these by indicating that they "pretended to be" or "masqueraded as" prophets. This was from the conviction that only one prophet, Moses, deserves the title until the promised appearance of one like Moses—the Taheb.

[35] Exod 23:1.

[36] 2 Kgs 14:29.

[37] 2 Kgs 15:10.

[38] 2 Kgs 14:17.

[39] 2 Kgs 14:21.

[40] 2 Kgs 15:27.

[41] In rabbinic tradition, Edom is a synonym for Rome. Rome was founded in 753 B.C.E.

sand footmen and three hundred horsemen. He divided them into three divisions and set a captain over each division.

Ninth Excerpt (Adler): The Assyrian domination

'Akabyah, 39 years

In the days of his priesthood, Menahem the son of Gadi reigned over Israel for ten years; [42] during his reign Pull the king of Assyria came over, and Menahem gave him a thousand talents of silver so that he might help him to strengthen his hold upon the kingdom.[43] And Menahem exacted the money from the wealthy men, fifty shekels of silver from every man to give to the king of Assyria.[44] Whereupon the king of Assyria turned back to his own land and did not stay in the Land of Israel. Then Menahem died and there reigned in his stead his son Pekahiah for two years,[45] being succeeded by Pekah[46] the son of Remaliah, his officer, who, with fifty men of Gilead, slew his master Pekahiah. In his time there came Tiglath-Pileser the king of Assyria and carried captive from there all the inhabitants of the land of Naphtali. Likewise, in his days, Jotham the son of Uzziah reigned over Judah for sixteen years.[47] All the while Isaiah, Hosea, and Micah were pretending to be prophets among the sons of Judah and Israel. Jotham's son Ahaz[48] reigned in his stead also for sixteen years like his father, so that Isaiah, Hosea, and Micah were active during his reign as well. At the same time, Hosrea[49] the son of Elah reigned over Israel, and in his days Shalmaneser, the king of Assyria,[50] came and imprisoned him. Thereupon the king of Assyria besieged the cities of Samaria[51] for three years and then carried Israel captive to Assyria. And these were the names of the princes exiled to Assyria with the High Priest 'Akabyah, who were left of the tribe of Ephraim and of the tribe of Manasseh, of the sons of Joseph the righteous; the sons of Ephraim: Joseph, Pamur, Harfif, Sallem, and Zarwand; the sons of Shuthelah: Karim, 'Ayin, and Haroham (Jeroham); the sons of Machir: Hamsit, Hako, Sa'ad, and Gideon; the sons of Manasseh: Sarbah and Sar of

---

[42] 2 Kgs 15:14.
[43] 2 Kgs 15:19–20.
[44] This is almost an exact quote of 2 Kgs 15:20.
[45] 2 Kgs 15:22–23.
[46] 2 Kgs 15:25.
[47] 2 Kgs 15:32–33.
[48] 2 Kgs 16:1–2.
[49] 2 Kgs 17:1.
[50] 2 Kgs 17:3–4.
[51] 2 Kgs 17:5.

the Machir family, Suf the son of Sered of the Gilead family, and Er and Dahag likewise of the Gilead family; these were the princes of the tribe of Joseph. In those days Tullus was king of Rome and reigned for thirty-two years.[52] After him Phanus Marsius[53] reigned for fifteen years and was succeeded by Tarquinius Priscus, who reigned for forty-eight years.

Tenth Excerpt (Adler): More prophets as pretenders

This excerpt also presents the episode of Numa, king of Rome.

Halal, 45 years

In the days of his priesthood, Hezekiah was king over the sons of Judah for twenty-nine years;[54] while Isaiah, Hosea, and Micah were active as [pretending to be] prophets. After him, Manasseh reigned for fifty-five years.[55] In those days, a new king reigned in Rome, whose name was Numa,[56] a native of Sabinia. Towards the end of his days, Numa retired to the wilderness and dwelt in caves all alone, no man being with him. And so two men of the princes of his people went to him to bring him back to the throne of his kingdom, but he refused to hearken to them. Afterwards, however, he went and sat once again on the throne of his kingdom until he completed forty-two years of rule. And his people wept for him like orphans for their father.

Eleventh Excerpt (Adler): Mention of a return

Seraiah, 50 years

In the twenty-first year of his priesthood, the children of Israel returned to the land of Canaan. In those days lived the wise man Salus, the philosopher.

Twelfth Excerpt (Adler): about the prophets Zephaniah and Jeremiah

Levi the son of Seraiah, 50 years

In the days of his priesthood, Amon reigned over Judah[57] for two years and was succeeded by Josiah, who reigned eleven years.[58] At this time lived also

---

[52] Tullus Hostilius.
[53] Adler suggests that this is a copyist's mistake for Ancus Marcius.
[54] 2 Kgs 18:1–2.
[55] 2 Kgs 21:1.
[56] Numa Pompilius.
[57] 2 Kgs 21:19.
[58] 2 Kgs 22:1, but there he is said to have ruled twenty-one years.

Zephaniah and Jeremiah the son of Hilkiah, of the priests of the Jews, who acted[59] as prophets. The next king was Jehoahaz,[60] who reigned for three months, after which the king of Egypt carried him away to his city, where he dwelt until he died. And there reigned for eleven years in his stead Eliakim,[61] whose name was changed to Jehoiakim by the command of Pharaoh the king of Egypt. He was succeeded by Jehoiachin, who reigned for eight years,[62] being replaced by Zedekiah,[63] the brother of Jehoiakim. In those days, the king of Rome was Serpius Tullius,[64] who reigned for forty-four years.

Thirteenth Excerpt (Adler): The destruction of Jebus by Nebuzaradan

This excerpt contains a very close quotation of 2 Kgs 25:5–7.

Nathanael, 52 years

In his days, Nebuchadnezzar king of Assyria came up against the city of Jerusalem,[65] which is Jebus, encamped over against it, built a wall around it, and besieged it. And the Chaldeans pursued the king of Judah[66] and overtook him after all his army had scattered away from him. They captured him and brought him up to the king of Babylon at Riblah, where they first slew his sons before his eyes and then put his eyes out. Thereupon the king ordered him to be bound in fetters and brought to Babylon. This Nebuchadnezzar ascended to the royal throne in the fourth year of Jehoiakim king of Judah, and in the nineteenth year of his reign he sent his servant Nebuzaradan, the captain of the bodyguard, to the city of Jebus, which is called Jerusalem. And Nebuzaradan burnt the house of the golden ark, which is the Tabernacle made by King Solomon the son of David, and the king's house, and all the houses of the city; every great house he burnt down, and the walls around the city they demolished, while the rest of the people who were left were exiled to the cities of Babylon.[67] As for the doors of the Tabernacle and all its furnishings, they broke them and carried them to Babylon. The king of Rome in those days was Tarquinius the

---

[59] "Pretending to be."
[60] 2 Kgs 23:30–31.
[61] 2 Kgs 23:34.
[62] 2 Kgs 24:6, 8.
[63] 2 Kgs 24:17–18.
[64] Servius Tullius.
[65] 2 Kgs 25:1.
[66] Here 2 Kgs 25:5–7 is quoted almost verbatim.
[67] 2 Kgs 25:9–11.

second,[68] who reigned for twenty-four years, after which the kingdom of Rome became a consulate; that is to say, the men of Rome put two men over them who were called consuls and served as judges for twenty-one years, extending into the days of the priesthood of Azariah. Three years after the consulate was set up over Rome, a great civil war took place in it, accompanied by exceedingly heavy famine.

Fourteenth Excerpt (Adler): Another description of the three communities into which the Israelites were divided

Azariah, 35 years

This Azariah, together with his entire community of Keepers, was carried off by the king of the Chaldeans[69] from the land of Canaan to a distant land in the East. This took place in the tenth year of his priesthood, so that their stay in the Holy Land between the first captivity and the second came to one hundred and thirty-one years. In those days the army of Nebuchadnezzar[70] came and besieged Tyre for thirteen years, that city being then built upon a wall; before that it had been built in an open field. Thus the land at that time became desolate of all (its inhabitants) the children of Israel, the children of Judah, and the community of Jehoiakim.[71] And the king of Assyria[72] brought in foreigners and settled them in the land of Canaan in place of the children of Israel. And at that time Ezekiel, Nahum, and Daniel were acting[73] as prophets; they were scattered in the land of Babylon.

Fifteenth Excerpt (Adler): A quarrel between high priest and ruler

This excerpt tells of the quarrel between the high priest Abdiel and Zerubbabel over the location of the restored temple and the proper place of worship. It states that the king of the Babylonians recognized the superiority of the Samaritan Torah.

Abdiel the son of Azariah, 40 years

---

[68] Tarquinius Superbus. The usual date for the consular arrangement is ca. 509 B.C.E.
[69] The *Tulida* says it was the king of the Greeks.
[70] Ezek 26:7.
[71] See in this threefold designation part of the Samaritan identity.
[72] Nebuchadnezzer.
[73] "Pretending to be."

In the thirty-fifth year of his priesthood, he returned from captivity to the Holy Land, and with him three hundred thousand men of the children of Israel, fifty-five years having elapsed from the beginning of the captivity till their return to the Land of Canaan. The prince of the sons of Joseph at that time was Uzzi the son of Simeon. Also at that time the princes of the tribe of Judah came to Abdiel the priest at Haran—having come from the cities of Kush—and likewise the inhabitants of Galilee: the children of Hananiah, the children of Benjamin, the children of Zechariah, and the children of Tobiah. A great number of people came also from Babylon—namely, the children of Merari—and they wrote to other men who likewise came, making a great multitude that arrived at Harran. With them was also Zerubbabel[74] the son of Sarsar, the prince of the sons of Judah. And they said to Abdiel the High Priest and to Uzzi the son of Simeon, the prince of the children of Joseph, "Come, let us all go together to Jebus, the city of King David." And Abdiel the High Priest and Uzzi the son of Simeon, the prince of the sons of Joseph the righteous, rebuked them, saying, "Why should we do this thing? Go rather and your seed with us to Mount Gerizim, the holy House of God, which the LORD has chosen to make His name dwell therein, and let us all return to the LORD our God. Perhaps He will then return to us and deliver us from the wrath of the judgment of our enemies, for the thing which you have spoken is an abomination and unacceptable. How long will you cling to this evil thing and fail to be persuaded by all the misfortunes which have befallen all of us of the community of Israel?" And when Zerubbabel heard their words, he grew angry, and a fierce quarrel broke out between the princes of the sons of Joseph and the princes of the sons of Judah until the Babylonians heard of it, as did also the king's household, who thereupon reported it to him. And the king sent after them to summon them to his Chamber of Assembly and asked them about the things which he had heard; and Abdiel the High Priest recounted to him what had taken place between them and the sons of Judah. Then the king ordered them to assemble before him and requested each party to display the evidence that it claimed in the Holy Torah, so that he might search after the truth between them. And the community of the Keepers, that is, the sons of Joseph, brought the Scroll of the Torah and recounted before the king the evidence contained therein in favor of Mount Gerizim and in proof that it was the chosen place. The sons of Judah likewise brought a book which they said was the book of King David, and Zerubbabel approached to speak before the king, saying, "King David commanded

---

[74] Zerubbabel, in biblical tradition, led back the first contingent of exiles ca. 536 B.C.E.

us to the effect that the threshing floor of the Jebusite[75] which is in the city of Jebus is the chosen place." The king, seeing that the truth was not with Zerubbabel and his community but clearly with the sons of Joseph, grew angry with Zerubbabel and commanded that sacrifices be brought on Mount Gerizim and not in Jebus. He thereupon imprisoned Zerubbabel and all his followers in the cities of Babylonia while letting Abdiel the High Priest and the princes of the sons of Joseph and all their followers go to the Holy Land. And they went and came to Mount Gerizim Bethel and worshiped the LORD their God upon it with joy and gladness. The number of those from all the tribes of Israel who came back at that time was three hundred thousand men. And it came to pass after these events that the king of Babylon died, and his son reigned in his stead for thirty-six years, and all that time there was exceedingly great enmity between the sons of Joseph and the sons of Judah by reason of the previously mentioned matters. And in those days a war broke out between the (Tar)quins and the men of Rome.[76]

Sixteenth Excerpt (Adler): The deceit of Zerubbabel, Nehemiah, and Ezra

This excerpt tells how Zerubbabel, Nehemiah, and Ezra used deceit to alter the words of the Torah and compiled additional writings.

Hezekiah, the son of Abdiel, 30 years

In the days of his priesthood, Zerubbabel, Nehemiah the priest,[77] and Ezra the priest came and gave to the king of Babylon a large bribe and petitioned him for an edict to rebuild the House which Solomon the son of King David had built in the city of Jebus. The king issued such an edict, and they came and built the house of the Ark, the house of the king, and all the city. Likewise in his days there lived in the land of Greece a wise philosopher named Hippocrates and also another wise man of the community of the children of Israel who were Keepers in the cities of Babylonia, named the wise Aaron. There was yet a third philosopher named Democritus, and also a fourth named Lazan. The priest Ezra, after his coming to the city of Jebus, which is called also Jerusalem, sought for a Scroll of the Law but could not find any among the men of his community, for the king of Assyria

---

[75] 2 Sam 24:24–25.

[76] This event seems to be chronologically out of place with the earlier mentioned consulate.

[77] Nehemiah is not present in Abu'l Fath's rendition of this episode.

had burned all the books of the sons of Judah. Whereupon Ezra used deceit to obtain an ancient torn Torah from a man who was one of the community of the children of Israel who were Keepers of the Truth.[78] At that time the Jews no longer knew the holy tongue, nor the holy letters thereof; indeed all of them knew no language save that of the Assyrians in whose cities they had dwelt for seventy years in captivity. Therefore Ezra the priest assembled his friend Nehemiah[79] and all the princes of his community, and they wrote the book of the Holy Torah in the tongue of the Assyrians and in their letters, and he altered many things in the text of the Holy Torah out of hatred for the community of the children of Israel who are Keepers of the Truth, that is to say, the children of Joseph the righteous, adding some things and subtracting many others;[80] for he did not keep that which the LORD had commanded by the hand of His servant Moses: "All this word which I command you today, you shall not add to it nor diminish from it."[81] Moreover, many errors were made by him in the book of the Torah, which neither he nor his people perceived or understood. In addition to this, he gathered many sayings and writings composed by former authors and prophets, such as suited his aims and desires, and he and his colleague Nehemiah commanded his community to keep them all. And Ezra said to all his community, "Thus did the LORD God command me to do." But He whose Name is to be blessed commanded him nothing; rather he did all these things of his own design. And all the words of Ezra and what he had done are written in the Book of Chronicles.[82] But the LORD knows best.

Seventeenth Excerpt (Adler): The story of Esther

Hananiah, 24 years

In the days of his priesthood, there were two men, princes of the sons of Joseph, which is the community of the Keepers. The name of one was Jomakim[83] and the name of the other was Jehozadok;[84] both were possessed of very great wisdom and understanding. And the community of the

---

[78] The Samaritans.

[79] In the *Annals,* it is Ezra who is blamed for altering the law.

[80] Often the SP is characterized as including expansions on the MT. Emphasizing the Jewish "subtractions" may be an apologetic on behalf of the Samaritans.

[81] Deut 13:1.

[82] I.e., the *Annals.*

[83] Neh 12:10.

[84] 1 Chr 6:15.

Keepers sent the two previously mentioned princes, by the command of the High Priest Hananiah, to serve the king of Babylonia. Accordingly, they went and served him, and he delighted in them, and his heart was inclined towards them. In those days, Esther, one of the daughters of Judah, became the wife of the king of Assyria, who loved her very dearly. He also had for his viceroy a man of the community of the Jews whose name was Mordecai, Esther, the wife of the king at that time, being his niece. They did many favors to the community of the Jews who resided in the land of Canaan.

CHRONICLE II (SEPHER HA-YAMIM)

Chronicle II, also known as *Sepher ha-Yamim,* presents Samaritan history from the time of Joshua up till the beginning of the twentieth century. The work exists in at least two versions and is a compilation incorporating and modifying materials available to the editors of a section. As a compilation, it is impossible to date, but some scholars have suggested that parts of it at least are of "a very old chronology of unknown date, possibly derived from a pre-MT version of the Biblical Text possessed by one or more north Palestinian (Samarian) families."[85] To this early material, updates were sporadically added, with major revisions in the late fourth century and again in the late seventeenth century.[86] Finally, the story was continued to include major events to the beginning of the twentieth century.

Chronicle II has attracted occasional scholarly interest throughout the twentieth century but has yet to be translated completely into English.[87] John Macdonald published an English translation of portions of *Chronicle II* in 1969, as did J. Cohen in 1981.[88] Although partial, both translations provide to the general reader a good sense of the style and content of the chronicle as well as notes and comments explaining textual issues raised in it.

One of the interesting questions to confront the student of *Chronicle II* is the use of Jewish Bible material (primarily Joshua, Judges, Samuel, Kings, and Psalms). The writers of the chronicle do not accord the material the same status as their Torah but have no qualms about using the documents when it

---

[85] John Macdonald, *The Samaritan Chronicle II* (or: Sepher Ha-Yamim). From Joshua to Nebuchadnezzar. (BZAW 107; Berlin: Walter de Gruyter, 1969), 8. Used by permission.

[86] Ibid.

[87] See J. Cohen, *A Samaritan Chronicle* (Leiden: E. J. Brill, 1981).

[88] Macdonald, *Chronicle II,* translated early portions of *Chronicle II* that are concerned with episodes also largely found in the Jewish Bible. The translation and notes of Cohen, *Samaritan Chronicle,* concentrate on the part of *Chronicle II* concerned with the career of Baba Rabba.

suits their purposes. Investigations into the use of the LXX, MT, and DSS traditions of the Hebrew Bible by the writers of *Chronicle II* will be able to occupy scholars for the forseeable future.

Chronicle II has been criticized for its historical inaccuracies and internal inconsistencies.[89] But the reconstruction of history, at least as thought of in the modern West, was not the intent of the writers of *Chronicle II*. R. Coggins, who understood this, concluded that the value of *Chronicle II* is not in its historical reconstruction but in the way it uses Old Testament material and, perhaps most important, in the "theological standpoint it reveals."[90]

As that theological story evolves, the definition of the Samaritan community is given shape. Several episodes of definition scattered throughout the chronicle help to form a composite of the Samaritan identity. The first of these is the division that occurred with the apostasy of Eli and Samuel.

Excerpts 1–11 below are Macdonald's translation. His italicizations and ancillary insertions were not retained. The descriptions and explanations are the present authors'.

CHRONICLE II (SEPHER HA-YAMIM): EXCERPTS

First Excerpt (Chron II): The deception of Eli

In this excerpt, Gerizim and the worship there serve as major characteristics of what will be later referred to as "true Israel."[91]

Now Eli was ambitious, and he let it be known that he wanted to take over the position of high priest. He was already overseer of the entire treasury of silver and gold which the Israelites used to offer to the Lord. It was he who would receive and issue for all the people of Israel. The High Priest Uzzi had his dwelling in the sanctuary, as the Lord had commanded his servant Moses: "Neither shall he go out of the sanctuary."[92] Eli won over to himself many of the Israelites by saying to them, "Is it right that I should minister to a youth? I do not want such a status for myself, and I expect you

---

[89] Macdonald (*Chronicle II*, preface i), however, is impressed with what he calls an "astonishingly accurate chronology" in portions of *Chronicle II*. See also ibid., appendix 5.

[90] Richard J. Coggins, *Samaritans and Jews: The Origins of Samaritanism Reconsidered* (Atlanta: John Knox, 1975), 131.

[91] Macdonald, *Chronicle II*, 111–13.

[92] Lev 21:12.

to share my opinion and follow me." Eli went on to write to all the cities in the neighborhood of Mount Gerizim Bethel, and he addressed the above words to them. These all gathered to his side and they addressed him as follows: "We accept what you have said; we will not disobey your orders. Everything you command us we will do." They made a covenant with him accordingly. Evil desire entered within Eli and he, along with all his men— the ones who had made the covenant with him—kept this matter secret.

After these things Eli one day offered an offering on the altar, but in error without salt.[93] The Lord did not accept the pleasing odor of this offering, and when the High Priest Uzzi realized that the offering was not acceptable to the Lord, he was angry at Eli and spoke to him very severely. There- upon, Eli was furious and sent word for his men—the ones who had cove- nanted with him—to be summoned, and he reported to them what had been said.

At that particular time the Israelites who dwelt in the cities of Shechem, the cities of Philistia and the cities of Jebus, were divided in two. One side followed the High Priest Uzzi the son of Bahqi, and the other followed Eli the son of Jephunneh. The latter became evil minded and they all followed their own inclinations and did as the Lord said in the holy law: "Jacob shall eat and be satisfied. But Jeshurun waxed fat, and kicked; you waxed fat, you grew thick, you became sleek; then he forsook God who made him, and they scoffed at the Rock of his Salvation. They stirred Him to jealousy with strange gods; with abominable practices they provoked Him to anger."[94] The Josephites followed the High Priest Uzzi the son of Bahqi, and the Judahites followed Eli the son of Jephunneh. The Ephraimites and Manas- sites drove out Eli and his community from the chosen place Mount Gerizim Bethel.

Eli and his community, with their families and cattle, departed to sojourn in the territory of the tribe of Judah at Shiloh. Eli dwelt there in that place and he made himself an ark of gold based on the structure of the ark of the tes- timony. He made himself also a mercy seat, cherubs, a table, a lamp stand, and altars just like those of the sanctuary of Moses, which is to be found in the chosen place Mount Gerizim Bethel.

Eli wrote letters, sending them to the chiefs of the Israelites, addressing them as follows:

---

[93] Lev 2:13.
[94] Deut 32:15–16. The first part of the quotation is lacking in the MT.

"Let whoever desires to see signs and wonders come to me at Shiloh, for the ark of the testimony containing the tablets is in my hands."

He put into the ark the books of the law which were the version of Ithamar the son of Eleazar son of Aaron the priest, peace be upon him. A good many Israelites gathered to him and he built at Shiloh a tent based upon the design of the tent of meeting. This Eli did not change a single word of the holy law, but he revised the order of words.[95] Eli went on sacrificing the offerings on the altars which he had made. Every one of his festivals was in accordance with the commandments of the holy law.

Second Excerpt (Chron II): The division between Jeroboam and Rehoboam

A second defining episode occurs with the chronicler's treatment of the division between Jeroboam and Rehoboam. In the description of this event, four groups emerge. First are the Samaritans themselves, loyal to Gerizim and the books of Moses. The second group is composed of those who worship in Jerusalem (Jebis). They are recognized as a large group, much more populous than the Samaritans themselves. The third group is identified with the city Pir'aton and worship the strange gods of the nations round about the true Israelites (Samaritans).[96] They are the "Forsakers," a name seemingly intended to contrast with the Samaritan self-designation (the "Keepers"). The final group is the "rebellious," those who followed Jereboam in his split from Rehoboam. Though occupying the same territory as "true Israel" (the Samaritans), the other groups are not codeterminative, and so an important clue is given to the essential apolitical self-definition of the Samaritan sect. This excerpt tells of the division of the kingdom.[97]

Jeroboam did what was evil in the sight of Solomon the son of David. Solomon sought therefore to kill Jereboam, but he fled into Egypt, to Pharoah king of all Egypt whose name was Shishak, and was in Egypt until the death of Solomon. Then Solomon died, a worshipper of the Baals, forsaker of the law of Israel, who walked in the way of the Gentiles by worshipping alien gods, inclining his heart to eat and to drink and to be merry and to do what was evil in the sight of the Lord, the God of Israel. And the time that

---

[95] Descriptions of the variant Torah are interesting, as in these descriptions critiques of the Samaritan Torah are answered.

[96] The identity of this city is still disputed. It may be intended to be symbolic of those living in apostasy; Coggins, *Samaritans and Jews,* 123.

[97] Macdonald, *Chronicle II,* 152–60.

Solomon reigned over all the tribes of Israel was forty years in the city of Jebis which he called Jerusalem. They buried him there, and his son Rehoboam reigned in his stead. . . .

In the time of the priestly reign of High Priest Jair the son of Daliah above mentioned, came Rehoboam the son of King Solomon, and the whole tribe of Judah and all the people of all the tribes of Israel who followed their allegiance, to the holy city, the city of Shechem, in order to make Rehoboam the son of Solomon king over them in the place of his father below the Lord's sanctuary, which is below the chosen place Mount Gerizim Bethel, the Mount of Blessing, the place of inheritance and the Divine Presence, which is opposite Gilgal. Now ever since Eli the son of Jephunneh went to Shiloh and made for himself there a sanctuary and altars modeled on the tent of meeting and for all the community which came with him to Shiloh, they had forsaken Shiloh during the days of King David the son of Jesse, and had brought the ark of gold to the city of Jebis, Aelia, which they called Jerusalem, where Solomon the son of David had built a temple to represent the Lord, and which he had called Beth Miqdash. But it was not in these two places that they made anyone king over Israel, but all the elders of the tribes of Israel came to the city of Shechem. They set up the king whom they made to rule over them below Mount Gerizim Bethel and they seated the king on the stone which Joshua the son of Nun had erected there, and they anointed him there below the mountain in the presence of all the chiefs of the tribes of Israel. They called out there "Long live the King!" The reason for this was the saying of the Lord in his holy laws through the lord of the prophets, his servant Moses: "Thus (the Lord) became king in Jeshurun, when the heads of the people gathered, all the tribes of Israel together."[98]

And the Israelites sent and called Jereobam the son of Nebat and all the chiefs of the tribes of Israel, and the chiefs of the House of Joseph, chiefs of the tribe of Ephraim and the tribe of Manasseh, along with those associated with them from the rest of the tribes, (all these being) the community of the Samaritan Israelites. They invited the king to the city of Shechem, and they all came to Shechem.

Then Rehoboam the son of King Solomon came to the city of Shechem in order that they might anoint him king there below the sanctuary of the Lord. There gathered to him the Samaritan Israelites, that is, the children of Phinehas the High Priest, and the chiefs of the Levites and the chiefs of

---

[98] Deut 33:5.

the tribe of Ephraim and the tribe of Manasseh, the Josephites, and the chiefs of the men who were associated with them from the rest of the tribes. They summoned to them Jeroboam the son of Nebat, who had fled from King Solomon the son of David to the land of Egypt. He and all his community came with the community of the Samaritan Israelites to Rehoboam the son of King Solomon. They said to him, "Your father made our yoke heavy. Now therefore lighten the hard service of your father and his heavy yoke upon us, and we will serve you, and walk with us according to the commands of the holy law." He said to them, "Depart for three days, then come again to me." So the people went away.

Then Rehoboam the son of King Solomon gathered the old men, who had stood before Solomon his father while he was yet alive, saying, "How do you advise me to answer this people?" And they said to him, "If you will be a servant to this people this day and serve them, and speak good words to them when you answer them, then they will be your servants forever." But he forsook the counsel which the old men gave him, and took counsel with the young men who had grown up with him and stood before him. And he said the them, "What do you advise me that we answer this people who have said to me, 'Lighten the yoke that your father put upon us'?" And the young men who had grown up with him said to him, "Thus shall you speak to this people who said to you, 'Your father made our yoke heavy, but do you lighten it for us,' thus shall you say to them, 'My little finger is thicker than my father's loins. And now, whereas my father laid upon you a heavy yoke, I will add to your yoke. My father chastened you with whips but I will chastise you with scorpions.'"

So the community of the Samaritan Israelites and Jeroboam the son of Nebat and the chiefs of his community came to Rehoboam the son of King Solomon the third day. And the king answered the people harshly, and forsaking the counsel which the old men had given him, he spoke to them according to the counsel of the young men who had grown up with him, saying, "My father made your yoke heavy, but I (will add) to your yoke; my father chastised you with whips, but I will chastise you with scorpions." So the king did not hearken to the people. And when all the chiefs of the community of Jeroboam the son of Nebat saw that Rehoboam did not hearken to them, they answered Rehoboam,

"What portion have we in David?
We have no inheritance in the son of Jesse.
To your tents, Oh Israel!
Look now to your own house, son of David.

Not one man among us remains with you. You are no king for us and we are no servants for you. Judge the tribe of your father, Rehoboam, at the city of David"—which is the city of Jebis, which they call Jerusalem.

Third Excerpt (Chron II): But he reigned over the cities of Judah alone

So Rehoboam the son of King Solomon returned. Then he sent messengers from him, Adoram, who was over the forced labor, accompanied by men of Rehoboam's officials, to the Israelites, that they might come over to him (and) that he might deal with them according to the counsel of the old men. But all the Israelites rose up and stoned Adoram to death with stones. Now when Rehoboam was in one of the cities of Judah, he heard about this happening, how the Israelites had slain the representatives of Adoram and had stoned him to death with stones, and that the men accompanying him had fled from them. Rehoboam was very much afraid and made haste to mount his chariot, to flee to the city of Jebis—namely Aelia in which his father Solomon had built the house to represent the Lord, which they called Beth Miqdash, in place of the sanctuary which is the tent of meeting made by Moses in the wilderness at the command of the Lord, the God of Israel.

Jeroboam the son of Nebat was established in the city of Shechem. Now Jeroboam the son of Nebat had been second-in-command to King Solomon the son of David in the city of Jebis, and he was a violent man. And when King Solomon saw that Jeroboam was a violent man, who did not obey the law, neither it statures nor its ordinances, he gave him charge over the house of Joseph, that is, the tribe of Ephraim and the tribe of Manasseh, son(s) of Joseph, the community of Samaritan Israelites, to be judge over them, but Jeroboam the son of Nebat rebelled against King Solomon the son of David. So Solomon made things difficult for him and went up against Jeroboam the son of Nebat. So Jeroboam fled from King Solomon the son of David to Egypt, and Jeroboam dwelt with Pharaoh king of Egypt. King Solomon the son of David did not send orders for Jeroboam to be brought from Egypt from Pharaoh king of Egypt, because the daughter of Pharaoh was the wife of King Solomon the son of David, and Solomon loved her very much, although she was the daughter of a foreigner.

After the death of King Solomon the son of David, the elders of his community sought to anoint Rehoboam king over all the Israelites in the place of his father in the place where kings were anointed in the city of Shechem, below the Lord's sanctuary, (on) Mount Gerizim Bethel, the mount of blessing and inheritance and the Divine Presence. They sent to Jeroboam the son of Nebat and all the chiefs of his community, the Samaritan Israel-ites, came to the city of Shechem, and they sought of Rehoboam the son of King Solomon that he should lighten the yoke upon them which King Solo-mon the son of David his father had made heavy, but he replied to them in a hard manner in accordance with the advice of the young men who had grown up with him. They became very angry as a result, and they rebelled against Rehoboam the son of King Solomon.

After Rehoboam came to the city of Jebis, he ruled over the tribe of Judah only. Jeroboam the son of Nebat was established in the city of Shechem, and he ruled over the rest of the tribes of Israel, and he ruled also over our ancestors, the community of the Samaritan Israelites, with a tight grip and with considerable violence; just as it had been in the days of Solomon, so he dealt with them. He made their life bitter and threw their flesh to the dogs.

During that period the Israelites were in four divisions. The first division believed in Mount Gerizim Bethel—for it was the mount of blessing, the chosen place, the mount of inheritance and the Divine Presence; they were the community of the Samaritan Israelites, who were descendants of Phinehas the son of Eleazar the priest and the descendants of Joseph—along with some Levites and some from the rest of the tribes who were as-sociated with them—a small number.

The second division consisted of those who substituted for the sanctuary on Mount Gerizim Bethel the one on the city of Jebis, which King David had captured and in which King Solomon the son of David had built the house, the name of which is called Beth Miqdash; the name of the city they called Jerusalem. They were the tribe of Judah, along with a very large num-ber who followed them from the rest of the tribes.

The third division consisted of those who were in the city of Pir'aton. These are men who followed strange (gods) of the gods of the nations which lived round about the Israelites. They worshipped them and sacrificed to them, forsaking the holy law and its commandments and ordinance. The Israelites called them the Sect of Forsakers.

The fourth division consisted of the rest of the tribes of Israel who fol-lowed Jeroboam the son of Nebat, and rendered obedience to him. The Israelites called them the Rebellious.

Jeroboam the son of Nebat moved away from the holy city of Shechem to the city of Samaria, which is nowadays called Sebaste. They erected two calves of gold at the command of Jeroboam the son of Nebat, one calf in the city of Samaria, that is, Sebaste, the other in the territory of the tribe of Dan. It is said the secret which they contain lies in the second one.

And Jeroboam said to his community, "You have gone up to Mount Gerizim long enough to worship there a god whom you do not see, nor do you know what he is; the same holds true of your going up to the city of Jebis. Behold your gods, Oh Israel, who brought you up out of the land of Egypt." And this thing became a sin, for eight of the tribes of Israel went after Jeroboam the son of Nebat, while the tribe of Judah and a large number from the tribe of Benjamin went after Rehoboam the son of King Solomon, but the tribe of Ephraim and the tribe of Manasseh and a small number from the tribe of Benjamin and a few men from the rest of the tribes remained steadfast to the truth of the law; and the descendants of Ithamar the son of Aaron the priest and the Levites were dispersed among all the tribes of Israel, but the descendants of Phinehas the son of Eleazar son of Aaron the priest remained with the Josephites. These had the high priests, and were supported by a small number from the Ithamarites and the Levite priests.

Rehoboam the son of King Solomon dwelt in the city of Jebis, which they call the city of Jerusalem, and he built cities for defence in Judah. He built Bethlehem, Etam, Tekoa, Bethzur, Soco, Adullum, Gath, Mareshah, Ziph, Adoraim, Lacish, Azekah, Zorah, Aijalon, and Hebron, fortified cities which are in Judah and in Benjamin. He made the fortresses strong, and put commanders in them, and stores of food, oil, and wine. And he put shields and spears in all the cities, and made them very strong. So he held the whole tribe of Judah, and a great number from the tribe of Benjamin sided with the Samaritan Israelites.

Rehoboam the son of King Solomon took as his wife Mahalath the daughter of Jerimoth the son of David; and she bore him sons, Jeush, Zechariah, and Zaham. And he took also Abihail the daughter of Eliab the son of Jesse. After her took Maacah the daughter of Absalom, who bore him Abijah, Attai, Ziza, and Shelomith. And Rehoboam took eighteen wives and sixty concubines, and had twenty-eight sons and sixty daughters.

When the rule of Rehoboam was established and was strong, he forsook the law of the Lord, and had served other gods in the house which King Solomon had built and which they called Beth Miqdash, Shishak king of Egypt came up against the city of Jebis, with twelve hundred chariots and sixty thousand horsemen. And the people were without number who came with him from Egypt. And he took the fortified cities, and came as far as the city of Jebis, that is, the city of Jerusalem. So Shishak king of Egypt came up against the city of Jebis; he took away the treasures of the house which Solomon had built, and the treasures of the king's house; he took away everything. He also took away the shields of gold which Solomon had made; and Rehoboam made in their stead shields of bronze.

Rehoboam the son of King Solomon was forty-one years old when he began to reign, and he reigned seventeen years in the city of Jebis, Aelia. His mother's name was Naamah the Ammonitess, being of the Ammonites. And Rehoboam did evil in the sight of the Lord, as Solomon his father and all his people the people of Judah and the people of Benjamin like him had done. For only ten years during the time of Solomon did they serve the Lord in the house which King Solomon had built. Afterwards they served the Baals.

And Rehoboam the son of King Solomon died; and Abijah his son reigned in his stead. His people anointed him in the city of Jebis, being unable to come to the holy city of Shechem, to the place where kings are anointed below the sanctuary of the Lord (on) Mount Gerizim Bethel, which the Lord had chosen out of all the tribes of Israel to put his name there, for there was great animosity between Jereboam and his people and Rehoboam and his people.

Fourth Excerpt (Chron II): The repugnance of the Jerusalem temple

Part of the Samaritan self-conception is their repugnance for the temple established by David and Solomon in Jebis (Jerusalem). An often repeated description of that temple is that it is "to represent the Lord."[99] For the Samaritans, this is a direct and serious denial of the self-revelation of the God of Israel expressed eloquently in Joshua's "hymn of praise" in chapter 16 of the SJ. The following excerpt speaks about the temple in Jerusalem (Jebis).[100]

After these things the chiefs of the people assembled and said to David, "Make us a house for the ark of gold which Eli made to replace the ark of the testimony"—in which he had placed, instead of the tablets and the book of the law which is the one written by the lord of the prophets Moses, the books of law written by Ithamar the son of Aaron the priest, peace be upon him—They said, "Let us make for it a temple in Beth

---

[99] In addition to the selection below, see Macdonald, *Chronicle II,* 161, 186–87.

[100] Ibid., 134–35.

Maqdish inside Jebis"—that is, Aelia, the name of which they called Jerusalem and to this day they all incline to it. From that day they forsook Shiloh, which Eli the son of Jephunneh had chosen.

David said, "This is a better place than Shiloh in which to build a temple for the ark of the testimony, (and) to sacrifice all the burnt offerings and peace offerings on the altars we shall construct here."

When the High Priest Jair the son of Jehonathan and all his people, the Samaritan Israelites, heard all this, they were exceedingly angry, for David used to send all his personal contributions, his votive offerings and freewill offerings and all his tithe offerings to the chosen place Mount Gerizim Bethel. The High Priest Jair the son of Jehonathan sent a letter to David. In it, he enquired of him about this matter, informing him that the temple and the Divine Presence could not be in any place but in the chosen place Mount Gerizim Bethel, as the Lord had commanded through his servant Moss the son of Amram. He set out for him evidences which further expounded this matter from the holy law—for up to that time there was but one law held in common by all the tribes of Israel, with neither addition nor subtraction (on either side). For they all read the books of the law by one method of reading and one vocalization, which is in accord with the whole law possessed by us up to this day.

David was afraid at the dictum of the High Priest Jaire the son of Jehonathan, and he stopped building the temple for the ark in Beth Maqdish in the middle of Jebis, that is, Aelia. The chiefs of his people came to him and said, "Why have you put an end to the building of a temple for the ark?" David answered, "My son Solomon shall build the house for the ark, for I have shed much blood."

Then Solomon began to build a house representing the Lord in the city of Jebis, the name of which they called Jerusalem, at the place that David his father had appointed, on the threshing floor of Ornan the Jebusite. . . . [101]

He set up pillars in front of the temple, one on the south, and the other on the north; that on the south he called Jachin, and that on the north Boaz, according to the names of Baals.[102]

---

[101] Ibid., 145.
[102] Ibid., 146.

Fifth Excerpt (Chron II): The name "Samaritan"

The name "Samaritan" is not the label claimed by the Samaritans themselves. This excerpt, which makes clear that "true Israel" or "Samaritan Israelites" (i.e., the "Keepers") are not to be equated with all who live in the environs of Har Shomron, also tells of the purchase of Shemer and the name "Shomronim."[103]

> In the days of Omri a man of the community of the Samaritan Israelites, of the tribe of Ephraim the son of Joseph, went and he bought Samaria from Shemer for two talents of silver; and he fortified the city and called its name after the name of Shemer, the owner of the hill of Samaria. It had previously been a fortress belonging to the community of Jeroboam the son of Nebat, which the Amorites had dispossessed them of and had demolished.
>
> Now this noble man went and bought it and afterwards he began rebuilding it. So he and all his people, the descendants of Ephraim the son of Joseph, inhabited it and all the cities which lay round about it. They called its name and the name of the cities which lay round about it Har Shomron. The Israelites who dwelt in these cities were named Shomronim after the name Shomron and its cities. And Omri died, and Ahab his son reigned in his stead.

Sixth Excerpt (Chron II)

The way in which *Chronicle II* portrays prophetic figures in the following excerpts is a fascinating study. Elijah is described as a false prophet who brought about the death (murder?) of the son of the widow of Zaraphath, whose food he mercilessly stole. Amos, Joel, and Hosea are sorcerers up to no good. Jeremiah, too, is a false claimant who deserves the stoning that was his fate. G. Fohrer may have identified the reason for the recasting of the prophets, at least compared with the Hebrew Bible traditions.[104] He suggests that the Samaritan disparagement of these prophetic figures is a result of their insistence that Moses stand unique, at least until the appearance of the Taheb, the prophetic figure who will restore the divine favor. Elijah accumulated fame and comparisons to Moses in both rabbinic and New Testament

---

[103] Ibid., 163.

[104] Georg Fohrer, "Die israelitischen Propheten in der Samaritanischen Chronik II," in *In Memoriam Paul Kahle* (ed. Matthew Black and Georg Fohrer; BZAW 103; Berlin: de Gruyter, 1968), 129–37.

traditions, and so he is especially targeted for negative press to correct these Jewish and Christian misconceptions. This excerpt tells the story of Elijah.[105]

> Now Elijah the Tishbite, of Tishbe in Gilead in those days called himself a prophet, claiming that the Lord spoke with him. Elijah came to Zaraphath, which belongs to Sidon, to the house of a widow; and he called to her and said, "Bring me a little water in a vessel, that I may drink." And as she was going to bring water for him, he called to her, "Bring me a morsel of bread in your hand." And she said to him, "As the Lord lives, I have not a morsel, only a handful of meal and a little oil, and I want to use them for myself and my son, that we may eat it, and die." And he said to her, "Fear not; go and do as you have said. I shall eat and so will you two. If you give me to eat of them, the meal shall not be spent, and the oil shall not fail." And the widow went and did as he had said, and Elijah wolfed the whole lot and ate them, and he went on his way from the widow. After the departure of Elijah, the fatherless son of the woman starved to death.

Seventh Excerpt (Chron II): The story of Elisha[106]

> Then the king [Jehoram] sought a messenger to go to Elisha the soothsayer and kill him with the sword, for he was the cause of that affliction. But Elisha and all his disciples had fled from the king of Israel and settled down in another land.

Eighth Excerpt (Chron II): The stories of Hosea, Joel, and Amos[107]

> In the thirty-second year of the priestly reign of the High Priest Amram Jerobom the son of Joash began to reign over the eight tribes of Israel, and he reigned forty-one years. In his days appeared Hosea, Joel and Amos. It is said of them throughout all Israel that they were sorcerers.

Ninth Excerpt (Chron II): The story of Jeremiah[108]

> In his time appeared Jeremiah. Now he was the son of Hilkiah the priest. He dwelt in the city of Anathoth in the land of Benjamin near Jebis. It is the city to which King Solomon drove Abiathar the priest, depriving him then

---

[105] Macdonald, *Chronicle II,* 163–64. See also the description of Elijah the sorcerer, ibid., 171.
[106] Ibid., 170.
[107] Ibid., 175.
[108] Ibid., 187–88.

of the priesthood. In the thirteenth year of Josiah's rule he began to claim for himself that he was a prophet of the Lord, the God of Israel, but many of the people of Judah conspired against him, stoning him to death.

Concerning all the prophets, as expressed by the king of Assyria:[109]

The king of Assyria assembled all the elders and chiefs and officers of the community of the Judeans to him, and he said to them, "Consider what I said to you in the time of battle. Since this has taken place, the truth of my words is revealed, for the men who said to you, 'We are prophets from the Lord for you,' have misled you by that statement, for they were sooth-sayers, sorcerers, diviners. They were no prophets! Did they deliver you that day from under my hand and the hand of my people, as Moses the son of Amram delivered you in the land of Egypt from Pharaoh and all his servants, when he led your fathers out of the land of Egypt with a strong hand and outstretched arm?" They answered the king, "What the king says is true."

Tenth Excerpt (Chron II): The centrality of Gerizim and the Torah

This excerpt tells the story of the Samaritan exile after the Assyrian conquest. The community is tragically forced to leave Shechem and its environs, well aware of the terrible cost of its departure.[110]

In the days of Hoshea the son of Ela king of the eight tribes of Israel and in the days of the High Priest Akbiah, and in the days of Hezekiah king of Judah, the king of Assyria came to the city of Samaria and besieged it for three years. He removed all that was in it and its cities to the cities of Babylonia. Later he came to the city of Shechem and assembled all the elders of the community of the Samaritan Israelites—that is, the descendants of Phinehas the son of Eleazar the priest, and the descendants of Joseph who believed in the chosen place Mount Gerizim Bethel—and he said to them, "Arise, go off to Haran." And they enquired of the king how long it would be before they should all gather and leave; but the king of Assyria did not heed them, and he said to them, "Any man who is found in this place within the next three days shall die."

The High Priest Akbiah arose and took the holy vessels and he concealed them in the chosen place Mount Gerizim Bethel. He wrote in the book of

[109] Ibid., 184.
[110] Ibid., 182–83.

his people concerning the place where they were hidden. He took the book of the holy law, which was written by his lord Abisha the son of Phinehas, and gave it to the Levite priests to look after it and keep guard over it, for they were expecting that they would return soon to their lands.

So they, with all they possessed, went forth under compulsion, mourning, wandering in the land. Their exit took place on the twenty-fourth of the month Nisan. They left open the doors to the temple—the community of Samaritan Israelites had rebuilt it after King Saul's men had destroyed it. They went forth, looking back, leaving behind the chosen place Mount Gerizim Bethel, mourning with tears because it was receding from them, saying,

"Peace be upon you from us, O Mount of Blessing.
Peace be upon you from us, O House of God.
Peace be upon you from us, O Gate of Heaven.
Peace be upon you from us, O Chosen Place.
Peace be upon you from us, O Mount of Inheritance and the Divine Presence.

We indeed are guilty. Therefore all this distress has come upon us, and the Lord has removed us so that we do not dwell in your midst, O House of God, O Mount Gerizim Bethel."

The Abisha Scroll reads,[111]

The king of Assyria took the books from the Israelites, and also the book of the holy law written by our lord Abisha the son of Phinehas, son of Eleazar the priest. He put them in the tower of Nineveh.

Eleventh Excerpt (Chron II): Hezekiah's Passover (2 Chr 32) and Sennacherib's Invasion (2 Chr 32)[112]

The writer responsible for the sections of the chronicle that concern the seventh and sixth centuries B.C.E. made fairly extensive use of the biblical book of Chronicles. As might be expected, changes in point of view are present; for example, prophets from the south are ignored or critiqued, and there is no sympathy for the political interests originating from Jerusalem.

---

[111] Ibid., 185.
[112] Ibid., 180–82.

In the tenth year of the priestly reign of the High Priest Halel, Hezekiah the son of Ahaz began to reign over the people of Judah, and he reigned twenty-nine years. This Hezekiah opened up the houses which King Solomon the son of David had built in the city of Jebis, which they called Jerusalem, to perform the Passover offering in it. He sent letters to all Israel, from Beer-sheba to Dan, that people should come and keep the Passover at the city of Jebis. Hezekiah's messengers went about with the letters of the King of Judah from city to city, and they came to the cities of Samaria; but the eight tribes laughed them to scorn. Then later they came to the city of Shechem and handed the letters to the chiefs of the community of the Samaritan Israelites. The chiefs of the Israelites replied to the King of Judah, saying, "How can we substitute evil for good and forsake the chosen place Mount Gerizim Bethel, the Mount of Blessing, the Place of Inheritance and the Divine Presence, and come to you at the city of Jebis to perform the Passover offering there? Rather do you hearken! Walk in the right way, by coming to the chosen place Mount Gerizim Bethel to perform the Passover offering here, as the Lord, the God of Israel, commanded."

So the messengers came to Hezekiah King of Judah saying . . . . the letter of the people of Ephraim and Manasseh—that is, the community of the Samaritan Israelites. But he refused to listen to them, and the people of Judah performed the Passover offering in the city of Jebis in the second month by themselves.

It came to pass after these things that Sennacherib king of Assyria came and invaded Judah and encamped against the fortified cities, and he managed to win them for himself. And when the king of Judah saw that Sennacherib had come and intended to fight against the city of Jebis, he planned with his officers and with his mighty men to stop the water of the springs that were outside the city; and they helped him. A great many people were gathered, and they stopped all the springs and the brook that went through the land, saying, "Why should the kings of Assyria come and find much water?" They built up all the wall that was in ruins, and raised towers upon it. He made another wall outside it, and he made implements of war in abundance; and he said to the commanders of the army, "Be strong and of good courage. Do not be afraid or tremble before the people of Assyria."

After this Sennacherib king of Assyria sent his servants to the city of Jebis, saying, "Thus says Sennacherib king of Assyria, 'On what are you relying, that you stand siege? Do you not know what I and my fathers have done to all the peoples of other lands? Were all the nations of those lands at all able to deliver their lands out of my hand? Who among all the gods of those nations which my fathers utterly destroyed was able to deliver his people from my hand, that your God should be able to deliver you from my hand? Now therefore do not let Hezekiah persuade you or mislead you, and do not believe him, for his god is not able to deliver you from my hand."

And they shouted with a loud voice in Hebrew to all (the people of) Jebis who were upon the wall, to frighten and terrify them, in order that they might take the city. So the king of Assyria returned to his own land. Then Hezekiah died, and Manasseh his son reigned in his stead.

Excerpts Related to the New Testament

Chronicle II contains a short discussion of Jesus and early Christianity. This part of the chronicle has also been translated and is the subject of scholarly investigation.[113]

First Excerpt

It corresponds, likewise, to the year 655 after the King 'Askander who ruled over all the nations, and to the year 308 after the appearance of Jesus son of Miriam, wife of Joseph the Carpenter, a descendant of King David, against whom some Judeans arose and they crucified him.[114]

Second Excerpt

During the period of his (Yehoqim's) high-priesthood was born Jesus the son of Joseph the carpenter of the Judaist community. The number of years from the creation of the world up to the advent of Jesus the son of Joseph the Nazarene, concerning whom the Judaist community assert that he was the son of Joseph the carpenter and that this Joseph lay with Jesus' mother Mary before he took her for his wife, was four thousand (two hundred) and ninety.[115]

Here is the genealogy of this Jesus the Nazarene. Judah was the father of Perez and Zerah by Tamar his daughter-in-law adulterously; for Judah was told, "Tamar your daughter-in-law has played the harlot; moreover

---

[113] John Macdonald and A. J. Higgins, "The Beginning of Christianity according to the Samaritans," *NTS* 18 (1971): 54–80. Reprinted with the permission of Cambridge University Press.

[114] The translation is from Macdonald and Higgins, "Beginning of Christianity," 75.

[115] Macdonald (Macdonald and Higgins, "Beginning of Christianity," 73) computes the date to 20 C.E.

she is with child by harlotry":[116] and (Judah) said, "Bring her out, (and) let her be burned."

Perez was the father of Hezron, and Hezron the father of Ram, and Ram the father of Amminadab, and Amminadab the father of Nahshon, and Nahshon the father of Salmon, and Salmon the father of Boaz by Rahab the Canaanitess, the harlot, for (Moses) said in connection with the spies that "they came into the house of a harlot,"[117] and Boaz was the father of Obed by Ruth the Moabitess who lay with Boaz[118] at midnight[119] before he had taken her for his wife; Obed was the father of Jesse, and Jesse the father of David and David was the father of Solomon by the wife of Uriah the Hittite. Now David lay with her and she became pregnant, before he had taken her for his wife. Solomon was the father of Rehoboam, and Rehoboam the father of Abijah, and Abijah the father of Asa, and Asa the father of Jehoshaphat; Jehoshaphat was the father of Jehoram, and Jehoram the father of Uzziah, and Uzziah the father of Jotham, and Jotham the father of Ahaz, and Ahaz the father of Hezekiah; Hezekiah was the father of Manasseh, and Manasseh the father of Amon, and Amon the father of Josiah, and Josiah the father of Jechoniah, and Jechoniah the father of Shealtiel, and Shealtiel the father of Zerubbabel; Zerubbabel was the father of Abiah,[120] and Abiah the father of Eliakim, and Eliakim the father of Azor, and Azor the father of Zadok. Zadok was the father of Jachin, and Jachin the father of Elihud, and Elihud the father of Eleazar, and Eleazar the father of Matthan; Matthan was the father of Jacob, and Jacob the father of Joseph the carpenter, the husband of Mary, of whom the Judaist community said that he lay with her before his betrothal to her, and that she became pregnant from the adultery, as a result of which, they said, she gave birth to Jesus the Nazarene.[121]

The birth of this Jesus took place in Bethlehem in Judea in the days of King Herod. When Jesus the Nazarene grew up, he called himself a prophet. Later he called himself divine, in the town of Nazareth, where many men from the Judaist community gathered to him. These were his disciples. The Judaists hated him very much and they sought him in every place, in every

---

[116] Gen 38:24.
[117] Josh 2:1.
[118] Ruth 4:13.
[119] Ruth 3:8.
[120] Cf. the genealogy found in Matt 1:3–16.
[121] The description of the conception of Jesus presented here is somewhat different from the irregular and presumably immoral episodes associated with Tamar, Ruth, and the wife of Uriah.

corner, with a view to executing him. They asserted that everything he did and the way he lived was in direct opposition to all that was taught in the books of their prophets and elders.

When Jesus the Nazarene had disciples, he would send them to various towns or cities. These disciples included Simon, who was called Peter, Andrew his brother, these two having been fishermen before they joined up with Jesus the Nazarene; James the son of Zebedee and John his brother, who also were fishermen before they joined up with Jesus the Nazarene; Matthew, whose dwelling-place was in the custom house before he took up with Jesus the Nazarene; Judas, nicknamed Ish Qeriyyot and Philip who belonged to Bethsaida, that is, from the same town as Andrew and Peter; Nathanael, Nicodemus, Thomas, Mark and Luke.

These were all the men who were Jesus' disciples. Now of these he sent Peter to the Romans, and Andrew to the Ethiopians. This Matthew who was with him wrote a gospel in the forty-first year after the execution of Jesus the Nazarene.[122] He wrote it in the village of Yehudit. He sent Thomas to Babylonia and he sent Philip to QRW'L and Africa. He sent Paul to Aelia and its surrounding villages.

Now this Paul was named Saul before he joined up with Jesus. He was born in Tarsus, one of the cities of Cilicia. It is stated concerning him that he belonged to the tribe of Benjamin, but he was really from the tribe of Judah. To him (are ascribed) fourteen letters; the first he sent to the Romans fifty-eight years after the execution of Jesus the Nazarene. The second, to the Corinthians, which he sent fifty-seven years after the execution of Jesus the Nazarene. The third, also (was sent) to the Corinthians in Macedonia fifty-eight years after the death of Jesus. The fourth, to the Galatians, which he sent to them fifty-five years after the execution of Jesus. The fifth, to the Ephesians, which he sent to them sixty-three years after the execution of Jesus. The sixth, to the Colossians, which he sent to them sixty-three years after the execution of Jesus. The seventh to the Phil(ipp)ians, which he sent to them sixty-two years after the execution of Jesus. The eighth, to the Thessalonians, which he sent to them fifty-two years after the execution of Jesus. The ninth, also to the Thessalonians, which he sent to them fifty-three years after the execution of Jesus.[123] The tenth, to

[122] The Samaritan calculation for the crucifixion places the event in the year 23 C.E., making Matthew's gospel date to the year 64 C.E.
[123] The Thessalonian letters are assigned early authorship, just as they are in modern scholarship.

Titus, which he sent to him sixty-four years after the execution of Jesus. The eleventh, to Timothy, which he sent to him sixty-three years after the execution of Jesus. The twelfth, also to Timothy, which he sent to him sixty-four years after the execution of Jesus. The thirteenth, to Philemon, which he sent to him sixty-two years after the execution of Jesus. The fourteenth, to the Hebrews, which he sent to them sixty-five years after the execution of Jesus. These are the fourteen letters (ascribed to Paul). Now Mark wrote a gospel-book, and it is said concerning him that he was a disciple of Peter. He wrote his gospel at the dictate of Peter to the Romans forty-eight years after the death of Peter his teacher.

Luke pursued his profession as a physician in the cities of Antioch and SBYWS. Luke was a foreigner, a pagan; he was a disciple of Paul from the time he came to believe in Jesus the Nazarene. Concerning Luke it is said that he wrote his gospel in the city of Basia. This Basia was a great city of the Greeks, Thebes (TBYS), being the seat of government.

John, whose birthplace was Beth-Sidon a town in Galilee, was the son of Zebedee and Salome. In his youth he was a fisherman, and Jesus the Nazarene made him one of his disciples whom we have already mentioned. This John too wrote a gospel-book in the year one hundred and one after the death of Jesus. It is said that he wrote it in the ninety-seventh year after Jesus' death, John's lifespan having reached a hundred and fifteen years. Concerning him it is stated that he wrote his gospel-book partly in the city of Titus and partly in the city of Ephesus after his return from Titus. He started writing his gospel-book in the sixty-fourth year after the execution of Jesus, continuing the task until the ninety-seventh year after Jesus' execution.

We return to the mention of Jesus the son of Mary, of whom the Pharisaic community, that is, the Judaists related to him, state that he was the illegitimate son of Joseph the carpenter. It is stated that King Herod sought to execute him, but he fled from King Herod and became a fugitive in the land, hiding himself from King Herod. So he became a fugitive in the land, hiding himself from King Herod and from the elders of the Pharisees, that is, the Judaist community.

During that period the high priest Yehoqim died. The favor and forgiveness of the Lord be his, Amen! In his stead the high priest Jonathan reigned. The whole period of his reign as high priest was twenty-seven years.

In the time of this high priest Jonathan they took Jesus the Nazarene before Pilate to exact vengeance on him. The elders of the Pharisees accused him before Pilate, but Jesus made no reply.[124] Pilate said to him, "Have you not heard their testimony against you?" But he made no reply at all. Now during that festival (pilgrimage) it was Pilate's practice to release to the Judaists any one prisoner they liked. At the time they had a notorious prisoner called Barabbas. Pilate asked them, "Whom do you choose that I should release to you, Barabbas or Jesus?"[125] They replied, "Barabbas!" Then he asked them, "What am I to do with Jesus?" They all said to him, "Let him be crucified." So he released Barabbas to them, and he had Jesus whipped. Then he handed him over to be crucified.

Some of Pilate's soldiers took hold of Jesus, divested him and bowed down on their knees before him. They mocked him, saying, "Greetings to you, King of the Judaists!" They spat in his face, took a reed cane and struck him with it on his head. While they were on their way, they came across a Cyrenian called Simon, whom they forced to carry Jesus' cross, and they went on to a place called Golgotha, which means the Place of the Skull. They gave him some vinegar, boiled with gall, but he refused to drink. Then they crucified him. They passed in front of him, mocking him, wagging their heads and saying to him, "You who are the destroyer of the temple and will rebuild it in three days, save yourself. If you are God's son, come down from the cross. Surely you who can save other people can save yourself. If you are the king of Israel, come down from the cross and then we shall believe in you." Yet he made no reply to any of them, but raised his voice and wept.

That is what we have heard about Jesus from the Judaists by word of mouth, that this is what happened to him when he was crucified. It is said that two criminals were crucified with him, one on his right and one on his left. That event took place in connection with Jesus the Nazarene in the city of Jebis, which they called Jerusalem, at the command of Pilate the governor of the Pharisaic community, that is, the community of the Judaists. Now Jesus the Nazarene did not consult the community of the Samaritan Israelites at any time in his life. He did not stand in their way, nor did they stand in his way. They did not impose upon him, nor he on them in any way.[126] He was, however, the subject of vengeance on the part of his own people, his own community, from whom he rose, that is, the Judaist com-

---

[124] The following account follows closely that appearing in Matt 27:13–33.

[125] The Matthew account includes a reference to Jesus as "the Messiah." The Samaritan account does not include the title either here or in the dialogue to follow.

[126] This statement of Samaritan nonparticipation in the trial and execution of Jesus is remarkable. Although Jesus is clearly not owned as the Messiah, the Samaritan writer nevertheless makes certain that the Samaritans are not incorporated in the role played by the Judaists.

munity. They hated him wholeheartedly, so much so that they were the cause of his execution, his crucifixion

The Judaists were also the cause of the execution of John the disciple of Jesus by getting him to make King Herod disturbed over an attractive young woman. They made a present of her to King Herod with adultery in mind, so that when he saw her King Herod would desire her and love her passionately. Now she requested from him John's head and because his passion for her had captivated his whole heart this affair troubled him in no way, but he speedily issued orders that John should be summoned to the city of Samaria. He decapitated him there, for at that time King Herod was in that city. This John was known as John the Baptizer, for the Judaists had at first said of him, "He is a righteous man," and they had believed in his righteousness and had been baptized by him. Then they realized that he was attracted to Jesus the Nazarene, the son of Mary. When they told him not to baptize him, he paid no heed to them. He took him off and, sitting in the Jordan (or 'dwelling in Jericho'), he baptized him there. When the Judaists saw John baptizing Jesus the Nazarene, they forbade everyone to be baptized by him, namely by John. Now the Judaists had previously said that anyone who was baptized in the waters of Jericho (or the Jordan) was cleansed of all uncleanness, of every abominable deed and of every sinful act. From that time onwards, the ordinance of baptism has been carried on by the community of the Nazarene, but the Judaist community has rejected it from the time that Jesus the Nazarene was baptized by him right up to the present time. In the place of baptism, they instituted immersion in the water, which is a tributary of the Jordan River. They asserted that anyone who entered into the Jordan waters would be cleansed of all their uncleanness and sinful acts. From that time the entire kingdom of the Nazarenes emerged, that is, from the baptism in the Jordan waters.[127]

Literature of the Kingdom of the Nazarenes

This section of *Chronicle II* was written, according to the accompanying colophon, in 1616 and provides an interesting list of the documents that the Samaritan editor believed to be commonly used by the Christian community. The list is fascinating for several reasons.

The first observation is about the dates that are assigned to the composition of some of the Christian documents. The letters of Paul are all dated according to the number of years following the crucifixion of Jesus.

---

[127] Translation from Macdonald and Higgins, "Beginning of Christianity."

According to most, Samaritan chronology places the crucifixion of Jesus in either 20 or 23 C.E. Thus a list dating Paul's letters can be produced:

1 Thessalonians: 52 years after Jesus' death (+ 20 or 23) = 72 or 75

2 Thessalonians: 53 years (+ 20 or 23) = 73 or 76

Galatians: 55 years (+ 20 or 23) = 75 or 78

1 Corinthians: 57 years (+ 20 or 23) = 77 or 80

2 Corinthians: 58 years (+ 20 or 23) = 78 or 81

Romans: 58 years (+ 20 or 23) = 78 or 81

Philemon: 62 years (+ 20 or 23) = 82 or 85

Philippians: 62 years (+ 20 or 23) = 82 or 85

Ephesians: 63 years (+ 20 or 23) = 83 or 86

Colossians: 63 years (+ 20 or 23) = 83 or 86

1 Timothy: 63 years (+ 20 or 23) = 83 or 86

2 Timothy: 64 years (+ 20 or 23) = 84 or 87

Titus: 64 years (+ 20 or 23) = 84 or 87

Hebrews: 65 years (+ 20 or 23) = 85 or 88

With the exception of Philippians (dated by moderns to 52–53) and Ephesians (dated by moderns to 80–90), if the Samaritan dates for the composition of the Christian documents are driven down by the 20 or 23 years added to account for the Samaritan reckoning of the date of the death of Jesus, the dates indicated by the Samaritan chronicler are remarkably close to dates for composition assigned by modern scholarship.

Likewise, two New Testament gospels can be dated:

Gospel of Matthew: 41 years after Jesus' death (+ 20 or 23) = 61 or 64

Gospel of John: begun 64 years and completed 97 years after Jesus' death (= completed 117 or 120)

Most modern New Testament scholars date Matthew to anywhere from 60 to 90, and John is frequently dated to the 90s. The Gospel of Luke is undated by the Samaritan. The Gospel of Mark is dated to the death of Peter

(48 years after his death, but the year of Peter's death in Samaritan reckoning is unknown).

The second and perhaps more fascinating observation about the Samaritan list of Christian documents is the list itself—what is included and what is excluded. In addition to the canonical gospels and the writings of Paul, thirty-five additional gospels are listed by the Samaritan writer:

The first: the gospel-book of the Egyptians[128]

The second: the gospel-book of the Birth of Mary, the Good Virgin

The third: the gospel-book of Saint James the Chief

The fourth: the gospel-book of the Infancy[129]

The fifth: the gospel-book of Leucius and Seleucus

The sixth: the gospel-book of Saint Thomas[130]

The seventh: the gospel-book of Truth[131]

The eighth: the gospel-book of Judas, nicknamed Ish Qeriyyot

The ninth: the gospel-book of Nicodemus

The tenth: the gospel-book of the Eternal

The eleventh: the gospel-book of James the Great (or 'Elder')

The twelfth: the gospel-book of Saint Barnabas

The thirteenth: the gospel-book of Saint Philip[132]

The fourteenth: the gospel-book of Life

The fifteenth: the gospel-book of Saint Andrew

The sixteenth: the gospel-book of Saint Bartholomew

The seventeenth: the gospel-book of Apellus

---

[128] Probably early second century.
[129] Early second century.
[130] Early second century.
[131] Mid–second century.
[132] Third century.

The eighteenth: the gospel-book of Valentinus

The nineteenth: the gospel-book of Saint Judas

The twentieth: the gospel-book of Tatian (Tasinus), which is the gospel of the Encratites

The twenty first: the gospel-book of the Syrians

The twenty second: the gospel-book of Basilides

The twenty third: the gospel-book of Cerinthus

The twenty fourth: the gospel-book of the Hebrews[133]

The twenty fifth: the gospel-book of the Simonites

The twenty sixth: the gospel-book of the Pleroma

The twenty seventh: the gospel-book of Matthias

The twenty eighth: the gospel-book of the Death of Mary the Virgin

The twenty ninth: the gospel-book of Tatian (Tisanus)

The thirtieth: the gospel-book of Eve

The thirty first: the gospel-book of the Gnostics

The thirty second: the gospel-book of Marcion

The thirty third: the gospel-book of Paul

The thirty fourth: the gospel-book of the Great and Little Questions of Mary

The thirty fifth: the gospel-book of the Birth of Jesus the Nazarene[134]

Many of the books in this list are unknown according to the title assigned by the Samaritan scribe. At least one of the books, the gospel-book of Philip *(Gospel of Philip),* is known only in fragmentary form and was thought to be "almost completely unknown from Late Antiquity, through the Middle

---

[133] Early second century.

[134] Translation from Macdonald and Higgins, "Beginning of Christianity." The text from which this excerpt is taken contains a colophon that dates the manuscript to 1616 C.E.

Ages, and down to the present day, until it was discovered as one of the documents in the Nag Hammadi Library."[135] Excluded from the list of Christian documents are the Acts of the Apostles, the letters of Jude, James, John, and Peter, and the Revelation of John. Perhaps it is coincidental, but only Peter lacks any mention in the list of documents (although perhaps Peter resides behind the group called the Simonites).

A third observation may relate to the second. The Samaritan scribe is aware of factions within the kingdom of the Nazarenes, at least as reflected in the titles of the literature. At least four subgroups are identified: the Encratites, Hebrews, Simonites, and Gnostics, with perhaps the addition of two more groups that are identified regionally: the Egyptians and the Syrians. Certainly, the kingdom of the Nazarenes, as understood by the Samaritan writer, was not a monolithic whole but admitted to variation and perhaps competition. Since the Samaritan holds all of the Nazarene literature to be false, he has no obvious bias that would lead him to favor one or more of these factions, and so the Samaritan list may provide a valuable and fairly objective comment on the structural makeup of the kingdom of the Nazarenes.

---

[135] Bart Ehrman, *Lost Scriptures: Books That Did Not Make It into the New Testament* (Oxford: Oxford University Press, 2003), 38.

Part Two

Samaritan Theology and Worship

Chapter 5

Tibat Marqe (Memar Marqe)

CONTENT

Tibat Marqe (Memar Marqe, also called *Memar Marqah),* a primarily theological work, is a treasure for Samaritans and scholars because it contains a rich variety of literature, its origins are relatively early, and later additions reflect the development of Samaritan languages (Hebrew, Aramaic, and Arabic) and thought.

Samaritans have used it extensively to expand, articulate, and sanction their theology, liturgy, and interpretation of the physical world. Later liturgies, chronologies, and theological works are enriched by their explicit and implicit citations of *Marqe.*

The fully developed Samaritan creed states, "We say: My faith is in thee, YHWH; and in Moses the son of Amram, thy servant; and in the Holy Law; and in Mount Gerizim Bethel; and in the Day of Vengeance and Recompense." Although *Marqe's* early creed simply endorses those who "believed in YHWH and in Moses," the additional articles of the longer creed have rich roots in *Marqe.*[1]

Tibat Marqe was originally written by Marqe in the third or fourth century C.E. God in *Marqe,* as in Jewish and Christian theology of the same period, often seems garbed in Hellenistic dress, and *Marqe's* philosophical bent is generally recognized.[2] The widespread Hellenistic culture of the Roman period provided the vocabulary for most religious and philosophical

---

[1] John Macdonald, ed. and trans., *Memar Marqah: The Teaching of Marqah* (2 vols.; BZAW 84; Berlin: Töpelmann, 1963), I, 34. Did this brief affirmation come (later) from Islam, or did Islam take it from the Samaritans (or the general culture)?

[2] Alan D. Crown, "The Byzantine and Moslem Period," in *The Samaritans* (ed. Alan D. Crown; Tübingen: J. C. B. Mohr, 1989), 63. A. Broadie (*A Samaritan Philosophy: A Study of the Hellenistic Cultural Ethos of the Memar Marqe* [Leiden: E. J. Brill, 1981]), argues that Marqe arranges his ideas in Hellenistic patterns like those of Philo. Macdonald (*Memar Marqah,* 1:XXXVIII) and others note that Marqe uses terms in favor with the Gnostics, but Macdonald does not believe they endow them with the same significance.

discourse and the basic context in which it could be understood. The interpretive traditions of each religious community provided subtleties and nuances of sectarian meaning.[3]

The exaltation of Moses and his teachings are the central concern of Marqe, and he enhances even the basic story of the Torah without being lured into Hellenistic content. He maintains the distinctive Samaritan frame of reference, the Torah. The two great songs of Moses, Exod 15 and Deut 32:1–43, receive special attention, focusing books 2 and 4.

Mount Gerizim receives no consideration in book 1, the most exclusively Marqan work, or books 3 and 6, but it receives lengthy attention in book 2 and consideration in books 4 and 5.

Likewise, early evidence of eschatological passages concerning the day of vengeance and recompense is problematic.[4] Relevant passages occur only in the chronologically later books 4–6.[5]

In addition to theological and philosophical exposition, *Marqe* is rich in hymns, many of which found their way into later liturgical works. Half of the almost forty hymns in *Marqe* are in book 1, lending strong support to their early origin. None are found in book 3, but books 2, 4, 5, and 6 each have a handful.

Scientific speculation, a theology of the natural world, also plays a significant part. Marqe created a thoughtful synthesis between primitive animism or pantheism, which attributed life and even divinity to various aspects of nature, and rigorous monotheism, which reserved divinity for the one God and in some forms, such as Gnosticism and neoplatonism, tended to ignore nature in the quest for the distinctly spiritual. Unlike Gnosticism and neoplatonism, Marqe was clearly not otherworldly. He affirmed and expanded on the physical concreteness of the biblical narrative, where he (Marqe) enhanced the natural forces of fire, wind, cloud, water, and earth with an interpretation that gives them a power and purpose shaped by the will of God. These forces are particularly significant in books 2 (§§ 32–34), 4 (§ 87), and 5 (§§ 124–125). In a sense, Marqe anticipated the desire of contemporary process theology to "re-enchant" the physical world without returning to animism.

Samaritan scholars have mined *Marqe* for clues to the development of Samaritan traditions, beliefs, and worship. Comparing *Marqe* with later works

---

[3] Thus developed Talmud, halakah, and midrash in both the Jewish and the Samaritan communities and their parallel commentaries in the Christian community.

[4] Ferdinand Dexinger ("Samaritan Eschatology," in *The Samaritans* [ed. Alan D. Crown; Tübingen: J. C. B. Mohr, 1989], 282–83) suspects interpolations and doubts that the passages about the day of vengeance and recompence belong to Marqe.

[5] Macdonald, *Memar Marqah*, 1:94, 104, 108–13 (a major section) (book 4); 1:119, 120, 126, 127 (book 5); 1:133, 140, 146 (book 6).

such as the *Asatir,*[6] Joshua, the liturgies, and the chronicles helps to chart the changes in beliefs and even in practices. It has provided clues to the similarities, differences, and possible borrowing, between the Samaritans and Jews, Christians, and Muslims. Passages in *Marqe* also offer clues to the development of Samaritan eschatology.[7] Finally, *Marqe* has facilitated understanding of the various stages of the Aramaic used by the Samaritan community.

MANUSCRIPT WITNESS TO *MARQE*

In the mid–nineteenth century, when the Samaritan community had decreased to a minuscule number and most of the world was oblivious of its existence, an occasional European scholar journeying in the Holy Land would come upon its members.[8] A German, Heinrich Petermann, visited their community at Nablus, observed their burial, marriage, and worship customs, and described them in his *Reisen im Orient.*[9] He also undertook pioneering study of their linguistic idiosyncrasies. Petermann solicited copies

---

[6] Moses Gaster found two copies of the anonymous Arabic work *Asatir,* one on parchment and the other on paper, during a visit to Nablus in 1907. Gaster, an English scholar, therafter became very interested in Samaritan materials and had copies of many texts, including the *Asatir,* made for him. He published the *Asatir* with its commentary, the *Pitron,* in both Hebrew and English. The *Asatir* is an annotated chronicle of the biblical events from Adam to Moses that occasionally provides new interpretations of Samaritan theology and history. Gaster dated it to the third century C.E., but subsequent observations by Ze'ev Ben-Hayyim and Abraham Tal imply a date in the second half of the tenth century C.E. The present form of the work was fixed by the twelfth century. For dating see Abraham Tal, "Samaritan Literature," in *The Samaritans* (ed. Alan D. Crown; Tübingen: J. C. B. Mohr, 1989), 413–67, here 465–67. Abraham Tal sanctions and underscores Ben Hayyim's dating in this article. The anonymous work *Pitron* is a commentary on the *Asatir.* The *Pitron,* written in Arabic probably in the fifteenth century C.E., is somewhat lengthier than the *Asatir.* More a free association with issues mentioned in the *Asatir* than a focused commentary, it is particularly preoccupied with the story of Balaam, whom, unlike the biblical story, it characterizes as conspiring with Balak to destroy the Israelites. This negative assessment of Balaam can also be seen in later Jewish writings and in the New Testament. The *Pitron* cites Marqe several times and tells the story of Moses' death mostly in Marqe's words.

[7] Dexinger ("Samaritan Eschatology," 270) particularly compares Marqe and Abisha and also notes the beginning of the Rahuta (Period of Divine Favor) with Joshua in *Marqe* in contrast to the SJ and the *Asatir,* which have it begin with Moses (p. 277).

[8] There were likely fewer than two hundred.

[9] Julius Heinrich Petermann, *Reisen im Orient: 1852–1855* (2 vols.; Leipzig, 1860–1861; repr., 1865; repr., Amsterdam: Philo Press, 1976), Citation 1, 274–76 (in 1865 edition).

of some of their manuscripts, and it was his copy of *Tibat Marqe,* brought to Berlin in 1868, that first provided European scholars with a glimpse of this work.

Because there were few Samaritan scholars, publication of the work was slow. From 1888 to 1898, books 1, 2, 5, and 6 were published.[10] Book 4 was published only in 1934, and John Macdonald published the complete work in 1963. Ze'ev Ben-Hayyim was prominent in the study of *Marqe* in the latter part of the twentieth century.[11]

Prior to this, there had been two earlier periods of transmission, the fourteenth to the sixteenth century and the eighteenth to the nineteenth century. In 1909 Paul Kahle obtained a text that he called K, which he (and Macdonald) presumed dates from the late fourteenth century. The relative absence of syntactical problems is part of the argument that the K text was dictated from memory.[12] The migration of desperate Samaritans from Damascus to Palestine during the invasions of Tamerlane (1336–1405) and the bubonic plagues that struck in 1348 and 1360 may have triggered the rebirth of *Marqe* manuscript production.[13] Written before 793 A.H., K has a colophon and parallel columns of Aramaic and Arabic in Samaritan script. Unique characteristics of K are the long *a—alif tawila*—and the prosthetic *alif.*

The colophon identifies the scribe as Pinhas b. Ithamar b. Aaron, b. Ithamar b. Aaron b. Ab Ozzi b. Pinhas b. Eleazar b. Netanel, Eleazar, the high priest. He was in Damascus and witnessed the sale of several manuscripts of various works between 1404 and 1416.

There follow the early-sixteenth-century text L (Levitical) 1 originally copied in 1531 and a hiatus in the seventeenth century separating the two periods of transmission. Then two D (Danfi) manuscripts, D 1 and 2 (A&B) appear in the middle of the eighteenth century and a few more in the nineteenth century: L 2, L 3, and D3.

The variants in the *Marqe* manuscripts are of several types: (1) orthographic variants, (2) the exchange of consonants, (3) the inversion of consonants, (4) variants resulting from the use of synonymous Aramaic expressions, (5) variants resulting from a variety of designations for the deity, and (6) vari-

---

[10] Macdonald, *Memar Marqah,* 1:XXII–XXVI.

[11] Ze'ev Ben-Hayyim, *Tibat Marqe: A Collection of Samaritan Midrashim* (Jerusalem: Israel Academy of Sciences and Humanities, 1988); and, in anticipation, "Towards a New Edition of Tibat Marqe," in *Études samaritaines: Pentateuch et targum, exégèse et philologie, chroniques* (ed. Jean-Pierre Rothschild and Guy Dominique Sixdenier; Louvain: Peeters, 1988), 161–78.

[12] Macdonald, *Memar Marqah,* 1:XXIII.

[13] Ibid., 1:XXI.

ants in the use of *alef* as a *mater lectionis*.[14] Ben-Hayyim emphasizes our lack of a chronological Aramaic dictionary to help us date the various parts of *Marqe* and the fluidity in interpolation and placement of texts. When subsequent copyists tried to update to current Aramaic, they often left compromises that are no longer understandable.[15] Ben-Hayyim criticized the Macdonald text as arbitrarily eclectic and needing help with the Aramaic,[16] and he subsequently published his own edition based on a 1531/1532 text (presumably L.1) and parts of an older version.[17]

AUTHOR

A discussion of texts quickly establishes that *Tibat Marqe* is not a unity, and it is not easy to locate the seams between different authors and different time periods represented in the work. There is precedence for this phenomenon. The New Testament writers Paul and John set a literary and theological tone that shaped the works of followers, resulting in Pauline and Johannine "schools." Similarly, later Samaritan writers sought the sanction of Marqe for their own ideas but also believed they were writing in the spirit of a Marqan "school," appropriately expanding Marqe's canon. These later writers cannot be identified.

Marqe himself was a third- or fourth-century scholar, poet, and philosopher. Some would emphasize the last and call Marqe a Greek philosopher in Samaritan garb.[18] Tradition says that his father, Amram b. Sered, possibly a high priest and certainly a leader of the Samaritan community, had a dream in which he was instructed to name his son Moses. This name was precluded by the Samaritan exaltation of the uniqueness of Moses (see Deut 34:10–12), but the name "Marqe" has the same numerical equivalent, 345, when the letters are converted into numbers and totaled. Marqe in turn had a son, Nanah (Latin, *Nonus*). Several clues suggest a setting in the late Roman period rather than Byzantine times. He uses Greek words and Aramaized Roman names, expresses a philosophical and scientific outlook, and reflects early midrashic material. The early sections show no Islamic influence.[19]

---

[14] Macdonald (ibid., 1:XXXVIII) believes that variants in texts are related to scribal families (Levitical, Danafi, Marhabi).

[15] Ben-Hayyim, "Towards a New Edition," 162.

[16] Ze'ev Ben-Hayyim, review of John Macdonald, *Memar Marqah*, *BO* 23 (1966): 185–91.

[17] Ben-Hayyim, *Tibat Marqe*.

[18] Alan D. Crown, "Samaritan Religion in the Fourth Century," *NedTT* 41 (1986): 29–47, here 45.

[19] Macdonald, *Memar Marqah*, 1:XIX.

Marqe was likely a teacher in a Bit Sifra, holding a position parallel to that of a Greek philosopher, a Hebrew *hakam,* or a Muslim *ulama.*[20] Teachers or sages are not in the forefront of Samaritan narratives, but there are intriguing connections. Simon Magnus, sometimes identified as a Samaritan, was an early advocate of Sophia, a feminine personification of Wisdom, sometimes identified as the Holy and called by Simon the spouse of the Lord. Proverb-like sayings occur in *Marqe:*

There is no hardship that has no end.

Let every teacher get on with what he does in school.[21]

The content of the latter saying could be another hint that Marqe is a teacher. The teachers in Islam, the ulamas, bore many honorific titles: "people of the bench" (presumably outside the mosque, where they might engage in religious discussion), "best of the community," "trustees of the prophets," "trustees of God over Creation," and "lamps of the earth."[22] Several Samaritan honorific titles have similar implications: particularly חכימה ("sage") and מור כל חכמתה ("dispenser of all knowledge"). The Muslim ulamas were a distinct class of learned men in the ninth century, the period in which Ben-Hayyim locates the editing of *Marqe.* The editors could have imposed the role on Marqe.[23] The role of the ulama was often a volunteer activity or underwritten by family or community, and probably in many communities it was a kind of hidden unemployment. Since major sources of wisdom would be age and experience, such teachers could be "retired" members of the community. In the second century B.C.E., Ben Sira's was the first explicit school. Subsequently there were other Jewish schools. Such a school among the Samaritans was likely the base from which later writers added to the Marqan canon.

Marqe books 3–6 were likely written or significantly reedited in later centuries. Ben-Hayyim's English preface to *Tibat Marqe* sees selections of book 1 as dating from the eleventh to the thirteenth century and the later books as reedited in the ninth century.[24] The authors of these later writings or interpolations are unknown to us, and the status of the Samaritan community in these later times is too sketchy to be in dialog with the uncertain layers of *Marqe* from that time. It is also likely that modifications were made to *Tibat Marqe* during the Samaritan renaissance of the fourteenth century.

---

[20] Also inferred by Macdonald, ibid., 1:XLII.

[21] Ibid., 1:13.

[22] Hamid Algar, " 'Ulamā,' " *ER* 15:115–17, here 115.

[23] Ibid., 15:116.

[24] Ben-Hayyim, *Tibat Marqe,* v.

HISTORICAL CONTEXT

The historical context for Marqe's life, the latter part of the third and possibly the early part of the fourth century, was most fortuitous. The Roman grip on Palestine was slipping, and Christian Byzantium was not yet in control. A rather large population of Samaritans[25] had reasonable freedom. They were accepted by the Jews as fellow Jews, and it is likely that Samaritan practice and doctrine were primarily affected by the common Hebrew heritage.

Marqe's father, Amram, was a purported associate of Baba Raba, the charismatic leader of an extensive Samaritan revival. Amram served on the newly restored council of sages (hukama) that Baba Raba established. The majority of its members were laity. A struggle between priestly and lay factions is common in many religions. Samaritanism tended to veer in a priestly direction, so this was a unique historical moment. With more power in the hands of the laity, the Samaritans were able to disperse further from Gerizim and the priestly class. Baba Raba established an official text of the SP and generally facilitated the separation of Samaritanism from Judaism.[26]

Marqe played Ezra to Baba Raba's Nehemiah. That is, like the biblical Nehemiah, Baba Raba effectively reorganized the Samaritan community and supervised an extensive building campaign, and Marqe, like Ezra, infused a new spirit or soul into the rebuilt and restructured community.

SOURCES

The sources for *Marqe* are the Pentateuch, the New Testament, Jewish (non-Torah) documents, and certain Muslim documents.

The Pentateuch

The biblical tradition represented in the SP and Targum (Aramaic paraphrase of the Pentateuch) was the major source utilized by the author(s) of *Tibat Marqe*. The Moses stories are used far more than the patriarchal or preflood stories. There are good reasons for expecting the Samaritans to favor the Pentateuch's E traditions over the J traditions.

---

[25] Crown ("Samaritan Religion," 35) cites an estimate of three hundred thousand.

[26] Ibid., 33.

Classic source criticism of the Pentateuch produced the Documentary Hypothesis,[27] a positing of four basic layers of tradition and editing in the construction of the Pentateuch. The earliest layer, dating from the tenth century B.C.E., is J, a southern Palestinian tradition telling the epic story of Israel's past with a focus on the exodus. A century later, after the separation of Israel into northern and southern kingdoms (Israel and Judah), the second layer, E, evolved in the north. Since the Samaritans have their origins in the north, it would be logical for them to have had more familiarity and more partiality for the E telling of the Mosaic story over the J telling.

John Macdonald has made the only focused attempt to evince evidence tying the Samaritans directly to the E tradition. The more plausible arguments follow: J attributes miracles to God; *Marqe*, like E, attributes them to Moses.[28] E is the chief source of the information that Moses is from the priestly house of Levi, which is important to the Samaritans; it associates Aaron with Moses in the account of the family of Amram and Jochebed. E, like *Marqe*, is well versed in Egyptian issues.[29] In J, the Lord saved Israel; in E (and *Marqe*), there is a Hebrew savior, Moses; in E, the power of miracle is innate in Moses, God reveals His name only to Moses, and Moses has powers that no other human being has.[30] E, like the Samaritans, avoids anthropomorphism: God communes with Moses through direct mystical union. E is not interested in the ordinary deeds of Moses.[31] Like *Marqe*, it is preoccupied with two figures, Abraham and Moses. And like the Samaritans, it is preoccupied with professional priestly matters and sacred institutions; E has the germ of theocracy. Macdonald picks up Robert Pfeiffer's comment that J is a sculptor, E is an architect.[32] The fundamental Samaritan belief about the Sabbath is in E (Exod 20:8–11) rather than in J, D, or the Covenant Code or P; the Sabbath is a gift of God through Moses to Israel (Exod 20).[33]

Two issues close to the heart of the Samaritans would have strong roots in the E document. The ark of the covenant was the central religious artifact of the southern kingdom and is supposed to have been in the holy of holies of the temple at Jerusalem; but the Samaritans condemn the reign of David

---

[27] For a basic explanation of the Documentary Hypothesis, consult a Bible dictionary or an introduction to the Old Testament.

[28] John Macdonald, *The Theology of the Samaritans* (London: SCM, 1964), 182.

[29] Ibid., 188.

[30] Ibid., 188, 196–197.

[31] Ibid., 197.

[32] Ibid., 198.

[33] Ibid., 188, 299, 302.

(who brought the ark to Jerusalem),[34] and the E document never mentions the ark of the covenant. The Samaritans instead focused on the tabernacle and may never have had a temple, but the J document never mentions the tabernacle or tent of meeting.[35]

Since J and E cover much of the same material, Macdonald has a particular burden to show a Marqan preference. But tough questions challenge such a hypothesis. In what form would the E tradition have survived for the Samaritans to be familiar with it apart from their Pentateuch, which, like all late versions of the Pentateuch, obliterates any recognizable documentary seams? Indeed contemporary scholars are not in agreement on the boundaries (or even the existence) of J and E.

The extensive use of J in *Marqe* puts in some question the intriguing examples pointed out by Macdonald. For example, the burning bush with the affirmation that there is no prophet like Moses, together with the appearance of angels, is from the J account.[36] Likewise the hymn "So Moses took a wife" is based on J, and the increase in the burden of the Israelites by their having to provide their own straw, together with their subsequent resentment of Moses, is told in J.[37]

There is the likelihood of a direct relationship between the SP and the Septuagint, particularly Codex Alexandrinus, evidenced by similar zigzag patterns at the end of biblical books, the marking of parallel texts, the Decalogue's structure, and the use of *kai/waw* symmetry.[38] The impact of this relationship for the Pentateuch is not evident in *Marqe,* but if the Samaritans were aware of the Septuagint, particularly Alexandrinus, they would also have been aware of the New Testament, which is attached in that codex. This awareness could have influenced a number of features that are present in *Marqe*. In addition, Samaritan *Chronicle II* lists the four gospels and Paul's letters as well as other Christian literature.

---

[34] The chronicler Abu'l Fath says, "The erroneous people all came together to celebrate his (David's) birth, and agreed upon . . . Jerusalem [as the Holy Place]" (Paul Stenhouse, ed., *The Kitab Al-Tarikh of Abu'l-Fath, Translated with Notes* [Sydney: Mandelbaum Trust, University of Sydney, 1985], 540).

[35] Richard Friedman (*Who Wrote the Bible?* (New York: Simon and Shuster, 1987; repr. New York: Harper & Row, 1989) underscores these different foci of religious place. He also argues that E has more material and greater reverence for Moses (p. 79). This would fit with the great Samaritan and Marqan attention to Moses.

[36] Macdonald, *Memar Marqah*, 1:5.

[37] Ibid., 1:11, 13.

[38] Alan D. Crown, "Studies in Samaritan Scribal Practice and Manuscript History, III: Columnar Writing and the Samaritan Massorah," *BJRL* 67 (1986): 349–81, here 373–75.

The New Testament

Marqe has written essentially a "gospel" of Moses. The gospel genre was invented by Mark, the earliest New Testament gospel writer. Marqe shares more with Mark than just the general genre. Both omit birth narratives (Jesus, Moses), emphasize miracles (healing miracles, the assault on Pharaoh), detail leaders' responsibilities (the disciples' manual of Mark 7–8; *Marqe* 3 on the priesthood), set out teachings (of Jesus, of Moses), and dramatically emphasize a death and assumption (of Jesus, of Moses). Some would argue that Mark is a northern Palestinian source,[39] making it more likely that it would be available to the Samaritan community.

This presents an interesting irony. David Strauss in the nineteenth century proposed that the gospel writers applied "Moses Theology" to Jesus, that the gospels were built on a paradigm of Moses' life to present Jesus as a second and superior Moses.[40] In light of the rigorous missionary activity of Christians toward Samaritans, already described in the book of Acts of the first century, *Marqe's* basic story may be influenced by a paradigm of Jesus' life to present Moses as a superior Jesus, and thus *Marqe* may apply Christian theology to Moses.

Not only was Samaria the earliest mission field of the church of Acts; the New Testament records several incidences of relationship between Christians and Samaritans.[41] The two communities shared a common geography and culture. Macdonald cites many examples of Marqan sensitivity to Gospel materials and notes that the Samaritans are never critical of Christians or Christianity.[42] Later Christianity could have influenced later interpolations in *Marqe.*

The Gospel of John is another likely northern source. It is distinguished from the other gospels by its relatively long theological discourses, a feature that *Marqe* shares. In general, Samaritan scholars have seen this gospel as the one most explicitly aimed at the Samaritans, and like Mark and *Marqe,* it does not have a birth story. John Bowman, among others, believed that John was intentionally creating a bridge between Samaritans and Jews in the person of Jesus. Salvation may be from the Jews, but it is for all Israel. Therefore John used notions of "light," the ten words, and other Samaritan terms

---

[39] E.g., Willi Marxsen, *Introduction to the New Testament* (Philadelphia: Fortress, 1970), 143.

[40] David Frederick Strauss, *The Life of Christ Critically Examined* (trans. Marian Evans; 2 vols.; New York: Calvin Blanchard, 1860, 1870), 1:65–69.

[41] Even so, Crown thinks that Christianity was an insignificant influence on Samaritanism in the time of *Tibat Marqe.* In his view, Judaism was by far the greatest influence (Crown, "Samaritan Religion").

[42] Macdonald, *Theology of the Samaritans,* 450.

to facilitate receptivity.[43] Jesus' ultimate audience is the "Israelites," the total of the twelve tribes, perhaps inspired by the vision of Ezekiel. Further, John implies that Jesus was rejected only in Jerusalem, not in Galilee and Samaria, and there is a conscious attempt by John to relate Galileans and Samaritans.[44]

There is little to suggest that the Samaritans used Pauline literature (assuming Hebrews is non-Pauline), but a few observations should be made. Like Paul, Marqe is no longer the storyteller but the commentator on the story, and like Paul, he selects a few major personages upon whom to hang his conceptual message. Paul uses Adam (humanity as material untouched by the holy), Abraham (who sees God and has faith), Moses (who tries to codify the faith in law), and Jesus (who by his act allows salvation for humanity in spite of its inability to follow the law). Marqe emphasizes Adam, Abraham, and particularly Moses. The *Asatir* defines the four "Foundations of the World" as Adam, Noah, Abraham, and Moses.[45]

Comparison with the Letter to the Hebrews, which has been called a homiletical midrash (on Ps 110) and coincidentally is a book many would associate in several ways with the Samaritans, is also appropriate. It addresses the "Hebrews," the preferred term of the Samaritans, and includes an extensive encomium that includes only heroes of the past who would be acceptable to Samaritans.

Jewish Documents (Non-Torah)

During times of shared oppression, the Jewish and Samaritan communities were fairly close. Although the literature of one was always available to be read by the other, there is no evidence that the Samaritans borrowed from Judaism.[46] There is no criticism by one group of the other's scriptures that would compare with the fight between Catholics and Protestants in the seventeenth century.[47] They, of course, shared a common scriptural heritage.

---

[43] John Bowman, "Samaritan Studies, I: The Fourth Gospel and the Samaritans," *BJRL* 40 (1958): 298–327, here 302.

[44] James D. Purvis, "The Fourth Gospel and the Samaritans," *NovT* 17 (1975), 161–98, here 170.

[45] Noted by Abraham Tal, "Samaritan Literature," in *The Samaritans* (ed. Alan D. Crown; Tübingen: J. C. B. Mohr, 1989), 413–67, here 466.

[46] Macdonald (*Theology of the Samaritans,* 452) states emphatically, "The Samaritans did not borrow from Judaism."

[47] Shelama ben Jakob of Damascus expressed a classic criticism of an Arabic translation of the Torah: "It is the translation of the Jewish scholar al Fayoumi who truly erred in using the right Arabic idiom." But this criticism is not focused on content or interpretation.

The Samaritans did utilize Jewish writings in other instances; for example, in the Damascus Diaspora, Jews and Samaritans shared the Jewish-initiated concept of the 613 precepts. Since *Marqe* uses commonly shared material, it is impossible to identify distinctively Jewish contributions. There are in *Marqe*, however, many cases, such as the traditions on the death and ascension of Moses, that are quite different.

Muslim Documents

The Samaritan liturgy startles us with frequent use of Muslim religious slogans such as the Muslim (Arabic) *Bismillah* and the Samaritan (Hebrew) *Bashem Yhwh*, "In the name of God." Macdonald has attempted to identify Islamic influences on Samaritan thought.[48] His generalization is that works from early fruitful periods of Samaritan thought, particularly *Tibat Marqe* and the *Defter,* are pre-Islamic and devoid of Islamic ideas whereas works of the productive and post-Islamic eleventh and fourteenth centuries reflect strong Muslim influence.

Utilization of Muslim ideas and expressions was inevitably facilitated as Arabic replaced Samaritan Hebrew and Aramaic in daily usage. Common Arabic greetings and salutations became part of the Samaritan vocabulary: *in sha Allah, Allah a'lam, Bismillah ar-rahman ar-rahim* ("God willing," "Eternal God," "In the name of God, the merciful, the compassionate").[49] After the eleventh century, Samaritan personal names were no longer exclusively taken from the Bible but were adopted from Muslims: Ghazal, Salih, Abdullah, Abu Sarur, Said, and Ibrahim. By the sixteenth century, this included the adoption of Muslim family names. To be intelligible to others as well as themselves, the Samaritans needed at least a modicum of Arab culture.

Islam facilitated an articulate expression of monotheism in Samaritanism, affirming an unchanging God. "God having neither species nor genus, can have no equal."[50] It is likely that the model by which Samaritans pray to Moses, their prophet, comes from the Muslim prayer for Muhammad, since neither Judaism nor Christianity has a prayer for its respective prophet.

The Shem ha-Mitparesh, a few columns on strips of parchment listing the names of God in the Pentateuch, is a parallel to the ninety-nine names of Allah. Judaism had a similar list, the Shem ha-Mephorash. Macdonald also

---

[48] John Macdonald, "Islamic Doctrines in Samaritanism," *MW* 50, no. 4 (1960): 279–90.
[49] Ibid., 283.
[50] Ibid., 284.

notes the Samaritan attribution of "logos," or "word," of God to Moses and believes it is inspired by Qur'an 7:144: "He said: O Musa! Surely I have chosen you above the people with My messages and with My words."[51] It could as well have come from John 1 or even directly from Greek philosophy. The phenomena of listing the names of God and the use of "logos" by the Samaritans likely were latent or subdued in Samaritan thought (they were not visible in the ninth century) and brought to the forefront when Samaritanism met Islam.[52]

Samaritans, like Muslims, avoid deifying the prophet (in contrast to much of Christianity) or humanizing God (in contrast to Judaism). An illustration of the latter would be the Samaritan change of the text in Exod 15:3 from the Jewish יהוה איש מלחמה ("YHWH is a man of war") to the less anthropomorphic יהוה גבור מלחמה ("YHWH is the mighty one of war").

Ramadan and the Samaritan Yom Kippur exhibit prayers much more similar to each other than to anything Christian or Jewish.[53] Macdonald notes that Samaritans have prayers for Moses as Muslims do for Muhammad, in contrast to Jews and Christians, who have no prayers for Moses or Jesus.[54]

CATEGORIES

A striking common element among the six books in *Marqe* is the presence of the encomium. With the exception of book 5, each has at least one list of "Good People." Book 5 is so focused on Moses that recognition of other good people may have been considered a distraction. After Moses, Abraham is the most cited person. There is a brief chiding of Moses in book 1 after he tries to put off God's call: "O my servant, who knows that I have done all these things, why have you answered me in all these words?"[55] But Moses is extravagantly praised in each of the books. Adam, Enosh (who is, curiously, cited in both the good and bad categories in book 6), Joseph, and Noah share wide acclaim (cited in books 1–4, 6). Enoch, Isaac, and Jacob are in the next tier of popularity. The priests Aaron, Eleazar, and Pinhas follow. Those mentioned infrequently include Abel, Judah, Joshua, Levi, Issachar, Miriam, Rebekah, Sarah, Serah, Simeon, and Reuben.

---

[51] M. H. Shakir, trans., *The Qur'an* (Elmhurst, N.Y.: Tahrike Qur'an, Inc., 1990).

[52] Ibid., 285.

[53] Ibid., 287–89.

[54] Ibid., 284.

[55] Macdonald, *Memar Marqah,* 1:10.

Less prevalent are lists of "Bad People." They occur only in books 3, 4, and 6. Surprisingly for Christians, Adam is nowhere to be found. The Sodomites are the only people on the "bad" list in all three books. Book 4 is heaviest into condemnation, citing Amalekites, the tower builders, the Egyptians, Cain, and Korah (each three times) and the calf makers, the people of the flood, the Sodomites, Enoch, Nimrod, and (twice) Reuben (with the qualification that he is later redeemed).

TYPES OF LITERATURE

Since each of the six books is distinctive in content, *Marqe* provides a broad range of genres and topics. Texts from *Marqe* are most commonly described as midrashim, elucidations of biblical text for both understanding and application. Jewish rabbinical literature provides many examples, and the Letter to the Hebrews in the New Testament, as mentioned earlier, is a midrash on Ps 110. Hebrews is closer to the midrashim found in *Marqe* because, unlike the more systematic rabbinical midrashim, Marqe does not provide us with a continuous midrash and, like Hebrews, his style is often homiletical. He selects only parts of the biblical story of the flight from Egypt and the death of Moses. As noted above, the Samaritans may have been familiar with the book of Hebrews, particularly if, as some believe, it was written with Samaritans in mind. Marqe quotes relevant biblical texts from the Samaritan Hebrew texts and from no-longer-extant Samaritan Targumim (translations of the Samaritan Hebrew into colloquial Aramaic, probably in the third or fourth century C.E.).

Books 3 and 4 contain haggadic midrash on Moses's teaching, and *Marqe* sometimes also deals with halakah in a homiletic fashion. Alan Crown sees *Marqe* as "philosophical" and halakic literature venerating the elders, particularly Joseph.[56]

Hymns are a significant part of the work. Most use the literary device anaphora, beginning each line or stanza with the same opening words. Some may have been written to enrich contemporary services, and *Marqe*'s hymns would become a standard part of later Samaritan liturgies. In the spirit of the old "myth and ritual" school, popular in the mid-twentieth century, the extensive use of poetry, hymns, responsive readings, and chants could be an indication that book 1 was used in services—perhaps even as a lead into the Passover service. Kippenberg has proposed that books 1 and 2, minus their

---

[56] Alan D. Crown, "The Byzantine and Moslem Period," in *The Samaritans* (ed. Alan D. Crown; Tübingen: J. C. B. Mohr, 1989), 63, 69.

more obvious interpolations, are a haggadah for Passover and the "Feast of Massot."[57]

Doxologies interposed in the work, particularly in book 2, may mark different parts of a subsequent liturgy.[58] Eventually hymns of other writers were included in the liturgy, and *Marqe*'s role in the liturgy diminished.

BOOK 1

Book 1 is written in fourth-century Aramaic and is probably the original, essential *Marqe*. It is called in the title the ספר פליאתה, "Book of Wonders," and follows the order of the Moses story in Exod 3–14, from the story of the burning bush to the Red Sea, incorporating some early nonbiblical poems.

As noted above, *Marqe*'s story of Moses begins with the call rather than the birth of Moses. Some scholars speculate that the birth was treated elsewhere or is lost.[59] *Marqe* thus presents an interesting parallel with the Gospel of Mark (whose name in Latin, Marcus, Marqe shares). Both begin with a call, contain a listing of miracles by the religious leader, and move on to instructions for the other leaders. John, the Gospel most closely associated with the Samaritans, also lacks a birth story.

The call of Moses follows the biblical story. The presence of the angel of the Lord is a J feature that must be considered if one views E as a unique source. *Marqe* cites the precedence for angels: three appeared to Abraham, two to Lot, and one to Joseph. Neither of the intermediate patriarchs, Isaac and Jacob, is mentioned. Subsequently *Marqe* lists the precedents for the dual call "Moses, Moses," noting that Abraham and Jacob were also called twice; Lot and Joseph are not included. Isaac is missing from both lists of precedents. In the biblical story, he serves mainly as a link between Abraham and Jacob and, particularly because of his associations with the extreme south of Palestine, would have had less significance to the Samaritans.

---

[57] Hans G. Kippenberg, *Garizim und Synagoge: Traditionsgeschichtliche Untersuchungen zur samaritanischen Religion der aramaischen Period* (Berlin: de Gruyter, 1971), 218–22.

[58] Doxologies separate the occasions of wind and earth and earth and water (Macdonald, *Memar Marqah*, 2:32), conclude an enumeration of events of power and preface the song of Moses (1:42), and divide the comments on Edom and Moab (1:45).

[59] Moses Gaster, *The Asatir: The Samaritan Book of the "Secrets of Moses" Together with the Pitron, or Samaritan Commentary, and the Samaritan Story of the Death of Moses* (Oriental Translation Fund NS 26; London: Royal Asiatic Society, 1927), 135.

Moses is commissioned to "return the sheep" and "govern the stars of Abraham." The former is the major task of delivering the Hebrews from Egypt. "Stars of Abraham is a reference to Exod 32:13: 'Remember Abraham, Isaac and Israel . . . how you swore to them, "I will multiply your descendants like the stars of the heaven."' The image is used again by Marqe as a reference to the Hebrews leaving Egypt: 'They were graceful, Abraham's stars.'"[60]

The story of Moses' rod, a unique Samaritan tradition, emerges when Moses resists the call. The Bible (Exod 4:2) implies that Moses already had the rod with him. *Marqe* implies that the rod is something from the fire that emboldens Moses and will act as a rod to his eyes.[61] Elsewhere in Samaritan tradition, the rod has a different history. *Malef* 48–49 says that when Adam was driven from Eden, he had the rod of God.[62] *Asatir* 228 and *Malef* claim that the true calendar, the Book of Wars, the Book of Signs, and the Book of Astronomy were written upon the rod. Noah received the rod, and seven years after Adam's death, he took three mystical books from it and handed them with the rod to Shem's sons, one of whom, Arpachshad, retained them and passed them on to Jethro, who gave them to Moses.[63] The Taheb, an eschatological prophet "like Moses," will receive the rod at the time of the Second Kingdom. These mystical books become a less attractive alternative to the personal mystical experience in *Marqe* to explain the source of Moses' wisdom. The biblical story also reports the transformation of the rod into a serpent.

The Taheb receives more attention in other books of *Marqe,* but an impressive poem is interjected amid the comments about Moses in book 1:

Let the Taheb come in peace and reveal the hidden [power], which has become strong in the world.

Let the Taheb come in peace and separate out the enemies who have angered God.

Let the Taheb come in peace and offer a legitimate sacrifice acceptable at Bethel.

Let the Taheb come in peace, and YHWH console [humanity] and reveal his grace, and [let] Israel sacrifice regularly.

---

[60] Macdonald, *Memar Marqah,* 1:25.

[61] Ibid., 1:7.

[62] Macdonald, *Theology of the Samaritans,* 319. The *Malef* is a likely nineteenth-century catechism that may reflect earlier traditions.

[63] Macdonald, *Theology of the Samaritans,* 319.

Let the Taheb come in peace and separate the chosen from the rejected and turn this oppression to relief.[64]

Macdonald believes that Marqe downplays God's anger with Moses, claiming, for example, that Marqe passes over Exod 4:13–14a because it is J. But downplaying Moses' shortcomings may have more to do with later attitudes toward Moses than with the sources used or not used. By the time of Marqe, the Christian Jesus had provided another paradigm, and the perfection of Moses is likely an intentional Samaritan parallel to adoration of Jesus.

In accord with J (and thus contrary to Macdonald's position), Moses in *Marqe* is instructed to go to Egypt, and he takes a wife, Zipporah (Exod 2:21; 4:25). Only eventually, however, is she acknowledged by E (Exod 18:2).

When Marqe envisions Moses, the personification of human perfection, and his brother, Aaron, approaching Pharaoh, the personification of human evil, he makes sure that the contrast is noted. Moses and Aaron make a stately entry, and even Pharaoh's counselors are so impressed that they exclaim, "These are good men!"[65] This is reminiscent of Luke 23:47, where even one of the Roman soldiers putting Jesus to death had to exclaim, "Certainly this man was innocent."

Marqe uses poetry to tell much of the story of Moses, from the calling through the flight from Egypt. These are the core poems:

And He said, "Moses, Moses!" And he replied, "Here am I." Marvelous secrets and all revelations were given.

And He said, "Moses, Moses!" He made known to him his compassion and peace.

And He said, "Moses, Moses!" He revealed to him that he would be clothed in prophethood and the name of God.

And He said, "Moses, Moses!" He made known to him that he would set free the Hebrews and kill the Egyptians.[66]

I am who I am, who was and will be, a root that has no beginning.

I am who I am, who existed in the beginning and at Mount Sinai.

---

[64] The primary texts upon which these translations are based are found in Macdonald, *Memar Marqah,* vol. 1, and CW 26349. Since the latter is not easily accessible to the reader, explicit citation will be made to Macdonald, *Memar Marqah* (here 1:22).

[65] Macdonald, *Memar Marqah,* 1:14.

[66] Ibid., 1:3.

I am who I am, calling [into existence] the world and calling for its creatures.

I am who I am, who formed the body and incorporated the soul.

I am who I am, who established the garden and repaid Sodom.

I am who I am, who cultivated life and destroyed death.

I am who I am, the God of righteousness and Lord of the Hebrews.[67]

See I have placed you as a God to Pharaoh, and Aaron your brother will serve as your prophet.

See I have placed you as a God to Pharaoh in order that you penalize him appropriately on behalf of the congregation.

See I have placed you as a God to Pharaoh in issuing destruction of his possessions and all his people.

See I have placed you as a God to Pharaoh with a rod, which I gave you to reveal wonders.

See I have placed you as a God to Pharaoh in my wish that all Egyptians be destroyed in the twinkling of an eye.

See I have placed you as a God to Pharaoh; I give him into your hand and you will kill him in judgment.

See I have placed you as a God to Pharaoh; you are the redeemer of the blood of the children of peace.

See I have placed you as a God to Pharaoh; you shall not be afraid of him because I have given him into your hand.

See I have placed you as a God to Pharaoh; he is conquered in your presence and there is no need for [other] help.[68]

And Pharaoh turned and entered his house; his spirit was overwhelmed and irritation dwelt within.

And Pharaoh turned and entered his house, an enemy of the world and a foe of the creation.

---

[67] Ibid., 1:8.
[68] Ibid., 1:13.

And Pharaoh turned and entered his house after vexing the speakers and the silent.

And Pharaoh turned and entered his house, and all the Egyptians were bound by him in oppression.

And Pharaoh turned and entered his house, and the sins of the living and the dead were piled upon him for seven days.[69]

Ten times the Egyptians were killed in the sea because they ignored the ten miracles.

The chariots of Pharaoh and his army were mired in the sea. Their blood poured into it as it did into the river of Egypt.

The depths covered them just as the frogs had covered them.

They sank in a heap like stones just as the insects sank into their flesh.

You pour out Your rage; it consumes them like stubble just as when flies ate their corpses.

With the wind from Your Nose you caused the water to heap up just as the hand of YHWH shook up their cattle.

They went up like a dam just as they stood in the judgment of boils.

The depths congealed in the heart of the sea just as hail congealed in the fields.

You blew with Your breath. The water covered them just as when the locusts covered them.

They sank like lead in the great waters just as they sank in the dim darkness.

You raised your right hand; it swallows them just as when the Destroyer swallowed the spirits of their first born.[70]

Another powerful literary device used by Marqe is the imagery of the river. It is employed for several purposes both in the story of the plagues and in the crossing of the sea. The two events are tied together by the hymn above that parallels the Egyptians in the sea with the plagues. When the Nile is turned to blood in the initial plague, Pharaoh, head bowed and unable to

---

[69] Ibid., 1:17.
[70] Ibid., 1:27.

approach the river, is told by God that it is a tributary of Eden that will no longer nourish Pharaoh. Marqe says that the Tigris and Euphrates rivers were anxious to come to the aid of the Nile but were prevented from doing so. God assures them that he will redeem the blood.[71]

A relatively obscure heroine focuses a surprising share of the narration for the initial stage of the exodus, when the pillars of cloud and fire stopped their progress and they could not leave Succoth:

> Moses and Aaron observed and were frightened. The whole congregation was stupefied by this mysterious thing. Moses said to Aaron, "I think there has been some foolish act in the congregation." "Let us call to the sages," they said to one another, "and ask them to evaluate this evil." The sages approached Moses and Aaron and their hearts were desolate. "Go in peace, sages of the assembly, and ask of each tribe about this mystery. I do not think that enchanters are able to bind the children of the Oath with their enchantment. This is nothing but a secret we have not come upon. The truth is near. It will reveal a reward."

> The sages dispersed among the congregation and began questioning each tribe. When they came to speak with the tribe of Asher, Serah came out quickly to meet them. "There is no sin to you in this. I will explain this puzzle for you." They considered her worthy and brought her to the great prophet, Moses. She stood before him. He was like a full moon. She said, "Peace be with you, O honored among men. Listen to me on this matter about which you ask. Praise to those who give light to those in darkness. You would have forgotten him [Joseph] except that the pillar of cloud and the pillar of fire stood still. You would have gone out and he would have been left by the river in Egypt. I [recall] the day of his death, and he made a vow with all his people as they went up from here with them."

> The great prophet Moses said to her, "Fair art thou, O Serah, luminous among women. From this day onward your greatness will be noted." Her voice was spread in the congregation and they were told, "Joseph will go up from here with us." Serah left and all the tribe of Ephraim acted on her [word].

> Moses and Aaron went after them until they came to the place where he was buried. She stood there, and they uncovered the ark and they carried it. Serah parted from Moses and Aaron. The great prophet Moses opened the ark with his right hand, and he touched it and he kissed it. He wept and began to shed tears in his memory.

---

[71] Ibid., 1:17.

And he said, "Your spirit is sweet, O Honored one of the house of his father." And all of the congregation stood weeping for him and said, "Your spirit is sweet, O Joseph, possessor of freedom." The great prophet Moses raised his voice and said to him, "Joseph, your spirit knows you will be borne by my hands and six hundred thousand who extol you. The cloud and the fire will lead you, and your progeny will serve as your bearer. After a hundred and forty years covered in the land of Egypt and after all these years, a return to the land which was allotted to you has come to pass. Your spirit is sweet, fruitful son, Joseph, king who was clothed with freedom, for whom was made a great and powerful renown and also glory and praise both in life and after your death. In life you were praised with greetings, and the children of your two wives adored you. After your death, you were praised more than then."

When the great prophet Moses finished weeping, he said to the house of Ephraim, "You will bear him." Joshua preceded and carried him. He called out and said, "Your spirit is sweet, O father, honored of the house of his fathers." As soon as he was lifted up in the hands of his children, the cloud and fire went before them.[72]

Serah was the daughter of Asher (Gen 46:17; Num 26:46; 1 Chr 7:30) and granddaughter of Jacob and Zilpah, Leah's handmaiden (Gen 29:24). Her name appears in every genealogical list of Asher. In addition, she was among the seventy people who descended into Egypt with Jacob (Gen 46:8–27), and she is in the census list of the clans of Asher (Num 26:46). It is possible that she became the ancestress of one of the prominent clans of Asher. There are many stories in Jewish tradition to explain her renown.[73] Marqe gives us a Samaritan explanation for her prominent position. The incident gives a focus to Joseph, whom the Samaritans see as their distinctive ancestor among the sons of Jacob.

The encomium, the praise of a person or persons, is well represented in book 1. The "Hymn of 10 Days" is an encomium, reaching a climax on the tenth day with praise of Moses.[74] A major theme of all the encomia is the extolling of Moses. The patriarchs Abraham, Isaac, Jacob, and Joseph are also strongly highlighted. Abraham at one point is upbraided for crossing some "border"; a later comment on a ritual border may be a clue. Moses is chided for whining that he cannot speak. But these criticisms are lost in the sea of

---

[72] Ibid., 1:25–26.
[73] Claude F. Mariottini, "Serah," *ABD* 5:1104.
[74] Macdonald, *Memar Marqah,* 1:27.

adulation. Aaron and his descendants, particularly Pinhas and Eleazar, also receive much attention.

Book 1 specifies or implies several attributes of God: "Power," "Knowledge," "Majesty," "Glory," "Living One," "Who does not die," "Unchanging," "No Beginning or Source," "Eternal," "Never Observed," and, as can be seen from the readings, the most popular, "True One."

Moses' feelings receive special attention in *Marqe*. Consider the episode of the rod turning to a snake (Exod 4) as told by *Marqe*:

> "Now cast it from your hand to the earth and indeed see, my prophet, what will happen in consequence." With good intention, he quickly threw it to the ground at the command of his Lord. Moses had hardly finished throwing it from his hand when it became a snake, an awesome sight. He gasped and moved away and from his strong fear Moses fled from it and stood in great awe. There was nothing like it. He had great fear in his heart. He was unable to go near it. Then he spoke and his heart was full of confusion from this incredibly bewildering event. "It is not in me to understand this great power—a dead branch becomes a snake moving before me, fearsome to my mind, and I cannot understand such an extremely unusual thing. Dust is not anything. All that comes from it is desolate. No one expects a powerful fearsome deed from it. I am quivering from it. I can't comprehend it, and had it not been for the glory of YHWH, I would have fallen. I would not have been able to rise to face it. I would have had to flee so that I would not see it. The great fear in my heart made me avert my eyes from the path of its form."[75]

This expression of feeling, unstated in the biblical text, is akin to Jeremiah's confessions (e.g., Jer 23:9–10), Job (e.g., Job 9:28–31), Ahaz shaking like a tree in the wind (Isa 7:2), and the subjectivity of many of the Psalms.

BOOK 2

The core of book 2 is the song of Moses, or song of the sea (Exod 15), an epic poem affectively describing the deliverance of the Hebrews from bondage and implying their certitude of divine providence.[76] For Jew and Samaritan alike, this deliverance of the Israelites from bondage is the central focus of the Torah. In abbreviated form, the song was carved in marble for

---

[75] Ibid., 1:9.

[76] Three different versions of it are found on a compact disk: Samaritan Singers Ensembles, directed by Benyamim Tsedaka, *The Sounds of Samaritan Music*. It is produced by the A.B. Institute of Samaritan Studies, P.O. Box 1029, Holon 58110, Israel.

the lintels of synagogues, and in the liturgy it sustained the community through its centuries of oppression.

Appearance of sections in Samaritan Hebrew rather than in Aramaic and the interpolation of various midrashim disturb the sense of order and uniformity found in book 1. The Aramaic parts of books 1 and 2 likely were a unity, but as they were expanded with interpolations, the book was divided.[77] The importance of the song of the sea explains why book 2 invited more interpolations than book 1. This is the pivotal story to which the rest of the Pentateuch is attached. For Christians, the parallel would be the passion narratives, to which the rest of the gospel pericopes are attached. Jews, for example, found it hard not to add sections to the book of Job as well. Exodus 15 is the Hebraic faith in sharpest focus and regularly invited commentary, and book 2 is an exegetical midrashic and poetical commentary on Exod 15.[78]

A little essay on the nature of humanity, quite different in temper from anything in book 1, forms a prelude to the book. The distinctive feature of humanity is an implanted (innate?) wisdom,[79] presumably deduced by Marqe from the Genesis story of the eating of the fruit of the tree of knowledge of good and evil. From the same source, he can affirm that all of the other creatures were made for humanity. Catching the spirit of the J tradition in which this story was told, Marqe exalts the nature of humanity. There are echoes later in book 2, where Marqe is at strong odds with contemporary (both to him and to us) Christian interpretation: "Adam is the best thing in creation; the Mount (Gerizim, from whose dust Adam was made) is the best part of dry land."[80] Adam is listed among the seven best things in the world.

> The world lives on the deep spring of Eden. Let us stand in understanding to drink from its water. We are thirsty for the waters of life and great rivers are before us. Blessed be God, who brought forth all kinds of creatures on behalf of humanity. Glorious is the form, which is in the image of God. The form of the heart is not the form of the body. He divided all kinds of beings into four groups, three for the sake of the fourth group. He implanted this [last] body with wisdom in order that it fully illuminate the heart. Not one [of the other three] can stand against a man. He gave a

---

[77] Kippenberg, *Garizim und Synagoge*, 218–22.
[78] Macdonald, *Memar Marqah*, 1:XL.
[79] The later Samaritan work *Asatir* distinguishes humanity by an image within (Gaster, *The Asatir*, 191–93).
[80] Macdonald, *Memar Marqah*, 1:46. The *Asatir* sees men of merit stemming from Abraham rather than Adam (ibid., 303). It also depicts Adam spending a hundred years in repentance after the fall.

perfect law to his servants, life and length of days because the soul desires in keeping it, and as the posture of the soul, so the body desires. And as the man reflects the soul, so the soul reflects the law because a man does not live by bread alone, but man lives by everything that comes forth from the mouth of YHWH.[81]

A second step preparing us for the central story is a long discussion of how the elements (fire, wind, water, and earth) served Israel a total of thirty-three times. Again water is of particular interest. It was central in the story of the plagues, the flight, and the early nourishing of Moses. The Egyptians are defeated by the water in six ways. They will even burn in the water.[82]

The Red Sea is the locale for two fascinating conversations. The first is between Moses and Pharaoh, although Moses does all the talking. Citing the fate of Cain, the generation of the flood, the tower builders, Nimrod, and the people of Sodom, Moses reminds Pharaoh of the consequences of wickedness. Pharaoh is speechless.[83] Moses then converses with the sea (which resists having itself polluted with Egyptians). The sea, however, is submissive (obedient) and allows Moses to dominate it. Macdonald points out the parallel of Jesus calming the sea (Mark 4:39).[84] The sea becomes a device to contrast the value of Moses and Pharaoh, both of whom enter the sea and experience quite different fates.

Continuing the theme, book 2 will conclude with meditations on water, including a hymn on the "Waters of Life," and a litany of three mysterious waters:

> Water, which causes every tree to grow well, which, is of pure body from its germination. That was in a time of only pure things. Moses dipped in a basin of wonders seven months. This is the purity of holiness, chosen water that purifies all who are unclean.

> The second water is milk of purity which he sucked from his mother and not from an outsider.

> The third water is from the Euphrates, which has hidden [powers].[85]

The scene is set for the song of Moses, whom Marqe introduces with a meditation on the word "then," impregnating it with the connotation of the

---

[81] Macdonald, *Memar Marqah,* 1:31.
[82] Ibid., 1:42, 44.
[83] Ibid., 1:34–35.
[84] Ibid., 1:35.
[85] Ibid., 1:51.

beginning of creation. It is a moment of *kairos* that includes all beginnings. Curiously, Marqe takes off not from the biblical אв but from the hellenized Aramaic *tet* (from the Greek *tote*).

In a unique Samaritan spin on the story, Moses and the host of Hebrews, though standing on the Sinai Peninsula, face Mount Gerizim as they sing. The expected focus is Sinai, not Gerizim. Later in this book there are longer sections related to Mount Gerizim. Exodus 15:17 offers an opening to talk about Gerizim: "You brought them in and planted them on the mountain of your own possession, the place, O LORD, that you made for your abode, the sanctuary, O LORD, that your hands have established." It is not surprising that Marqe does not miss this opportunity to speak about the center of the Samaritan world, one of its seven wonders.[86] He tells us the thirteen names of Mount Gerizim and the events that happened there. It is the "Mountain of the East," site of Eden, source of the dust to create Adam. It is the place where Abram brought Isaac for sacrifice, and it was revered by Adam, Enosh, Enoch, Noah, Abraham, Isaac, Jacob, and Joseph, and "Woe to those who alter the True One in lie, who choose for themselves a place of worship apart from it."[87]

> See how he begins after "in the sea," making known his prophecy to the inhabitants of Canaan. He announced their destruction to Israel. They could not stand when Moses said it. God commanded him to write it, and he pronounced the truth of the prophecy of Moses. He made known that he would do what he had promised at the beginning to the first of the righteous: "I will give this land to your seed" (Gen 12:7).
>
> He built an altar there. Where did he build an altar except at the established House of the Powerful One? Its previous name was the Mount of the East. Why Mount of the East? Because it and the Garden of Eden are twins. They were revealed when dry land was exposed.
>
> From this [dust] the form of Adam grew when God created him from the dust of the good Mount. Adam is the best of the creation. The good Mount is the best of dry land. The body of Adam was created by the hand of God and finished with a holy spirit and an expressive soul. It began in a holy place on a holy day. All best things are assigned to be holy; nothing in it can be unclean. Every best thing recognized by the hand of man is associated with the great and glorious Holy Name. Therefore the body of Adam could

---

[86] The others are light, Sabbath, Adam, two stone tablets, Moses, and Israel. The seven are put into a little hymn, ibid., 1:46.

[87] Ibid., 1:47.

not be taken from any but the Holy place. Because of this God said about him, "To work the land from which he was taken" (Gen 3:23). The good Mount is holier than any other Mount. From the beginning of creation it has been exalted with holiness. Jacob in holiness learned and encountered it when he saw what he saw and said, "This is none other than the House of God" (Gen 28:17).[88]

There are seven best things in the world that the True One chose and set apart as divine: light, Sabbath, Mount Gerizim, Adam, two tablets of stone, the great prophet, Moses, and Israel. Light is from fire because it is the beginning of everything. In it is order and life. The two stone tablets have their base in God. He brought them forth in power by the will of his mind. The Sabbath is the best of all the days because He set it exclusively apart. Adam is the best of all creatures because from him prophets and righteous men rose in the world. Mount Gerizim is the best of the Holy things because He made it a dwelling for His glory. Moses is the best who magnifies all the best things. Israel is the best of all peoples. God chose her and made her his selection.

So God wrote in His Scripture on behalf of Enoch, "And Enoch walked with God" (Gen 5:22). He knew the place of the True One and ran to his side just as Abraham had hurried in the time of his calling. He said to Abraham, "To the land that I show you" (Gen 12:1). What did he show him except the Good Mount? And He spoke words to him again in the time of his trial when He asked for Isaac and revealed His Holiness. He said, "To the good and blessed land of the vision" (Gen 22:2). Abraham knew it and hastened to it knowingly.

Hear now a question regarding what was said to Abraham. What is the meaning in the saying of the True One to him when He asked for Isaac "to be sacrificed as an offering upon one Mount which I will tell you" (Gen 22:2)? He made it known from the beginning of His speech. Turn your mind to the question and listen now. The answer does not need any second [source] of knowledge on its behalf. When he came supported by righteousness and truth, he asked about the place, which God had chosen. He looked at the site from a distance. He turned toward it and prayed, and when he had finished praying, he raised his eyes. He did not raise his eyes except to worship because it was the time to stand for Morning Prayer.

---

[88] Ibid., 1:46.

And in what direction would he pray except toward Mount Gerizim? When he prayed devoutly, he saw in his enlightenment that you do not say, "in regard to that which I said to you," that it is something which is coming, but to what is long since past because the word "which" made it known and revealed the meaning of this statement. Now I set for you real evidence that the word "which" is used so that you may know it refers to that which is long since past. When God proclaimed the Ten Words, He did not say there, "who brought you out" (Exod 20:2). If he referred to what is to come, Israel would not have gone out from Egypt and would not have stopped to listen.

It is good that you know that Adam worshiped in its presence and that Enosh proclaimed in the name of God on it and Enoch knew it and hastened to it and Noah built an altar there and stood by it and gave praise to the Lord of the world. So it is said about him, as it was about Abraham, "And Noah built an altar" (Gen 8:20) "And there Abraham built an altar" (Gen 12:9), just as surely as Noah had done. So Abraham truly exalted our God, who set secrets in the hearts of good men that they might illuminate them and they might reveal them. The hearts of good men are tied with their Lord. Righteousness sees them through and truth increases their goodness.

Isaac saw it, Jacob knew it, and Joseph possessed it. In full completeness it was inherited from their fathers [and passed on] to their sons. Good is the one who possesses and good is the one who inherits. A fugitive or deviant son was not [found] among them. Rather they were all good from beginning to end.

O, world full of blessing. It was a time when the great prophet Moses was seen. Let us enhance our world by praising our Lord, and let us not cease so we do not come to an [untimely] end. Let us make a shield in the face of all impurity so that we may dwell in His favor. Let us be aided by faith in YHWH and in Moses, his servant, because except for the great prophet, Moses, the law would not have been revealed and no commandment would have come down. Let us magnify our Lord and believe in him, and let us witness and say, "There is no God except One."

It is special that a blessing is returned from our Lord, who is compassionate and merciful, who is good to those who love him. Let us consider Moses, a man of God, who spoke a great prophecy at the sea, "On a Mount of Your own possession" (Exod 15:17). What is His possession? Israel is His possession. As He said, "Israel is His allotted possession" (Deut 32:9). The appointed place of your dwelling has two parts. The first is the Holy

Dwelling, and the second is that the angels of God did not cease going up and down in it (Deut 27:12). From this it is the House of God, the dwelling place of his glory. The Divine Presence is nowhere except in it. As He said, "You seek for the Divine Presence" (Deut 12:5). There is no sacrifice except before it, no oblation except before it, no heave-offering except in its presence, no free-will offering, no tithe, no first fruit, no deliverance, and no blessing received away from it forever, because it is the place of the Presence of the True One and the dwelling place of His great glory. Woe to those who alter the True One in lies, who choose for themselves a place of worship away from it. Say to them, "What is this wicked turning aside, in which you have strayed to the place where Abel sacrificed his offering and not to the place where the Divine Presence is raised?" And if you say, "Who appointed it as a dwelling place?" and if you say, "Who built it?" woe to the mind that turns from the True One and reveals discontent with all its might.

O chosen of all peoples, in the True One hold fast and do not deviate from him and do not abandon him. That would not be fitting. It is good for us to walk in accordance to the will of God and understand the sayings of the great prophet, Moses, "O YHWH your hands have established" (Exod 15:17) in the Holy Dwelling. As he said, "And I will dwell in the midst of the children of Israel" (Exod 29:45). There He dwells and His will is done. Also he repeated the words of the great prophet, Moses, "Let them build for Me a sanctuary where I may dwell in your midst" (Exod 25:8).

With no offering what is the sense of it? Or the sense of an offering that is without His will? So spoke the great prophet, Moses, "O YHWH your hand established it," a great prophecy because it was not established until after the desolation.

Let us extol our Lord at all times and praise Him in every place and exalt Him in every way, and let us believe in Moses the prophet, who made life known to us and warned us of death and taught us what is good.

The Lord will rule forever and ever (Exod 15:18): His kingdom is permanent and will not change.

The Lord will rule forever and ever: woe to the person who is an enemy to Him.

The Lord will rule forever and ever: [it will be] good for those who believe Him.

The Lord will rule forever and ever: [it will be] good for those who draw near to Him, but woe to those who distance themselves from Him.

The Lord will rule forever and ever: He gathers together those who remember the Name of YHWH and Mount Gerizim, making known that the place He has chosen from the day that God created it, its holiness continues until the day of judgment.

There are thirteen names for it in the Law, and each name announces its glory.

The first: The Mount of the East because the God of the East had acquired it from the days of Creation. Then He revealed dry land. There are seven trustworthy witnesses for it who are revealed in the Ten Words from the mouth of the Mighty One by the hand of the faithful, righteous prophet.

O YHWH your hand established it, YHWH will rule forever and ever.

The second: Bethel, because the mighty and revered God is a shield and help to those who believe in Him. He made it a shelter, an escape for all who return to God.

O YHWH your hand established it, YHWH will rule forever and ever.

The third: House of God because Your Holy angels did not cease singing praise to their Lord in it. They sought God in it.

O YHWH Your hand established it, YHWH will rule forever and ever.

The fourth: The Gate of Heaven because all who turn to it to seek God will find him near. It is the place of the Nazarites, the tithes and offerings, the vows, the blessings, the sacrifices, the gifts and the burnt offerings, and all offerings.

O YHWH Your hand established it, YHWH will rule forever and ever.

The fifth: (It's name was Luza in the beginning) formerly Luza because of its glory and light. As Jacob said, "How light is this place!" (Gen 28:17).

O YHWH Your hand established it, YHWH will rule forever and ever.

The sixth: He made it a sanctuary like a Holy Place, a place for the dwelling of holiness where a holy people could turn. He said Holy to God, glorious in holiness as the holy prophet said, "You have made, O YHWH, a sanctuary" (Exod 15:17).

O YHWH Your hand established it, YHWH will rule forever and ever.

The seventh: Mount Gerizim, place of blessing, as he said, "You will give the blessing on Mount Gerizim to place his Name there. There I will come to you and bless you" (Deut 12:5 and Exod 20:24).

O YHWH Your hand established it, YHWH will rule forever and ever.

The eighth: The house of YHWH, as he said, "You shall bring to the House YHWH your God" (Exod 23:19; 34:26). Just as there is no associate with the lord of this name, there is no place like this among all the Mounts.

O YHWH Your hand established it, YHWH will rule forever and ever.

The ninth: The Good Mount because all good things come to it, beginning with Abel. So God said, "All your chosen offerings and all your service to God [is done] upon it.

O YHWH Your hand established it, YHWH will rule forever and ever.

The tenth: The Chosen Place, because he said on its behalf, "It is the place which YHWH will choose."

O YHWH Your hand established it, YHWH will rule forever and ever.

The eleventh: The Eternal Hill, the first of the mountains of the east, highest above all mountains in holiness and glory.

O YHWH Your hand established it, YHWH will rule forever and ever.

The twelfth: One of the Mountains in One of the Tribes. As He said, "In one of your tribes, selected from the land for all the children of Adam" (Deut 12:14).

O YHWH Your hand established it, YHWH will rule forever and ever.

The thirteenth: From Abraham calling it the place that YHWH would see to; he made it known that none who seek a request upon it will be turned back empty-handed.

O YHWH Your hand established it, YHWH will rule forever and ever.[89]

Marqe meditates deeply on the story of the exodus and is in reverie about not only the awesome deliverance of the Israelites but also the incredible defeat of the powerful Egyptians. He details Pharaoh's camp and includes an illustra-

[89] Ibid., 1:46–49.

tion of it, a perfect square with a division of Egyptian soldiers on each side. In the middle are Pharaoh and his god, Baal-Zephon. Marqe bases his narrative on Exod 14:9–10 in a Targum that reads, "In front of Baal Zephon. When Pharaoh made offering."[90] The biblical text does not mention Pharaoh making an offering, and there Baal-Zephon is understood as a place name.

In book 2 there is a set of four hymns more reminiscent of the style of literature in book 1.[91] They are joined throughout book 2 by a scattering of other hymns.

Using the Torah to elaborate on Moses and Mount Gerizim, book 2 does not neglect the other fundamentals of Samaritanism, God and the Taheb. We are informed that all the names of God are attributive save the Tetragrammaton. Attributes of God may be used in reference to other beings as well. The Tetragrammaton is the essence of God—"There is none like it."[92] At the end, the Taheb will glorify the dead. They will come from the four corners of the world.[93] Macdonald notes the parallel with Mark 13:26–27: "Then they will see 'the Son of Man coming in clouds' with great power and glory. Then he will send out the angels, and gather his elect from the four winds, from the ends of the earth to the ends of heaven."

Further exaltation of Moses may also be inspired by New Testament adulation of Jesus. "If it had not been for Moses, the world would not have been created," says Marqe.[94] Parallel words are spoken of Jesus in John 1:3, "All things came into being through him, and without him not one thing came into being," and Col 1:16, "For in him all things in heaven and on earth were created." Whether or not Marqe was aware of these particular scriptures, he could have been aware that this was a way that Christians talked about Jesus, and he could have wanted to emulate it.

Commentary on Exod 15:15 turns away from a backward look at Egypt in anticipation of encounters with Edom and Moab: "Then the chiefs of Edom were dismayed; trembling seized the leaders of Moab, and all the inhabitants of Canaan melted away." Marqe is aware of both occasional animosity between Moab and Israel and the relationship of the Hebrews to the Edomites through Esau, the purported founder of Edom. Marqe joins with Exod 15 in ignoring the later story (Num 20:14–21; 21:10–20) in which neither the Edomites nor the Moabites seem to be intimidated and the Edomites flatly refuse to allow the Israelites to cross their territory.

---

[90] Ibid., 1:38.
[91] Ibid., 1:39–40.
[92] Ibid., 1:43–44.
[93] Ibid., 1:51.
[94] Ibid., 1:46.

God made war forty years, twenty in Egypt and twenty in the sea. In the great song[95] He said, "Is it not your father who created you through wonders that He revealed on your behalf?" And the great prophet, Moses, gathered them in the section [of the song], "For ask now" (Deut 4:32) in seven words. It is in the trials because God tested His enemies so that He would not be good to them later, as He would be for His loved ones.

By signs because they gathered many excellent and amazing works of a creative Lord.

By wonders because the magicians became weary from doing the like of them which were the works of a great and awesome God.

And by war because He battled with them until He delivered the children of righteousness.

And by a strong hand by which many souls died in the marvelous act and it turned very severe.

And by an outstretched arm He divided with his right hand all the starting fruitful roots from wormwood.

And by great terrors containing everything amazing to the sight of the eye, not in the hearing of the ear.

The prophet is exalted and revealed great marvels that had not been created in all the earth or in all the nations.

YHWH our God is one alone, and there is no prophet like Moses, his faithful one and his servant.

All the names of God are names of like attributes except the name YHWH, which has no correspondent to it. So the great prophet Moses says in this song, "YHWH is his name." There is no other name like this name.

There are twenty praises in this song. The great prophet praised the great YHWH: "Blessed is the One who raised all, who lifted the Egyptians so they could see the Israelites go out in safety." So Moses said in this song, "Pharaoh's chariot and his army He saw enter into the sea. And the warriors, beside their charioteers, strengthened by their officers' third men, sank in the sea of reeds. And afterward Israel saw the Egyptians go down to death in the depths like stone." The great prophet, Moses, said, "Your right hand O YHWH is glorious, by which heaven and earth are borne.

---

[95] The song of Moses in Deut 32.

Your right hand, O YHWH, broke your enemy." When he sees the eminence of YHWH, he trembles uncontrollably. In your great eminence is the shooting of arrows of His judgments, which are upon them. He overthrew his opponents in the blink of an eye.

Great is the Strong One who burned their bodies in the midst of the sea and the water did not drip into the fire. God overturned the truth of the world on behalf of Israel in every place. Natural water seeks [to go] down, but in the Sea of Reeds He set it to go up because the waters piled up like a water dam, like great mountains to prepare a way for Israel to walk. The enemy said, "I will pursue, I will overtake, I will divide the spoils"—all the cattle and possessions. From this the great power of Pharaoh, King of Egypt, was made known because no enemy could take the spoils of his foes until after he had killed them. Pharaoh said he would slay them after he took all the spoils. With your breath you blew a wind of anger. Water covered them, abandoning them to the deep. He likened it to lead because it sank quickly and quickly burned. In the awesome waters—they were great waters, they were not able to extinguish the fire, which consumed them.

Who is like you among the gods, O YHWH? Who is like you, O Maker of all that is brought forth, whom none is like. Who is like you glorious in holiness, who does just, righteous, holy, and pure things quite apart from what unbelievers say? Awesome in praiseworthy deeds, doing wonders. To Him are great names and attributes. No other is associated with Him. Doing wonders, forty miracles in Egypt and in the Sea of Reeds, and all His works are great wonders.

You stretched out Your right hand, the earth swallowed them (Exod 15:12). There are two parts in this matter. The first, the ground of the sea was divided and swallowed chariots and his horsemen, and second, a saying that when the Egyptians died, the sea threw them upon its bank. Therefore it is said that "Israel saw the Egyptians dead upon the shore of the sea" (Exod 14:30), and their faces were turned upward. Israel knew them and confronted them with their evil. And after, the seashore split and swallowed them.

The people heard and were afraid. This is a true prophecy from the mind of God. He was strengthened in it. The great prophet, Moses, is true in what he said, "The kingdom of Israel has been created now." The peoples heard and feared because the Kingdom of Egypt had been abolished. In their understanding, it was a great kingdom. Therefore, they were frightened by what they heard.

Two works were done then, each one greater than the other: the dividing of the sea and what happened to the Egyptians in it. This shocked all the peoples, and they said in their hearts, "As the Egyptians were wasted, so shall it be with us!" It was as [if] the True One told them from on High, "Wait, because for you greater than this will fill the world." They displeased the True One by what they did. The world will make a great supplication on behalf of the evil that was done in it. Their supplication ascends to the dwelling on High, just like their prayers when they prayed from the midst of great oppression. God looked attentively in His compassion and came near and delivered. Woe to those who turn away, for what is prepared for them. Beneficence for the good people, for what is in store for them.

When the Taheb comes, he will reveal the truth and God will glorify the dead. From the four corners of the world they will come. Woe then to the inhabitants of the world. If you fear from the deed that happened there, it is appropriate that you know that it was the True One who did it. What is prepared for them will also be for you.

Praise the Powerful One who in the strength of His goodness filled the minds of the glorious ones with true wisdom. We see how the great prophet, Moses, said on behalf of the inhabitants of Palestine as He said in His Holy Writings, "Cramping has seized the inhabitants of Philistia" (Exod 15:14). In this great prophecy he revealed the deliverance of Isaac and established His promise. He was ransomed with pangs from the garden, and the land of Palestine was given to him, as he said, "Travel in this land and I will be with you and I will bless you because is it not for you and your progeny I will give all this land?" (Gen 26:3). The great prophet, Moses, set in motion here a lifting up of Isaac, his father, and teaches that pangs would afflict all the inhabitants of Palestine.

How great is your greatness, O Israel, because on your behalf I have caused great wonders. Exalted is the great prophet, Moses, whom his Lord taught in what he would be glorified. He glorified all the generations of the world who were near to God as Moses was near, who listened to God as Moses listened, or stood where Moses stood, or saw what Moses saw, or believed what Moses believed, or petitioned or attained or said and did for Him what pleased Him, or were crowned with knowledge like Moses, or whose image was clothed with light.

He was made a storehouse of wonders and his tongue flowed with blessings. His Lord did for him what He has not done for any other person. Hidden things were awakened for him into revelations. Creations exulted in him. Heavens rejoiced at his word; the earth was sparked by his words. Mind heard. He nourishes the living and magnifies the dead. Where is there one like Moses and who is like Moses, a prophet like none who has risen and will not rise forever?

Now the chiefs of Edom are astonished. All of it connects; as the trampling of Edomites, so the Moabites, the former in astonishment, the latter in fear from the announcement of these wonders. So God said, "Now the chiefs of Edom are astonished," because the Edomites expected that their kingdom would stand. When Israel went out, they knew that their kingdom would be changed.

Jacob approached Esau with great honorable intent, and Esau came out to meet him. The two of them embraced, and their hostility was set aside and afterward turned into love. When the Edomites heard this, their enmity returned as it had been in the beginning, and their hostility doubled, remembering what had passed and imagining what was to come because of the books of their fathers that were in their hands and also in the hands of Israel. When Moses reported the books of the fathers before the children who came after, they believed in the True One and knew that the True One had sent Moses. When the Edomites heard this, they were astonished, and they became hostile, and they knew they would be destroyed by their hands. They would stand before them in great dread. So Moses remembered here the leaders as the True One had instructed him in this prophecy when He said, "These are the kings" (Gen 36:1). Moses said these words and replied then by the command of the True One, "It is good for you if you know you are the writer of their books and stand by the mystery of my hidden statement. You will gain power by this among all creatures."

Praise to the King who is enduring in His presence, who watches over all who love Him and continues His guardianship in all times.

It is fitting then that we bow down before Him to the ground with hearts full of faith, honor, and remembrance of a faithful prophet who has power over all creatures and let us see how he gained his prophethood.

In prophecy he spoke in the heart of the sea, and the True One supported him. The world magnified him for what he said when he loosed dread among the Moabites. So the True One said, "The honorable ones among the Moabites are seized with dread" (Exod 15:15).

Where did Moses get this knowledge? If it had not been for his prophetic ability, he could not have said it then. So the True One wrote what Balaam said on behalf of Israel, "It will crush the corners of Moab" (Num 24:17). The great prophet, Moses, [said], "Woe, O Moab" (Num 21:29). There was knowledge of the destruction in his words, "You perish, O people." They are like yesterday's yesterday. Moses words, "Woe to you," here imply complete destruction.

They were filled with dread when they heard that the sea had killed the Egyptians and the kingdom of Pharaoh had been scattered in fear by good men who were in the hand of the Presence. O world, confirm what has been done in you and in what is yet to come in the second generation. The third generation is the generation of the repentant, in which no confusion and no apostasy will be found. Woe to the generation that is to come. All of its judgments and punishments will be strong. It is appropriate that we should not meet this generation nor see what will happen to it. From this it follows that we should feel guilty for turning from wisdom that enhances life. If we hurry and seek the True One and learn wisdom, no apostasy will be seen in us unless we run in every case for the guidance of the wicked. That would strengthen darkness in our hearts. Woe to us and what has happened to us because of judgment. We can't comprehend it. Let us set ourselves to return to the True One, and let us trust in YHWH, our Maker and our Lord, and also in Moses, our prophet and our deliverer. Except for Moses the world would not have been created and none of these wonders would have been seen.[96]

Finishing the story of the Torah, Marqe comments, "This is a great moment; there is none like it; it is divided into three sections, the first visible, the middle section in a dream, and the third is like the first."[97] It is also known as the moment of Abraham, also with three parts: "YHWH made it known to Abraham, ten sections in the first part, clarified like the light of the sun; in the middle thirteen sections dealing with the first Kingdom of Israel; and, after that, ten sections that narrate the deeds of the Kingdom." Macdonald suggests that the first part could be the period of the patriarchs whereas the second deals with the first kingdom of Israel, initiated by Moses, and the third deals with the second kingdom (the final period of divine favor to be initiated by the Taheb).[98] Hans Conzelman discerns a parallel three-stage saga in what he calls Luke's salvation history: the time of Israel, the earthly

---

[96] Macdonald, *Memar Marqah,* 1:43–46
[97] Ibid., 1:49.
[98] Ibid.

life of Jesus, and time of the church. Conzelmann thinks Luke is thereby making sense of the delay of the Parousia.[99] Marqe could have utilized the pattern to explain the delay in the coming of the Taheb.

In the concluding section of book 2, Moses is exalted in many of his body parts and his overall superiority. He is a perfect priest. One wonders if Marqe is arguing with the author of the Letter to the Hebrews, who acknowledged that Moses was great but did not compare with Jesus, the perfect priest.

Numerology is important in Marqe, particularly book 2. Four elements save Israel three, ten, fourteen, and six times. Water defeats the Egyptians six ways, earth four. (Sometimes there is a discrepancy in the repetition of the numbers.) God wages forty wars, twenty in Egypt and twenty in the sea. There are twenty praises in song and seven best things. Gerizim has thirteen names. The Great Saga of Abraham has three sections with ten, thirteen, and ten parts. In the discussion of the Ten Commandments, a little meditation on the number ten עשרה is included.[100] Moses was crowned with ten wonders. All of these numbers are significant in Judaism, Christianity, and Islam.[101]

BOOK 3

Book 3 is a midrash on a pericope in Deut 27:9–26, the direction from Moses to utter blessings and curses. The purpose is to teach the laws. Parallel to the counsel of Mark 7–8 to the followers of Jesus, Marqe outlines the responsibilities of the leaders, that is, the priests. Here we are likely no longer dealing with Marqan authorship, as the revival of Samaritanism under Baba Raba, Amram, and Marqe was lay-oriented. Book 3 may be a subsequent addendum reclaiming the authority of the priesthood while accepting the need for reform.

The first two books belong to Moses, but "if Moses was exalted in his prophethood, Aaron was honored in his priesthood,"[102] and this book belongs to Aaron. It is a sanction of the priesthood, appointed by God to fifty tasks—among them, performing services, receiving offerings, and wearing appropriate clerical attire. The high priest is set above the other priests with special garments, privileges, and responsibilities. No specifics are listed.

---

[99] Hans Conzelmann, *The Theology of Saint Luke* (Trans. Geoffrey Buswell; New York: Harper, 1960). This is a thesis found throughout the book.

[100] Macdonald, *Memar Marqah,* 1:47.

[101] See, e.g., Annemarie Schimmel, "Numbers: An Overview," *ER* 11:13–19.

[102] Macdonald, *Memar Marqah,* 1:55.

From the great treasures that fill the life of the world, let us partake so that we truly live in the world.

Great is the treasure of the True One. It is all a blessing, and great is the man who is satisfied with it.

Possessions are not comparable to it. Possess wisdom, and it is the door to knowledge of the treasure.

If Moses was exalted in his prophethood, Aaron was honored in his priesthood from the day it was said to the great prophet, Moses, "Aaron, your brother will be your prophet" (Exod 7:1). The two of them departed in peace, and at a certain place an agreement was made that they be sent to Pharaoh. Aaron was not assigned to the priesthood at that time but [only] after Israel was delivered. And they came to the Mount of God in majesty in the third month, and they were told, "You shall be to me a kingdom of priests and a holy nation" (Exod 19:6). Then Aaron was appointed to the priesthood, and he was set apart in it and his seed after him.

Moses made known that the tribe of Levi, all of it, were brought up to be priests because his ancestor established it on behalf of the one who came from it and he was appointed to YHWH in his great zeal. As he said, "All the sons of Levi gathered to his side" (Exod 32:26). And when it was said to the great prophet, Moses, "You and Aaron with you and the priests" (Exod 19:24), it was not said except on behalf of his descendants. So God spoke with a strong voice, "And also let the priests who stand before YHWH consecrate themselves lest YHWH make it dramatically known among them.

Because of this, Aaron and his sons were clothed in priesthood and set apart in it.

Let us prepare ourselves for wisdom in order that we possess honor. We are not told, "You will be empty because every place is empty. There is not a will in it." The name of an empty place is not written except the Pit of Joseph. This only has honor to it. He said in another place, "You may not destroy great trees for food" (Deut 20:20).

It is a duty upon us. Let us be a great good tree to be seen, full of good fruit. Let us dedicate ourselves to possess wisdom and fill our souls with the teachings of the True One. It is not fitting that we abandon ourselves as an empty land with nothing in it or like a great tree with no fruit. An end must be made of it. We are not created except to learn the wisdom of our ancestors about what is fitting.

When Aaron was honored with the priesthood, God reminded him and revealed how He would glorify him in it. God called to Moses from the midst of a cloud and set him in his place. He saw the likeness of a tabernacle, and He commanded him to build it. He gave Aaron fifty labors, forty inside and ten outside it; ten related to clothing, ten for works, ten for ministering, and ten for offerings. Look at each one of these and praise the King who is eternal in Oneness.

The ten ministries: See what they are because all of them are done inside the tabernacle. The basin in which one washes before approaching the Holy Work and altar for burnt offerings, the table, the lamp stand, and the gold altar for the time after morning and evening, the burning fire upon the altar which is never extinguished, the sprinkling of blood, the incense from inside the curtain, and the blood upon the place of atonement and before it.

There are other ministries for him before he may draw near.

Each of the offerings is made at the right time with intention: the first month, votive, free will, burnt, Passover, firstfruits, seventh month, Day of Fasting, Feast of Booths, and eighth day. Praise be to the One who commanded these.

The ten vestments: the breastplate, ephod, robe and sash, turban, checkered coat, head gear, two stones, holy crown, and two other garments: a linen garment and a specially woven garment for ministering.

The ten sections other than these do not need our concern. See this glory in which Aaron was manifest when he was given two positions, prophethood and priesthood. When Aaron was ennobled, he was a partner to the great prophet, Moses, time and again. The will of the True One made visible the glory of Israel, teaching them, reproaching and warning them, showing them visually, not conceptually, the greatness of the blessing and the warning of the curse.

Moses and the Levitical priests said, "Look at these words. Cling to them in your mind, how the great prophet, Moses, sought, priest to priest, right deeds leading to a good reputation so Israel would know that no acts should be done except by their hands alone. From the beginning they shall learn that all deeds are from them and they are superlative among all tribes.

He did not say here, "Moses and Aaron said" (Exod 16:6), as before, but we see Aaron in partnership with him in the things he did before Pharaoh and in other places as well. You do not remember the Levitical Priests. The great prophet, Moses, hoped that they would be here first to reveal their greatness and Israel would know their high status in which they are honored among all generations of the world.

Therefore he said here in this place, "And Moses and the Levitical Priests spoke" (Deut 27:9) words to all Israel, saying good things, all of it helpful.[103]

The models for right worship are Adam, Enoch, Enosh, Noah, Abraham, Isaac, Jacob, Joseph, Moses, Aaron, Eleazar, and Pinhas.

The blessings begin at Deut 27:12, and the tribal elders who do the blessings define the status of the various tribes. Simeon, Levi, Judah, Issachar, Joseph, and Benjamin, all children of Jacob's two wives rather than their handmaidens, do the blessings from Mount Gerizim. Joseph and his descendants are special in the eyes of Marqe, though they do not stand out above the other blessed ones in the biblical texts. The curses are uttered from Mount Ebal by Reuben, Gad, Asher, Zebulun, Dan, and Naphtali.

This division of the tribes into those worthy of uttering the blessings on Mount Gerizim and those designated to utter the curses from Mount Ebal creates some problems, which the author explicitly addresses. In order to have an even division of six and six, two of the sons born to Rachel and Leah (Reuben and Zebulan chosen for wrongs they did) must be included with the sons of handmaidens on Mount Ebal. The nonchalant inclusion, without comment, of Judah on Mount Gerizim may reflect a period of good relations between Samaritans and Jews in the author's time.

The rubric of questions and answers is particularly popular in book 3. Five explicit questions are asked and answered, mostly in rather obscure and convoluted fashion. This section becomes very catechetical or halakic.[104] The questions are these: (1) Can a defiled priest be made pure again? (2) Can a foreigner ascend Gerizim? (3) Is Asher an exception? (4) How do we know Noah sacrificed only at Gerizim? (5) When were the blessings made to Noah, Abraham, Isaac, and Jacob?[105]

This device is used more subtly in book 2, where Marqe asks, "Why should the wonders done in the Red Sea precede the wonders done in Egypt in this song?"[106] and, "Hear now a question in connection with what was said to Abraham here. What is the meaning of the True One's saying to him when He requested Isaac, 'Offer him [there] as a burnt offering upon one of the

---

[103] Ibid., 1:55–56.
[104] Ibid., 1:58–102.
[105] Ibid., 1:58–64.
[106] Ibid., 1:37.

mountains that I shall tell you'?"[107] Sometimes the technique seems akin to Paul's use of rhetorical questions to anticipate objections to what is being said. Sometimes it is employed to reinforce the information.

One section on blessings announces that the Taheb is buried in the land.[108] It implies that the one buried is Moses, and Macdonald wonders if Marqe is saying that Moses is the Taheb. Ben-Hayyim sees the puzzle and asks if it is Asher who is buried there.[109]

Marqe is more self-conscious than the author of the book of Judges about the credibility of using Gerizim or Ebal as a pulpit to be heard throughout the land. The latter without apology states that Jotham stood on Mount Gerizim and spoke to the people of Shechem (Judg 9:7). "How can one man speak and his voice be heard throughout the camp?" Marqe asks.[110] He assures us that Moses and Aaron had very powerful voices.[111] The description of their voices not only assures that they could be heard but underscores the power of the message that was being proclaimed. Later, in book 4, Moses is again described as opening his mouth with great might.[112]

There follows a long homily focused on the curses included in Deut 27:15–26. Keep far from the curse, Marqe admonishes; otherwise you will "have forsaken Sarah and her righteousness and walked after Naᶜamah[;] . . . Rebekah[,] . . . and followed Tamar[;] . . . Miriam, . . . and walked after Cozbit[;] . . . Gerizim, . . . and gone unto Sodom[;] . . . Moses, and gone astray with Korah[;] . . . Pinhas[,] and clung to Zimri." Women are set forth in a positive way in this litany.

Reuben utters a curse and Levi a blessing although these are not stated in the Bible. Reuben is the first person mentioned on Mount Ebal, but Simeon is mentioned before Levi on Mount Gerizim (in both the Samaritan and Masoretic texts). Marqe underscores Reuben's bad reputation.[113] In any case, Reuben utters the first curse, and it is against idols. Marqe cites the episodes of the making of the golden calf (Exod 32) and Baal-Peor (Num 25). Divinity, prophethood, and priesthood can make the curse effective.

---

[107] Ibid., 1:47.

[108] Ibid., 1:62.

[109] Macdonald, *Memar Marqah*, 2:97, Ze'ev Ben-Hayyim, "Towards a New Edition of Tibat Marqe," in *Études samaritaines: Pentateuque et targum, exégèse et philologie, chroniques* (eds. Jean-Pierre Rothschild and Guy Dominique Sixdenier; Louvain-Paris: E. Peeters, 1988), 161–78.

[110] Macdonald, *Memar Marqah*, 1:63.

[111] Ibid., 1:65.

[112] Ibid., 1:85.

[113] Ibid., 1:67.

O Congregation, be worshipful and give thanks to God always for the glory that is in the House of your Lord. You are living in great splendor. You have slain your enemies. You have heard a blessing. Take care for yourself not to depart to right nor to left, for a curse is before you. Take care for yourself and keep watch over yourself. Keep far from it with all your strength lest you stand in a great curse and become naked among all creatures. You would then be shamed and rejected. Everything would come to an end for you. Favor would become hidden from you, and the True One would be taken from you. Righteousness would flee from you, and wickedness would dwell in you. You would have forsaken Sarah and her righteousness and walked after Naᶜamah. You would have abandoned Rebekah and the search for her and followed Tamar. You would have forsaken Miriam, the prophetess, and walked with Cozbit. You would have forsaken Mount Gerizim, the House of God, and gone unto Sodom. You would have abandoned the great prophet, Moses, and gone astray with Korah. You would have abandoned Pinhas and clung to Zimri.

Why this time in which you have abandoned your good fathers, with whom you were [once] joined? Far be it from you to forsake your holy status and be profaned forever. Would you leave your place a desolation when it is possible that it not be so? Far be it from you, O glory, that you be rejected, and, O priest, that you be defiled.

Why this significant time of hiding your intelligence and revealing that you have turned around and act like a man who does not comprehend and does not hear? It is fitting for you now that you put yourself where you can hear the words of the curses. And be warned inside and out and know which actions are advantageous to you, and through which you possess a blessing, and through which you possess a curse.

O this blessing is before you and this curse is before you. Give it thought. Do not forsake the blessing of which you are the son and it enhances you. Turn from the curse because it is not for you and it is not fitting for you to draw near to it. Your fathers are the righteous of the world. They increased by blessings and it has come upon you also. Therefore it is not fitting for you to be a son apart from them so that it is said of you, "You are their son literally, but a son not in the likeness of the father. Who is he like in the world?" Do not abandon the True One because God has chosen you. Therefore we do not cease from praising Him in all times and periods. Let us give thanks to the Mighty One and worship His greatness and let us be humble before Him in what we hear of Him. Let us be quick to learn and not forsake Him, but stand up to what we are to do.

Reuben stands and opens his mouth and utters words of the curse because I hear a man of many words and he speaks to us in order to hear an answer to what Reuben started to say. Shall not another say to us, "There is no need to discern these words"?

Hear the answer from those who were told what he was told, or heard what he heard, or did what he did. All men do what is customary in the world so that they know what to expect. A man does not seek what is not fitting for him, like Korah when he sought a status that had not been given to him. See how he was paid back. There is no need to say more.

When Levi stood and began the blessing, that was his place, he was assigned to it. Reuben rises and speaks words of reproach to the congregation and is speaking to himself, and he says a word. God appears and speaks with a powerful voice, "Cursed be the man who makes a graven image" (Deut 27:15) or any image. He seeks to make it firm with a curse. On Mount Sinai He said, "Do not make a graven image for yourselves." They went out and made a calf. And He said, "Or any image." They sacrificed and they worshiped Baal Peor.

Here he made it stronger with a curse so that there would be no deliverance for the maker of it. God knew and He made it known to the great prophet, Moses, that He would conceal His favor from them because of their wickedness. And He abandoned them to their own spirit. If they did this, they deserved the curse. The twelve tribes stood to listen, and they knew that this action would hurt them because it was said only of the doer if he should do it.

Woe [to us] from it. The words of Jacob our father will not stand for us in the last days because all the tribes know what will follow from it and what will be the consequence of the deed. Woe to us now in this place. O for a fitting act or a report we could speak as a warning. We fear that it will not happen. Amen. It is the end. It is an acronym for three witnesses.[114] Righteousness, greatness, glory, divinity, prophecy, priesthood—perhaps they will be aroused.

We give thanks to the Powerful One who remains forever in Himself, retaining life for those who carefully consider the truth. MEM[115] reveals great glory. It is not in the power of a man to estimate its glory. It established a

---

[114] The three consonants of "Amen," *alef, mem,* and *nun,* represent God, Moses, and Aaron.

[115] The Hebrew letter equivalent to *m.*

worthy peace for us. It is revealed for us in all generations and remains forever as if it were a witness for us. So it shall be for us. Woe to us if we
cross over this great boundary because we would stand in a desolate place.
Woe to the man who stands in it. Let us turn ourselves from workers of
evil and swear at all times that we will not ever draw near to it. We fear
lest we perish in sin that increases and catches up with us. As the angels
said when they met Lot, "Consider your life lest you be destroyed" (Gen
19:17). They were forceful about that and he was delivered. They did not
abandon him until they came to the place that he asked of them. So deliverance will be with us if our spirit does not quiver.

O Congregation, be worshipful and give thanks to God always for the glory
that is in the House of your Lord. You are living in great splendor. You
have slain your enemies. You have heard a blessing. Take care for yourself
not to depart to right nor to left, for a curse is before you. Take care for
yourself and keep watch over yourself. Keep far from it with all your
strength lest you stand in a great curse and become naked among all creatures. You would then be shamed and rejected. Everything would come to
an end for you. Favor would become hidden from you, and the True
One would be taken from you. Righteousness would flee from you, and
wickedness would dwell in you. You would have forsaken Sarah and her
righteousness and walked after Naʿamah. You would have abandoned
Rebekah and the search for her and followed Tamar. You would have forsaken Miriam, the prophetess, and walked with Cozbit. You would have
forsaken Mount Gerizim, the House of God, and gone unto Sodom. You
would have abandoned the great prophet, Moses, and gone astray with
Korah. You would have abandoned Pinhas and clung to Zimri.

NUN.[116] Know what its glory is. Seek it with your whole mind. Let us not
depart from it and let us not forsake it, and from its honor let us not cease
or desist [acknowledging it]. At all times let us magnify it by whose hand we
are delivered from all wounding judgment. Woe to us if we do not know
what is good for us in it and set ourselves toward what He has commanded
us. If you seek wisdom, teach yourself, and do not leave your heart to
turn from wisdom. Seek for yourself what your Lord seeks for you, and
do not let yourself be far from your Lord. Know that He is merciful and
gracious, not accepting sinners until they repent. We finish the first word
(Deut 27:15).[117]

---

[116] The Hebrew letter equivalent to *n*.
[117] Macdonald, *Memar Marqah,* 1:66–67.

The sermonic explication moves on from Deut 27:15 to 27:16: cursed be he who dishonors father and mother. In Marqe's imagination, this provokes two imaginary conversations: one between Heaven and Earth as the nourisher and bearer of humanity, and the other an admonishment of Heart by Mind. Heart acknowledges that Mind is the first of created things in an angry exchange between Mind and Heart, with Body caught trembling in between. Subsequently Joseph, Ephraim, the Angels, and Glory all speak in praise of emulating "father" Joseph.

> We address the second word (Deut 27:16). They are stunned by what they hear, a fearsome statement for all who hear it. When God proclaimed the Ten Words, He did not warn them at each word of a curse. Let us say "Amen" to what we say. Our Lord knows what we do not know of the evil of our doings. Woe to us. Our minds do not know what our Lord asks of us. He does not ask of us anything except what is good for us, not what will harm us. Let us give thanks to Him for this. Let us worship before His greatness upon all His glory, and let us humble ourselves before His strength so that He will be pleased with us.

> Cursed is the one who belittles his father and mother. This word incorporates ten commandments: one from heaven and one from earth, one from the heart and one from the mind, two magnifying the body in its being, one from your ancestor, one from your ancestress who lived in dependence of you and also in your teaching, one from Joseph and one from Ephraim (these two are incredibly great), one from the angels and one from the glory. They complete what has been done for Israel. Observe each one of these. They speak words of wisdom that enrich the learner.

> Heaven speaks: "I give you suck with good milk, and in my storehouse are good things from which you are supplied. Do not set me shaking [my fist] at you and bring great punishment unto you. After this will there be healing upon you? Will I leave you grieving and forsaken in the world? This is the word I heard about Cain when he inquired of the Lord and asked, "Where will I go and where will I hide from your anger?" Whoever is driven from land to land is not hidden from me in any of them. Where a man goes, I shadow him; whether in [the broad] creation or in cities, you stand under me in exceedingly great judgment."

> Earth said, "I am the one who bore you and bring forth my glory for you in all times and establish for you in all times your hopes for life. Do not abandon me with nothing. For what would give you shape? I would rage in your face until it would be the end of you and you would stand in misery with no pity, in distress with no deliverer, in judgment with no redeemer, and

under a curse with no one who is merciful. Reprove yourself inside and out, and do not be drawn to evil deeds for which you will stand under a curse. Whoever is cursed is done in by it. He will never be accepted because, in the place of pardon and the place of blessing, witnesses have stood against the apostates who have turned from their understanding of the word. They will deliver by mouth a witness to what they have heard, and they will not be able to be delivered from it."

When Heaven and Earth had finished speaking with the congregation, Heart began and spoke with Mind words of great reproving, one to the other, and Body stood between them in fear and amazement at what they said.

Mind said to Heart, "Prepare yourself and bind your extremities for what you are about to hear. Set your mind. Do not be distracted so it all becomes confused and they stand in great adversity. It would not be fitting for you and you would not be able to do it, lest you see destruction return to you because it is not in your power to repel it from you. If you place yourself in this torment, I will seek your blood. As He said, 'Your blood from your life, I will ask' (Gen 9:5). You would then be in a great and powerful trouble. Do what is fitting for you. Turn yourself away from evil and keep the laws, and you will not suffer from evil deeds and become weak and not be able to heal yourself. Rather it is fitting upon you to keep your health, as He said to you, 'And keep your soul' (Deut 4:9); in doing good works, you deliver yourself and deliver others. Thus He said when He asked you to love YHWH your God for your good."

Mind said to Heart, "Listen to these words."

Heart answered, "O Mind, we receive succor from you. You are the bubbling spring from which we drink, and from you we prepare pure olive oil so your light extinguishes all darkness because you are before body and soul and spirit. About you it is said with our minds and our strength, 'You are the first of the created things. Who has qualities like you?'"

Thanks be to the Powerful One who filled you with this and made you to be filled with all glory. "Do not reprove me until you have reproved yourselves. Out of you and in you I live, and I and the five [senses] depend on you. When you appear, we leave." O we have heard the words of these two.

It is appropriate that we listen now to fully beneficial words. As Abraham said to his son, "On your behalf the True One enriched me in the things asked from Him. My prayers and many requests continued to stand, as I knew how to do. It happened that my Lord accepted me and has considered you and has revealed to me a secret. All of it is good. It is fitting to give thanks to the Great One concerning it because it is all from Him and it will all return to His hand. By His word it is done, and by His great will it is given to me.[118] Should this great bounty now be turned from truth to falsehood by evil? Should my prayers be reduced from many to few in number, and the longevity of Isaac be trashed along with what he possessed and the deliverance he had, his blessing which was heard from heaven, and the exalted decrees with him, and the oaths that were sworn to him? Will all of this be changed because of you?"

Far be it from the seed of Abraham that it should be rejected by the world and driven from any place; after holiness, shall it be profaned; after a blessing, shall it be cursed; after purity, shall it be stained? This is a deed that shall not be. It is not fitting for you and not a proper deed for you, and not for your fathers either.

Note what work is for you. Remember it and do not forget it. At the beginning your enemies were killed through miracles. They were crushed while you, with all your honor, stood. Why then this long delay? Far be it from you then to turn honor into evil. Do not forsake how God has honored you. You would be removed from yourselves, and enemies of the True One would rejoice, and you would stand in severe judgment, hoping for all good and not getting it. You would say that you are good, but it is not so. God is more righteous than you in everything you do. Let us give thanks to our Lord, who endures in Himself in all times and places, and let us fulfill ourselves with what our Lord has given us.

See Joseph and Ephraim speaking with all Israel in total reproach of them. Joseph was saying to them, "Come to my house and do as I do. Those who act differently from the good deeds I did will not dwell in my house. Those who observe the deed that Abraham did will go up to the place. He prayed and observed what he observed and did not wander from it. When he was tested there, he was comforted. He was made great with the blessing."

Whoever learns humility from Isaac will stand in a place of extended morning. Those who observe what Jacob observed will rest where he rested and will become great in what he saw. These are companions of the True One

---

[118]One manuscript reads אל ("not") rather than לי ("to me"). In this case, "not" would go in the following sentence, and it would be a declarative statement rather than a question.

who loved their Lord and He loved them. Now you possess the place. Do not do any deed that upsets God. Let us praise the Merciful One whose mercy is abundant and who is strong and good to those who are faithful.

See Ephraim answer to his father, a totally fine answer, "If you seek men who are good and set a place and went to it, let them be ones who worship, are exalted and faithful as they were in the beginning. Not those who turn away from the path of the True One, but like those who preceded them who trusted in God in truth and as their fathers acted, so did they act. They did not turn from what was asked of them and held up [to them]. I fear the evil acts that will come forth for all judgment. It will be destructive and tormenting with intense cursing and destruction to all who have been warned. After a time of complete deliverance there will be a time of total destruction."

Now let us be in awe before the words that the angels explained and also its glory. Glory said, "The great name is inside me, and I am not hiding from those who do rebellious acts. When one turns aside, I apprehend him, and so it is said about me, 'He will not lift up your sin because my name is in him'" (Exod 23:21).

The angels were also saying, "O Congregation, cleave to your Lord and serve faithfully, for deliverance is in our hands, destruction is in our hands, rest is in our hands, weariness is in our hands, killing is in our hands, and love is in our hands. All of this is in our hands. Guard yourself and learn the way of the True One. You do not need to inquire what we did from Adam to Noah and with Abraham, Lot, Isaac, the men of Sodom, Jacob, Joseph, and the great prophet, Moses, in all that he did.

"We stood with Adam. We magnified his origins. We appeared with Noah and honored him. We were with Abraham in his proclamation and with Isaac when he was made great with goodness. For Jacob, too, we met in a group. We were not commissioned except to these good, perfect ones. You do not need to inquire about the act of Lot and the people of Sodom because these are revealed before you. If you ask knowledge of what was in their hands, come to Jacob. We were ascending and descending on the ladder in his dream, and Glory was standing upon it. A great blessing was announced. In the sojourn with Laban and meeting with Esau, we counseled him, and the Glory magnified him and blessed him in the Yabbok and at Luz and announced to him the coming and going, and all of this was perfect for him and for his descendants after him, generation after generation."

If you maintain this status, you will prosper in both worlds. But if you deviate from the way of the True One, the act done to the men of Sodom will happen to you, too. So the True One wrote, "Like the overthrow of Sodom and Gomorrah" (Deut 29:23).

We shall come and reveal it, and we will not appear until very severe judgment is made—there will be no shortage of it. Great is the One who is able to make us witnesses. Let us witness in truth before the True One and stand here in every right deed, no lack in it and all of it a comfort.

Glory again spoke, "O congregation, Guard yourselves from me because no great deed is before me. I killed, tormented, destroyed, and brought to life. With you I did all these deeds when I stood at the sea and showed you wonders and had you cross over with great miracles by the great power of God. Look at these deeds and set your heart. Do not rebel from me or against me. Do not go near evil so that your Lord may make you great and be honored by me. If not, I will banish you from the world of the living. I will put you under a variety of curses, and I will subject you to great affliction. Reprove yourselves inside and out in secret and in the open, and you will be in the upper world, a holy and elect people, and what was said to your fathers will stand with you because our Lord is merciful and compassionate. He defines himself so."

Let us give thanks and praise to the Great One, and let us worship his Godliness, and let us serve Him at all times and love Him at all times because He is our Maker, Former, and Creator.

Let our mind be set on these words and hear them in great trust and humility, and let us be quick to praise God, of whom there is no likeness. Nothing stands forever except His power. Happily he puts glory upon us and delivers us from this evil because he gives ease to those who love Him and He remembers them. Let us say with fear and humility that there is no God but One.[119]

The admonition of Deut 27:17, not to move the neighbor's landmark, is expanded by Marqe and given specific application for priests, princes, judges, and the congregation.

The third warning: Cursed is one who changes his neighbor's boundary, and all the people will say, "Amen!" See these words and know their secret. Do not deviate to the right or to the left because it contains ten

---

[119] Macdonald, *Memar Marqe,* 1:67–70.

significant sections, five for the priests, one for the princes, two for the judges, and two for the congregation. Praise to the One who spoke and revealed these words.

The five that are for the priests: Let there not be any change in their service from the ministry which God decreed upon them. What is the benefit of changing it except a fall, and far be it from a priest to fall. What has been set aside for them in every land is their share of all the goods of Israel. And what has been given to them by this distribution you should extend to each one according to his work. Do not leave any out from eating of the bread of his Lord. Do not deceive your companion so that he goes to his place in shame.

What was said for the princes: See how it is and learn it so that your knowledge is increased. Let no one rise to speak falsely. It will become an enemy to destroy the soul, and his neighbor's place will be a place of desolation, and it will be rooted up unto one for whom it is not fitting.

What was said to the judges: Consider how it is and learn it with all power. You will prosper in works if you do not snub the poor and adorn the face of the wealthy. Your status would fall and you would be separated from me because of that.

What was said to the congregation: Look and increase your knowledge about it until you are exalted, and make it a shield before you. It will protect you from all evil men. It is the word that he wrote before you. You shall love your neighbor as yourself. You shall be at peace at all times. This is the end of the words for us. Set it before you like a beaming light.

Set your heart. Do not alter these words so there is any lack. You will stand in calamity. Do not let your heart be preoccupied by possessions and make it difficult. I will empty everything that is in your hand. Do not let your eye covet what belongs to your neighbor. It would be a sin for you. Do not take what belongs to a Levite. I am your judge. Do not raise a voice to a priest in your sanctuary. I am his portion and you will fall. Do not use your strength against the three weaker types, the poor, the widow, and the orphan. My ability is greater than yours. There are five things you will not seek; among them you will not search. If you seek wealth, I will give you poverty; if you take into your hands what has not been assigned to you, if you seek to increase what is in your hands, if you act unjustly and you suppress truth and you raise your hand and withhold your words and you love yourself—all of this is evil and I will repay you for it.

If you grasp outstretched hands in your hand, do anything that afflicts, if you seek to increase what is in your hand, I will impoverish you. If you act unjustly, I will be a true judge. If you hold back your words, I will reveal your destruction in the blink of an eye. If you love yourself in evildoing, I will loathe and destroy it. My great power does not show favor except to make truth stand.

I have not forsaken these words with stipulations, but I have strengthened them with a curse so that you would not deviate and stand in punishment. Whoever dies in it, I will penalize for it. If he worked covertly, none of his works are hidden from me. To me the hidden creation is like the revealed; no deed done is a secret to me.

Let all of us know this mystery; let us not turn from it. Praise to Him who says and does all that He wills. Let us give thanks to the Mighty One, and before His greatness let us be humble. Let us say there is no God except One.[120]

Social ethics become the focus of Marqe's homily beginning at Deut 27:18. Concern is expressed for misleading a blind man (and Marqe explicitly understands "blind" to be a metaphor), and in 27:19 concern is expressed for the sojourner, orphan, and widow, which Marqe says also has significant inner meanings.

We present a section which shines like a lamp before us and enfolds all darkness because its depth appears and strengthens us in great knowledge—good for those who possess it. See the mystery of this great word. Take hold of it and never deviate from it.

Cursed is the one who misleads a blind man on the way, and all the people say, "Amen!" with a loud voice. These words gather twelve commandments. Look at them and understand their meaning. These are not words for those who do not have sight but for men who see and hear.

[When] a man asks about the truth, do not let his question be ignored; [when] a man seeks to ask about knowledge, do not leave him without teaching; [when] a man strays in the path of evil, do not abandon him [or] you receive his sin. [When] a man speaks words of blasphemy, do not rejoice in him [or] you receive his sin; [when] a man strays from words of shame to hear evil, do not receive him and I will not be hesitant to destroy him. If a man stands in the presence of his guilt and does not know its

---

[120] Ibid., 1:70–71.

meaning, turn him from his path; [when] a man leaves himself empty of knowledge, do not rejoice for him in this. [When] a man hastens to stand with evil, turn him from his path and cut off his judgment. [When] a man speaks words and he does not know them and is shamed by them, turn him to the truth; [when] a man stands in a place of desolation and does not know how it is, turn him from that place to another; [when] a man teaches you something he does not know, make truth known and do not let him go astray; [when] a man does not know the meaning of what he is doing, set him upon truth and take his coins.

If there is not one of these who will take heed to hear and not turn, I will be a true judge. He will be turned from the Blessing and stand in the Curse. In this world I will penalize him according to his deeds according to what he did. [If] a man asks about truth and hears it answered, but is not changed, I will exact his fruit from him. [If] a man places himself in righteousness and truth is revealed to him and he does not see, he is not righteous and not worth noting. [If] he stands in misery in his life and in his death, I will not ever receive his cries. He is worse than Pharaoh when he asked the great prophet, Moses, "Who is YHWH?"—a good question. When the light was revealed to him, he turned and said, "Who is YHWH?" His evil heart devised an evil thing. So I worked with him in revealing all wonders, turning his heart as it had turned from the beginning.

[If] a man is bound up concerning knowledge, teach him. If he changes, his actions will be good. If his actions are false, a curse will be upon him. I am more righteous than he is. Take a look at his penalty and what I will do to him. He will see himself under an exceedingly great Curse and later mighty penalties. If a man walks in the way of evil and doesn't know it and you abandon him, you will receive the sentence of the Curse and he will turn from it because you did not turn him. And if he does turn and does not listen to what you said to him, it will return upon him, and if he does not turn and listen to your words, watch how I am able to penalize him, setting him among the creatures in great and small reprisal. I am more righteous than he is.

If a man speaks words of blasphemy and knows it, I will make judgment upon him. There is no need for you to reproach him among men. I will reproach him with many misfortunes. If he does not know what he said and he learns it from you, it is good for you and good for him. If he knows what he said, but did not listen to the words, truth will be removed from him, and the Curse will be upon him who completely tore out my great fence.

On Mount Sinai I warned of it and judged that it should never be done. Now I have bound him with a curse.

No deceiver in the world will stand. A deceiver of men is a deceiver of his Lord because he has deceived Him. Because of the magnitude of what he says, he shall not stand before me. I will blot out his memory under heaven because he altered my word. I will destroy his life.

[If] a man utters a shameful word and does not know its truth, I will punish him so that no man will walk in his place. If he walks in the way of truth, good for him. If he does not learn today, he will be killed in judgment.

A man who stands in sin, if he does not drop it, it is not taken from him because it was made known to him and he turned away from it. Trifles do not cause desolation to rise; it is the sin that you do. Judgment is revealed from generation to generation.

Whoever shows his fornication will be judged because he reveals his sin. He is not able to hide it. Everyone will know his sin and turn from him. His repentance will be accepted. If one sees a thief, he will not look the other way. If he does withdraw, he [still] knows about this.

There is no sin except what I have taught you. [It makes] the heart unclean, and turns the mind away, and turns a man from honor to shame, and gives a man a bad name. He sees a light and he is not able to walk in it. If he does this deceitfully, I will raise my hand and kill him by my power and put him in severe punishment. He will not be able to escape from it forever.

[If] a man turns from knowledge and he asks and you do not teach him as I said to you, you will stand [responsible] for this. If he does not ask and forsakes knowledge, the consequences will be upon him.

A man who hurries to the side of a doer of evil, if he does it consciously, will receive the Curse. His sin is great because he performed an act that affronted my greatness. I will do with him as he intended to do with his good brothers. He put himself in sin, and he will see himself in great torment. I will consume him, and there will be no memory of him in the world.

If a man speaks words he does not understand, and they are shameful words whose innuendo he does not know, and you ignore him without teaching what the implications of what has been spelled out before you, it truly shall be your [responsibility]. But if he is unwilling to hear instruction, he shall be cursed and you will be in the right.

Look at the statements he makes, not knowing the innuendoes, and set your heart. Let them have no standing with you, and do not trust in them or hold to them—[i.e.] words of diviners, snake diviners, enchanters, false prophets who make their sons and daughters pass through fire, idol worshipers, owners of spells, necromancers, soothsayers, seekers of the dead. Rid yourself of all of these with all your strength because there is no good in them.

If a man stands in a totally desolate place and suffers harm living in it and doesn't know it himself, look at that place and recognize it as a place of an alien god. He fully warned about it on Mount Sinai, and in the valley of Moab He revealed it in a song. These [alien gods] are the sun, moon, and stars and all the heavenly powers and all the images of things above and below, male, female, beast, reptile, and fish of the sea. All of these are places you should not dwell. You would harm yourself, cause your mind to go astray, and turn your heart because there is no place to worship except the place that God chose for His glory.

If you hear a man or his wife go to one of these places, do not abandon them. Your hand shall be with them at first, and the hand of all the people at last. Then you will not bring its curse upon you. Know that these places bring together many shameful things, each one more shameful than the other. An image or any likeness is not fitting for you to look at. You should not feast your eyes on an evil altar. You shall not stand in an evil congregation, and you will not go near them because your Lord warned you about all these.

[If] a man gives you a blasphemous report, don't listen to his words. He is a man about whom I warned you because he brings together seven evils. He likens himself to the righteous, who have passed on, to whom I revealed in dreams of the night what would honor them. He says that he is like Moses in performing a wonder or miracle. And it could be that you would then depart from the light of truth and you would forsake your fathers, the righteous ancestors. Abraham would not pray for you. I established the like of it in his dream and in his speech. Isaac will not have compassion upon you. You abandoned his place and I chose a place for you. Jacob will not love you. You altered all his stability.

[If] a man does not know the innuendoes of a deed that he does, keep away from him until you are far from the Curse, and do deeds that will bring you close to God.

[If] a man who is not poor does not distribute what I ordered, I will exact his fruit from him and destroy everything that is in his hand. Thanks be to God, who is good to those who love Him and reveals to them what will benefit them. At all times let us give thanks to the Great One, therefore, and let us praise His name according to the ability of our speech, not by what He deserves by His ability.

We offer a section that will increase light, and we will go from there to a boundary completely of faith. Its teaching is life. Its ending is death. It will be good for those who learn it and woe to those who forsake it.

Cursed is the one who pushes aside justice for the sojourner, the orphan, and the widow. He encounters ten evil deeds. See how He puts the sojourner first and returns to remember the orphan and the widow. Consider the significant inner meanings that this statement brings together. On behalf of the sojourner, seven rules. On behalf of the orphan, seven; and on behalf of the widow, six.

These reveal to you those on behalf of the sojourner. See what they are, and know that the deeds of our God are entirely good.

You shall not oppress [him] in speech or in action so that the sojourner is sorry about what he has left behind and hates where he has come.

Like the settler among you, do not do deeds that were done in former times. This one collection contains three very glorious commandments. Let him read in the teachings of the True One until he learns instruction, all of it a blessing.

Second, he will do what comes to him with perfection; if he withdraws, let him be judged in it like you.

Third, he should not move from His order or withdraw from His decree. [There is] one justice for him and for Israel. You should not descend from good to evil, rejoicing in it, nor should you abandon him. Let him join with you in all your rejoicing, and let him rest with you when God gives you rest. All this [is for] the sojourner. It is not fitting for you to abandon him because God chose him among His seven. It is not fitting for a priest or a judge to pass him over, but they must stand in truth as your Lord commanded you. You should not ever abandon him because I have commanded the unfolding of all of this.

The seven for the orphan: Set your heart; do not withdraw from one of them. See the beginning of them and focus your eyes and discern what you hear. Your heart will not speak if you do things that do it harm. Do not abandon the heartstricken, but join with him in your house and also in my House and in the place of my Sanctuary and my Festivals and all my glorious things in which I have glorified you. That which was to those who loved him shall be for him from the least unto the greatest. What I have taught you, you shall teach him that he not be brought up deficient in knowledge, because I set myself and the prophets also as teachers for you from the day when I made my voice heard on Mount Sinai and showed you my power. I commanded Moses to engrave the law and revealed its secrets to him. Where is there one like Moses whom YHWH sent, a righteous messenger, faithful to the hidden and to the revealed. On behalf of the widow he spoke true words from God. Truth about the orphan and the widow is in six rules. Thanks to the King who endures in Himself, who does not change. Let us give thanks with a sincere heart, full of awe, and magnify His power, and let us witness and say, "There is no God but One."[121]

Deuteronomy's curse on sex offenses (sex with one's father, animals, daughter, or mother-in-law [Deut 27:20–23:]) is notable because it focuses again on Reuben (for sleeping with his father's concubine [Gen 35:22]) and also for the comment "Woe to the man who is a doer of this wicked deed and commits adultery in his mind," which could be alluding to Matt 5:28. The subsequent dark days of punishment are described.[122]

We offer a totally comforting section before we go up to the city. At the beginning and the end the Great One reproved. He spoke a word that is very helpful in this world and the next, warning against the doing of evil deeds. It contains ten shameful things.

"Cursed is the one who lies with his father's wife" (Deut 27:29). This is a great shame. Woe to the man who approaches such an evil deed. See the shameful things it comprises, and each one of them deserves a mortal punishment. He makes the bed of his father unclean and leaves him an adulterer. If he has children, they are children of adultery, adultery in the father and also in the mother, and he joins the flesh of the two as one. He has revealed the nakedness of his father and lain with his mother.

A question. Listen to it. What is the deceit of a man who lies with her? Go to the outskirts and proclaim it. For your sake, a man should know the innuendoes of this. The announcement spoken to all is, "Do not draw near to uncover nakedness" (Lev 18:6). This is a shame. It is the nakedness of a

---

121 Ibid., 1:71–74.
122 Ibid., 1:76.

man himself. Let him not bring himself to an evil justice because God has spoken many words about many impurities: "You shall not uncover the nakedness of your brother's wife" (Lev 18:16). He made firm with words, "She is the nakedness of your brother."

Let us return to the word "lies with." It implies it is done with a virgin who is not betrothed and sleeps with him. If a man lies with a woman, her progeny are also promiscuous. A man who lies with a woman who is menstruating . . . (all of these are witnesses of this [incriminating] statement).

There is no need for you to be concerned further about this. All ten have been remarked on before you. Hear them and give praise to your Lord, who warned you about approaching shameful things. Do not taint or profane the bed of your fathers or reveal an act that is not fitting in the world. Is it not that such a deed kills oneself and cuts off one's fruit? His father is cursed in all time and falls from high status, and his fathers fall with him. So Jacob said, "Reuben, my first born, you have defiled my bed in this evil deed" (Gen 49:4).

Consider this statement and separate yourself from it forever because the angel said it and revealed to him that the like of this shame would not come near him and it greatly stunned him. He did not come to him at any time except to put his heart at rest and to have pity on him in everything he did.

Men make statements about this deed of Reuben: "Will not this evil deed continue? Descendants from this deed will arise forever." His father reproved him and made known his fall when he said, "My firstborn, you are the first to go from his loins, and think therefore of high status." His mind was changed, and he profaned his status, and he wrote to him of shame that will never be erased.

It is fitting upon us to keep far from this evil deed and not let the dread of it come upon ourselves lest we be destroyed by this great evil and we be greatly cursed by God and by our fathers. Let us smite ourselves before our Lord and humble ourselves before His mercy and compassion. He will not reject one who asks. Let us give thanks for His greatness because of his abundant mercy and goodness, and let us say, "There is no God but One."

Cursed is the one who sleeps with any beast. This is an exceedingly evil deed that brings together twelve unclean evils. Each one is a mortal sin, tainting a decree, breaking a covenant, destroying a species and profaning the seed, mixing waters, putting everything in the wrong place, destroying semen, causing a falling of self, deviating from good to evil, denial of the wish of his Lord and departure of the Blessing and the coming of the Curse upon him because he desired what had not been established for him.

Observe all that He wrote before you and do not depart from it. You will perish from tainting the law. It will not come to you forever. You will be slain in judgment; whoever breaks a covenant will be slain, as He said, "That person will be cut off from his people. He has broken my covenant." He who destroys his species will be rooted up, as He said, "A man who sets himself to lie with an animal will be slaughtered." Whoever profanes his progeny will be killed, as He said, "Defiling my sanctuary and profaning my Holy Name" (Lev 20:3). Whoever mixes the waters raises [condemnation] "because he destroys a soul for a pledge" (Deut 24:6), and whoever destroys his soul shall be killed. And whoever puts anything in a forbidden place will be judged accordingly.

Six more with their interpretations: Whoever sows his seed in evil will reap for himself thorns and thistles, and it will be revealed to him that it is an evil land which has no advantage to it. So I will show that deed to you so that this statement will not be wasted on you. If evil people come to you and present you with a false statement, do not be silent before them about it. Whoever lies with an animal will not live because of this evil deed. He will be killed and likewise the animal, and likewise the inhabitants of the land who favor this deed will be killed. The land will be burned and disappear from memory.

Who departs from the way of the True One and goes to another will be burned in his place because God asks that the land [be free] from such. Whoever does the act of the Sodomites will be burned like them. Whoever lies with an animal will not be pleased with his deed but will be destroyed, and his animal with him. Whoever covers the fence of the righteous and does what his fathers did not do will come up to a curse. Thanks to Him whose kingdom remains unchanging, completely His own and leading to His presence. He is to be praised and exalted forever. There is no God but One.

"Cursed is the one who lies with his sister" (Deut 27:22). He warned against this evil before, and here He curses the one who does it.

We present a very important section: Let us fill our heart with the light of knowledge that we may be crowned with all its glory. Here is a statement much like the preceding statement.

"Cursed is the one who lies with his mother-in-law" (Deut 27:23). This act comprises very great evil, it contains ten evil deeds. Who does [such a deed] drives himself away from righteousness. Woe to the man who does this evil deed and envelops himself in ten evil things, all of them shameful. He taints the body of his mother-in-law and reveals her body and transforms her bed and commits adultery himself. He brings together three fleshy things, each one of them a great adultery. He raises bad fruit and adulterous children and burdens the world with evil. He profanes two seeds and owns a curse with great condemnation.

After this there is no need for you to be concerned or speak further about it. Woe to the man who is a doer of these evil deeds and commits adultery in his mind and abandons the True One, losing the blessing and receiving the Curse in the world and torment in the next because his Lord warned him and he did not take the warning. He withdrew from the True One and deviated from the path of righteousness and walked in the way of the men of the flood, about whom it was said, "Is it not that all flesh found on the earth is corrupt?"[123]

The remaining curses—on one who strikes down a neighbor in secret, or who takes a bribe, or who disobeys the words of the Mosaic law—are enumerated.

Men come and fill your minds with what is explained before you, true words that are wholesome.

"Cursed is the one who strikes his neighbor in secret" (Deut 27:24). Whoever lies in wait for a man on the path to strike him like a cursed snake comes upon a curse. Whoever attacks his neighbor in secret and topples him from his position passes on to a curse. Whoever sees his neighbor enter into the way of evil and does not return him crosses into a curse. Whoever knows that there is an evil being in the path that his neighbor is entering and does not inform him about this takes his curse and receives his sin. His Lord shakes [in anger] and will never find him acceptable.

Let us warn ourselves about these deeds and turn from being drawn to them because we are children of good people who loved the True One, who kept the covenant and forsook evil. Let us not ever deviate from their way. Let us stand with them, and let us give thanks to our Lord, who has filled us so and let us magnify His greatness in all times and places, and let us continually affirm, "There is no God but One."

---

[123] Ibid., 1:74–75.

We present a section concerning this statement, all of which is a significant teaching and righteousness for ourselves.

"Cursed is the one who takes a bribe to strike a person" (Deut 27:25), positioning himself to kill him with his hand. This deed is worse than when Cain killed his brother in anger. He seeks his own well-being and does not know the penalty for killing. He has done evil and will not be accepted or given what he asked. He hides himself from the mercy of our Lord. He is completely forsaken and despised. He is fully punished in ten ways. He deserved nothing else.

Woe to a man who receives possession of this portion. In the beginning is the Curse and a loss in the value of the land and the produce of it. It is a sin far from acceptable, and he will be driven from the face of the earth and will never be acceptable. His fruit is uprooted and he is in exceedingly great torment, the likes of which never existed. The heavens oppress him and the earth holds back from him.

Thus He reveals that such a one cannot withdraw from righteous blood. He taught you and He wrote out before you that he will not withdraw from the blood of Abel and His action with Cain is an act that teaches that you are not to act like him ever. Whoever commits the act of Cain, I will not withdraw him from the ten punishments, one for each part of the act. Whoever kills his neighbor, I will make his children orphans. What he did to his neighbor is evil. I will do the like of it. Whoever takes the share of his neighbor which I gave to him, I will take it from him to retrieve it, and whoever hardens himself and kills his neighbor, I will kill him with many punishments. If there was hostility between them and he enforced the punishment with his own hand, he is an enemy to me. Woe to him in this matter. If he expects to be raised to a higher status, I will drop him to lower status. If he expects to receive a reward for what he did and he has not held fast to me, he will see my power. If he seeks by this to reveal the power of his hand, I will show him the weakness of his hand. If he seeks to make known his strength, I will make known my strength. If he expects that his fruit will be according to his desires, I will [keep] him from it. If his secret thoughts are evil, I will reveal his desires to all men of his generation so that no man do a deed that that will sorely offend God and men will know that there is no failure in my creation.

Let us be humble before His greatness, and let us worship and turn away from men who do these deeds and think evil thoughts in their minds. Woe to them for what they have done to themselves. Let us not be pleased for them in this, and let us never learn from them, but let us know that our

Lord is merciful and compassionate. He knows the secret of every heart and what is hidden in it. There is no power apart from Him, whether for good or for evil. If a seeker seeks Him with a pure heart, he will find Him. If he seeks with evil intent, He will not listen to him and will return a curse to him.

Observe Pharaoh when he questioned Him with evil intent. He wrote concerning him, "He made Pharaoh's heart rigid." See the nature of this rigidity and broaden your mind in what you know. He did not make his heart firm except for three deeds He did before him, terrifying wonders that put him in great fear. He made his heart hard until he stood in great dread, awesome to all who saw it. The third relates to the statement that was made to Abraham, "Is it not that the sin of the Amorites is not yet complete?"

Greatness to the Powerful One, who remains to Himself through generations and their changes. Let us give thanks for His Greatness and be humble before His strength and say, "There is no God, but One."[124]

There are no hymns in this book, and few in the next. The content of these books did not lend itself to liturgical use.

BOOK 4

Book 4 is a midrash on the other great song found in Deut 32 and attributed to Moses. Bowman thinks that the central focus is Deut 32:34–35, which he considers the source of teachings on the day of vengeance and recompense. Book 4 indeed climaxes on these verses.[125] Macdonald believes that the book reflects the higher spiritual teachings of the Samaritans in the Roman period.[126] Most scholars suspect that this book is not part of the work done by Marqe and postdates the Roman period.

Like many old-time Christian preachers and, more to the point, like many cabalists, the author uses extensive wordplay throughout the book.[127] For example, in the long play with *way-dabber* ("And he said"), the author lifts out significant letters such as *bet resh* at the end, for which he notes that *bet* is the first letter used in the Torah and in combination with *resh* is the

---

[124] Ibid., 1:75–76.

[125] This passage is included in John Bowman, *Samaritan Documents Relating to Their History, Religion, and Life* (Pittsburgh: Pickwick, 1977).

[126] Macdonald, *Memar Marqe,* 1:XL.

[127] Esp. ibid., 1:83–98, 112–13.

beginning of the word "blessing." The expression *haš-ši(y)ra(h) haz-zo(ʾ)t* ("this song") is made into an acronym by the author. *He,* the Hebrew letter that is also the number five, represents the five books of the Torah. *Shin resh* (Shemah rabbah) is the great name. *Yod,* the Hebrew letter that is also the number ten, stands for the Ten Commandments. *He* is the seal. In the second word, *he* represents God's name, *zayin* (seven) is the Sabbath, and *alef* (the first letter in Elohim) is divinity. The final *tav* is the preparation for truth *tav, ayin, tav, yod, dalet,* "preparation" (תעתיד from עתד). There is an acronym or acrostic on "faithfulness."[128] For Deut 32:3, the author plays with the word *waw, bet, he, waw,* saying that the *waw* (six) represents the six days of creation, *he* represents God, *bet* (two) stands for the two worlds, and the second *waw* is the end.

> Ten Foundations are revealed in Genesis. They stood there to amplify and also to perfect. Great is this prophet, the like of whom has not risen since Adam and will never rise again. See how it is in Genesis and count the letters. Six for the six days; each is like its neighbor and the name which revealed all created things to complete it. Therefore he said, "God completed." *Bereshith* is the starting point and God completed it. Six days, the Sabbath and Holiness. Therefore the great prophet, Moses, proclaimed at the beginning *Ki* (because or for), since these things came in the name. *Ki* made prophecy powerful. *Bereshith* is a beginning, and so *Ki* is a beginning, and God is in the beginning and the end because it is with His name that he is clothed and strengthened. Therefore he began and said, "*Ki* in the name."
>
> Observe how great is his knowledge. What he did in the name is a mystery. It established the glory with which our Lord clothed him. YHWH said it of the form of Adam because, by it, it was established and by God it was perfected. "YHWH, God formed Adam." "For in the name of YHWH I will proclaim" is renewed in Genesis, and the name with which he was clothed, and the great name whose secret he taught. He increased greatly in knowledge, all of it in faith. The foundation of Genesis, know what it is: the great name and the word *Ki* were heard from the mouth of Moses.
>
> The mouth of the divine and the mouth of the prophet were one. We have seen a word that the True One wrote, *Bara'.* What is the meaning of it? He wrote, "In the beginning . . . ," and Moses, in his beginning, said, "For in the name." *Bara'* was said there because the True One appointed and created by His will. Moses said, "By His great knowledge, I will proclaim," just like the word *Bara'.*

---

[128] Ibid., 90–91.

Genesis contains six days and all the decrees that are written in the law. Praise to the Lord of the world, who alone remains and does not ever change.

Grant greatness to our God. The great prophet, Moses, made it a gate to all praise. The order of it and what it is like are in Genesis. [The letter] *Wav* is the six days and all that was created in it. [The letter] *He* is the name in which all creatures rose. [The letter] *Bet* is two worlds, the first world and the second world. [The letter] *wav* is the end.

He made known that one is like the other, and he increased the speaking of the end. When he said, "Great," he sought to strengthen the word with holiness. When Creation and Sabbath were gathered to him, he increased its holiness with [the letters] *gimel* and *dalet* and completed it with [the letter] *lamed*. This is a city all of which is great, at the entrance of which is written, "YHWH our God, YHWH is one." Those who dwell in it are content. He causes all to have favor.

The great prophet, Moses, lived in it and had honor. He fed himself from it, and in its goodness he made himself great. No one like him has lived in it, and no one has been illuminated like him.

Men, learn from him and go after him and delight in his word and do not forget his decrees. Woe to whoever obscures it and turns from its light. His teaching is forgotten, and they have gone far from it. They do not draw near to it and destroy themselves. God is more righteous than they are. They cry out, but He does not answer.

Greatness to God, who bears sins and rolls them away in His mercy so that they repent.

The Rock (Deut 32:4). He said, "The Rock that bore you." He began with the one and finished with the other. The first word is a [virtual] schoolhouse completely [full] of praise like the Paradise that Abraham planted. "The rock that begat you" lifts up the son who flees and is defiant. Woe to the son who does this. So Isaac in his holiness restored a Paradise of righteousness. The fathers and all the wise men of the city rejoiced in it. A son who flees and is defiant ruins his Paradise. Fathers and all the men of the city turn away from him.

The image of Adam is honored above all. His Lord made it stronger than all forms. From four elements he established it. Therefore Moses used this word first. The first element is water that everything needs. The second is a handful of dust mixed with water with great know-how. Since these were made the origins of creation, so they were made the origins of the body. Therefore the great prophet, Moses, said, "Listen O heavens" (Deut 32:1), and further he said, "Listen, O earth." Two elements began to call out. These are heaps of wind and light.

[It is] good to bear to do as he did. [It is] good to enter into the service of his master. Fire is a part of all works, since at the creation it was a basis for everything. Everything is made from four elements; the genus of each one expanded in the making.

[There are] four [types] of water, four of dust, four of wind, and four of fire.

See how the elements of water are divided into four types. Go to the garden and see how one is distinguished by sweetness and its change and one is distinguished by bitterness and its change. Likewise fire is like this. In the sanctuary it was made so upon the menorah. Aaron did well with the fire on the altar that is continuous and is not put out. [There is] the fire that is for kindling, about which it is said, "Fire from the presence of YHWH." Apart from this, no other fire goes up to the sanctuary. When it is lit, it makes a great illumination. The fire that the sons of Aaron placed on the altar was quenched when the great prophet, Moses, drew near to it.

Dust is also of four types: dust of the earth, dust of the garden, dust of the heavens, and dust of the floor of the sanctuary.

Wind is also of four types: wind from the presence of YHWH, the east wind, the desert wind, and the blowing wind. Let us magnify our Lord and let us be humble before His Greatness; let us trust in Him and Moses his prophet, who said the word "rock" and joined it to the word "perfect" (Deut 32:4). The body was completed from form and mind and set apart from all creatures of creation. So *tav* is here made a primary [thing]. *Tav* magnifies all perfection. He put *yod* in the middle of the *mems*. The first [*mem*] is a sign of the elements of creation and the ten wonders and words of the covenant and mercies. The second *mem* is the portion of the days of fasting. So he wrote *yod* between the two and enhanced its proclamation with the word "his work," which he used to conclude the words of praise.

At the beginning He remembered His creation and also at the end He magnified Adam's form. He blessed the origins with two words, "His work is perfect."

Greatness belongs to our Lord. He has made known in His wisdom that which He brought into being because our Lord in His great power made all forms. He created and established and made very great creatures. Everything is made by His hand. Everything is from Him. Everything is by His command, "Come!" By His power it was apportioned, and in His goodness it was made strong and magnified by His glory.

Elevated and good is one who draws near to Him and does not stray from Him because He is near to all who seek Him and responds to all who love Him. He is a strong shield for those who have faith in Him because He is merciful and compassionate.

So He testified of Himself, "YHWH, God, is merciful and gracious."[129]

Book 4's wordplay—for example, in the form of acronyms—is a new element in *Marqe*. This device seems very cabalistic in style and may date from the same later (late medieval and early Renaissance) period.

A handful of hymns appear in book 4: "Apply the mind," "His greatness deals justly," "The Lord called Israel," "I, even I, am He," and "Where is the one like Moses?"[130]

Although even in this book we are told that Adam transgressed, it is Cain who brought about death: "he made death necessary when he slew Abel his brother."[131] Samaritan theology explicitly differs from Christian thought on this point.

A God of faithfulness. The word "Kingdom" is never changed. It was said ten times. None began with these except Moses, the prophet. In the first he called out, "Enter," and in the last for comfort. In the time of Miriam he made a request for deliverance, and she stood with him and got what he asked. He made a petition here. She reveals what arose there. God is before the world, with it and after it, a staying power, an extraordinary king, a faithful God.

He teaches us here that there is faithfulness in perfection, as he said, "The faithful God." So the True One said, "My servant Moses is faithful about hidden things, and revealed things are entrusted to him." Further, in the beginning and on the Day of Judgment, his faithfulness is perfect and his sovereignty is forever. The words "The Faithful God" [mean] the God who possesses eternal life, the God who is before the beginning, the God who is after the Day of Judgment, the God from whom everything comes and to whom it returns.

---

[129] Ibid., 1:86–88.
[130] Ibid., 1:86, 89, 105, and (the last two) 111.
[131] Ibid., 1:90, 92.

Here is a reading, all of which is significant. Here is wisdom, all of which is relevant. Here is faithfulness, all of which is perfect. Here is a position that does not change. Here is a ruler who never waivers. Here is a power that is not understandable. Here is a power without end, a God who destroys all foreign gods, a God who shepherds all good people, faithful in His greatness, who endures in Himself. Divinity, prophethood, creation, priesthood, and writings are completed in the union of these.

In the beginning of these it is revealed, and they are *alef* [132] for divinity, *mem* for prophecy, *wav* for creation, *nun* for priesthood, *he* for the five books that Moses put forth.

Here I add for you wisdom so that there will not be any weakness in your heart for lack of wisdom. *Alef* is the great name that makes known that it is one. His writing and his name are alike, like one another. *Mem* is the number of years of Favor in the days of the great prophet, Moses, when two were united, when the world was made great. *Wav*, whose greatness is in its fullness when he descended, his face clothed in light. *Nun* is the number of the divisions of the priests. There is no need to pay attention to *He* because everything in it is great and it concludes the great name.

Therefore the great prophet, Moses, spoke these words, making known by them what [the phrase] comprised, because it is a good analysis. There is none like it.

God remains forever. Preexistence is His. Antiquity is His. Kingship is His. Sovereignty is His. Divinity is His. Unity is His. Power is His. Greatness is His. Eternal life is His and all life he brought out of His own.

Who is able to praise Him for what He is or know what He is? Let Him be praised with a sincere heart because He is one with Himself. Look at the words which the great prophet, Moses, spoke after he spoke the unchanging word and he said the word "iniquity" (Deut 32:4). As it was in the beginning so it will be at the end. He does not show a partial face. There is no iniquity in Him. There is no iniquity in "Surely you must die!" There was no iniquity when He called to Adam. There was no iniquity there when He punished Cain. There was no iniquity there when He clothed Eve with distress. There was no iniquity there when He scorched the ground. There was no iniquity when He punished Lamech. There was no iniquity when He

---

[132] Again each of the Hebrew letters stands for something—e.g., *alef* is the first letter the Hebrew word for "God," and *mem* is the number 50 in Hebrew, explained in the following paragraph.

scattered the men of Babel. There was no iniquity when He burned Sodom and Gomorrah and overturned them. There was no iniquity there when he destroyed Pharaoh. There was no iniquity when He killed the Egyptians. There was no iniquity when He destroyed those who made the calf. There was no iniquity there because in each of these He did to them what they had done first.

Adam transgressed a command; he was justly punished. When he heard the voice of his wife, he was truly dumbfounded. Cain killed his brother; he was justly punished. Lamech honored evildoing; he was justly punished. When the men of Babel offended God, they were justly punished. When the men of Sodom increased their sin, they were justly punished. All of these who offended God were justly punished.

Let us praise the One who changes things but remains unchanged, who judges evil doers and punishes them and [judges] doers of good and rewards them; when Noah did well, his deeds were revealed, and it was said about him that he was a righteous and perfect man. Abraham, when he was called and came with a good heart, was justly rewarded. Likewise, all of them, when they submitted themselves to their Lord in righteousness, were justly rewarded.

Where is the like of Moses, and who can compare to Moses, whose Lord revealed to him what He had not revealed to any other? He should be thanked for his many goodnesses and exalted for his gifts. Let us fear His strength, and let us tremble at His anger, and let us be humble, and let us say, "There is no God but One."

The mind of Moses was strengthened when he said, "God of Faithfulness" (Deut 32), and completed [those] two words when he said the words "without iniquity" and returned and said, "Righteous," a perfect word, turning from any deficiency. Adam said it when Abel was killed. His Lord gave him comfort, and when he returned to the side of his wife and when he said it, his heart was strengthened and made righteous. From him Seth rose, and when he was named by it, Noah was set free and was a second Adam because this is a great statement, totally beneficial. In it Israel is blessed. Now the True One has established it. He commanded you to walk after it.

Consider the beginning and the end of it. When *He* was said to Noah, it was completed with *Yod,* but when it was uttered by the mouth of the True One, there was no *Yod* in it. When Moses said it and strengthened God with it, he placed a *Yod* in it because it is the beginning of the great name and establishes the creation. He proclaimed righteousness and by it commanded Israel, "In righteousness you will judge and righteousness, righteousness you will pursue."

When God called the great prophet, Moses, to gather men according to number, the first were you and Aaron, Nadab and Abihu, Eleazar and Ithamar, and seventy of the elders and twelve leaders of the Israelites, and Joshua and Hur—these ninety. After [the letter] *dalet* because it brought to the sanctuary great glory and the two tablets and angels. All of these gathered there to magnify Moses. The letter *qof* lifted Abraham and raised his joy at the birth of Isaac, the son of Abraham. Abraham was an innovator in what he did. He established what his maker commanded of him, and planted a paradise with all the great trees. God was pleased with what he did. When the angels came to announce it, he prepared from it a meal, and they gathered around it and were cooled by the trees.

Therefore the great prophet, Moses, renews memory of all of them for the sake of comfort. "Turn from your strong terror," in your memory of good men. The mind of Moses is exalted in what he revealed, a great mind focused on deliverance, pity, and compassion.

Honesty is a word set apart; it has no equal. Its beginning and also its end [encompass] God and Moses. It does not have such association with any other. Its beginning is a creation that reveals great power, and its end is prophethood that is made great by the True One. There is no need to be concerned about these words any further.

Therefore make your hearts sincere and open your eyes and stir your mind and establish yourself with your God. You will then find the gate of freedom open before you. Enter completely into it and learn from it what Moses, the chief of the prophets, taught you that you may attain a status that no one apart from you can attain who does not have knowledge.

What will happen with such? He will return to his house and not stand in the sanctuary. A priest who has a blemish shall not approach the sanctuary. How can one who knows wisdom not stand in the sanctuary? A blemish in a man is either in an eye or in a limb; it is not in him. There is no need for him to help the congregation; it is not in his power. God will help them when they listen. YHWH will burst forth. There is no need for the wise to attack them. The great prophet, Moses, did not cry out to the wise except to teach the congregation. Moses sat to teach with his people. He taught the wise men and the wise men taught them.

Watch and I will make a division. They are the wise men who received a portion of the truth, and it worked for them. What will be done with those who do not have a portion? They are removed and they stand in confusion.

And when the great prophet, Moses, came to forcefully strike [the rock] to cause water to come forth from it, his Lord said to him, "Surround yourself with the elders of Israel." Blessed is our Lord, who exalts His loved ones and watches them in all their paths. It is fitting upon us that we walk in the way of life, and do not leave the True One, and look upon the sayings of Moses, His man.

"And upright" (Deut 32:4). He changes and strengthens with the word [*hu*ʾ] ("He"). He revealed in this mystery that He is the Ancient One with no beginning. He is the One who stood above the silent abyss. He is the One who created when He willed and desired. He is the "I am" who [continues] after the world as He was before. So He will be the last. Let us humble ourselves and let us say in awe and great faith, "There is no God but One."

See the great prophet, how he stood and began to reprove the world and Israel listened. He did not reprove unless the word was pleasing to God. The good are enriched by it. He included the powers of heaven and earth and put them first as God had made [them]. Preparations that are for life are enriched by what it is. From the beginning it is prepared to help the heart of man. So God said, "Life and Death." It prepared Adam and it prepared Moses. Adam tasted death prepared. Moses fasted for life prepared.

"They have acted corruptly" (Deut 32:5). Adam and Eve [were corrupted] by the word of the serpent who came in his cunning and spoke blasphemy, "And you will be like angels." It is the words "they acted corruptly" that make known that it was not the word of truth. Therefore He said, "It is not for him" (Deut 32:5), in wisdom, as a great rebuke. "They acted corruptly" gathers the statement of the serpent in his cunning and in his insolence. He divided their minds until he brought forth death and distress. What is this great transformation that took place in the world? Destruction through death for Adam and his seed and distress for Eve, as was said, "In distress you will bear children." They were corrupt in their desires and their eating of all of it. "They acted corruptly" is what was said of the act of Adam that was done as the beginning of evil, before which no act had been done that offended the True One because He had warned them.

"The children of blemish" (Deut 32:5). Woe to Cain, who was born in a thoroughly offensive time. He did two evil deeds. He destroyed the firstborn and he sinned unto death. He destroyed the firstborn in not defending the firstborn, and he sinned unto death when he killed Abel, his brother. The year of Adam would have been good, but he did not make it perfect. The year of Cain would have been good, but he did not make the year of Adam perfect. He set a blessed dish for himself, humility, when he transgressed the commandment "YHWH, God, caused to grow from the ground every perfect tree." He forsook it and ate to his death. Cain, in his year, profaned the best and forsook the dish and returned ruined and despised. The best is what remained, and he wasted it.

So Israel in the first year forsook life and went to death. In the first year she heard from the Lord of the world, "I am YHWH, there shall not be another god." They forsook him and made a molten calf. In the second year the sanctuary was built. They hid the secret until they came to Baal Peor and did what they did. Therefore the great prophet, Moses, said, "They have acted corruptly" (before God and the "sons of blemish" supported it).

"A perverse generation" (Deut 32:5) are the unclean apostates who bring evil, who profane the Holy and build an evil house in the name of an alien god who has no place in the world. The enmity of the apostates of God will return upon themselves, and the significance of the great prophet Moses will be revealed. He includes here ten prophecies. He reveals them in this song. They are all [related] to the worship of an alien god which the apostates come and erect with all power in their hand in an exceedingly great rebellion. There are ten rebukes in it to rebuke Israel, ten alerts to shake the entire congregation, ten warnings to warn, ten judgments he revealed before them, ten comforts he taught them, and ten honors to honor them.[133]

In commenting on Deut 32:16, the author is moved to unusual hostility:

"They stirred him with strange [gods]" (Deut 32:16). He revealed, with illumination from the mind of the True One, that the evil apostate comes and performs abominations that make God jealous. He comes to the place of the True One, but he hides it and sets up another place and evokes jealousy with it.

O world, finish him and let him stand no more. Do not strengthen him with strength, nor let him be very fruitful. Like the people of the flood, let

---

[133] Macdonald, *Memar Marqe*, 1:90–92.

him perish; like the people of Sodom, burn him. Like the Tower Builders, spread him out like the Egyptians, uproot him, and afflict him like Pharaoh. Like Amalek, slay him, and like Korah, kill him, because your Lord desires this. [134]

The sanctuary on Mount Gerizim had a long history of being both ignored and destroyed. Joshua purportedly built a temple, an altar, and a fortress on the mount, and they were later destroyed by Saul. Eli is chastised for moving the sanctuary from Shechem to Shiloh. John Hyrcanus destroyed the sanctuary in 128 B.C.E. Hadrian preempted the Samaritans from building a temple in the early second century C.E. by building a temple to Zeus. In the fifth century, Zeno drove the Samaritans from Gerizim and built a church on the highest peak. The Samaritans destroyed that church, but Justinian built another church in 530. It is difficult, however, to identify the author with any one of these periods, and he may be venting frustration at the continual desecration of the mount.

This expression of the author's anger leads nicely into a condemnation of the evil ones and an inspirational buildup of Israel. The day of vengeance is bad news for those who do not hear, obey, read, pray, and supplicate,[135] but not for the true Israel. Moses fasted and wrote "what the Lord had told him—we are not descendants of Cain, Enoch, Cush, Nimrud, tower builders, Sodom, Egypt, Amelkites, or Korah." Reuben rebelled but was saved by Joseph's intercession. "We are descendants of Noah, Abraham, Jacob, and Joseph."[136]

> The sixth word: "Because the Day of Calamity draws near" (Deut 32:35). Leave me that I may destroy them, and I will erase their name. You who lie with your fathers—and whatever is done afterward—and turn after alien gods do evil and will die by the True One. O what an evil future for evil people! O what a harsh punishment will be administered on the Day of Judgment!
>
> O what a good future, as [also] was said, "They depend on your footsteps, receiving your words." O what great richness! O what eternal sovereignty; for all who love God, it enriches them.
>
> Let us begin to utter words that perfect the minds of the righteous. Praise be to the Merciful One, who remains in all generations forever in His greatness. O world of light, world of righteousness, a great order, fully

---

[134] Ibid., 1:93.
[135] Ibid., 1:94–95, 101–4.
[136] Ibid., 1:95.

prosperous. A world that has in it the great prophet, Moses, whose light makes all his world beautiful. Honored is he, the great prophet, who opened his mouth and said this:

The seventh word: a word that contains comfort and judgment. The word is, "Their future hastens to them" (Deut 32:35). For those who do evil, their reward is punishment, and who do good, their reward is in like manner. As he said, "Doing good to thousands who love me and observe my commandments and remember the sin of their fathers upon the third and fourth [generation] of those who hate me."

It is fitting for us that we renew our repentance so that we have rest and security from all of the punishments of the Day of Vengeance, from all penalties. The Day of Recompense is for all the good people, the Day of Rising for all men, the Day of Repentance for all evil people, a Day of Thought upon all activities, a Day of Rewards for good and for evil, a Day of Asking after the blood in the activities of all creatures, a Day of Trembling for all feet, a Day of Renewal for all limbs, a Day of Thought about all actions, a Day in which all people receive rewards, a Day of Judgment, a Day of Tears, a Day of Deliverance, a Day of Gathering, a Day of Truth, a Day of Fear, a Day of Standing, a Day of Coming out of the ground, a Day of Grief for all evil doers, a Day of Rejoicing for all who obey, a Day in which the Lord of the World is revealed and proclaims, "I, I am He and there is no other with me."

He will call out to his creatures as He wishes. Earth will be split with great terror, and all of them will spread out in the blink of an eye. They will stand at one time before Him. Earth will be renewed, and its split will be changed where it was split. The aroma of precious perfume will rise from it to the high Holiness.

And the evil, the smell of their dust will go up, as He said, "It will return to earth." It returns, and with it sulfur and fire. When these assemble, notice the difference between the two.

The good, their aroma is accepted and their garments are renewed, as He said, "Your mantle is not worn out upon you." Adam and Noah and the righteous of the world are before them, and the angels of Favor surround them, and dewdrops of mercy are sprinkled on them. Light shines on them and the great prophet, Moses, glorifies them. Aaron, the priest, rejoices on their behalf, and his son, Eleazar, exults with them, and Pinhas extols them, and Joshua and Caleb and the seventy elders magnify them, and the favor of

YHWH dwells upon them and proclaims them. "So Israel dwelt in security alone" (Deut 33:28).

These are the things that define the good, the possessors of righteousness who observe the decrees that God commanded and did not withdraw from them.

The corresponding evil, when their evil smell ascends from the barren dust, sulfur and fire are mixed with it and it is not acceptable. Their clothing is humble and their faces are dejected. They say to them, "Why are your faces evil today?" Cain, Lamech, the people of the flood, the people of Babel, the people of Sodom, the Egyptians, the Amalekites, Korah, and all his congregation bring them to an end by their hands. They are united against them. The angels of terror surround them, and dust and ashes come down upon them, and their eyes become weak. The great prophet, Moses, is more righteous than they are. And Aaron and his sons raged at them, and a great fire consumed their bodies, and God has no pity on them. They are weeping and the world closes in around them. And the True One says, "I will make my arrows drunk with blood, and my sword will consume flesh" (Deut 32:42).

These are the definitions of the sinners on the Great Day of Judgment.

The good will rejoice, and none of their clothes will wear out upon them because they loved the stranger and gave him bread and clothing. Their faces shine because they did not turn their faces from seeking. Their hands are full of light because they did not close them from righteous acts. Their hearts were full of light because they did not speak wrong things. Their souls are pure because they loved their Lord with their soul and heart and body, as He said, "You shall love YHWH, your God." Their feet have not scattered off because they walked after YHWH, as He said, "You shall walk after YHWH." All of this will be revealed on the Day of Recompense.

The evil will be in great strife, and their clothes will be humble because they took in pledge the widow's garment. Their faces are blackened because they turned from every poor and needy one. Their hands are cut off because they closed them from doing righteous acts. Their hearts are desolate because they did not serve YHWH with a joy and a good heart. The sons of Belial ruled over them. Their souls are hidden because they were not fully after YHWH. Their minds are troubled because they committed adultery after them. Their strength is weak because they did not cleave to the commandments. He struck them from foot to head because they walked in slander and they did not fear, from doing this, the Day of

Vengeance which is prepared for all these deeds. Whoever does evil in the world and does not turn back from it, there is no escape for him then. Woe to the sinner because of what he had done to himself. A devouring fire is prepared which will consume his soul. Happy are the righteous in what they own. Dew and well-being give him rest: dew from the garden and well-being from heaven. One gives him coolness, the other gives him rest. O, a great portion is the portion of righteousness. Whoever is despised will be in great glory in this world and the next.

The great prophet, Moses, is glorified because his Lord sanctified him and placed him in a status not attained by any of the seed of Adam, before or after, forever.

The eighth word is awesome to everyone who hears it. "Where are their gods"? (Deut 32:37). This [refers] to those who worship an image made with man's hands. He who makes an image and worships it, his image will be changed on the Day of Judgment. Whoever worships a created thing and makes it a ground of trust—when the True One comes, who will deliver him? Who makes much of something other than his Maker—when he stands on the Day of Vengeance, who will save him?

Let us return from the errant path and go on the righteous path, the path of rest for all who seek it. How glorious is that way. It is fitting upon us that we walk in that place because He calls us there, "Come because I am before you, do not fear." Let us listen to those words from the mouth of the True One. Let us never turn aside from them so that we may trust in the place of honor He has given us.

The ninth word. "Let it be a hiding place for you" (Deut 32:38) on the great day. The Lord of the world will come among all the peoples who worship the stars, sun, moon, fire, and all the images, the worshipers of Baal-Zephon, the makers of the calf and Baal Peor. When all these people come, they will see them fall. The True One will say to them, "These are your gods," after which you go astray in your minds. Let them stand; let them support you and be a protection for you! I am the One who was a shield for Abraham in Sodom when he said, "I raised my hand to the Strong One on high who rules heaven and earth. What is in the hands of your gods to do today?

Now receive your penalty! In terror you will be tormented. O Fire, burn them "because they have made me jealous with their non-god; they have offended me" (Deut 32:21) with their shameful acts. They have besmirched my dwelling and profaned my holiness. Their faces have revealed shameful things. They have multiplied their haughtiness before me; they have revived wild vines; they have ruined my House; they have removed themselves from the True One, hidden my will. They have gone away from me and observed what is my enemy's. How can I reward them with good things or listen to their cry or answer them in the day of their affliction in the world? I called them and they did not come. I warned them and they did not listen. I informed them; they were foolish. I honored them; they revolted. I taught them; they forgot. I lifted them up; they fell. I treated them well; they became evil. How can I have pity upon them? How can I show mercy to them? How can I be sorry for them? How can I watch over them? I have taken my mercies from them. My good treatment is being withheld. When they forget me, I abandon them. When they reject me, I leave them. I reward all doers according to what is done.

These words are not for other men in creation, only for us. Woe to us if we do not learn them. We will be rewarded according to what we have heard. We are children of the good people. The oath of the True One walks with us. Let us not hide from the True One, nor act shamefully, nor stray from the law of God. That which God taught us, let us not forget, and what He instructed us, let us not forsake so that His grace may appear in the world and security and peace return to His own. We will rest and not tremble, and have trust in our homes. Will not the great prophet, Moses, pardon because the law is a standing memorial to him enriching life? Will not Aaron bless us because the commandments are before us? There will be no excuse for us when the True One asks us and the laws are in our hands. As He said, "[It is] in your mouth and in your heart for the doing." He wrote it with His hand, and He gave it with His hand.

Let us praise our Lord in faith, and let us be humble before the Great One in great awe, and let us witness and say, "There is no God but One."[137]

Ishmael is expressly excluded from a share in Israel.[138] If we assume that this book was written in the Muslim period, the author may be expressing anger at the Muslims, the purported descendants of Ishmael.

Macdonald points to very close parallels between a section of this book and the Gospel of John:[139]

His words were from the words of his Lord. (*Memar Marqah* 1:97)

---

[137] Ibid., 1:108–10.
[138] Ibid., 1:95.
[139] Ibid., 2:160, 162.

The word that you hear is not mine, but is from the Father who sent me. (John 14:24)

Believe in him—you will be safe from all wrath. (*Memar Marqah*, 1:97)

Everyone who believes in him may not perish but may have eternal life. (John 3:16)

He who believes in him believes in his Lord. (*Memar Marqah*, 1:97)

Believe in God, believe also in me. (John 14:1)

He who understands it knows that all was made by it. (*Memar Marqah*, 1:97)

All things came into being through him, and without him not one thing came into being. (John 1:3)

This is a true prophet sent by God. (*Memar Marqah* 1:98)

This is indeed the prophet who is to come into the world. (John 6:14)

The last parallel is found in a discussion in which the author underscores the rigorous monotheism of Samaritanism. The whole cosmos, he says, witnesses that there are no other gods.

The graphic description of the resurrection as both the good people and the bad come forth from the earth is a precedent for both Muslim and Christian fundamentalists, furious at the licentiousness of the world and assured of a reward for their righteousness. The comment that we shall all rise in the wink[140] of an eye echoes the expression Paul uses for the resurrection in 1 Cor 15:52.

The description of the distinguishing characteristics of the good and the bad emerging on the day of judgment is noteworthy, focused on clothing, light, and hands. The clothes of the good will not wear out, and their faces, hands, and heart will be full of light. The evil will be in ragged clothes, and their faces will be dark, their hands cut off, and their hearts grieving. Presumably the light is the illumination of God, parallel to the brightness of Moses' face when he descended Sinai. Evil people are so far from God that their faces are dark.

The Taheb will come to rule in the "places of the perfect ones" (Macdonald's translation) or "the city of the perfect" (Bowman's translation), which Bowman compares with Rev 21:2. There are also parallels in Heb 11:10 and 16. The nature of the place is not defined in the Aramaic.

---

[140] Bowman, *Samaritan Documents,* 254, translates it "twinkling."

In general, book 4 has been preoccupied with issues less significant than the previous books, which could be an indication of a different author and a later date, but book 4 ends with a great challenge to be loyal to God.

BOOK 5

Book 5 contains the most touching narrative in *Marqe*—the death of the hero. To highlight the singular hero of the Samaritans, no other encomia are given in this book. The death, ascension, and assumption of Moses are described with many midrashic details.[141]

The Samaritan account has many parallels to nonbiblical Jewish and Christian traditions related to the end of Moses' life. The most extensive and closest work is the *Testament of Moses* (also known as the *Assumption of Moses*). It has been variously dated to between 168 B.C.E. and 135 C.E.[142] and located in Palestine. R. H. Charles concluded that it was written by a quietistic Pharisee who was looking forward to the return of the northern ten tribes.[143] Focus on the northern tribes evokes thoughts of Samaritans, and some scholars think the Samaritans are better candidates for authorship than the Pharisees.[144] James Purvis carefully compares the *Testament of Moses* with both *Tibat Marqe* and the *Asatir* (and notes contrasts with the Samaritan chronicles and the SJ) and concludes that although the *Testament* is a Jewish document, it represents a school of Jewish thought that was very close to Samaritan thought.[145]

A Jewish midrash, *Petirat Moshe,* witnessed by many recensions from the seventh to the ninth century, presents a dialogue between God and Moses' soul in which Moses' soul expresses a reluctance to leave.[146] In *Marqe's*

---

[141] The death of Moses is described in a very similar way in the later Samaritan work *Asatir.* See Gaster, *The Asatir,* beginning at p. 303.

[142] John Priest, "Testament of Moses," *OTP* 1:920.

[143] R. H.Charles, ed., *The Apocrypha and Pseudepigrapha of the Old Testament* (2 vols.; Oxford: Oxford University Press, 1913), 1:lv–lviii; 2:407, 411.

[144] Klaus Haacker, "Assumptio Mosis: Eine samaritanische Schrift?" *TZ* 25 (1969): 385–405.

[145] James Purvis, "Samaritan Traditions on the Death of Moses," in *Studies on the Testament of Moses* (ed. George W. E. Nickelsburg Jr.; Cambridge, Mass.: Society of Biblical Literature, 1973), 93–117.

[146] Cited by Mathias Delcor, "La légende de la mort de Moise dans le *Memar Marqah,*" in *New Samaritan Studies of the Société d'Études Samaritaines: Essays in Honour of G.D. Sixdenier* (ed. Alan D. Crown and Lucy Davey; Sydney: Mandelbaum, University of Sydney, 1995), 25–45, here 29. Further parallels with Jewish traditions are pursued in this article.

account, the congregation of Israel is reluctant, but Moses' soul is willing to leave and meet the Lord.

Finally, Moses disappears into a cloud and subsequently a cave, leaving the question of whether he died.[147] Jewish tradition is more ambiguous than Samaritan tradition. Josephus, apparently as part of an apologia to the Romans, implied that the disappearance of Moses was akin to that of Aeneus and Romulus.[148]

The Letter of Jude in the New Testament reflects a tradition that the archangel Michael fought with the devil for Moses' body, and an Ethiopian tradition has Moses helping the angels dig his grave.[149] Jesus' final disappearance is full of parallel mysteries.

> The great prophet Moses was standing before his Lord. He heard all the requests on his behalf from all the creatures that death not come to him. The Lord of the World answered all of them, "The day of his passing away has come; no pleas are accepted today."

> It was a bitter moment when the great prophet Moses heard these requests that were made on his behalf and how the Lord of all answered them. "Expect the end of my prophet, Moses, today. Your wishes on this are to no avail." How fitting to see the great prophet, Moses, when he heard all these proud words. He implored before his Lord and worshiped and extended his hand toward His Holy Dwelling. Tears came from his eyes like rain, great weeping began, not for himself but for the congregation. He cried out and said in a loud voice, "Woe upon you, O congregation. I am going to leave you. You will go astray after my death. Who will plead on your behalf? Who will appeal for you? Who will pardon you? Who will have compassion on you after me? I am turning from life and will be thrown into the pit that Adam dug. I will not go up to the good land. I am prohibited from it. I reach the end of my journey, and today I depart from the world and die. My spirit has no more time. I am transformed from my dwelling by the word of the serpent, by the eating of Eve, and by the deed of Adam. There is no hope for me forever. Righteousness is Yours, my Lord. The crown of life is Yours. You do not hide justice. You do not show anger to prophets or to the righteous. Righteousness is Yours, O True One. Righteousness is yours, O judge who is full of truth and faithfulness."

> After this worship the great prophet, Moses, stood at the door of the Tent of Meeting and called to Joshua, the son of Nun. He repeated all the mat-

---

[147] Macdonald, *Memar Marqah,* 1:124, 126.
[148] Delcor, "Légende de la mort," 34, *Ant.* 4.8.48.
[149] Ibid., 38.

ters and said, "O my protégé, Joshua, son of Nun, go quickly to the house of the priests and make known what is happening." And he said to Eleazar and Ithamar and Pinhas, "Come quickly that we may be filled with their peace."

These words were spoken to Joshua by the great prophet, Moses, at the Door of the Veil that he set up outside the camp at some distance from the camp. From this he called it the Tent of Meeting. Joshua, the minister of the great prophet, Moses, left and went quickly to the place of the Holy Dwelling and stood before it weeping copiously until the three, Eleazar, Ithamar, and Pinhas, came out from it. They looked at Joshua, who stood there weeping, and they said to him, "What is the matter? Why are you weeping?" He spoke to them, his tears flowing like rain, "Today, my lord, Moses, wishes to die." These words were upsetting to the holy priests, and they were greatly distressed when they heard this announcement from Joshua.

They quickly went, and all the house of the priests with them, and they came to the great prophet, Moses. When they got to his side, they kissed his face here and there and they fell at his feet. Pinhas the son of Eleazar carried a trumpet in his hand, and he stood weeping before them. The great prophet, Moses, said to him, "O son of the son of my brother, you and Ithamar stand at the door of the meeting place with the trumpet in your hand and blast an alarm until all the congregation hears, and they will come here and arrange themselves before me and I will greet them."

Ithamar and Pinhas stood and blew an alarm at the door of the place of meeting. When the congregation heard the sound of the trumpet, they were puzzled and trembled and said, "What is this blast at this hour? It is not the time of offering, nor is it the time for setting up camp." The sound of the trumpet sounded in the tent of the great prophet, Moses, and the entire congregation were afraid and terrified.

It was a bitter moment when the news arrived and it was said that Moses, the prophet, was going to die. When this news was given to the tribe of Jacob, they were grieved along with all the inhabitants. When they heard the report among the tribes that Moses wished to go up onto Mount Nebo to die there, all of them gathered and went quickly, tribe after tribe, until they came to the tent of Moses. All the tribal heads, the judges, the elders of the congregation, and the seventy elders walked until they reached the tent of the great prophet, Moses, and stood before him.

Moses, the man, stood before them as they were arranged in rows, and recounted to them what God said. They were arranged before him as they were the time when he proclaimed the Song. He made for himself a box and stood up on it so he could see all of the congregation seated before him and all of them could see him. Were not they filled with the sight of him weeping with tears like rain coming down from heaven? He taught them proclamations, great faith, penalties, judgments, and all the commandments that God had ordered him. Joshua the son of Nun listened to all this and learned what he heard with a heart full of wisdom, as was said, "Joshua the son of Nun was filled with the spirit of wisdom."[150]

The great prophet, Moses, was standing like the moon in its fullness, reproving and teaching and weeping for the whole congregation of Israel, and his weeping rose into the heavens, and he said in a loud voice, "O inhabitants of Machpelah, O righteous of the world, rouse yourselves! O let your spirit know, O good father, son of Terah, O beginning of righteousness and peace, that the fences of your Paradise that you planted are broken in pieces by sin and rebellion.

"O Isaac, the holy sacrifice, an offering who was not immolated and its blood not shed. O let your spirit know that your possessions that were restored in your righteousness are going to the sword in sin, taken away in a downpour of cursing and planted in apostasy.

"O Jacob, father of the beloved tribes. O let your spirit know that the tribes that rose from you were delivered from the hand of the Egyptians by the power of God and they heard the voice proclaiming from the place of fire the Ten Words. They saw what he did on their behalf and how the mouth of Balaam changed. He said, 'How good are your tents, Jacob, and your dwelling place, Israel, like wadis that stretch out' in great glory, 'like gardens beside a river' in great mercy, like a tabernacle set up by YHWH in holiness, 'like a cedars beside the waters,' raised above all these coming glories, and all of them will be brought down by apostasy.

"After this His Favor will be hidden, and evil will become very strong. The dwelling of God will be concealed, and Mount Gerizim will become unclean. Apostasy will rest in every place, and none will be jealous for God." . . . [151]

---

[150] *Asatir* 11:15–42 describes Moses as he prepares for death, copying the law, predicting the next 3,402 years, and uttering oracles regarding an unidentifiable prince who is to come. These go beyond the account in *Tibat Marqe*. Please see the extract from the *Asatir* at the close of chapter five.

[151] Macdonald, *Memar Marqah*, 1:118–20.

When the great prophet, Moses, finished commanding the congregation, he stood on his feet and saw six hundred thousand men, women, children, and babies in formation. The earth shook a moment when he got to his feet. He went out, wanting to climb Mount Nebo and die. Eleazar the priest held his right hand and Pinhas, his son, held his left hand, and Ithamar and Joshua and all the house of the priests went before him with great weeping.

At the moment that the great prophet, Moses, reached the base of Mount Nebo, all the tribes presented themselves, tribe by tribe. They kissed his hand and greeted him, all the congregation of Israel, one after another until the whole congregation was done.

Eleazar, Ithamar, and Pinhas approached him, and they embraced him and kissed his face. Then Joshua, the son of Nun, his minister, drew near, kissed his face, touched his feet, and said,

> Peace be with you, O faithful one of the house of God.
> Peace be with you, O storehouse of prophecy.
> Peace be with you, O one who tore the veil.
> Peace be with you, O one who sought the flame.
> Peace be with you, O one who approached the darkness.
> Peace be with you, O wearer of the corona of light.
> Peace be with you, O receiver of the two tablets.
> Peace be with you, O one with whom YHWH spoke face to face, visibly, not in riddles.
> Peace be with you, O one like whom none has ever been and none will ever be.
> O chief of the prophets, it difficult for me to release you today.

After this the great prophet, Moses, raised his voice and said, "O congregation, be at peace, be at peace. After today, I will never exchange with you again." When the congregation heard these words, they were greatly grieved by them. They raised their voice in weeping and said,

> By your life, O messenger of God, stay a moment with us.
> By your life, O seal of the prophets, stand with us a little (but God called secretly, "Make haste!").
> By your life, O great prophet, Moses, stay just a moment with us (but his Lord called secretly, "There is no time").
> By your life, O great prophet, Moses, do not go. Stay with us another hour (but the angels from heaven called, "Hurry!").

When the congregation understood the situation, all of them said, "Go in peace, O prophet; go in peace, O deliverer; go in peace, O honored one; go in peace, O faithful one; go in peace, O priest of the hidden. Peace be with you, O crown of righteousness of the world. Peace be with you, O shining light of prophecy. You, the likes of whom has not risen since Adam and will not rise again. At this time you are going from us, and we will not see you again. Woe to the congregation after you. Who will pray on our behalf after you and lift wrath from us? Peace upon you from us forever.

The great prophet, Moses, went up to Mount Nebo with great majesty, crowned with light, and all the host of exalted angels gathered to meet him. At the moment that he parted from the congregation and began his ascent, the congregation cried out an extremely great bitter cry that went up to the heavens.

He went up a little way and looked behind him, and from his eyes tears poured down like rain from heaven upon the congregation behind him.

He went up a little way and looked behind him like a mother to her suckling children, who did not have one to care for them after her.

He went up a little way and looked behind him and blessed the congregation with a blessing which he had said on Mount Sinai: "May YHWH, the God of your fathers, increase what you are a thousand times and bless you as He has said to you."

He went up a little way, and his soul rejoiced to meet his Lord. Looking toward the top of the Mount, he saw the exalted angels ready to meet him.

When the great prophet, Moses, reached the top of Mount Nebo, he saw a range of angels placed there to meet him. All the congregation of Israel below had their eyes on him. And as they could see him, so could he see them.

It was a bitter moment when the great prophet, Moses, went up into the cloud and became an inaccessible light. When the great prophet, Moses, was hidden from the eyes of the congregation of Israel, every one of them was in distress and weeping, and they were all saying to one another, "Moses, the prophet of peace, is hidden. Peace be upon him from us forever."[152]

---

[152] Ibid., 1:122–24.

BOOK 6

Thanks be to the God of Gods, Possessor of Divinity, Owner of Eternity, Enduring in Sovereignty, Lord of Unity, One, Unequaled, Great, Awesome, Faithful, Designer, Orderer of All by His Word, Unassisted, Unaccompanied, Alone, Supreme, and Peerless. Exalt Him and praise His power over His complex works.[153]

This imperial, extended address to God at the beginning of book 6 is likely influenced by parallel introductions to Muslim works.

Marqe wrestled explicitly with the relationship of science and religion,[154] and the initial discussion of book 6 is a dissertation on the creation. The primary witness to God, the author says, is light. The four independent seasons represent the distribution of light throughout the year and the four parallel characteristics of people: desire, idea, conscience, and reason. A list of good and bad people—that is, those who know and who don't know the above wisdom—follows. (Enosh makes it to both lists.)[155]

The author agrees with current wisdom that the earth derived from the mass of the sun, and he presses the question—whence the mass of the sun? He answers that it is the pre-creation light, a major feature of Samaritan theology.[156] In a very modern insight, matter and energy are equated. Two factors lead Macdonald to confirm an early date for this section of *Marqe*. First, it reflects neoplatonic thought of the early first millennium, and second, the existence of a primordial light is repudiated in the fourteenth century by Abdallah b. Solomon.

He created ten witnesses in His strength, and they make known His greatness and power: a period of light and a period of darkness (two witnesses never listed), four seasons which He commissioned by His power, established as four witnesses. So these four elements from which forms grow.

Note these and know that they are witnesses testifying that He is One in Himself. He revealed light, and it was seen by the whole world. He established it in His Greatness, and the light of the sun was drawn forth from it and also that of the moon and the stars. Then He set a time for light and a time for darkness, each in its place. There are four distinct seasons.

---

[153] Ibid., 1:131.
[154] Ibid., 1:XLII.
[155] Ibid., 1:131–33.
[156] Ibid., 1:133.

The first season is like a good mother bearing children and caring for them because they are vulnerable. They need a shelter, or else danger comes and they all perish in the blink [of an eye].

The second season is like a good father who raises his children worthily until they are grown and it is seen that all their fruit is desirable to look at and good to eat. If the hand of a warrior reaches them, no fruit would appear and be plucked.

The third season is a time of completion, when all that has been done in the [first two] is fulfilled. If there is a weakness in its power then, all of it would perish, it could not stand.

The fourth season develops the elements of all these seasons that have been mentioned.

See the place of these four and know that it is necessary that you will be like them. Learn from them and set your mind to receive illumination.

Notice the four [elements from] which develop forms, and know that an important witness is in you. When the form is completed from the four elements by the will of its Maker, He brings them forth in His greatness. He has made four portions in you so that you can exist and grow in power.

[These four are] desire, response, intuition, and reason hidden within you. He who created them knows their truth. Each one of them has strong control in your body and in your understanding.

O seeker of wisdom, look within your soul and learn what is good for you in it. Do not go far from your Maker in doing what will harm you, for you would be an enemy of the True One and all impurity would dwell in you. Cry out in all time in your heart and soul, "There is no God but One."

Righteous, Upright, Glorious, Hidden, Revealed. What king is able to stand up to Him? His crown is eternal life. Life emerges from Him for a time, and He rules all times because He created everything and formed everything. He maintains everything in His great power. He set the heavens without pillars and crowned them with various marvels. He acts on its needs from it and within it so that He makes known by that His great power because the earth produces of itself and it needs a hand from the Spirit of heaven.

Do not say in your mind that earth sits on the depths of water. By His great power He set your mind and gave it wisdom so that your words upon this matter are fitting. The world does not stand upon water but upon fire and water. If it were only on water, its essence would destroy all that is in it, from strong trees to herbage. Many things are similar to this. If trees had power to extend their existence and fire did not mix with water, its wetness would harm everything that is in it, trees, herbage, grass—everything. But they do not establish the elements nor enrich their growth.

Men say our Lord drew His work from the substance of the sun. Answer them now: You have not been lacking in saying this. You have not spoken except from knowledge. Where was the essence of the sun drawn except from a greater light and the fire from it? The light of power clothed it because it is not in the power of an essence to stand against it. Tell him that and search this out along with him on this. You do not need to be concerned further. It is good for you to understand this and know the greatness of the Creator who created this. O great and powerful creation! It is not in the power of one who knows to know the greatness of the Creator. O powerful Creator, great is the Creator. It is not in the power of one who knows to know its greatness. O high Creator, who is wise enough to know that the Creator is great and strong? We cannot know His power. O great divinity, O powerful sovereign, O eternal King, O prolonged greatness, O extended strength. Who is able to stand against you, or who can be compared to Him? Who has creations like Him, or wonders like His wonders, or stunning acts like His stunning acts? His power is in heaven above and on earth below. There is no place to turn from Him who made all places and fashioned and perfected and formed and prepared them. He supplied their needs.

What is in the heavens is in the heart, so even what is on the earth is in the eye. What is in the four elements is in reason. What is in all places is in insight. Who can establish who He is or know how He is? From His creation He is known. From His works He is understood. Let us be sincere before Him, and let us worship His greatness, and let us say, "There is no God but one."[157]

According to the author, the Hebrew letters appeared at the time of the creation, and most of book 6 is a dialogue between Moses and the Hebrew letters—or a representation of them. Only about half of the alphabet appears: *alef, bet, gimel, dalet, he* (these five collectively at the end) and *tav, nun, samek, pe, tsade,* and *qof.* Each letter makes a case against its neglect, and each is appeased with statements showing its importance. The whole exercise underscores the significance of words in Hebrew thought.

---

[157] Ibid., 1:131–32.

Tet said, "Why is there no mention of me like my companions in the beginning sections, for my name is not at the beginning of Genesis? Was I not a crown crowning all good, standing to receive Adam at the time when he was choosing every choice thing, and standing with the righteous and setting their hearts as a dwelling place for me with greatness? Did I not run to the side of Joseph and magnify him in the land of Egypt? Did I not stand with you to magnify you in every place in which God set you? When I had no place in the proclamation of words which God proclaimed on Mount Sinai, I repeated the request until it was revealed to you. God appeared and wrote me before you. Why was I not written at the beginning of the section like letters before me? From your enlightenment comes enlightenment for the whole world. So it was when everything was made by your hand. Your words are the words of God, and all that you revealed He did."

The great prophet, Moses, answered and said to him, "Your greatness, O *Tet,* is known in everything.[158] What was made for you in the world was for you, as I was the beginning of anxiety in the world which the serpent enhanced and revealed to all generations. As your strength evolved, you later returned in the proclamation. The Proclaimer illumined me, and I took you from the beginning of Genesis and made you great as God has shown, and by your hand He made the world great. It was revealed with great illumination, and He commanded me to make the generations great on your behalf. This great honor that has been done to you is a remembrance of children growing in the womb, and all who are born by your hand are in peace with everything because you develop them until they are grown."

So I taught Israel what God commanded me, and proclaimed before them The Ten in greatness so that your days might be long and you may prosper. Woe to the man whose days are prolonged in great evildoing, turning from good to exceedingly great affliction! Of Jacob it was said, "He possessed righteousness." He was supported by ten significant actions. In the announcement to his mother about him, she knew he was outstanding. When he came into the world, his standing was high, and when he possessed himself, he possessed all wisdom. His ancestor, Abraham, built a dwelling, and he (Jacob) did not leave the dwelling of Isaac, his father, empty. It was said about him on his behalf, "Jacob was a perfect man." He lived in tents, and God blessed him and his father also. He made a vow and he stood by his vow, and the heart of his brother was turned to peace and his hostility was turned to compassion.

---

[158] As the first letter in the Hebrew word for "good," *tet* is important in many contexts.

Do not be confused by any action except the deeds which his four [children] did at four [different] times. The first was at the hand of Reuben, the second by Simeon and Levi (the third also by their hands), and the fourth by Judah. The first deed, done by Reuben, was to taint the bed of his father as a bed of adultery. The second, at the hands of Simeon and Levi, was that they destroyed the city and killed its kings. Jacob feared from this action that the hand of strangers be sent against them. The third is what they did with Joseph, stressing him and harshly afflicting him. They did not hide themselves from the ire of God, and they did not have compassion for his childhood in what they did. They committed ten offenses, and their acts were taught to their children. Therefore God said on behalf of their children, "They have tested me ten times."

Look at the offenses they have committed against Joseph. They changed their thinking from good to evil, and they thought cunningly to kill him, and they cast him into a cistern. These are strange hearts. They hoped they could cover the sun that rises from Jacob. They sat to eat bread with great ruthlessness because they needed it and they had been left with it. They stood before him in great fear and sold him. It was an evil deed that they did. They ate his silver. O evil deed that they revealed to their father! Their perplexity of heart stood them in great shame. They denied it to their father. They were like Cain when he went to a strange place and killed Abel. They did not know that the heart of Joseph was righteous. No evil had ever come near him.

There was much unity among the four things that they did. They were an abomination and asked to be cut out. Because of the four things that they did, Pharaoh asked Jacob about [the number of] days of his life. Note how he reacted and answered. He did something Joseph had taught him, and he answered what God had commanded him. Far be it from Jacob to be evil in his days. Then he made known to his sons what was prepared for them in the area where they were and how the Divine Mercy would hit them.

Thus our Lord revealed to Abraham what we would say and that all our days we would walk in sin and not repent.

Tet was elated with what happened to it from the beginning to the end. When *Tet* knew the glory with which it had been honored, it lived in joy and knew why it was not written at the beginning of the section on the law and three great sections had been made for it. The first section, at the beginning of Genesis, the Lord of the world made as a crown for it. The second section extolled the righteous and increased them with all honor where they lived. The third section extolled children in the womb until they were complete and came forth into the world perfect. Set your mind upon this mystery and know what was spoken on behalf of *Tet.*

See how *Nun* comes speaking on its own behalf: "If *Tet* had all these definitions, then my Lord extols ten items in me. By my number the four [elements emerged]. Creation grew. If there are ten elements, God appears and divides them. I came to the Sabbath and stood and received it and was given a portion of its understanding. I came to Noah and joined him. His Lord ordered that he possess me and make me an element in his name.[159] He rejoiced in this and knew that it was an honor to him. I said to Moses, 'I came to you, and you were about to come to the river, and I did not allow a hand to come near you. I was revealed to you in great wonders, and I gave you strong power. I served you from one side of the sea to the other. I aroused your brother and was a holy crown upon him. His portions were in my number because they were exalted portions as there was not any impurity in them; all of them were holy. [I, *Nun*, am] in the name Aaron and "sanctuary," and both are made in my number. The God of all asked from Aaron and the sanctuary a high status. I promoted Pinhas and made a place for him, and I am never away from him because he is the beginning of deliverance. To him is the great priesthood and to his seed after him.'"

It is fitting for you to know your greatness, O *Nun,* because there is no other letter like you, needed in "prophet" and "priest,"[160] part of me (my role) and of my brother Aaron's, for as there is nothing like priesthood and prophecy, so there is nothing like you among all the letters.

The garment of Aaron was drawn out of my garments. From where did anything outside come to us? No outsider can come near to clothe himself in any garment made for Aaron. Each of his sons, who were anointed with the oil of greatness—will they not assist and stand with him?

God has revealed this glory to us in ten gifts. They were assigned to it. All of them were anointed with the oil of greatness, and an outsider who approaches it will be killed. He offers a true sacrifice, and his sons also with him. They all go to the place of the sanctuary, but the stranger does not come near. He offers a true sacrifice, and his sons with him, and they go up into the sanctuary and the stranger does not come near. Nothing that is left over will leave it, from land to animals, but the fire consumes it from

---

[159] *Nun* is the first letter in Noah's name.

[160] *Nun* is the first letter in the Hebrew word for "prophet" and the last letter in the Hebrew word for "priest."

their hands. No stranger is able to eat with them bread from the bread that was sacrificed by their hands. Likewise with the blessing which God taught them, the stranger does not associate with them.

They burn it in the sanctuary in fire. Who is able to draw near to this place? Who is able to stand before the Cherubim and have the voice of God speak with him? Who begins the words of pardon, and his sons with him? Who is able to be like them when they finish? Who is able to speak one word with them? Who is able to be pure as they are pure, or tainted as they are tainted? Who has as great status as they do? All of them wear the crown of prophethood. Where is the like of the priesthood that is revealed in the world?

Nun is the beginning and the end. What occurs to you is sufficient. You have no need for more. O men of this generation, grasp this and know, and know why I was not made at the beginning of the section: because I am the beginning of prophethood and the end of priesthood. The number of the divisions of the priesthood and the breadth of the sanctuary are in my number. So its length is double. Aaron needed to stand in the service of the Holy Place because the status of the priests is very great and the beginning of all glorious things is in your hands. Know, O *Nun,* all the glory with which God has honored you. The priesthood is placed in your hands forever and ever. Woe to the man before whom there is light and he walks in deep darkness. O light, light of the priesthood, that illuminates all of the congregation of Israel. They are ruled by it. It is not fitting that we should leave this great light which enhances us in all generations. Who is like Aaron in the world—or Eleazar or Pinhas or the base that goes out from them?

A covenant was made to enhance Israel, as God said, "Let there be for him and for his seed after him a covenant of eternal priesthood." Announce it to all Israel. All their enemies will be erased before them, as he said, "Dash the loins of the rebels!" (Deut 33:11). Let us give thanks to the merciful God, who honored the priests and exalted their status above every status. . . . [161]

See *Qof* as it hurries and reveals words overflowing in goodness. "Peace be with you, great prophet, because it is more fitting to you in that you possess honor from your Lord. God did not reveal Himself except to you, and our base is not apart from you. My glory is revealed in your presence since

---

[161] Macdonald, *Memar Marqah,* 1:138–40.

the holy day in which our Lord rested. He sanctified it in my name.[162] The True One[163] is also relevant to this, and I dwell in every heart. Great power was in the heart of Enoch. I passed through and revealed his perfection. In the mouth of Enosh I stood and revealed his goodness. I perfected the heart of Noah and expanded his glory. I greeted Abraham and completed his righteousness. I stood with Isaac and raised his status. I walked with Jacob and illumined his mind. I taught Joseph and increased his wisdom.

"This great perfection was made by me. I lived inside your heart and I did not go from you. When I went out, I was ruled by your light. I dressed Aaron with a crown from your holiness. In his request from you, your Lord acted brilliantly and attained it for you. So he made his progeny a priesthood, stable and unchanging forever.

"I dwelt in the sanctuary, enhancing the congregation. Why wasn't there any mention of me in the beginning sections so that I would be like my companions which were written and by which each section of the law began?"

Then the great prophet, Moses, answered in response to these words an answer that enriched his hearer. "For you O *Qof,* there is greater than that in that you magnified Abraham and his glory was perfected by your number, too.[164] The Sabbath day came, and you enhanced it and revealed its glory to all generations. On the day when the congregation of YHWH was delivered, you revealed deliverance that enriches its possessor. In it Israel, set apart in holiness, rejoiced."

The faithful prophet spoke words that were all beneficial. "Be at ease, O blessed letter, because in your existence is life and in your end is destruction. While you live, there is life, and when you cease, there is destruction. There is abundant peace for the congregation which is sustained for you, and loss for the congregation when it loses you. Woe to the generation in which you are obscured. It would not be a place of light, and none who repent of sin would be seen there."

It stood and answered him. "Maybe they would return to the place of the True One. Do not hidden and revealed things [belong] to YHWH? That

---

[162] The first letter of the Hebrew word for "sanctity" or "holiness" is *qof.*
[163] The first letter of the Hebrew word for "true" is *qof.*
[164] The numerical value of *qof* is 100, the age of Abraham when he fathered Isaac.

which He wishes, He does. This, O house of evil, is offensive, and all who are in this place are evil. O congregation, set your heart away from this house and do not go over to it because it is not in your power to change it. If you hate it, your glory will be above what it is, and if you love it, it will be the end for you. If you say, 'I will not cross over to its side,' you will be called by the name of YHWH, and all your enemies will fear you. The glory of your fathers will remain with you, and what they covenanted for you will not be changed forever. Be alert to what you know of healthy deeds that enrich the possessor. Men, be alert to this wisdom and learn it with a faithful heart. If you are empty, you will not be given the law, and you will have only this deed."

Let the Powerful One be exalted, who did not make you need to learn from outsiders or the wisdom of the impure but gave you writings full of life. He wrote it with His finger and handed it to a faithful prophet with His right hand. He crowned it with wonders, magnified it with miracles, and strengthened it with signs. This is a great moment. Moses was exalted by it and greatly ennobled above all men. The witness of his Lord about him is, "There has not risen anyone like him, and no such one will ever arise."

This is a prophet whose prophethood is a sign. It will not ever be taken from him or the world: the father of signs, store of wonders, companion of covenants, light of the worlds, sun of prophethood, like whom there is no prophet since Adam. The living listened to him, the dead feared him, and neither heaven nor earth ignored his words.[165]

The expulsion of the Jews from Spain and Portugal in 1492 and 1497 could have disseminated the teachings of cabala to the Levant. In the 1540s it was present in Safad in Galilee. Among other things, cabala played with the numerical value of letters, used letters as abbreviations of whole words, and interchanged letters; this esoteric section of *Marqe* may reflect that enterprise.

EXTRACT FROM *ASATIR* 11:15–42 ON THE IMPENDING DEATH OF MOSES

He began engraving the law on the third [day] and finished it on the fourth. He went up to the Tabernacle on the fifth [day]. The voice of the Living One came down from a Cloud of Glory: "O Righteous One, the work has

---

[165] Macdonald, *Memar Marqah,* 1:145.

prospered. This is the last day. The one who informed generations of what he, Moses the great prophet, revealed of what his Lord had commanded him." So it is said, "He sees the visions of YH." He spoke of what would happen in the next 3,204 years when you bear children and children's children. At the beginning of the Fanuta, the door to falling away, a man, a Levite, will rise and his name is עזרי [a permutation of Eli] the son of Fani, and a time of anger will begin by his hand. He will gather a sanctuary in his day. He will exchange the sanctuary of the Hebrews for a foreign sanctuary. He will cast dissension into the midst of the congregation. He will turn away order, and קרטם [a cryptic name probably representing Saul] the Benjamite will be established among them. In the world, by the drive of the House of Judah, a variety of decrees will cease. Hear, O YHWH, the voice of Judah. A fortress of shame[166] he will build in baseness. The congregation will ask for truth; it will be oppressed by a son born of a harlot [presumably Solomon]. He will be like the false prophet, Balaam. In his days, the worship of foreign gods will be established. In a few days, the foreign sanctuary will be destroyed by the hand of a nation with a strong face. And those of the house of שהמה [another cryptic name] and of the house of apostasy will be scattered in the earth. The congregation is guilty, and they will dwell in their place with great finality. The congregation will turn to strife and will stand, and the land will be worked by the chosen ones of אלינים [cryptic name]. Peace will be in the world, choice, strength, honor, and a good life. Later a change in writing[167] will be made. New words will be moved into the place of the old. YHWH your God will bring you up to the land your fathers inherited, and you will inherit it. Luz will be built. [There will be] a Jubilee of rejoicing and a second turning away. Sin will be seen among the innocent people. In the last days, on the Holy Hill, He will destroy the images and break the idols.

There follows in *Asatir* 12 a series of Mosaic oracles describing an unidentifiable prince who will arise:[168]

A prince will arise with a strong hand ten [years].

A prince will arise with strength from his people for five [years], and he will not be fulfilled.

---

[166] This is a reference to the temple at Jerusalem, according to Gaster, *Asatir,* 308.

[167] Likely referring to Ezra.

[168] Gaster, *Asatir,* 53–56, makes comparisons with the *Sibylline Oracles.*

A crowned prince will arise of shameful reputation. In his day they will be destroyed by the hand of foreigners.

A prince will arise with great truth. A great salvation of the congregation will occur in his day.

A crowned prince will arise. A yoke of iron will return in his day.

A prince will arise with great wealth. A house of war will be built in his days.

A prince will arise who will dwell in Luz. The inhabitants of the עמינדם [a cryptic people] will see stress.

A prince will arise with great knowledge of truth. The congregation will rejoice.

A crowned prince will arise. He will walk in darkness. His days will be stressful.

A prince will arise mighty in wealth. Rulers will secretly perish in his days. A hundred will flee to the borders of Shechem.

A prince will arise who will perish in grief. In his days the people will return to sin and abandon the covenant.

A prince will arise. Trials and weariness will precede this.

A prince will arise at the end of sinfulness. In his day desolation from a mighty land will bring a strong army.

A prince will arise who will increase the trials of the congregation.

A prince will arise by the darkness of divination. The temple at Shechem will be burned by his hand.

A prince, Gog, will arise after these.

A prince will arise who will scatter the land of the Hebrews. It will be no more.

A prince will arise by the hand of innocence. His days will be in wisdom.

A sinful prince will arise. In his days a foreign sanctuary will be put together in shame; at the end it will be burned with fire and brimstone.

A prince will arise who will betray circumcision. In his days he will suck the outpouring of the sea.

A prince will arise. [In his days?] the congregation will see נדם return in every place of dwelling in the land of גבעלה, and Israel will act strongly, and the top of the hill will be established in visions of faith.

A prince will arise from a part of the law writers. From the west, the messenger of peace will arrive at the gate of glory. The congregation will rejoice because they will worship our Lord in peace.

A prince will arise who will plunder the gentiles. He will come out of Jacob and will destroy a part of the city.

A prince will arise. In truth he will write the law. The miraculous rod is in his hand. There will be light and not darkness. May our Lord hasten this. Happy is the one who sees it and attains it.

Blessed be our God forever. Blessed be His name forever. Adam, Noah, Abraham, Moses. Upon them be peace forever.

Twenty six is twenty six [verses]. Praised is the one who understands what is hidden and revealed. May he be exalted.

Chapter 6

The Samaritan Liturgy

PHYSICAL DESCRIPTION

Unlike the many fine biblical texts, the Samaritan liturgical texts usually are not works of art. They are written on coarse paper rather than soft animal skin; watermarks in the paper, often bearing some combination of the capital letters "FF PALAZZUOLI" and three crescents, can be distracting; the page is much smaller than an average Pentateuch (ca. 22 × 16cm); and they are written in varying qualities of a cursive hand rather than the formal characters used in copies of the Pentateuch. Many copies are bound in native leather.

Liturgical texts are literally more colorful than biblical texts because several different-colored inks are used. Most of the text is written in black ink. Green ink is used sparingly, most obviously for texts that may be added or omitted in the service. Purple and, later, orange ink were used frequently for several functions: rendering alternative readings in a service, instructions, contrasting color in alternative verses, responses, and important words. The biblical passages, which form a large part of the liturgy, are usually written continuously in paragraph form in a single column without indentations. Sometimes they are written within a triangular shape with a closing "and so forth" in Arabic to abbreviate the text. Hymns are generally in double lines, forming two columns.

Headings are in colloquial Arabic and of no literary character. They vary by scribe and are often difficult to read or understand. Rubrics are a mixture of Arabic and Samaritan, often idiosyncratic and written in a corrupt and careless hand.

Nearly two hundred handwritten copies survive, although most of them were copied in the last three centuries. Without a broad chronological spread of manuscripts, the development of the liturgy must be traced through comments in the Samaritan chronicles and through deductions made from the vocabulary and style of the materials in the text.

HISTORICAL CONTEXT

It is likely that the early Samaritan liturgy consisted almost exclusively of readings from the Pentateuch.[1] In the fourth century C.E. under the reforming impetus of Baba Raba, hymns and prayers were added, perhaps as a way of modernizing the service and bringing in contemporary theological interpretations. This basic early collection of hymns, prayers, and Scripture became the backbone of the *Defter*.[2] The core literary works in the *Defter*, other than the biblical readings, are the revered hymns of Amram Dare, his son, Marqe, and grandson Ninna, whose work and stories will be presented below.

Two later periods of unusual productivity related to the liturgy were the eleventh to thirteenth centuries and the fourteenth century.[3] There was a great expansion and revision of the *Defter* and the institution of a service for the fifth Sabbath in the tenth and eleventh centuries.[4] These periods parallel the revivals and the production of other literary works, such as the chronicles and the standardization of the Torah. The authors from these periods as well as works subsequent to the fifteenth century are discussed below.

SERVICES

In the fourteenth century, the basic Samaritan prayerbook, the *Defter*, had expanded to accommodate all the services of the liturgical year. Different services and component parts had continued to develop, and the *Defter* had become unmanageable. So prayerbooks for specific holidays, such as Passover, were created, and the *Defter* became more exclusively dedicated to the weekly and Sabbath services. Still, it models the style and compositional units of all the services.

---

[1] John Bowman, *Samaritan Documents Relating to Their History, Religion, and Life* (Pittsburgh: Pickwick, 1977), 27; Reinhard Pummer, "Samaritan Rituals and Customs," in *The Samaritans* (ed. Alan D. Crown; Tübingen: J. C. B. Mohr, 1989), 650–90, 672.

[2] It is generally thought to be from διφθέρα, the Greek word for "leather," although others see it as an early Semitic word with wider connotations, indicating "texts." See Pummer, "Samaritan Rituals," 672.

[3] Arthur E. Cowley, *The Samaritan Liturgy* (2 vols.; Oxford: Oxford University Press, 1909), 2:xxxiv.

[4] Solomon Brown, "A Critical Edition and Translation of the Ancient Samaritan Defter (i.e., Liturgy) and a Comparison of It with Early Jewish Liturgy" (PhD diss., University of Leeds, 1955), XII.

Most scholars believe that proto-Samaritans from the Maccabean period onward began a liturgical development independent of Jews without abandoning their common biblical heritage. This is partially substantiated by the Qumran liturgical texts, which do not have comparable material, and also by the absence of focus on the temple, which is found in both early and late Jewish hymns.

Chief among the services is Passover, the celebration of the escape of the Hebrews from bondage in Egypt. It is for Samaritans, as for Jews, the major annual festival. Unlike the Jewish celebration, sheep are still slaughtered on Mount Gerizim at the point in the service when Exod 12:6 is read, "Then the whole assembled congregation of Israel shall slaughter [the lamb] at twilight." The dramatic pageantry attracts much attention to the modern Samaritan community.

Passover has not always been celebrated on Mount Gerizim—for example, when political situations made the mount inaccessible to Samaritans. And it has not always been celebrated in the same location on Mount Gerizim. The present site of the celebration was purchased in the late eighteenth century.[5] But it is likely that Passover has been continuously celebrated over the centuries.

Massot, the Festival of Unleavened Bread, overlaps Passover. It is one of three pilgrimage festivals of the Samaritans. The liturgical texts and the beginning site of the pilgrimage have changed over the years, as can be noted in the difference between the fourteenth-century texts and *Memar Marqe*.[6] There are also differences in the number of stations between the starting synagogue (whether in Nablus or on Gerizim) implied by *Marqe* and current practice.

The second of the pilgrimage festivals is Shavuot, celebrated on the Sunday of the eighth week after Passover. The "Day of Scripture," or "Day of Standing on Sinai," is celebrated on the Wednesday before Shavuot.

Sukkoth, celebrated on the fifteenth day of the seventh month, is the last pilgrimage festival. The sukkoth, or booths, are set up inside houses, a custom initiated under Muslim repression. The booth has only a roof holding many types of produce in patterned arrangement. There are no sides to the booth.

Here is the prayer of the patriarchs (sometimes labeled a *qetaf*) that is said at the beginning of Passover and the pilgrimage festivals:

God be praised. There is no God but One, no God but One. God be praised. There is no

---

[5] Reinhard Pummer, *The Samaritans* (Leiden: Brill, 1987), 21.
[6] Ibid., 24.

God but One, no God but One, no God but One. So in the Name of YHWH I cry

And give greatness to our God. His work is perfectly formed. So all His ways are just. A God of faithfulness

And no wickedness. He is righteous and upright. Blessed is our God forever and blessed is His Name forever. I am Who I am.

Remember your servants, Abraham, Isaac and Jacob. Lord, by their labors and the labor of Moses Your servant.

Do not turn unto our stubbornness, our evil and our sin. We are evil and sinful

Before Your greatness. And You are the God of mercy and compassion. For our good we ask Your loving-kindness and your goodness and Your mercy.

Your mercies inspire us to watch over the ones who keep Your statutes and Your commandments and judgements every day.

God be praised, There is no God except One. YHWH our God, YHWH is One.

God delivered them and brought them up from this land unto the land which He promised to Abraham, Isaac and Jacob. And God remembered his covenant with Abraham, Isaac and Jacob and he said, "I am the God of your fathers, the God of Abraham and the God of Isaac and the God of Jacob, their God and their Lord. Have mercy upon them in their passing and hear the sound of our cries in remembering their covenant. God be praised. There is no God but One.

YHWH, God of your fathers, God of Abraham and God of Isaac and God of Jacob. YHWH God of your fathers. He looked unto the God of Abraham and Isaac and Jacob because he trusted because he looked unto You Who are the God of our fathers, the God of Abraham and the God of Isaac and the God of Jacob. Their God.

Blessed is the One Who says, "I am YHWH and I appeared unto Abraham, Isaac and Jacob as God Almighty. I brought you unto the land that I lifted my hand to give to Abraham, Isaac and Jacob." Lord YHWH, turn from the heat of Your anger and have compassion upon the shepherds of Your people. Remember Abraham, Isaac and Jacob, O God.

Go up from here, you and the people who went up from the land of Egypt unto the land that I promised to Abraham, Isaac and Jacob and I will remember the covenant of Jacob and also the covenant with Isaac and also the covenant with Abraham, I will remember. Go and inhabit the land that I promised to your fathers, to Abraham, Isaac and Jacob, O God.

The children of twenty years and upward[7] who came up from Egypt will not see the land that I promised to Abraham, Isaac and Jacob. Go and inhabit the land that I promised to your fathers, to Abraham, Isaac and Jacob. And it will be that YHWH your God will bring you to the land that was promised to your fathers, to Abraham, Isaac and Jacob, O God.

Remember YHWH your God when He gave you power to do mighty things because He established his covenant that He promised to your fathers, to Abraham, Isaac and Jacob and because He established the word which was promised to your fathers, to Abraham, Isaac and Jacob. YHWH be praised. And the Lord YHWH will speak unto the humble among you and your inheritance which you redeem in Your greatness which You brought out of Egypt by your strong hand, remembering Your servants, Abraham, Isaac and Jacob, O God.

Because He established you today as a people for Him and YHWH became for you a God just as He said and just as he promised to your fathers, to Abraham, Isaac and Jacob. Because He is your life and lengthens your days to dwell upon the land that YHWH promised to your fathers, to Abraham, Isaac and Jacob. And YHWH said unto him, "This is the land that I promised to your fathers, to Abraham, Isaac and Jacob. I remember them for good forever, the righteous of the world, the first of the innocent, Abraham, Isaac and Jacob, who dwelt in a barren place multiplying all the prayers in our name." Receive their memory, O God and their Lord.

Our God, YHWH, God of Mercy and Comfort, patient in anger and great loving-kindness and faith be praised.[8]

To a dispossessed and oppressed people, the constant reiteration of the promise and the patriarchs who were the anchor for it was a sustaining ritual.

---

[7] Often a criterion for inclusion in a census in Israel. The particular reference here is to Num 32:11: "Surely none of the people who came up out of Egypt, from twenty years old and upward, shall see the land that I swore to give to Abraham, to Isaac, and to Jacob." (NRSV)

[8] Abraham Sedakah, *The Celebration of Passover by the Samaritans* (Tel Aviv: n.p., 1962), 1–3, provides the Samaritan text. The translations are Anderson's.

The feast of the seventh month is sometimes compared to the Jewish Rosh Hashanah, but it is not considered a New Year's Day by the Samaritans. It is a time of penitence and preparation for the Day of Atonement. The Day of Atonement is a time of fasting and prayer in the synagogue. There are also services connected with the rites of circumcision, marriage, and death.

With the expansion of other services into liturgical works of their own, the *Defter* became focused on the regular services, but elements of the *Defter* are characteristic of elements of all the services. The regular services usually include sections from the first story of creation in Genesis, a hymn by Amram often followed by a hymn of Marqe and a pentateuchal *qetaf,* among other prayers and readings.[9] This basic pattern is modified and focused by the particular service and the idiosyncrasies of the times or the scribe. Most copies of the *Defter* have this extended title:

> A collection from a collection of the words of praise and wisdom, establishing the Sabbaths and Festivals from the words of the priests and elders; the grace of YHWH be upon them. Amen[10]

Any Samaritan liturgical work might be likened to the hymnals and/or prayerbooks of many Christian denominations in that they contain a collection of hymns, prayers, and biblical readings from which any given service could be constructed. A substantial sampling appears below.

There are four services on the Sabbath, and these vary according to the place of the particular Sabbath in the month.[11] The first service begins the hour before sunset on the Sabbath eve and ends at sunset. The second begins between 3 and 4 in the morning. A prayer such as the following would be used on a weekday morning:

> When you rise in a part of the morning and you see the light come up and illumine all the world, all of you cry out and say, "Praise the Light which kindled for the world an illumination that does not dim. It passes through space and illuminates all the world by the mouth of the Lord of all. He kindled for the world an illumination that does not become dim. In the beginning He made a storehouse for light. Heaven and earth are their children who are not children of the Great Light like the foundation. Light at the break of each morning speaks to the world. Light cries to the children of

---

[9] See samples from the story of creation and the hymns below.

[10] Cowley, *Samaritan Liturgy,* 2:3.

[11] Pummer, "Samaritan Rituals," 676–77.

men, "Rise from your sleep, see the light and praise its Maker." Let God be praised. There is no God, but One.[12]

The Sabbath morning hymn consisted of two hymns, a brief exclamation of praise, a *qetaf* for Genesis, and a Gloria. This pattern would be repeated for each of the subsequent books of the Pentateuch.[13] The third service is a two-hour service beginning at noon. The fourth service, evening prayers, begins a half hour before sunset and lasts until sunset.

Each Sabbath (and festival) service begins with the following prayer, an affirmation of intention, said silently:

In the name of YHWH, the Great! In Him we begin and we end.

I stand before You at the door of Your mercies, YHWH, my God and God of my fathers, to speak Your praise and your glory in my poor strength and weakness. I know today, and I have put it upon my heart, that you, YHWH, are God in heaven above and on earth below. There is no other. Here before you, between Your hands, I stand and I face the chosen place, Mount Gerizim, House of God, Luza, Mount of Inheritance and the place You have made for You to dwell, YHWH, sanctuary of YHWH, established by Your hands.

YHWH shall reign forever and ever because YHWH is greater than all the gods. He is righteous and upright.

May this prayer go up to the place of life in the invisible [world] before the knower of invisible things. Where is there a God who helps his worshippers, except You. Blessed is Your Holy Name forever. There is no God, but One.[14]

This is usually followed by a shorter affirmation of intention:

My Lord, let us never worship except to You; let us not have faith except in You and Moses Your true prophet and at Your place of worship, Mount Gerizim, House of God, the Faithful Mount, Possession and Dwelling Place. Today we stand and greet "I am Who I am," YHWH, our God, YHWH is One. How great is His goodness and mercy. I stand between Your hands. I seek your love and mercy, speaking before You, O Lord of my heart and soul.[15]

---

[12] Cowley, *Samaritan Liturgy*, 1:41; CW 10312, p. 136. The CW items here and following are prayer books that were accessible in the Chamberlain-Warren collection.

[13] Bowman, *Samaritan Documents*, 29

[14] Cowley, *Samaritan Liturgy*, 1:3; CW 26343, p. 264.

[15] Cowley, *Samaritan Liturgy*, 1:3.

If it is the Sabbath, there follow another prayer and congregational response.

SCRIPTURE

At this approximate point in almost every service, there is an instruction to read the קשי הבריה, "sections from Creation," the paragraphs from the Genesis creation story of Gen 1:1–2:3. The biblical text is very uniform both among Samaritan pentateuchal manuscripts and between the SP and the Masoretic Text. Although, like other biblical texts, it is a substantial part of the service, it need not be reproduced here, since it is a familiar reading and is readily available in English translation.

Another common way of interjecting Scripture into the services is the use of triangular-shaped "boxes," each with the beginning of a biblical verse followed by "etc." For example, both CW 2486, pages 98–99, and CW 2480, pages 72–73 (repeated on pages 143–144) have thirty triangles in two columns. Alternate triangles are made in purple or black ink. The top of each column is as follows: [16]

Triangle written in black ink	Triangle written in purple ink
ואזכרה את	יעש יאותות
בר לכן אשר	לעינת העם
לבני יש	ויאמנו
אנץ	הקם
י	

When a new surge of hymns was introduced in the fourth century C.E., room had to be made for them in the services. One option was to use fewer scriptural texts. The Samaritans chose a unique response: they abbreviated the biblical texts in what became known as *qetafim*.

---

[16] The triangles essentially function as an extension of the *qetafim*. The triangle on the right begins with Exod 4:30, ". . . and [he] performed the signs in the sight of the people. The people believed; . . ." (NRSV) followed by the beginning word of another verse with a similar theme. The triangle on the left is focused on "remembering," the covenant (Gen 9:15), and the sons of Israel (Exod 28:12). The last word of the right triangle does not appear in Codex XII (John Rylands Library at the University of Manchester). Edward Robertson, *Catalogue of the Samaritan Manuscripts in the John Rylands Library* (2 vols.; Manchester: Manchester University Press, 1938–1962), 1:165.

The *qetaf* may have been modeled after the cento, a style of abridgement. In Greek and Roman times, a literary composition was sometimes created by joining fragments of a literary work. The literary work was thus shortened by excluding the intervening parts of the composition. For example, the Byzantine Greeks condensed Homer by adding a half line of one strophe to a half line of another strophe.[17] Romans later made similar condensations of Virgil. Samaritans did this with pentateuchal inscriptions in the Byzantine period. For example, the marble inscription CW 2472 contains Exod 15:3 immediately followed by Exod 15:11 with no intervening verses. Chapter 38 of the eighth-/ninth-century *Pirqe Rabbi Eliezer* makes reference to Samaritan law written in shorthand *(notarikon)*.[18]

Three major organizing ideas, whether intentional or not, can be observed in the *qetafim*. The first kind of *qetaf* is an abbreviated version of the law. There developed a *qetaf* version of each book of the Pentateuch (a *qetaf* for Genesis is cited below). The second assembled biblical passages with a common theme or based on the theme of a festival. To some extent, the *qetaf* for Genesis below illustrates this as well, focused on the theme of covenant. The third is a doctrinal *qetaf* that underscores basic precepts of Samaritanism—for example, focusing on Mount Gerizim. Since it is likely that most Samaritans would have known the Pentateuch very well, the *qetafim* could act as a mnemonic device to bring to mind a scripture already in the memory of the worshiper.[19]

Qetafim for each of the five books of the Torah are read in different services. The *qetaf* for Genesis is usually read on the Sabbath. Unlike the קשׁי הבריה, the creation paragraphs, which are from Gen 1, the *qetaf* for Genesis begins at Gen 2:8. The first section of the Genesis *qetaf* as it is found in service for the Sabbath of Unleavened bread in CW 2480 follows:[20]

> And YHWH, God, planted a garden in Eden in the East and He placed there the man whom He had formed. And YHWH, God, caused to grow from the soil every tree that was pleasant to see and good to eat. The tree of life was in the midst of the garden.[21] . . . From there it divided and

---

[17] Bowman, *Samaritan Documents,* 28.
[18] Ibid.
[19] Ibid., 30.
[20] It is not always the same. For a longer alternative, see ibid., 31–35; or Brown, "Critical Edition," 66–73. Most of the Genesis *qetaf* is from the J tradition (as is most of Genesis). The *qetaf,* however, seems to favor theology, such as covenants, over stories, such as Cain and Abel and the marriage of the sons of God to the daughters of men. In this sense, the *qetaf* leans more toward the P tradition.
[21] It skips to Gen 2:10b, omitting the tree of knowledge of good and evil.

became four sources. The name of the first is Pishon.[22] . . . The name of the
second river is Gihon[23] . . . and the name of the third river is Hiddekal
(Tigris)[24] . . . and the fourth river is the Euphrates.

YHWH Our God Be Praised. Blessed Be YHWH Our God.

And YHWH God took the man and led him into the garden of Eden to
work it and watch over it. And YHWH God commanded him.[25] . . . And
they heard the voice of YHWH God.[26] . . . A son was also born to Seth and
he called his name Enosh.[27] Then people began to call on the name of
YHWH. This is the Book of the generations of Adam. In the day God created Adam He made him in the image of God, male and female He created
them. He blessed them and called them man on the day that He created
them.[28] . . . Enoch walked with God.[29] . . . And Noah found favor in the eyes
of YHWH God. These are the generations of Noah. Noah was a righteous
man. He was perfect in his generation. Noah walked with God.[30] . . . I will
establish My Covenant with you.[31] . . . And Noah did according to all that
God commanded him; so he did.[32] . . . And Noah did all that YHWH commanded him.[33] . . . And only Noah remained and those with him on the
ark.[34] And God remembered Noah.[35] . . . It was the six hundred and first
year, in the first.[36] . . . And Noah and his sons went out by families from the
ark. And Noah built an altar to YHWH and he took from all the clean animals and all the unclean animals and made an offering on the altar. And

---

[22] It skips to Gen 2:13, omitting the description of the path of the Pishon.

[23] It skips to Gen 2:14, omitting the description of the path of the Gihon.

[24] It skips to Gen 2:14b, omitting the description of the path of the Tigris.

[25] It skips to Gen 3:8, omitting the creation of woman and the introduction of
the serpent.

[26] It skips to Gen 4:26, omitting the expulsion from Eden, the story of Cain
and Abel, and some subsequent genealogy.

[27] A scribal error in CW 2480 reads, "Noah."

[28] It skips to Gen 5:24, omitting a few generations in the genealogy.

[29] It skips to Gen 6:8, omitting more of the genealogy and the account of the
sons of God marrying the daughters of men.

[30] It skips to Gen 6:18, omitting the description of pervasive evil and the command to build the ark.

[31] It skips to Gen 6:22, omitting instructions on what to bring on the ark.

[32] It skips to Gen 7:5, omitting a second set of instructions on what to bring
on the ark.

[33] It skips to Gen 7:23b, omitting the sealing of the ark and the great flood.

[34] It skips to Gen 8:1, omitting a brief comment on the length of the flood.

[35] It skips to Gen 8:13, omitting the sending out of the raven and doves.

[36] It skips to Gen 8:18, omitting the command to leave the ark with the
animals.

YHWH smelled the pleasant aroma.[37] . . . All the days of the earth, seeding and harvesting, cold and heat, summer and winter and day and night will not cease. God blessed Noah and his sons. And he said to them, "Be fruitful and multiply."[38] . . . (Because He made Adam and them in the likeness of God.)[39] . . . Be fruitful and multiply, swarm over the earth and multiply in it.[40] . . . "Behold I am establishing My covenant with you; [I am establishing my covenant with you]."[41] . . . God said, "This is the sign of the covenant.[42] . . . And it will be for a sign of the covenant.[43] . . . I will remember my covenant and observe it. I will remember the covenant forever." And God said to Noah, "This is a sign of the covenant." And he said, "Blessed is YHWH my God."[44] . . . Shem, and Egypt, Put and Egypt he bore.[45] . . . And they settled from Mescha toward Sephar, the Mount of the East.[46] . . . And all the earth had one language and one vocabulary.[47] . . . So they called its name Babel because YHWH confused the language of all the earth there. From there YHWH scattered them across the face of the whole earth.[48] . . . Go! Go! From your land and your relatives and the house of your father unto the land that I will show you. And I will make of you a great nation and I will bless you and I will make your name great and you will be a blessing. I will bless those who bless you.[49] . . . Abram passed over the land to the place at Shechem to the oak of Moreh. The Canaanites were then in the land. YHWH appeared to Abram and said to him, "I give this land to your descendants." He built there an altar to YHWH who appeared to him. He advanced from there to the Mount of the East, unto

---

[37] It skips to Gen 8:22, omitting God's promise not to curse or destroy the world again.

[38] A curious skip back to Gen 5:1. It is in CW 2480 but not in all the *qetifim* of Genesis.

[39] It skips to Gen 9:7, omitting the conditions of the covenant with Noah.

[40] It skips to Gen 9:9, omitting the identification of the speaker (God) and Noah.

[41] An apparent dittography. It skips to Gen 9:12, omitting the promise not to destroy the world.

[42] It skips to Gen 9:17, omitting a description of the sign (the rainbow).

[43] These comments on the covenant are interspersed throughout Gen 9:8–17. This version of the Genesis *qetafim* has put great emphasis on the Noah story.

[44] This is a choppy and brief summary of the genealogy of Ham that begins in Gen 10:6.

[45] The summary. It skips to Gen 10:30 toward the end of Shem's genealogy.

[46] It skips to Gen 11:1 to pick up the tower of Babel story.

[47] It skips to Gen 11:9 to complete the bracketing of the Babel story.

[48] It skips to Gen 12:1 and the beginning of the story of Abraham, omitting Abraham's genealogical background.

[49] It skips to Gen 12:6, omitting the journey of Lot and Sarah, his wife.

Beth El, water[50] and Ai to the east. He built there an altar to YHWH and called on the name of YHWH. And Abram went further and departed to the Negev. Between Beth El and Ai to the place of the altar that he had made in the beginning.[51] . . . Rise, walk through the length and breadth of the land because I will give it to you.[52] . . . And Abraham went up.[53] . . . I have raised my hand to the God Most High, Owner of heaven and earth.[54] . . . Fear not, Abram, I am a shield for you and your reward will be exceedingly great.[55] . . . And he said, "Look, I pray, to the heavens and count the stars." And he said to him, "So shall be your seed." And he believed YHWH and He reckoned it to him as righteousness. On that day YHWH made a covenant with Abram, saying,[56] . . . You shall call on the name YHWH, the word God.[57] . . . And Abraham was a son of eighty-six years when Hagar bore Ishmael to Abram.

The first section of this long Genesis *qetaf* is interrupted at this point in CW2480 with other prayers, a not uncommon practice during the reading of the *qetafim*. The central place of Scripture in Samaritan services cannot be overstated.

The "Prayer of Joshua, the son of Nun; Peace be upon him forever," may follow the Genesis *qetaf*:

YHWH is a God of Love and Pity. YHWH is King and Eternal Witness. YHWH is God, there is no other beside Him. His name be praised and His might exalted. O Lord of compassion, have mercy on us. O Lord of forgiveness, forgives our sins. Let us fear Him in our hearts; He establishes the faithful in great honor because whoever magnifies God, glorifies himself. According to the deed is the reward. According to our strength we witness concerning You that there is none like You, our God. You are to be praised. According to what the prophet wrote, we say, "Give greatness to

---

[50] A reference to the Jordan? The allusion to a biblical text is not clear.

[51] It skips to Gen 13:17, omitting the famine visit to Egypt, when Abram tells Pharaoh that Sara is his sister.

[52] It skips back to Gen 13:1.

[53] The following words are unclear in context: והם בעלי ברית אברם. It skips to Gen 14:22, omitting the dissension with Lot and the battle of the kings.

[54] It skips to Gen 15:1 with first two letters reversed, omitting the meeting with the king of Sodom.

[55] It skips to Gen 15:5, omitting Abram's protestation.

[56] It skips to Gen 16:13, omitting the ritual of the covenant with Abram and Hagar's flight.

[57] It skips to Gen 16:16, omitting the statements of the etiology of Beer-lahai-roi and the birth of Ishmael.

our God, because greatness is Yours, our God." There is no service but for Him. We say it and we are blessed in what our mouths utter.

The prophet received the ten commandments and he explained the law with them. The first decree which God spoke was, "I am YHWH your God." We worship none except Thee forever, Our Lord, "I am Who I am." Be praised forever, who planted beautiful praises. Its fruits go up on high. Moses cried out at the sea, "This is my God and I will praise Him. We bless, we praise, we magnify and exalt You, O Lord of all holiness. We praise You, our God. Who is like You? None is like You. There is none like the God of Jeshurun. Praise God. There is no God but One. O Lord, hear our voice and receive our prayers because you are the merciful One who shows mercy without end. We do not turn our faces to any other except toward Your Kingdom and no physician can heal us except Your Goodness and Mercy. There is none like the God of Jeshurun.

Praise to our God, praise forever. Like the days of the heavens upon the earth, or again, like the days of fathers and children, all the days of the generations and the ones that follow, we will still praise You and we will still bless You because You are our God and the God of our fathers in all days. The God of Abraham be blessed. The God of Isaac be praised. The Name of the God of Jacob be exalted every day. We fear God and we trust in God. We praise God because the world is His. Like the days of the heavens upon the earth we praise the Lord who stands forever. Blessed are You, our God and the God of our fathers. Praise to You. Who can accomplish [anything] like your deeds and your victories?

O True One, God of the heavens and God of the earth and God of all the world be praised.

God of Abraham, God of Isaac and God of Jacob, merciful One, [sender of the] Taheb, be praised.

O Lord of the secret and the revealed, be praised.

Our God and the God of our fathers, be praised in all days.

The Good and Who does good, Who is merciful every day, be praised.

Who is righteous, eternal, true and sovereign, be praised.

Who is great, praiseworthy and asks for reverence, be praised. Who supports the supporters of the doers of good, be praised.

Who apportions justice, who gives much without counting, be praised.

The Healer Who heals, shields, and pardons sins, be praised.

The King whose words live and whose reports live and who stands forever, be praised.

Unto the One who stands forever and establishes all those who trust in Him, be praised. We fear and love Him and we worship and praise Him.

Who delivers us from sin, judgement and wickedness, be praised.

Who does justice and mercy and shows pity to all the world, be praised. The One Whom we fear and love, be praised. Who created all the world and gave order to its creation, be praised.

The One Who spoke the word and brought to pass what He willed, be praised. Blessed be He the like of Whom there will not be forever. Blessed is our God forever and blessed is his Name forever.[58]

A short series of blessings may separate the prayer of Joshua, or whatever prayer is used, from a series of biblical verses with congregational responses (responses indented), for example:[59]

We shall bless and praise and acclaim and cry out and exalt and give thanks and praise to the Lord of all the world. Let us say in a loud voice, "Our God we bless You! Our God we praise You! Our God we acclaim You! Our God we cry out to You! Our God we exalt You! Our God we give thanks and praise to You!" "I will be Who I will be." "Blessed is Your Name. There is no God but One."[60]

God blessed the seventh day and made it Holy. . . .
    Holy is His Name.
YHWH, God called unto Adam and said, "Where . . . ?"
    Greatness is Yours.
Noah built an altar for YHWH and he took from all the clean beasts . . .
    Praise to You.
After these words YHWH spoke to Abraham . . .
    Righteous is Your Name.
Isaac said to Abraham, his father . . .
    Strong is Your Name.

---

[58] Cowley, *Samaritan Liturgy,* 1:4–5.
[59] Sometimes the biblical text is fuller, and sometimes the given responses may differ.
[60] Cowley, *Samaritan Liturgy,* 1:7.

Jacob awoke from his sleep and said, "Certainly YHWH is in this place."
>   Awesome is your Name.
And He said, "I am the God of your fathers."
>   Powerful is Your Name
God said to Moses, "I am Who I am."
>   "I am" is Your Name.
This is My Name forever; it will be remembered from generation to
>   generation.
>   Holy is Your Name.
I made judgements among all the gods of Egypt; I am YHWH.
>   Judge is Your Name.
Keep this statue for the festivals from day to day.
>   Keeper is Your Name.
Who is like You among the princes, O YHWH, who is like You adorned
>   in Holiness?
>   Power is Your Name.
Listen to His commandments and keep all His commandments.
>   Healer is Your Name.
And it will be like a word to all the congregation of the children of Israel
>   and they shall turn to the desert.
>   Glory is Your Name.
And Yahweh said unto Moses, "Write this memory in a book. . . ."
>   Receiver is Your Name.
Because YHWH is the greatest of the gods.
>   Praised is Your Name.
YHWH said to Moses, "Behold, I am coming to you in a dense cloud."
>   Drawing Near is Your Name.
Moses came down from the Mount unto the people and said to them, . . .
>   Able is Your Name.
God spoke all these words saying, "I am YHWH your God."
>   Glory is Your Name.
Three times walk to me in a year.
>   They make greatness for you.
Aaron made atonement at the horns [of the altar] once a year.
>   Atoner is your Name.
My Lord, YHWH, turn your face from anger.
>   Comforter is Your Name.
Forgive our sins and trespasses and our lot.
>   Forgiver is Your Name.
Forgive again and again His house.
>   Exalter is Your Name.

Forgive again and again His house and slaughter the bullock.
> Atoner is Your Name.

Forgive again and again His house and again all the congregation.
> Forgive your people.

Forgive again and again the people and burn the fat of the sin offering on the altar.
> Deliver your people.

Assembly of YHWH which you call, these assemblies are a Holy calling to God.
> Thanksgiving is Your Name.

Seven complete Sabbaths will end after the next Sabbath, you will count five days.
> He Dwells is Your Name.

Moses spoke the appointed times of YHWH to the people of Israel.
> Mighty is Your Name.

I made the first covenant for them.
> Remembrance is Your Name.

YHWH bless you and keep you.
> Blessed is Your Name.

Let us remember them before YHWH your God.
> Saviour is Your Name.

Forgive, I pray, the sins of this people by Your great mercy.
> Forgive Your people.

YHWH said, "I will forgive according to your word."
> Slow to Anger is Your Name.

In the first month, you will bring a burnt-offering to YHWH.
> Receiver is Your Name.

This offering will be made each month.
> Praised is Your Name.

YHWH is a God of love and mercy.
> Merciful One is Your Name.

Blessed are those who say, "Keep the Sabbath."
> Holy is Your Name.

Who is God of heaven and earth?
> God is Your Name.

Turn to YHWH your God and listen to His voice.
> Exalted is Your Name.

Because God is exalted, YHWH is your God.
> Great Mercy is Your Name.

Six days you will eat unleavened bread and on the seventh day, a feast to YHWH your God, you shall not do any work.

May You be praised.
Bend down from Your Holy Dwelling in heaven.
Gift is Your Name.
YHWH our God, YHWH is One.
YHWH is Your Name.
May YHWH open his good treasures for you.
Thanks be to You.[61]

"This by the Holy Angels" is another frequently used set of prayers:

All of us stand and say to You that You are Our God and there is none beside You or after You. Teach us Your Decrees and Your Covenants. We do not hide Your Unity.

I am Who I am. King of all Kings. Answer us and listen to our voice so that the remembrance of Your compassion does not cease. Bind the stance of our enemies as we read in Your writings. To You we give thanks. With our works we worship You. Do not let us err. You are God of the past and the future establishing your teachings with all generations and enduring in truth, greatness and sovereignty.

Your works assure Your goodness and You possess them and order them and put them in their proper place according to Your pleasure. Further, You have no aide because You are head over all things. Holy Sovereign, be merciful. I am Who I am, King of all kings . . .

To You we make requests, O Lord, and before You we worship. When Your writings are read, they give Your greatness. O Merciful One, help us in Your mercy. O Merciful One, cover us with Your loving-kindness. Pardon us and our fathers with Your plentiful loving-kindness through the labor of your servant, Moses. Turn from the heat of Your anger as is your custom, goodness and compassion at all times, our God of mercy and compassion.

Our mouths will not stop from telling of Your wonders and our hearts will not forget Your fear. O Merciful One, help us in your mercy. O Merciful One, look attentively upon us with loving-kindness. Be righteous with us in righteousness and forgive us . . .

---

[61] Ibid., 1:7–9.

All of us are sinners before You and You know our wickedness. Unless You help us, who can help us except Your goodness and mercy. O Merciful One, help us . . .

For the labor of those who love You, remember and do not forget their seed. We give thanks and magnify and in Your Presence we worship. O Merciful One, help us . . .

O Judge of Truth, who does not take anger and does not reject supplication. From your Divinity, Lord, we ask. Accept [it] from us in Your mercy. O Merciful One, raise Your anger from us and spread Your mercy and compassion upon us and forgive us . . .

Before Your goodness, O Lord, we petition, worshipfully praying to Your Name, O Merciful One. Raise Your anger from us. O Merciful One, help us in Your mercy. O Merciful One, receive our supplications in your loving-kindness and forgive us . . .

To You we pray, O One Who hears prayers. Look attentively in Your mercy and answer us and hear the sound of our prayers. O Merciful One, help us in Your mercy. O Merciful One, hear our prayers in Your loving-kindness and forgive us . . .

Unity in your divinity, we praise You and exalt Your Name. We proclaim Your goodness, saying, O Merciful One, help us in Your mercy. O Merciful One, be righteous to us in Your Righteousness and look attentively upon us in Your loving-kindness and relieve us from this distress and forgive us . . .

Before the world, You existed in greatness, a foundation without beginning. When it pleased You, You created alone. With no assistant, You created the necessary things, revealing Your goodness. You worked without weariness. You rested, but not from weariness. You brought about in appropriate time all that was necessary forever. O Merciful One, help us . . .[62]

Following is the Kadishah, which has two different forms, depending on which Sabbath in the month it is used for. This example is used on the second and fourth Sabbaths:

Holy Glorious One Who has separated us Your holy ones and revealed to us Your chosen ones and given us Holy Sabbath for rest and the Book of Life with wisdom and glory and majesty. You have set up for us an altar to worship your Name in order that we know that you are our Maker, our God and

---

[62] Ibid., 1:9–11.

our Lord. O Merciful One, help us in Your mercy. O Merciful One, send Your blessing upon our houses and upon our hands. O Merciful One, turn aside all distress and all anger and all disease from us. O Merciful One, prevail against those who prevail over us. O Merciful One, [give us] trust against fear. O Merciful One, heal our wounds. O Merciful One, enrich our soil. O Merciful One, restore our sanctuary. O Merciful One, have mercy on our dead. O Merciful One, place a blessing on this Sabbath and every Sabbath that is coming and bless us. Make us righteous in righteousness and forgive us and our fathers in your great compassion. On behalf of Moses, Your prophet, turn Your Face from Your great anger as You will. Have mercy, treat us well and make us free, O Merciful and Compassionate God.[63]

HYMNS

Second only to the various uses of Scripture, hymns play a dominant role in the services. There are long midrashic hymns for Passover, Pentecost, the Feast of Booths, and Yom Kippur. They begin with the story of creation, may include a long astronomical excursus, at least mention the lives of the patriarchs, and finally underscore the legislation on Sinai, encouraging the saints and warning the sinners.[64]

Some prayers, poems, and songs share the rhythms of others, and appropriate instructions for this appear in the liturgy. For example, the congregation may be instructed, "This Tephillah (prayer), is to be repeated in the rhythm of the Tephillah of our master Abisha."[65]

There were lighter moments of celebration in which secular songs were imported into the liturgy. One collection of Passover prayers contains a series of poems that celebrate drinking wine (as in a poem by Ghazal al Rosi, identified as a Moroccan), sailing at sea, good conversations, flowers, and maidens.[66] They recall the sensuality of the Song of Solomon in the Hebrew scripture, the *Rubaiyat* of Omar Khayyám, and some works of Sufi mysticism in Islam. As happens with these other works, Samaritans could justify such poems by giving the elements religious interpretations, but a scribe in CW 2486 was willing to acknowledge, "We are willing to write a few verses of poetry on pleasure which

---

[63] Ibid., 1:11–12.

[64] James A. Montgomery, *The Samaritans, the Earliest Jewish Sect: Their History, Theology, and Literature* (Philadelphia: Winston, 1907; repr., New York: KTAV, 1968), 299.

[65] Robertson, *Catalogue*, 1:159.

[66] The poems begin in CW 2486, p. 177. All of these elements are found in a poem by the "Moroccan" in CW 2486, p. 179.

may be said during a time of relaxation and joy."[67] Codex XIV in the University of Manchester collection contains a poem in Arabic described by the scribe as "a jocular piece to be recited at a time of pleasure and merry-making." The scribe writes that another song in the same manuscript is "an elegant piece, from long ago, the author unknown to us. It is recited on eves of Sundays (first nights) and on occasions of pleasure and happiness, drinking wine. It is attributed to Sartor b. Sadden, may (God) in his mercy pardon him."[68] Salih b. Ibrahim b. Salih b. Murjan notes that in July 1842 there was a pilgrimage "to this exalted place of our master, Eleazar . . . where there was drinking of wine, feasting, reciting hymns of praise and stories."[69]

The First Period

Several hymns of Marqe, the earliest known hymn writer, are used during the service.[70] During the morning service of the first Sabbath of the month, the following acrostic hymn of Marqe is used:[71]

א You are our God and the God of our fathers; the God of Abraham, Isaac and Jacob.

ב In height and depth Your strength is great and sovereign; in the invisible and visible world you are a merciful God.

ג Your great power—who can see it or know it? Mighty and Awesome One to all generations forever!

ד Who was before the world was and established it in glory; You made it a witness to Your greatness, that You are a God forever.

ה Where is there one who is pleasing, good or anything like you? Or where are their possessions except for what you possess?

ו You, for Your greatness, are a God who does not change; whoever seeks apart from You, seeks and finds not.

ז Righteousness is Yours, the righteous love You; there is no time or season when we are silent about Your Goodness.

---

[67] CW 2486, p. 183.
[68] Robertson, *Catalogue,* 1:210, 208.
[69] Ibid., 1:232.
[70] Cowley, *Samaritan Liturgy,* 1:16–27, reproduces about a dozen.
[71] Each line of the poem begins with a subsequent letter of the Hebrew alphabet. The majority of hymns in the *Defter* are alphabetical acrostics.

ה You have spread out the heavens, You have ordered the world; You have sent dreams to comfort those who love you.

ט The world is good because You are the Lord and Manager; Your commandments are good and those who keep them are good.

י Unique One who was first, You will remain forever; Giver of gifts, thanks to You for Your greatness.

כ You see everything, nothing sees You; all Your works are good, Our Lord, and You are better than them.

ל Forever You are merciful; forever You are compassionate. We worship Your Glory, You who enhance those who worship You.

מ We are believers that You are our God and we are glad; from us to You are praises, from You to us is a gift.

נ Guide of the world, we walk after You; Observer of Life, in Your goodness, you draw near.

ס Your goodness is abundant, those who love You are many; they are plentiful, Your wonders—You are to be praised.

ע Your great works serve You; Your servants rule, all glory is in Your service.

פ You open Your treasures, You enrich the world; mouths [speak] Your praise without end.

צ We need You, the living and the dead; true prayers to Your Name should be said.

ק Before Your Holiness, we cry out, "O El Elyon!" You are near to those who worship You, to whom You do not show Yourself.

ר Beginning with no end, we praise You; love of all, Your love is life.

ש Your Name is awesome, because You are glorious and fearsome; Your messengers are strong and in their hands is a message from You.

ת You will be praised forever, because everything that is Yours praises You; You are blessed forever, there is no God, but One.[72]

---

[72] Cowley, *Samaritan Liturgy*, 1:17–18; CW 2480, p. 93; CW 2486, p. 133; CW 26344, p. 96; CW 26344, pp. 23, 70.

Marqe's father, Amram Dare, also known as Tutu (Titus) and Amram Serad, is among the most popular Samaritan hymn writers.[73] He was a contemporary of the Samaritan Reformer of the third century C.E. and a member of the council of sages. He may have been the originator of his distinctive style of poetry. Lines are not of uniform length or number, and there is no rhyming. The absence of Hebrew and Arabic implies a purer form of Aramaic.[74] His poems were called "a string of pearls," a play on Dare, which is literally "elder" but works as a pun for "pearl."

Amram Dare's poems, three of which are given here, are frequently part of the liturgy. The first is an alphabetical acrostic poem:

ע (for א)[75] Maker of the world, who is able to define Your majesty? You made it gloriously in six days.

ב In the great true teaching we read and become wise. Every day You appointed creations.

ג Great in Your wisdom, they make known Your greatness; revealing of divinity that there is no greatness except You.

ד You created without weariness; Your works are exalted which You brought forth out of nothing in six days.

ע (for ה) You made them perfect. There is no defect in any of them. You made known their perfection because You are the Lord of perfection.

ו And you rested (but not from weariness) on the seventh day. You made it a crown for the six days.

ז You called it Holy and You made it a beginning, a meeting place for all festivals and a guide to all holiness.

ע (for ח) You made it a covenant between You and Your servants. You have made it known that You observe those who observe it.

---

[73] They are found, e.g., in the following liturgical manuscripts: CW 2480 (many), CW 2486, CW 10312, CW 26343, CW 26344; Codex XI, Codex XII, Codex XIII, Codex XVIII, Codex XX, Codex XXVII (John Rylands Library at the University of Manchester).

[74] Moshe Florentin, "Amram Dare," in *A Companion to Samaritan Studies* (ed. Alan D. Crown, Reinhard Pummer, and Abraham Tal; Tübingen: J. C. B. Mohr, 1993), 13.

[75] An exchange of gutturals, in this case ע for א, is not uncommon in Samaritan texts.

ט Happy are the ones who rest, who are worthy of its blessing. His holy protection is rest to them from all weariness and exhaustion.

י High glory honors us among the exalted. He gives us His Sabbath that we may rest when He rests.

כ All their greatness which You raised, You revealed by the hand of Moses the prophet. You spread abroad Your Holy Scripture to Your faithful.

ל The tablets of Your covenant You spread to the son of Your house for life from the Lord of all the living.

מ Who brings to life, from Whom is all perfection; He said from the fire, "There shall not be for you [another] God."

נ Prophecy was for him from the days of creation; Moses was worthy to be clothed in its light.

ס The tablets of the covenant are a comfort to our lives, a comfort that will not cease forever and ever.

א (for ע) Where is there a God like the God of our fathers? Where is there a true prophet like the faithful One of God?

פ God spoke to the son[76] of His house face to face. He revealed wonders to him that He had not revealed to another.

צ Former Who formed the world and all that is in it, He commanded Moses to give life to the living.

ק Proclaimer Who proclaimed, "There shall be no [other] God for you." He proclaimed, "Keep the Sabbath day, to hallow it."

ר High Great One of all great ones; He made great the son of His house above all the sons of Adam.

ש Name to name He joined in greatness, YH[WH] God of the generations and Moses the prophet of all generations.

ת The Great One made a limit to His words; a limit to the words of Moses, a limit to the words of the Lord.[77]

---

[76] This reference to Moses as God's son shows an affinity of religious language with Christianity.

[77] Cowley, *Samaritan Liturgy,* 1:31–32; CW 26343, pp. 140–41.

A second alphabetical acrostic poem by Amram is this:

ע (for א) Maker of the world Who is to be worshipped and praised. The Maker Who made is not in the likeness of [another] maker.

ב You made new creations out of time in order that You make known that You are the first, not [existing] in time.

ג You are revealed to us in the hidden and concealed from us in the re-vealed. You are revealed to the mind, but concealed from the eye.

ד Because You are found in every place. Nothing like You is found any-where. Concealer and knower of every secret; none sees all like You.

א (for ה) You Who from of old are in every place and time; every place and time and all creatures are Your work.

ו You Who are not from anything; You who are not like anything; You made all of them without any image of them.

ז At the time that Your wisdom saw to create, Your power brought every-thing together by Your word.

א (for ח) You are the first cause, creator, establisher of all. You are the One by Whom and from Whom all is obedient to You.

ט Happy is the heart in which nothing dwells except You. Happy is the one who gives thanks to You on behalf of Yourself.

י Unified and original is Your Divinity in itself; of a single source with much loving-kindness and truth.

כ None of it can surround You, but You are found in everything. You are in every place and not in any one place.

ל No one can know where You are; where a man turns, there he finds You.

מ Who can know You except by Your works? Who can fully praise You except in righteousness that comes from You?

נ We know You from the creation of ourselves. We look for Your wisdom in ourselves and we worship Your greatness.

ס Your work is Your witness that You are one substance. They witness a truth that does not change.

א (for ע) O One Who is hidden from the sight of all who see; if it looks [appropriate] to You, look upon us in Your mercy.

פ Deliverer of the oppressed, Who is nearer to him than his heart, deliver us, because we have no deliverer except You.

צ The soul is righteous that has in hand what is Yours. Be righteous upon us from Your righteousness, righteousness from Your compassion.

ק We stand before You, standing with the poor. Do not cut off the voice of our requests if You see [fit].

ר You are merciful and generous. Because Your name is Merciful; Your Mercy is greater than the number of our requests.

ש Hearer of pleas, listen to the sound of our cries; You know what we ask before we speak.

ת Accept our repentence and forgive our sins. Do not close the gate of Your mercy in our face.[78]

The third poem is this:

א Merciful God, help us in Your mercies. Unless the Merciful One helps, who can help?

ב Look upon us with the eyes of Your mercy and loving-kindness. With the hand of Your loving-kindness, extend relief to our misery.

ג Mighty and Illuminated One, be praised forever. God of gods, be worshipped forever.

ד We fear You and are comforted by You. We fear Your anger and are comforted by Your mercy.

א (for ה) I am Who I am, Creator and Helper; do not subdue us because you are a house of refuge.

ו Do not reject us because You are our hope. Do not requite us because You are our trust.

ז Our cry to Your hand is the cry of the poor. They do not find relief for themselves except from You.

---

[78] Cowley, *Samaritan Liturgy,* 1:27–28; CW 10312, pp. 155–56; CW 26343, pp. 145–46.

א (for ה) We place our hope at the gate of Your mercy. Far be it from You to reject those who hope in You.

ט Happy is the one who draws near to You, O Far One Who is near. Woe to the one who is far from You, O Near One Who is far.

י Our sins are abundant apart from Your pardon. Our trespasses are many apart from Your mercy.

כ Every soul trusts Your abundant compassion. Every body trembles from the power of Your terror.

ל Do not hide Your mercies from those who stretch out their hands or Your pity from who cannot raise their face.

מ What are we in the hand of Your anger without Your mercy; how weak is dust to receive its kneader.

נ Our souls are Yours and our lives, Your righteousness; our comfort, Your loving-kindness and our hope, Your mercy.

ס Pardon us, my Lord, because we are living like the dead; speak to us of the covenant who are as alive.

ע Upon whom shall one who is with You cause to be trusted except in You? To whom shall one who has need ask except You?

פ Apportioner of life, extend mercy; open the hand of Your loving-kindness in righteousness upon the poor.

צ We need your mercy after our affliction. When in death we need You, in life more so.

ק Nearest of the near ones, who cannot be seen; receive our requests and answer our hopes.

ר Pity our fear on the day we stand before You; do not spare giving Your compassion and Your mercy.

ש How are we healed in the time of our renewal after our affliction unless You look upon us in Your loving-kindness?

ת Be praised, glorified, exalted forever. Be honored, blessed, worshipped forever.[79]

---

[79] Cowley, *Samaritan Liturgy,* 1:29–30; CW 2480, pp. 43–44; CW 2486, pp. 65–66; CW 10312, pp. 172–73. This hymn, labeled "Eluwem Remmanah," is found on a compact disk: Samaritan Singers Ensembles, directed by Benyamim

Marqe's grandson, Nanah, was also a significant hymn writer in this first period, but he has the fewest surviving hymns.[80] Cowley understands the name Nanah to come from the Roman name Nonus. Ben-Hayyim speculates that it is related to the Talmudic name Nanny. Only one undisputed hymn of his survives:

> In peace, the day of Sabbath went.
> The great crown for Israel.
> If you put it on, you are a king
> But if you set it aside, you are in great weariness.
> A slave's release is at six years
> And Israel's—every six days.
> Unless the Sabbath comes.
> And gives rest to Israel's labor,
> Truly, she would be surrounded by the hand of distress
> Which prevails exceedingly around her.
> Except for the gift of the Sabbath.
> Thanks and praise to God.[81]

Second Period

In the tenth and eleventh centuries C.E., the liturgy was expanded in a new surge of Samaritan activity that produced Pentateuchs and other manuscripts as well.[82] Previously many hymns had been anonymous. During this second period, hymns were attributed and identified by their authors, a handful of whom stand out as particularly productive or acknowledged.

Tabiah son of Darta is represented by one prayer in the *Defter*. A man named Darta helped restore a synagogue shortly after the death of the high priest Netanel in about 274 A.H., which would put him in the tenth century.

> O, He who is the Lord of all the world,
> Receive what is said before you.
> If we have sinned, forgive and comfort [us].
> According to—it is not in us to say—
> "I am Who I am."[83]

Tsedaka, *The Sounds of Samaritan Music*. It is produced by the A.B. Institute of Samaritan Studies, P.O. Box 1029, Holon 58110, Israel.

[80] E.g., in CW 10312, CW 26343; Codex XI, Codex XVIII (John Rylands Library at the University of Manchester).

[81] Found in CW 26343, p. 53; and Cowley, *Samaritan Liturgy*, 1:15.

[82] See Cowley, *Samaritan Liturgy*, 1:xxii–xxv.

[83] Found ibid., 2:78.

Ed-Dustan is a curious contributor because of his name or, more likely, his title, which has been understood as indicating a follower of Dositheus in a gnostic offspring Samaritan sect, but Cowley suspects no heretic would be included in the liturgy and thinks that this must be an eleventh-century figure.[84] Ed-Dustan is the purported author of three hymns in CW 26343 and others in Codex XI and Codex XVIII at the University of Manchester. The following hymn, used as a *manat* (hymn for a special situation), is attributed to him:

> How strong the one who seeks knowledge,
> Let there be understanding in its creation.
> Who seeks service,
> Let there be rest for him from it.
> Let us speak words to the world and let us serve those who speak them.
> The Strong One created Heaven and earth.
> They endure forever.
> One from them ministers who rises and illuminates; who ministers to mortals.
> Light is closed forever and darkness has dominion over them.
> Who aspires to judge those who do not cause sorrow, terror of rebellion is among them.
> When He devours rebels of works He began, He proclaims a full explanation that He has no need for them; we bless Him forever.[85]

Ab Hasda of Tyre is credited with the first Samaritan Arabic translation of the Pentateuch, although a thirteenth-century scribe, Abu Said, felt the text was so bad that it was really the work of the tenth-century al Fayoumi, also known as Joseph Gaon. A few hymns of Abu'l-hasan (Ab Hasda) survive.[86] This is a frequently used alphabetical acrostic poem by Ab Hasda:

> א Great God, like Whom there is none.
> God Who sees all who love Him.
> God of mercy and compassion, doer of good without end forever.

[There is a response after each verse: Because You are merciful; because you are merciful. Praise to Your great and victorious name. There is no God, but One.]

---

[84] Ibid., 1:xxii.

[85] Ibid., 1:69; CW 26343, p. 242.

[86] Hymns of Abu'l-hasan (Ab Hasda) of Tyre are found in CW 2480 and CW 26343; and in Codex XI, Codex XIII, Codex XIV, Codex XVIII, and Codex XX (John Rylands Library at the University of Manchester).

ב In Your great strength we trust.
In Your Divinity we are glorified.
We have none to trust save You.
Everything except You is nothing.
You are a God Who owns the heavens and the earth,
Who rules above and below forever.

ג Your greatness is glorified forever
because You made the world with no helper.
Your creations are glorious, new things every day
That do not perish, obedient and serving forever.

ד O One Whose power is praised, Doer of wonders.
Moses, the prophet, proclaimed Him Doer of wonders forever.
Who awes all peoples of the world forever
with one small miracle from You.

ה Where is there a God like You, my Lord?
How can another stand beside You?
You are the King of all kings Who looses the loins of the great,
Who causes change, but is not changed forever.

ו Because we know that there is no God, but You,
We proclaim before You that You are the Merciful One.
We serve You because You are compassionate.
You are merciful in your judgements
and compassionate in Your punishments forever.

ז You are righteous forever, My Lord.
Your rightousness fills all the world.
Cleanser of all sins and King of all kings.
The righteous worship You, the Righteous One.
And one who repents is not [?] found with You forever.

א (for ח) You [are] in Your Divinity, my Lord.
Alone in [the] lofty divine.
You are in Your kingdom, my Lord, gracious with all sins.
Compassionate, delivering, merciful and patient forever.

ט Your goodness fills all the world.
Your goodness is a gift forever
because you are good and cause good and do not cease.
You keep Your goodness for us forever.

' Hearts give thanks to You. Bodies serve You.
You are the God who created all the creation.
You created man and all his needs.
He acted wickedly before You and You pardoned him.
He feared You and You showed compassion forever.

כ All serve You, my Lord. All fear Your terror.
The greatness of the creation, all of it testifies to You.
The heavens and all their host,
the earth and its foundations, above and below, my Lord.
They are Your domain and all the holy angels exalt You forever.

ל There is no king like You and no one acts like You act.
What is there in heaven or earth that is not under Your Hand?
We trust in Your power; there is no trust like Yours.
No other stands beside you in goodness.
There is none like You and no lack is ever found in You.

מ We praise You, Lord with strength.
We exalt You with all our soul.
Who can glorify You according to Your glory?
Humbly accepting us,
You receive our weakness and knowledge forever.

נ We are brought to life when we do Your commandments.
Great joy comes to all worshippers of You.
Finding You for us everywhere forever.

ס You pardon sinners without growing weary.
Forgive our sin in Your mercy.
Your comfort and Your mercy form the hearts of those who repent.
Who desire Your kingdom forever.

א (for ע) You have revealed Your great faith to all the congregations of Israel so that they may observe Your restrictions according to our strength
and Your goodness accepting us in your mercy, my Lord.

פ Your wonders You have shown to past generations
and will show to generations to come.
We cross over and pass away and leave.
But You remain in greatness forever.

צ We need to give You thanks
because you supply us with all our needs.

You are God Who needs nothing.
You give us what we need, my Lord

ק Original One, Who existed before habitation.
Before your goodness, we offer our services.
Our spirits bow down before You.
We benefit ourselves when we do your commandments, my Lord.

ר Great is Your majesty, my Lord.
Great are Your wonders upon Your mercies.
You show mercy, do justice to their seed
and do not reject their petitions before You, my Lord.

ש Hearer of all prayers, listen to our voice and receive us.
YHWH Who redeemed our fathers,
look down from Your holy habitation
and receive our prayers forever.

ת Our souls are at rest again when we do Your statutes.
Our bodies are greatly exalted when we ask for Your mercy.
The world is good when the repentant and the perfect come and they are
pleasing to Your Holiness forever.[87]

This second poem of Ab Hasda is also an acrostic and has a regular response:

א O time of thanks for our Lord, O time of praise,
O time in which we repent and we worship in it.

[The response to each verse is, We seek relief for ourselves and that which
gives honor to us.]

ב A covenant full of gifts in word form His Kingship; compassion is upon us
everyday, so that His Name may be worshipped.

ג He reveals all the hidden [things] He sees; our bodies serve Him. His recompense is good to us; enhanced by praise He gave it to us.

ד He who goes after it does not sin, who labors with it is not disappointed.
Who trust in it does not fall, who fears it is not oppressed.

ה He brings freedom to all the world. He heals the creation in His mercy.
He is a merciful King. He helps the oppressed. He comforts all who suffer.

---

[87] Cowley, *Samaritan Liturgy,* 1:70–72; CW 26343, pp. 63–66.

ו There is no great God like Him and no enduring King except Him and no works like He did and no gift like He gave.

ז He calls to His creatures as He wills, splendor and high honor. We are called His works. He feeds us with His words.

א (for ח) He is praised in His works. He is exalted in His wonders. He is naked who deserves it. He who has need has a gift.

ט The dew of the heavens is dew; the earth is a gift. Happy is the mouth that praises Him. Happy is the heart that serves Him.

י Every mouth will thank You; bodies will serve You; lips will praise You; souls will love You.

כ Everything comes with wisdom. Everything is in His sovereignty, all order and position. All who speak will praise Him.

ל To Him is worship and exaltation; to Him heart and soul make request. We remember Him every day. There is no living God, but Him. We serve Him in faith.

מ He is king of all worlds. Who can estimate His praise? Who can supply words of His glory? Who is there to be praised like Him?

נ We worship Him Who is merciful. We serve Him Who is compassionate. He feeds our souls abundantly. He extinguishes the light of the wicked.

ס Who bears the world in strength, Who bears the creation with His words. He loves the order of His dwelling. Great praise we give to Him.

ע He sees our works. He knows the secrets of our hearts. He sees what is not seen. He sees sinners and He is compassionate with them.

פ He seeks works of truth. Works of light He glorifies. A work with no limit to what it gathers. It has no sustenance except Himself.

צ Righteousness He does without end; He receives the cries of orphans. Our needs are met from Him. We must praise Him.

ק He lives forever. The living serve Him. He receives life and blessings. Before Him we worship and serve.

ר He is compassionate and merciful. Compassion is near and anger is far. So wrote Moses, the prophet, for us, "YHWH is compassionate and merciful."

ש Heaven and earth He raised with His word. The Sabbath He created for glory. Walls of water He raised on their behalf. His name be praised forever.

ת The penitent one prepares to serve God in sincerity and truth, working diligently for the righteous and receiving their recompense.[88]

Third Period

Several hymn writers appear in the third period, which peaked in the fourteenth century. Among them were Joseph Ha-rabban, once referred to as עבתה דמשק ("minister of Damascus").[89] The title Ha-rabban was in common usage there. Pinhas the son of Joseph was the instigator of a religious revival and contributed several hymns, some of which are found in CW 10312 and in Codex XI and Codex XXVII in the John Rylands collection. Special services for festivals were developed at this time. This same Pinhas the high priest and his two sons, Abisha and Eleazar, contributed to the growing liturgical texts.

The following is a poem in the style of Marqe, rendered by Pinhas the high priest:

א God Who hallowed and blessed this seventh day be blessed, hallowed and glorified.

ב Blessed is YHWH our God and God of our fathers, God of Abraham, Isaac, and Jacob, Joseph and our lord Moses, our prophet.

ג YHWH revealed [that] this Sabbath day and those who keep it are Holy according to our lord Moses in His book, the Torah.

ד God said to Moses in the Ten Words, "Observe the Sabbath day to keep it holy."

ה This is the holy Sabbath; Blessed are all who keep it; they are called Keepers.

ו And now rest O Israel because it is the Sabbath of YHWH. Let no one go out from his place on the Sabbath day; pray and call and bless in the name of YHWH.

---

[88] Cowley, *Samaritan Liturgy,* 1:72–74.
[89] Ibid., 2:xxxii.

ז This is the holy Sabbath; how much glory and strength YHWH has stored up for those who keep it, for Israel, His people.

ח It is the garden of the world. YHWH, God, set it up for his people, His assembly, His congregation and His servant, Israel.

ט We are happy and blessed with what YHWH has given us in keeping this holy Sabbath. Thanks to YHWH, our God.

י This is the Sabbath day. How great and glorious. YHWH will not make a covenant with us unless He helps us to keep it.

כ The glory of YHWH is seen in it. Therefore, YHWH said in His book, "Surely you will keep my Sabbath because it is a sign between Me and you.

ל For your generations to know that I am YHWH Who sanctifies you. You will keep the Sabbath because it is holy to you."

מ Those who profane it will surely die because from any one who does labor in it, his soul will be cut off from the midst of his people.

נ We will observe this Sabbath, just as YHWH our God commanded by the hand of our lord, Moses, messenger of YHWH. May it be blessed and be a blessing upon us.

ס We will read the book of the Torah on this holy Sabbath, from evening to evening, with heart and soul.

ע We will do no work on this Sabbath day except the daily burnt offering and the Sabbath offering on the Sabbath.

פ We offer our prayers in the presence of YHWH on the altar of prayers. In stead of the Sabbath offering we will sanctify ourselves and praise and proclaim and rest from all work.

צ YHWH commanded us on the keeping of the Sabbath. From evening to evening we repose and rest.

ק YHWH proclaims in His book, "You will keep My Sabbaths and revere My sanctuary; I am YHWH."

ר The first of holy things, holy of holies, holy to Israel which is holy.

ש Keep the Sabbath day to make it holy, a Sabbath of rest, holy to YHWH.

ת The children of Israel will continually keep the Sabbath to do the Sabbath for their generations, an eternal covenant between Me and the children of Israel, an eternal sign.[90]

There are many hymns by Eleazar, the son of Pinhas.[91] On the basis of its appearance in many liturgical works, one of his most popular hymns follows. It is an alphabetical acrostic in which both the first and the second part of each verse begin with the appropriate letter of the alphabet:

א YHWH, the Glorious One, is one; there is none beside Him. Blessed be God Almighty for His great goodness and loving-kindness.

ב Blessed is YHWH, our God, Whose name is glorious. Praise the Creator as is fitting and done.

ג His greatness is greater than all greatness. His strength rules over all territories.

ד Select among the select and not like anything else. True, holy judge is His name above all names.

ה He was and will be. He is "I am Who I am," the great God Who kills and brings to life.

ו Give greatness to His divinity Whose word is above and below. Who is like Him among the strong, a God of light Who cleaves the darkness.

ז His arm is outstretched and His power is great and mighty. My song and my strength are found every day and [every] place.

ח His wisdom dwells with everything that dwells in goodness. Wisdom with full knowledge stands in enduring strength.

ט Exceeding great goodness, its glory cannot be measured; goodness of the world whose Lord and guide You are.

י He said, "Let there be," and it was; exceedingly good for all who saw. Glorified is this name Who does what is asked of Him.

כ Because in the name of YHWH we seek, our pardoner in all times; because YHWH will judge His people and be comforted by His servants.

---

[90] Ibid., 1:82–83; CW 26343, pp. 183–84.
[91] They are found in CW 2480, CW 2486, CW 26343, CW 26344; Codex XI, Codex XIV, Codex XVIII (John Rylands Library at the University of Manchester); Cowley, *Samaritan Liturgy,* 1:35–37, 180, 489.

ל There is no God beside Him. His hand is strong. There is no lasting strength except His strength and no one can do things like His work.

מ Moses, His servant, is a prophet. We trust in the strength of the name. Our Saviour saves and there gives us rest.

נ We worship and serve our Maker Who supplied our needs. We petition release from Him and a giving of blessing.

ס Pardoner, Comforter, deliver us with your Deliverance. Forgive us, O Lord, and our fathers in your loving-kindness.

ע We are Your servants and children of your servants. Do to us what is good in Your eyes according to Your faithful works.

פ We turn toward Your Face, O Lord. Unto Your refuge we come. We are afraid of Your wrath. Bear our straying and sin.

צ The shadow of Your roof is over us, O God of Hosts. Look from Your Habitation, Hearer of cries.

ק Possessor of heaven and earth, Warrior of warriors. Rise O YHWH and scatter them; turn to whoever will return.

ר Rider of the heavens, look. I have seen a revelation. My trust is in You. I hope in You for salvation.

ש Turn to us and bless us with many blessings. Break the yoke of injustice and lead us standing tall.

ת Be praised forever. Be sanctified and glorified. Be thanked in all time and Sabbath and feast day.[92]

Cowley divides the post-fifteenth-century hymn writers into three groups, the Levitical or priestly family, the Danfi family, and the Marhib family.[93] The

---

[92] Cowley, *Samaritan Liturgy*, 2:36–37.

[93] Ibid., 1:xxxiii–xxxiv. Chief among the Levitical family are Abraham b. Isaac, who died in 1732; Tabiah aka Ghazal b. Isaac, who died in 1787; Solomon b. Tabiah, who died in 1857; Amram b. Solomon b. Tabiah, who died in 1874; Isaac b. Solomon b. Tabiah; Pinhas b. Isaac, who died in 1898; Khidr b. Isaac; and Tabiah b. Abraham. Chief among the Danfi family are Isaak b. Musalama, Murjan I also known as Ab-Sakhwah b. Ibrahim, Muslim I b. Ab-Sakhwah (Murjan I), Muslim b. Murjan b. Ibrahim b. Murjan, and Abraham b. Jacob b. Murjan I b. Abraham. Chief among the Marhib family are Mufaraj Jakob Mufaraj, Mufaraj al Mufaraj (same as the preceding?), Marhib b. Jacob; the earliest mention of the family is the seven-

following are two works of Abraham son of Jacob son of Murjan I son of Abraham.[94]

> God of Abraham, in justice be with us in our affliction.
> God of Isaac, in watchfulness light our light.
> God of Jacob, in completeness, smite our adversaries.
> God of Joseph, in compassion, refresh us from our oppression.
> God of Moses, in prayerfulness, hear our prayer.
> God of Aaron, in priestliness, receive our petitions from us.
> God of Eleazar, Ithamar and Pinhas, assist and answer our requests.
> Swear help to us who tremble before serpents.
> O Merciful King, continue to help us.[95]

Most of the second hymn, related to Passover, is given here:

> We open our mouths in constant praise to the master of all power. Hear our prayer and make known hidden things and answer our requests, You Who are a merciful God.

> The Living One Who is set apart, Origin, Glorious One, Whose Glory continuously draws near [those] who give thanks and worship. [You are] slow to anger and majestic in loving-kindness, Who put the haughty in their place.

> How good is His work and how exalted is His glory. How perfect is His loving-kindness and how great is His mercy upon us. We send praise to Him alone. We speak with a pure tongue.

> How He loves us and we love Him. We hallow Him. We treasure Him. We are established as a holy people. We know and hear and do the Law of Moses.

> Until we glorify and are glorified when we set ourselves in the dwelling which He commanded to be worthy for us to receive good tidings.

> Our beginning is good news. Rejoice and be glad that in it we are renewed. There is a festival of rest every year for our renewal. Happy are those who call the Holy One. He discerns the congregation's success.

---

teenth century, and Abraham b. Ishmael (b. Joseph al-mufarriji) is the latest and was living in 1828.

[94] His works are included in many liturgical works, with several each in CW 2480, CW 2486, and CW 10312 and several in Cowley, *Samaritan Liturgy,* including pp. 1:141, 151, 155, and 206.

[95] Cowley, *Samaritan Liturgy,* 1:155; CW 2480, p. 29; CW 2486, p. 59.

By thought is observed the One Who created, Who watched, Who gave good news to Noah, Shem and those who crossed over to take possession of what is right, to disperse the owner of the vow whose living You turned back.

The peace of YHWH upon Moses, highest of all men, to him the Lord commanded that he go to the stubborn and deliver his people from bondage and he revealed to them their deliverance.

He did as he was charged and to his people he fled and by his hand they fled and he commanded them with authority. This is a holy month and service on the fifteenth is a sacrifice.

It is a rite continued every year. This month is the beginning the coming of joy, good news in a delightful feast, the Passover Sacrifice and a memorial to deliverance from all who hate.

I declare and bless and hallow this feast called holy, an eternal rite, never diminished; only You possess it, on the fourteenth day of the month for everyone every year.[96]

CONCLUDING COMMENTS

The Taheb, Mount Gerizim, and Moses are certainly not ignored in the liturgy, but attention to them is more subdued than the sharp focus they receive in *Marqe* and the chronicles. God in his many manifestations is the central focus of the liturgy. God is the "True One," Knower of hidden things, Creator, Power, One, Unique. There is no God but One. God does not get weary. Many of the attributes, names, and affirmations are shared with Islam. God is revealed in his works and in the law of Moses. Praise is the primary message directed to God, and the patriarchs are exalted. By contrast, there is strong emphasis on the sinfulness of humanity and the need for divine forgiveness.

Colophons appear frequently in the liturgical books, but other than notations about when various parts of the liturgy were completed, they contain no significant information. Late colophons witness a number of unique occasions. One year soldiers confiscated four hundred rams, precluding the sacrifice on Gerizim. Within a couple of years, there were unusual thunderstorms, "so that the world seemed on the point of

---

[96] Cowley, *Samaritan Liturgy,* 1:141–42; CW 10313, pp. 158–59.

destruction."[97] In April 1850 the Abisha Scroll was unrolled to check out the *tashqil* (literally, an elevated and separated text).[98] The colophon to Codex XIV exclaims, "This awe-inspiring sight dispelled all doubts. . . . They read in it and found a dittographed word, which they erased with a penknife." A colophon of June 1845 describes a series of recent hardships, including drought, locusts, and war.[99]

---

[97] Robertson, *Catalogue,* 1:231–32.

[98] The *tashqil* is an acrostic running through many Samaritan Pentateuchs, identifying the scribe, the date, the location, and occasionally some other data. This colophon is particularly important because it authenticates for the Samaritans that the scribe was Abisha, the great-grandson of Aaron, shortly after the entry into Canaan.

[99] Robertson, *Catalogue,* 1:233–35.

Chapter 7

Miscellaneous Texts

This book has focused on major Samaritan literary texts: the SP, the chronicles, the basic theological work *Tibat Marqe,* and representative prayers and hymns from the Samaritan liturgy. In addition to documents on paper and sheepskin, a few documents were engraved or molded into inscriptions and amulets. What are written in this form are not major literary works, although often they are quotations from the Pentateuch. But the additional effort taken to create such artifacts underscores their importance in the thinking of the Samaritan community and merits attention. In addition, there is an extensive body of astronomical texts. Again, they are not literary texts, but they do underscore important affirmations of the Samaritan community.

INSCRIPTIONS

Inscriptions are usually made in stone, often white marble, although they also appear as silver inlays in scroll cases and are embroidered into silk covers for Torahs; at least one inscription appears as a mosaic in the floor of a synagogue or church. Most inscriptions have been found in towns close to Nablus. Scroll cases were often manufactured in Damascus. Some Samaritan inscriptions appear as far away as Thessalonica and Delos. Marble and other stone inscriptions and the mosaic likely date from the third to the sixth centuries C.E. Metal and cloth inscriptions date from the fifteenth century to the present.

Biblical texts are the most popular subject of inscriptions. They lead us quickly to the texts that the Samaritans considered most significant. These include the Ten Words of Creation (an abridgement of Gen 1), the Ten Commandments (a conflation of the lists in Exodus and Deuteronomy), the core of the Passover story (Exod 12:13, 23), the focal account of the exodus in Exod 15, the priestly benediction (Num 6:22–27), and the scattering of Israel's enemies (Num 10:35).

The *qetaf,* a condensed scriptural reading, is a featured part of the Samaritan liturgy, as described in the previous chapter, and its parallel is seen in inscriptions that abbreviate longer biblical passages, such as Exod 15 (see below). A popular and longer inscribed condensation of Scripture is the Ten Words of Creation, which is the subject of the second Shechem inscription:

> In the beginning God created.
> And God said, "Let there be light." And God said,
> "Let there be a firmament," and God said, "Let there be a collection
> of waters." And God said, "Let the earth sprout forth."
> And God said, "Let there be
> Lights." And God said, "Let
> the waters swarm." And God said, "Let bring forth
> the earth." And God said, "Let us make
> a man." And God said, "Behold, I have given
> to you." And God saw all that He
> made and behold; it was very good and he said, "I am
> the God of your father, the God of Abraham
> and the God of Isaac and the God of Jacob."[1]

Both the subject, creation, and its place at the beginning of the Pentateuch make it worthy of attention.

A statement of Samaritan history, also the basis for the Passover liturgy, the most important festival of the Samaritans, is encapsulated in Exod 12:13, 23 and engraved on a number of inscriptions:

> In the name of YHWH, the Deliverer, [His word] spoken by the hand of Moses:
> "I will pass over you and you will not be smitten."
> YHWH will pass over the door and will not let the Destroyer
> enter into your house to smite you.[2]

Two aspects of YHWH are personified in this prelude to the flight from Egypt. YHWH is the Deliverer or Savior who will lead the flight from bond-

---

[1] Translated from plate 2 in James Montgomery, *The Samaritans, the Earliest Jewish Sect: Their History, Theology, and Literature* (Philadelphia: Winston, 1907; repr., New York: KTAV, 1968).

[2] Translated from the text in John Strugnell, "Quelques inscriptions samaritaines," *RB* 74 (1967): 573. This passage is also used in Moritz Sobernheim, "Samaritanische Inschriften aus Damascus," *Mitteilungen und Nachrichten des Deutschen Paläistina-Vereins* 8 (1902), inscriptions nos. 3 and 8; Hans H. Spoer, "Notes on Some New Samaritan Inscriptions," in *Poceedings of the Society of Biblical Archaeology* 30 (1908), inscriptions nos. 1, 5, 10, and 12; and an Emmaus inscription discussed by Melchior de Vogüé, "Nouvelle inscription samaritaine d'Amwas," *RB* 5 (1896): 432–34.

age. More important at this moment, YHWH is the Destroyer, sometimes known as the angel of death, who represents the destructive power of God, who makes flight possible by destroying the obstacles. This Hebrew personification of the God as Deliverer of good and Destroyer of evil is parallel to the Hindu presentation of Vishnu and Lakshmi as the beneficiaries of humanity and Siva and his consort as the aspect of God that wars against the demonic. The sense of a cosmic struggle between the forces of good and evil is quite visible in Samaritan theology, liturgy, and here in the inscriptions.

Exodus 15 is the poem that focuses the story of the exodus, the transition from bondage to freedom. It has been a source of hope for oppressed peoples, including Jews through the ages up to the Nazi concentration camps; African-Americans in the South, as evidenced in surviving sermons; and the Samaritans, as seen in several inscriptions.

> Yahweh is a hero in battle; YHWH is His name.
> Who is like Thee among the gods, O YHWH, who is like Thee?
> Majestic in Holiness, terrifying in glorious deeds.[3]

In terms of power and imagery, this poem is among the earliest and finest Hebrew writings. It expresses joy at the release from bondage, vindictive bitterness toward the former oppressor, and affirmation and confidence in the God who made escape possible.

Part of Exod 15 comes from a later time, since it describes events from the period following the exile as if they had already occurred. But the first eleven verses and the song of Miriam are contemporary with the events they describe, encapsulating the depth of feeling about the most profound event in Israel's life.

The present inscription circumscribes both the beginning and the end of that earliest poem; that is, it highlights the frame, verses 3 and 11. The ignored verses 1 and 2 are a later prologue. Knowing whether this choice of verses is coincidental, represents a sensitive selectivity, or reveals a vestigial awareness of the original compass of the poem could help us understand the text and the Samaritans. This conclusion to the first chapters of the book of Exodus could be a liturgical text that very early was read at certain festive occasions uniting subsequent generations around a common historical tradition. The Samaritans may have perpetuated this usage.

---

[3] Translated from CW 2472. The same text is found in the so-called Second Emmaus Inscription, described in J. M. Lagrange, "Inscription samaritaine d'Amwas," *RB* 2 (1893): 114–16. The first part is found on the inscriptions labeled Sobernheim I and Musil IV, in Alois Musil, "Sieben samaritanishe Inschriften aus Damaskus," *Sitzungsberichte der kaiserlichen Akademie der Wissenschaften in Wien, phil.-hist. Klasse 147* (1903), 1–11.

The Samaritan version of the Ten Commandments is often a shortened conflation of Exodus and Deuteronomy's version of the Decalogue with some unique Samaritan readings. The Leeds Fragment, the Beit al-Ma inscription, and Strugnell's inscription number 4, for example, read generally as follows:

> You shall have no other gods before Me.
> You shall not lift up the name of YHWH, your God, in vain.
> Remember to keep the Sabbath day Holy.
> Honor your father and your mother.
> Do not murder.
> Do not commit adultery.
> Do not steal.
> Do not testify falsely against your neighbor.
> Do not covet the house of your neighbor.
> Build there an altar for YHWH your God.[4]

The Decalogue, the major artifact of the covenant between YHWH and Israel, has a prominent visual as well as theological place in the life of the Samaritan community. It is the basic document that binds the community together with its God in a covenant.

Toward the end of the stay on Sinai, it becomes clear that the tenure of Moses' leadership is coming to an end, and preparation is made to pass political leadership on to Joshua and religious leadership to Aaron and his sons. Among the tasks assigned to Aaron and his sons is the blessing of the people. The Samaritans perpetuate the classic Priestly Benediction in their services and inscriptions.

> YHWH bless you and keep you.
> YHWH make His face to shine upon you and be gracious to you.
> YHWH lift up the light of His Face upon you and give you peace (Num 6:22).

This is inscribed, for example, on a fourth-to-sixth-century white-marble bilingual (Greek and Hebrew) plaque found at Thessalonica in Greece. The plaque also includes this inscription:

> God is one. Blessing to Siricius who has made this [it is not clear whether this refers to the plaque or the religious building of which it was a part] with his wife and children. Neapolis [Nablus] may prosper with all its friends.

---

[4] Translated from the text in Strugnell, "Quelques inscriptions," 571. The last commandment, sanctioning Mount Gerizim, is the most distinctive feature in the SP, as discussed in ch. 1 above.

Blessed be our God forever.

Blessed be His Name forever. [The blessing on His Name is particularly relevant because the priestly benediction is followed by the verse "So shall they put my name upon the people of Israel, and I will bless them."]

The Priestly Benediction is also found on CW 2465, a brass scroll case of the fifteenth century, among other inscriptions.

An ancient song to the ark of the covenant (Num 10:35), the special box built to transport the Law, receives special attention as the inscription across the six horizontal borders of a brass scroll case:[5]

When the ark departed,
Moses said,
"Rise,
O YHWH, and scatter
your enemies and cause
those who hate You
to flee from before You."

It is an appropriate inscription, since the scroll case is itself a special metal box to transport a copy of the Torah, or Law. The original ark not only carried the law but was considered the throne upon which YHWH himself sat. To transport the ark was not only to carry the Law, the conditions of the covenant, but to transport YHWH, who was seated upon it. Thus the Hebrews could bring YHWH with them from the desert into the promised land and also into battle with them "to scatter your enemies and cause those who hate You to flee before You."

The collection of inscriptions becomes a "mega-*qetaf*" highlighting the biblical passages of creation, the passover, the exodus from bondage, the Sinai covenant, the Decalogue, the transfer of leadership from Moses to Joshua and Aaron, and warfare led by the ark to take the promised land.

Not all inscriptions were biblical. We have already seen two dedications attached to a marble inscription of the Priestly Benediction. Two more inscriptions in Greek were found at Delos, one dedicated to Sarapion, son of Jason of Knossos, and the other to Menippos, son of Artemidoros of Heracleia, both for donations. The former is dated 150–50 B.C.E., and the latter to 250–175 B.C.E.

Strugnell cites another, longer dedication, presumably from Nablus:

---

[5] CW 2465.

In the name of the great YHWH,
This scroll case was restored for the scripture of Abisha,
The son of Pinhas, the peace of God be upon him, (..)[6] (..) (..)
(..) (..) Ab Zehuta, son of (..) (..) (..)
(..) Sadaqah of the Qabasa family among the inhabitants of Damascus
and also (..) (..) (..) (..) Jacob, son of (..)
(..) (..) (..) (..) Abraham of the Poka family
among the inhabitants of the land of Egypt. YHWH renew them
and give them their due. Amen. Amen.
In this world and the next. In the year 903
Of the reign of the Ishmaelites. I praise YHWH.[7]

The Abisha Scroll, believed by the Samaritans to have been written by Moses' grandnephew, is the most significant surviving artifact owned by the Samaritan community. It has been housed in at least three different scroll cases during its history. There is a record of the earliest known case. It was restored by two men, each from one of the largest cities of the Samaritan Diaspora, Damascus and Cairo.

One presumably early Samaritan inscription commemorates a significant first-century tragedy in the life of the Samaritan community:[8]

Behold.
In the springtime
Trajan came,
Cursed be his name,
into the land of Palestine
before Vespasian,
King of Rome.
And with him [was]
a great army.
They besieged us a month
on Mount Gerizim
until the rainwater was
exhausted and there was no
water to drink.

---

[6] Each parenthesis represents an honorific title attributed to the person described, in this case Ab Zehuta.

[7] Translated from the text in Strugnell, "Quelques inscriptions," 575. The most common surviving dating system for the Samaritans is the Muslim lunar calendar, starting with the year 622 C.E., when Muhammad fled Mecca (the Hegira). The year 903 A.H. is equivalent to 1497/1498 C.E.

[8] Only an impression of the inscription has been found.

They died by the sword,
about ten thousand
strong men.[9]

In *Jewish War* 3.7, Josephus apparently describes the same siege with more Samaritan dead (11,600), a somewhat different cast (Cerealis instead of Trajan), and a much shorter term for siege. The reason Josephus names a different Roman general is hard to explain. Josephus also may have exaggerated the number of dead. The Samaritans may have wanted to tell of a longer siege to demonstrate the integrity of their troops. Inscriptions of war often commemorate a great victory, but this inscription served as a memorial to the ten thousand who died.

AMULETS

Amulets represent a specialized form of inscription. Because their content is often similar to the inscriptions on synagogue lintels, they may share a similar function of soliciting healing and repelling enemies. The major distinction is that lintel inscriptions are on public buildings and speak on behalf of the community whereas amulets are worn by individuals or placed in individual residences for personal protection.

As a distinctive kind of personal adornment, often worn around the neck, they may have had their origins in jewelry. Most of them are made of metal, although more recent amulets are also made of paper and wood. Some date from Roman and Byzantine times, but the majority come from the eleventh and twelfth centuries and later.

As might be expected, some of the popular sayings on amulets are the same as those on inscriptions. Here are two common readings. The first is Exod 15:3:

YHWH is a warrior; YHWH is his name.

The second is Num 10:35:

Rise,
O YHWH, and scatter
your enemies and cause
those who hate You
to flee from before You.

---

[9] Translated from the text in Strugnell, "Quelques inscriptions," 562.

Exodus 15:26 is a common reading that obviously was intended to ward off illness:

> If you will diligently hearken to the voice of YHWH your God and do that which is right in his eyes, and give heed to his commandments and keep all His statutes, I will put none of the diseases upon you that I put upon the Egyptians; for I am YHWH, your healer. (RSV)

Deuteronomy 6:4 is the Shema, the common Jewish and Samaritan affirmation of God and God's oneness:

> Hear O Israel, YHWH, your God, YHWH is one and you will love YHWH, your God, with all your heart and with all your soul and with all your might.

Two other common scriptural amulets affirm the presence and power of YHWH. The first is Num 14:14:

> They have heard that You, YHWH, are in the midst of this people; for You, YHWH, are seen face to face and your cloud stands over them and You go before them in a pillar of cloud by day and a pillar of fire at night. (NRSV)

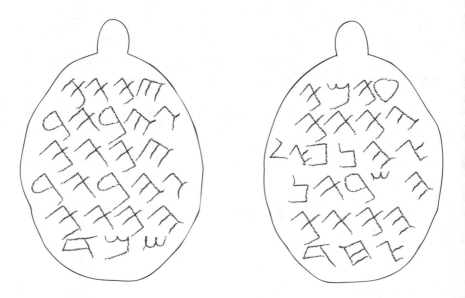

Figure 7. A Samaritan amulet of the Byzantine period, when such amulets were often made of brass and worn around the neck. One side, the left drawing, reads, "YHWH is a hero; YHWH is a hero; YHWH destroy." The other side reads, "Roar, YHWH, [There is] none like God, Jeshurun, YHWH is one." Used by permission of the Israel Exploration Society.

The other is Deut 33:26:

> There is none like God, O Jeshurun,
> who rides through the heavens to help you
> and in his majesty through the heavens.

Among the more esoteric amulets are various adaptations of the "magic square," familiar to many of us from puzzle books. The briefest form is the arrangement of numbers 1–9 in a 3 × 3 square so that the total of any line, horizontal, vertical, or diagonal, is 15:

8	1	6
3	5	7
4	9	2

Using a 5 × 5 square with numbers 1–25 would raise the totals of each line to 65:

23	20	12	9	1
7	4	21	18	15
16	13	10	2	24
5	22	19	11	8
14	6	3	25	17

Extrapolating from this principle, the Samaritans would take meaningful numbers, often the numerical equivalents of Samaritan letters that spelled a scriptural fragment, such as "I am Who I am," and work the numbers into a magic square. Robertson cites a 5 × 5 Samaritan magic square that has utilized this slogan. In Hebrew the text is

אהיה אשר אהיה

Translated into their numerical equivalents in Hebrew, the three words would read (reading with the Hebrew from right to left)

5–10–5–1   200–300–1   5–10–5–1

The total is 543, which can replace 65 for the totals of a 5 × 5 square by dividing 543 by 65. The result is 8 plus a remainder of 23. If each of the numbers in the basic 5 × 5 square is multiplied by 8, and 23 is added into each column and row, the new square incorporates the numerical value of the text "I am Who I am" and looks like this:[10]

184	160	96	72	8
23				
56	32	168	144	120
				23
128	104	80	16	192
			23	
40	176	152	88	64
	23			
112	48	24	200	136
		23		

An amulet may say, for instance, "Repel what is baneful," whether as a personal attack or as protection from military invasion or disease.[11]

Curiously, modern Samaritans claim that they do not wear amulets and probably never did. Purportedly they made amulets to sell to non-Samaritans. Some motifs found on amulets, such as a rider with halo, and Greek inscriptions could imply that at least some amulets were produced for Christians and Jews.[12] Contemporary Samaritan hesitancy to use amulets may have to do with concerns about idolatry of images (reenforced by the dominant Muslim culture) and the tendency of many cultures to feel that amulets, to be effective, ought not be visible. They may be concealed in clothing or small bags made especially for the amulet. It may

---

[10] Edward Robertson, *Catalogue of the Samaritan Manuscripts in the John Rylands Library* (2 vols.; Manchester: Manchester University Press. 1938–1962), 2:xxii.

[11] T. H. Gaster, "Amulets and Talismans, " *ER* 1:243–46, here 243.

[12] Reinhard Pummer, "Samaritan Rituals and Customs," in *The Samaritans* (ed. Alan D. Crown; Tübingen: J. C. B. Mohr, 1989), 650–90, here 654.

be the flaunting of the amulet rather than its use that concerns contemporary Samaritans.[13]

ASTRONOMICAL TEXTS

The astronomical texts are focused primarily on the establishment of
the Samaritan calendar and, like astronomical concerns elsewhere, imply that
the movement of heavenly bodies is a paradigm for right decisions of the
human community. Some of the texts describe the fate of the countries that
lie below particular astronomical features. They might predict famine, insurrection, natural disaster, war, and other events.[14]

In addition, it is important to the Samaritans that the calendar be
correct because the feast days ought to be celebrated at the right time.[15] The
establishment of the calendar and its secrets were entrusted to the family of
the high priest. Robertson cites a colophon on an astronomical codex presumably written for young priestly students:

> It was my intention to make further explanation, but I was fearful of the
> Christians . . . this knowledge is a heritage in the hands of the priests. It
> must not go forth ever, and he who reveals it will be excommunicate and a
> thwarter of the petition "May the Lord increase the Levites 'who bear the
> Ark of the covenant of the Lord,'" for this knowledge is restricted to them
> and is not for others. And to this there are many testimonies and tokens in
> the Beloved Book . . . . [16]

Robertson successfully deciphered their calendar system and published
it in 1939. The Samaritan calendar depends on both lunar and solar phenomena, so calculations relate to the relationship of the orbits of the moon
and the sun in relation to the earth and also the location of the "seven stars"
in relation to the zodiac.[17]

---

[13] Non-Samaritans could be awed and intrigued by the esoteric quality ren-
dered by foreign symbols or writing or signs that they do not understand. T. H.
Gaster reports opening the magical pouches of some African shamans and finding
European hairpins, scissors, cigarette butts, and bus tickets. Gaster, "Amulets and
Talismans," 245.

[14] Robertson, *Catalogue,* 1:366.

[15] A good discussion of the Samaritan calendar appears in Sylvia Powels, "The
Samaritan Calendar," in *The Samaritans* (ed. Alan D. Crown; Tübingen: J. C. B.
Mohr, 1989), 691–742.

[16] Robertson, *Catalogue,* 1:xxxiv–xxxv.

[17] The seven heavenly bodies that were significant in the Middle East at least
from Babylonian times were the sun, the moon, and the five visible planets, Saturn,
Jupiter, Mars, Venus, and Mercury.

According to Samaritan tradition the mystery of the calendar was revealed to Adam: "[Adam] saw the נגימו ("planets," "horoscope") of the days"[18]
and "began reading the book of signs."[19]

> And when Enoch was thirteen years, he learned the Book of signs which
> was given to Adam.[20]

> And when Noah had finished the division of the land by the astronomical
> calculation of the day, he found that there were still four thousand three
> hundred years less seven years to come after the flood, of the six thousand
> from the beginning of the creation and three hundred and seven since the
> flood.[21]

The advent of Islam was a significant influence on the Samaritans'
means of calculating astronomical phenomena. Before that time they may
have used earlier traditions, Babylonian technology or their own observations. With the coming of Islam and the Arab development of astronomy,
presumably with the aid of Indian precedents, Samaritans adapted the new
means of calculation.[22]

Two major Samaritan festivals, Simmut Pesach and Simmut Sukkoth,
refer explictly to conjuctions (Simmut). The liturgy for each refers to the
conjunction of the sun and moon. Each also refers to another conjunction
(meeting) that they do not share in common. Simmut Pesach refers to the
meeting of Moses and Aaron in Exod 4:27–28, and Simmut Sukkoth refers
to a meeting of Eleazar with his vocation, becoming a priest in Num
20:22–29. The calculation of the date for these festivals is the base from
which the remaining festivals can be determined.

Astronomical texts are more often charts than text. For example the
first few lines of Codex XXIII, an eighteenth-century astronomical manuscript in the John Rylands Library, reads in translation:[23]

[18] *Asatir* 1:22 and 2:17, in Moses Gaster, *The Asatir: The Samaritan Book of the "Secrets of Moses" Together with the Pitron, or Samaritan Commentary, and the Samaritan Story of the Death of Moses* (Oriental Translation Fund NS 26; London: Royal Asiatic Society, 1927), 198. The word נגימו is Gaster's transliteration of the Arabic *najm* ("star") into Samaritan Hebrew. The idea of horoscope is inferred from the context and confirmed by Arabic speakers and the word in Arabic, *tanjīm* ("astrology").
[19] *Asatir* 2:7 in Gaster, *Asatir*, 198; *Pitron* 2:11 in Gaster, *Asatir*, 196–97.
[20] *Asatir* 2:7, ibid.
[21] *Asatir* 4:19, ibid., 230.
[22] Sylvia Powels, "The Samaritan Calendar," in *The Samaritans* (ed. Alan D. Crown; Tübingen: J. C. B. Mohr, 1989), 691–742, here 720–21.
[23] Robertson, *Catalogue,* 1:391 and plate 5.

COURSE OF THE SUN IN DAYS AND HOURS

THE DAYS					THE HOURS				
Number	Zodiac sign	Degree	Minute	Second	Number	Zodiac sign	Degree	Minute	Second
1		59	8		1		2	28	
2	1	58	15		2		4	56	
3	2	57	24		3		7	24	
4	3	56	33		4		9	52	
5	4	55	41		5		12	19	

The chart continues through thirty days and thirty hours.

All of the writings discussed in this chapter reflect the Samaritan community's wide range of materials, skills, creativity, and affirmations over almost two millennia.

Bibliography

GENERAL WORKS

Anderson, Robert T., and Terry Giles. *The Keepers: An Introduction to the History and Culture of the Samaritans.* Peabody, Mass.: Hendrickson, 2002.

_____. "Samaritan Pentateuch: A General Account." Pages 390–96 in *The Samaritans.* Edited by Alan D. Crown. Tübingen: J. C. B. Mohr, 1989.

Ben-Hayyim, Ze'ev. *The Literary and Oral Tradition of Hebrew and Aramaic amongst the Samaritans.* 5 vols. in 6. Jerusalem: Academy of the Hebrew Language, 1957–1977.

Bowman, John. *Samaritan Documents Relating to Their History, Religion, and Life.* Pittsburgh: Pickwick, 1977.

Crown, Alan D. "Studies in Samaritan Scribal Practices and Manuscript History, IV: An Index of Scribes, Witnesses, Owners, and Others Mentioned in Samaritan Manuscripts, with a Key to Principal Families Therein." *Bulletin of the John Rylands University Library of Manchester* 68 (1986): 317–72.

_____, ed. *The Samaritans.* Tübingen: J. C. B. Mohr, 1989.

Josephus. Translated by H. St. John Thackery et al. 10 vols. Loeb Classical Library. Cambridge, Mass.: Harvard University Press, 1926–1965.

Montgomery, James A. *The Samaritans, the Earliest Jewish Sect: Their History, Theology, and Literature.* Philadelphia: Winston, 1907. Repr., New York: KTAV, 1968.

Rothschild, Jean-Pierre. *Catalogue des manuscrits samaritains.* Paris: Bibliothèque Nationale, Department des Manuscrits, 1985.

SAMARITAN PENTATEUCH

Anderson, Robert T. "Clustering Samaritan Hebrew Pentateuchal Manuscripts." Pages 57–66 in *Études samaritaines: Pentateuque et targum, exégèse et philologie, chroniques.* Edited by Jean-Pierre Rothschild and Guy Dominique Sixdenier. Louvain: Peeters, 1988.

_____. "Samaritan Pentateuch: A General Account." Pages 390–96 in *The Samaritans*. Edited by Alan D. Crown. Tübingen: J. C. B. Mohr, 1989.

_____. *Studies in Samaritan Manuscripts and Artifacts: The Chamberlain-Warren Collection*. Cambridge, Mass.: American Schools of Oriental Research, 1978.

Ben-Hayyim, Ze'ev. *A Grammar of Samaritan Hebrew*. Rev. ed. Winona Lake, Ind.: Eisenbrauns, 2000.

Bruce, F. F. *The Books and the Parchments*. Westwood, N.J.: Fleming H. Revell, 1953.

Cappelus, A. L. *Diatriba de veris et antiquis Hebraeorum literis*. Amsterdam, 1645.

Coggins, Richard J. *Samaritans and Jews: The Origins of Samaritanism Reconsidered*. Atlanta: John Knox, 1975.

Cohen, M. "The Orthography of the Samaritan Pentateuch: Its Place in the History of Orthography and Its Relation with the MT Orthography." *Beth Miqra* 64 (1976): 50–70; 66 (1976): 361–91.

Cross, Frank Moore, Jr. *The Ancient Library of Qumran and Modern Biblical Studies*. Rev. ed. Garden City, N.Y.: Doubleday, 1961.

_____. "History of the Biblical Text." Pages 177–95 in *Qumran and the History of the Biblical Text*. Edited by Frank Moore Cross Jr. and Shemaryahu Talmon. Cambridge, Mass.: Harvard University Press, 1975.

_____. "The History of the Biblical Text in the Light of the Discoveries in the Judean Desert." *Harvard Theological Review* 52 (1964): 287–92.

Cross, Frank Moore, Jr., and Shemaryahu Talmon, eds. *Qumran and the History of the Biblical Text*. Cambridge, Mass.: Harvard University Press: 1975.

Crown, Alan D. "The Abisha Scroll of the Samaritans." *Bulletin of the John Rylands University Library of Manchester* 58 (1975): 36–55.

_____. "Redating the Schism between the Judaeans and the Samaritans." *Jewish Quarterly Review* 82 (1991): 17–50.

Dexinger, Ferdinand. "Limits of Tolerance in Judaism: The Samarian Example." Pages 108–14 in *Aspects of Judaism in the Graeco-Roman Period*. Edited by E. P. Sanders, A. I. Baumgarten, and Alan Mendelson. Vol. 2 of *Jewish and Christian Self-Definition*. Edited by E. P. Sanders. Philadelphia: Fortress, 1981.

Eissfeldt, Otto. *Einleitung in das Alte Testament*. Tübingen: Mohr, 1934.

Fraser, J. G. "A Checklist of Samaritan Manuscripts Known to Have Entered Europe before A.D. 1700." *Abr-Nahrain* 21 (1982/1983): 10–27.

Gall, August von. *Der hebräische Pentateuch der Samaritaner*. 5 vols. Giessen: Töpelmann, 1914–1918. Repr., 1 vol., 1966.

Gerleman, Gillis. *Synoptic Studies in the Old Testament*. Lund: C. W. K. Gleerup, 1948.

Gesenius, William. *De Pentateuchi samaritani origine, indole, et auctoritate commentatio philologico-critica.* Halle, 1815.

Goshen-Gottstein, Moshe. "The Textual Criticism of the Old Testament: Rise, Decline, Rebirth." *Journal of Biblical Literature* 102 (1983): 372–75.

Greenburg, M. "The Stabilization of the Text of the Hebrew Bible in the Light of the Biblical Materials from the Judean Desert." *Journal of the American Oriental Society* 76 (1956): 157–67.

Hall, Bruce. "The Samaritans in the Writings of Justin Martyr and Tertullian." Pages 115–22 in *Proceedings of the First International Congress of the Société d'Études Samaritaines.* Edited by Abraham Tal and Moshe Florentin. Tel Aviv: Tel Aviv University Press, 1991.

Hjelm, Ingrid. *The Samaritans and Early Judaism: A Literary Analysis.* Journal for the Study of the Old Testament: Supplement Series 303. Sheffield: Sheffield Academic Press, 2000.

Hottinger, Johann Heinrich. *Exercitationes antimorinianae de Pentateucho samaritano.* Zürich, 1644.

Kahle, Paul. "Die überlieferte Aussprache des Hebräischen und die Punktation der Masoreten." *Zeitschrift für die alttestamentliche Wissenschaft* 39 (1919): 230–39.

———. "Untersuchungen zur Geschichte des Pentateuch-textes," *Theologische Studien und Kritiken* 88 (1915): 399–439.

Kennicott, B. *The State of the Printed Hebrew Text of the Old Testament Considered: Dissertation the Second Wherein the Samaritan Copy of the Pentateuch Is Vindicated.* Oxford, 1759.

Lagarde, Paul de. *Anmerkungen zur griechischen Übersetzung der Proverbien.* Leipzig: F. A. Brockhaus, 1863.

Moody, R. E. "Samaritan Material at Boston University: The Boston Collection and the Abisha Scroll." *Boston University Graduate Journal* 10 (1957): 158–60.

Morinus, Johannes. *Exercitationes ecclesiasticae in utrumque Samaritanorum Pentateuchum.* Paris, 1631.

Pérez Castro, F. *Séfer Abisha.* Madrid: C.S.I.C., 1959.

Pfeiffer, Robert H. *Introduction to the Old Testament.* New York: Harper & Brothers, 1941.

Pummer, Reinhard. *The Samaritans.* Leiden: Brill, 1987.

Purvis, James. *The Samaritan Pentateuch and the Origin of the Samaritan Sect.* Cambridge, Mass.: Harvard University Press, 1968.

———. "The Samaritan Problem: A Case Study in Jewish Sectarianism in the Roman Era." Pages 323–50 in *Traditions in Transformation: Turning Points in Biblical Faith.* Edited by Baruch Halpern and Jon Levenson. Winona Lake, Ind.: Eisenbrauns, 1981.

Sanderson, Judith E. *An Exodus Scroll from Qumran: 4QpaleoExod and the Samaritan Tradition.* Atlanta: Scholars Press, 1986.

Rothschild, Jean-Pierre. "Samaritan Manuscripts: A Guide to the Collections and Catalogues." Pages 771–94 in *The Samaritans.* Edited by Alan D. Crown. Tübingen: J. C. B. Mohr, 1989.

Skehan, Patrick. "Exodus in the Samaritan Recension from Qumran." *Journal of Biblical Literature* 74 (1955): 182–87.

Smith, Morton. *Palestinian Parties and Politics That Shaped the Old Testament.* New York: Columbia University Press, 1971.

Tal, Abraham. "Samaritan Literature." Pages 413–67 in *The Samaritans.* Edited by Alan D. Crown. Tübingen: J. C. B. Mohr, 1989.

_____. *The Samaritan Pentateuch, Edited according to MS 6 (C) of the Shekhem Synagogue.* Tel Aviv: Tel Aviv University Press, 1994.

Thomas, D. W. "The Textual Criticism of the Old Testament." Pages 238–63 in *The Old Testament and Modern Study.* Edited by H. H. Rowley. Oxford: Clarendon, 1951.

Tigay, Jeffrey H. "An Empirical Basis for the Documentary Hypothesis." *Journal of Biblical Literature* 94 (1975): 327–42.

Tsedaqa, Abraham and Ratson. *Samaritan Pentateuch.* Holon, Israel, 1965–1968.

Waltke, Bruce. "Prolegomena to the Samaritan Pentateuch." PhD diss., Harvard University, 1965.

_____. "Samaritan Pentateuch." Pages 932–48 in vol. 5 of *The Anchor Bible Dictionary.* Edited by David N. Freedman. 6 vols. New York: Doubleday, 1992.

Wise, Michael, Martin Abegg, and Edward Cook. *The Dead Sea Scrolls.* San Francisco: Harper Collins, 1996.

Würthwein, Ernst. *The Text of the Old Testament: An Introduction to the Biblia hebraica.* Translated by E. F. Rhodes. Grand Rapids: Eerdmans, 1979.

SAMARITAN JOSHUA

Crane, Oliver T. *The Samaritan Chronicle; or, the Book of Joshua the Son of Nun.* New York: John Alden, 1890.

Crown, Alan D. "A Critical Re-evaluation of the Samaritan Sepher Yehoshua." PhD diss., Sidney: University of Sidney, 1966.

_____. "New Light on the Inter-relationships of Samaritan Chronicles from Some Manuscripts in the John Rylands Library." *Bulletin of the John Rylands University Library of Manchester* 54 (1972): 282–305.

Hottinger, Johann Heinrich. *Exercitationes antimorinianae de Pentateucho samaritano.* Zurich, 1644.

_____. *Smegma orientale.* Zurich, 1657.

Juynboll, T. W. J. *Chronicon samaritanum.* Leiden: S. & J. Luchtmans, 1848.

KITAB AL-TARIKH (THE *ANNALS* OF ABU'L FATH)

Gaster, Moses. *The Samaritans: Their History, Doctrine, and Literature.* Schweich Lectures for 1923. London: For the British Academy by H. Milford, 1925. Repr., New York: Gordon Press, 1980.

Jost, J. M. *Geschichte des Judenthums und seiner Secten.* 3 vols. Leipzig: Dörffling & Franke, 1857–1859.

Lowy, Simeon. *Principles of Samaritan Bible Exegesis.* Leiden: Brill, 1977.

Neubauer, A. "Chronique samaritaine, suivie d'un appendice contenant de courtes notices sur quelques autres ouvrages samaritains." *Journal asiatique* 14 (1869): 385–470.

Nutt, John. *Fragments of a Samaritan Targum, Edited from a Bodleian* MS, *with an Introduction Containing a Sketch of Samaritan History, Dogma, and Literature.* London: Trübner, 1874.

Payne-Smith, R. "The Samaritan Chronicle of Abu'l Fath, the Arabic Text from the MS in the Bodleian Library," *Deutsche Vierteljahrsschrift für englisch-theologische Forschung und Kritik* 2 (1863): 304–35, 430–59.

Sacy, Silvestre de. *Chrestomathie arabe.* Paris: Imprimerie Impériale, 1806.

_____. *Notices et extraits de divers manuscrits arabes et autres.* Paris: Imprimerie Royale. 1829.

Stenhouse, Paul, ed. *The Kitab al-Tarikh of Abu'l-Fath, Translated with Notes.* Sydney: Mandelbaum Trust, University of Sydney, 1985.

_____. "Samaritan Chronicles." Pages 218–65 in *The Samaritans.* Edited by Alan D. Crown. Tübingen: J. C. B. Mohr, 1989.

Vilmar, E. *Abulfathi Annales samaritani.* Gotha, Germany: F. A. Perthes, 1865.

ADDITIONAL SAMARITAN CHRONICLES: *THE NEW CHRONICLE (CHRONICLE ADLER)* AND *CHRONICLE II*

Adler, E. N., and M. Séligsohn. "Une nouvelle chronique samaritaine." *Revue des études juives* 44 (1902): 118–222; 45 (1902): 70–98, 160, 223–54; 46 (1903): 123–46.

Coggins, Richard. *Samaritans and Jews: The Origins of Samaritanism Reconsidered.* Atlanta: John Knox, 1975.

Cohen, J. *A Samaritan Chronicle.* Leiden: E. J. Brill, 1981.

Fohrer, Georg. "Die israelitischen Propheten in der samaritanischen Chronik II." Pages 129–37 in *In Memoriam Paul Kahle.* Edited by Matthew Black and Georg Fohrer. Beihefte zur Zeitschrift für die alttestamentliche Wissenschaft 103. Berlin: de Gruyter, 1968.

Macdonald, John. *The Samaritan Chronicle No. II.* Beihefte zur Zeitschrift für die alttestamentliche Wissenschaft 107. Berlin: Walter de Gruyter, 1969.

Macdonald, John, and A. J. Higgins. "The Beginning of Christianity according to the Samaritans." *New Testament Studies* 18 (1971): 54–80.

Stenhouse, Paul. "Samaritan Chronicles." Pages 218–65 in *The Samaritans.* Edited by Alan D. Crown. Tübingen: J. C. B. Mohr, 1989.

TIBAT MARQE (MEMAR MARQE)

Algar, Hamid. "'Ulamā.'" Pages 115–17 in vol. 15 of *The Encyclopedia of Religion.* Edited by Mircea Eliade. 16 vols. New York: Macmillan, 1987.

Ben-Hayyim, Ze'ev. Review of John Macdonald, *Memar Marqah. Bibliotheca orientalis* 23 (1966): 185–91.

_____. *Tibat Marqe: A Collection of Samaritan Midrashim.* Jerusalem: Israel Academy of Sciences and Humanities, 1988.

_____. "Towards a New Edition of Tibat Marqe." Pages 161–78 in *Études samaritaines: Pentateuque et targum, exégèse et philologie, chroniques.* Edited by Jean-Pierre Rothschild and Guy Dominique Sixdenier. Louvain: Peeters, 1988.

Bowman, John. "Samaritan Studies, I: The Fourth Gospel and the Samaritans." *Bulletin of the John Rylands University Library of Manchester* 40 (1958): 298–327.

Broadie, A. *A Samaritan Philosophy: A Study of the Hellenistic Cultural Ethos of the Memar Marqe.* Leiden: E. J. Brill, 1981.

Charles, R. H., ed. *The Apocrypha and Pseudepigrapha of the Old Testament.* 2 vols. Oxford: Oxford University Press, 1913.

Conzelmann, Hans. *The Theology of Saint Luke.* Translated by Geoffrey Buswell. New York: Harper, 1960.

Crown, Alan D. "The Byzantine and Moslem Period." Pages 55–81 in *The Samaritans.* Edited by Alan D. Crown. Tübingen: J. C. B. Mohr, 1989.

_____. "Samaritan Religion in the Fourth Century." *Nederlands theologisch tijdschrift* 41 (1986): 29–47.

_____. "Studies in Samaritan Scribal Practice and Manuscript History, III: Columnar Writing and the Samaritan Massorah." *Bulletin of the John Rylands University Library of Manchester* 67 (1986): 349–81.

Delcor, Mathias. "La légende de la mort de Moïse dans le *Memar Marqah*." Pages 25–45 in *New Samaritan Studies of the Société d'Études Samaritaines: Essays in Honour of G. D. Sixdenier.* Edited by Alan D. Crown and Lucy Davey. Sydney: Mandelbaum, University of Sydney, 1995.

Dexinger, Ferdinand. "Samaritan Eschatology." Pages 266–92 in *The Samaritans.* Edited by Alan D. Crown. Tübingen: J. C. B. Mohr, 1989.

Friedman, Richard. *Who Wrote the Bible?* New York: Simon and Shuster, 1987. Repr. New York: Harper & Row, 1989.

Gaster, Moses. *The Asatir: The Samaritan Book of the "Secrets of Moses" Together with the Pitron, or Samaritan Commentary, and the Samaritan Story of the Death of Moses.* Oriental Translation Fund NS 26. London: Royal Asiatic Society, 1927.

Haacker, Klaus. "Assumptio Mosis: Eine samaritanische Schrift?" *Theologische Zeitschrift* 25 (1969): 385–405.

Kippenberg, Hans G. *Garizim und Synagoge: Traditionsgeschichtliche Untersuchungen zur samaritanischen Religion der aramäischen Periode.* New York: de Gruyter, 1971.

Macdonald, John. "Islamic Doctrines in Samaritanism." *Muslim World* 50, no. 4 (1960): 279–90.

_____. *The Theology of the Samaritans.* London: SCM, 1964.

_____, ed. and trans. *Memar Marqah: The Teaching of Marqah.* 2 vols. BZAW 84. Berlin: Töpelmann, 1963.

Mariottini, Claude F. "Serah." Page 1104 in vol. 5 of *The Anchor Bible Dictionary.* Edited by David N. Freedman. 6 vols. New York: Doubleday, 1992.

Marxsen, Willi. *Introduction to the New Testament.* Philadelphia: Fortress, 1970.

Petermann, Julius Heinrich. *Reisen im Orient, 1852–1855.* 2 vols. Leipzig, 1860–1861. Repr. Leipzig, 1865. Repr. Amsterdam, Philo Press, 1976.

Priest, John. "Testament of Moses." Pages 919–934 in vol. 1 of *The Old Testament Pseudipigrapha.* Edited by James H. Charlesworth. 2 vols. New York: Doubleday, 1983.

Purvis, James D. "The Fourth Gospel and the Samaritans." *Novum Testamentum* 17 (1975): 161–98.

_____. "Samaritan Traditions on the Death of Moses." Pages 93–117 in *Studies on the Testament of Moses.* Edited by George W. E. Nickelsburg Jr. Cambridge, Mass.: Society of Biblical Literature, 1973.

Schimmel, Annemarie. "Numbers: An Overview." Pages 13–19 in vol. 11 of *The Encyclopedia of Religion.* Edited by Mircea Eliade. 16 vols. New York: Macmillan, 1987.

Shakir, M. H., trans. *The Qur'an.* Elmhurst, N.Y.: Tahrike Qur'an, Inc., 1990.

Stenhouse, Paul, ed. *The Kitab al-Tarikh of Abu'l-Fath, Translated with Notes.* Sydney: Mandelbaum Trust, University of Sydney, 1985.

Strauss, David Friedrich. *The Life of Christ Critically Examined.* Translated by Marian Evans. 2 vols. New York: Calvin Blanchard, 1860, 1870.

Tal, Abraham. "Samaritan Literature." Pages 413–67 in *The Samaritans.* Edited by Alan D. Crown. Tübingen: J. C. B. Mohr, 1989.

THE SAMARITAN LITURGY

Ben-Hayyim, Ze'ev. *A Grammar of Samaritan Hebrew.* Rev. ed. Winona Lake, Ind.: Eisenbrauns, 2000.

Brown, Solomon. "A Critical Edition and Translation of the Ancient Samaritan Defter (i.e., Liturgy) and a Comparison of It with Early Jewish Liturgy." PhD diss., University of Leeds, 1955.

Cowley, Arthur E. *The Samaritan Liturgy.* 2 vols. Oxford: Oxford University Press, 1909.

Florentin, Moshe. "Amram Dare." Page 13 in *A Companion to Samaritan Studies.* Edited by Alan D. Crown, Reinhard Pummer, and Abraham Tal. Tübingen: J. C. B. Mohr, 1993.

Pummer, Reinhard. "Samaritan Rituals and Customs." Pages 650–90 in *The Samaritans.* Edited by Alan D. Crown. Tübingen: J. C. B. Mohr, 1989.

———. *The Samaritans.* Leiden: Brill, 1987.

Robertson, Edward. *Catalogue of the Samaritan Manuscripts in the John Rylands Library.* 2 vols. Manchester: Manchester University Press, 1938–1962.

Sedakah, Abraham. *The Celebration of Passover by the Samaritans.* Tel Aviv: n.p., 1962.

MISCELLANEOUS TEXTS

Gaster, Moses. *The Asatir: The Samaritan Book of the "Secrets of Moses" Together with the Pitron, or Samaritan Commentary, and the Samaritan Story of the Death of Moses.* London: Oriental Translation Fund, 1927.

Gaster, T. H. "Amulets and Talismans." Pages 243–46 in vol. 1 of *The Encyclopedia of Religion.* Edited by Mircea Eliade. 16 vols. New York: Macmillan, 1987.

Lagrange, J. M. "Inscription samaritaine d'Amwas." *Revue biblique* 2 (1893): 114–16.

Musil, Alois. "Sieben samaritansiche Inschriften aus Damaskus." *Sitzungsberichte der kaiserlichen Akademie der Wissenschaften in Wien, phil.-hist. Klasse 147* (1903), 1–11.

Powels, Sylvia. "The Samaritan Calendar." Pages 691–742 in *The Samaritans.* Edited by Alan D. Crown. Tübingen: J. C. B. Mohr, 1989.

Reinhard Pummer, "Samaritan Rituals and Customs." Pages 650–90 in *The Samaritans.* Edited by Alan D. Crown. Tübingen: J. C. B. Mohr, 1989.

Robertson, Edward. *Catalogue of the Samaritan Manuscripts in the John Rylands Library.* 2 vols. Manchester: Manchester University Press, 1938–1962.

Sobernheim, Moritz. "Samaritanische Inschriften aus Damascus." *Mitteilungen und Nachrichten des Deutschen Paläistina-Vereins* 8 (1902), 70–80.

Spoer, Hans H. "Notes on Some New Samaritan Inscriptions." in *Proceedings of the Society of Biblical Archaeology* 30 (1908), 284–291.

Strugnell, John. "Quelques inscriptions samaritaines." *Revue biblique* 74 (1967): 555–80.

Vogüé, Melchior de. "Nouvelle inscription samaritaine d'Amwas." *Revue biblique* 5 (1896): 432–34.

Index of Modern Authors

Index of Subjects

Index of Ancient Sources